ECONOMICS OF SPORT

The Sport Management Library offers textbooks for undergraduate students. The subjects in the series reflect the content areas prescribed by the NASPE/NASSM curriculum standards for undergraduate sport management programs.

Titles in the Sport Management Library

Case Studies in Sport Marketing
Developing Successful Sport Marketing Plans
Developing Successful Sport Sponsorship Plans
Economics of Sport
Ethics in Sport Management
Financing Sport
Fundamentals of Sport Marketing
Legal Aspects of Sport Entrepreneurship
Media Relations in Sport Organizations
Sport Facility Planning and Management
Sport Governance in the Global Community
Sport Management Field Experiences

Sport Management Library Titles Forthcoming in 2001

Financing Sport (2nd Edition)
Fundamentals of Sport Marketing (2nd Edition)
Sport Facility Planning and Management (2nd Edition)

NEW Related Titles from Fitness Information Technology

Directory of Academic Programs in Sport Management
Sport Tourism

ECONOMICS OF SPORT

Ming Li
GEORGIA SOUTHERN UNIVERSITY

Susan Hofacre
ROBERT MORRIS COLLEGE

Dan Mahony
UNIVERSITY OF LOUISVILLE

Fitness Information Technology, Inc.
•
P.O. Box 4425
•
Morgantown, WV 26504-4425

Library of Congress Card Catalog Number: 00-136499

ISBN: 1-885693-27-3

Copyeditor: Sandra R. Woods
Cover Design: James Bucheimer
Developmental Editor: Brenda Pitts
Managing Editor: Geoffrey C. Fuller
Production Editor: Craig Hines
Proofreader/Indexer: Maria den Boer
Printed by Sheridan Press

10 9 8 7 6 5 4 3 2

Fitness Information Technology, Inc.
P.O. Box 4425, University Avenue
Morgantown, WV 26504 USA
800.477.4348
304.599.3483 phone
304.599.3482 fax
Email: fit@fitinfotech.com
Website: www.fitinfotech.com

Acknowledgments

Writing a textbook requires the assistance of countless people. We want to thank all those who contributed to the process and in particular the following individuals.

Dr. Brenda Pitts was the project editor of this book. Her guidance and continuing encouragement were crucial to bringing this project to closure. Our appreciation goes to Andy Ostrow and the editorial board for supporting the vision of a Sport Management Library.

We are indebted to Dr. Christine Brooks and Dr. Tim DeSchriver who reviewed the book and provided us with many valuable suggestions that greatly facilitated the completion of the project.

Our gratitude is extended to those outstanding researchers and scholars whose work in the economics of sports has made possible this text. In addition, our sport management students challenge us to know and be able to clearly explain the concepts we present here.

Finally, completing a text such as this requires tremendous personal support. Our spouses, Wan Chen and Laura Mahony, provided the courage, confidence, and comfort that made it possible. Henry Eisenhart, Mark Eschenfelder, Scott Branvold, Dave Synowka, Dan Funk, Mary Hums, and Anita Moorman patiently listened and encouraged. Thanks.

Contents

Detailed Contents

Preface

Sport is a major part of our business and cultural environments. A wide variety of people follow sport actions, sport statistics, league standings, and sport superstars through watching sports on TV, reading newspapers, attending games, buying sport merchandise, and betting on sporting events. Millions of people also participate in sports, fitness, and recreational activities daily. Bookstores are filled with books about elements of the sport industry. So why write a text on the economics of sport?

It is often difficult to understand why the sport industry operates as it does. Why do governments in some countries directly support sport programs, facilities, and athletes, while other governments do not or do it in an indirect manner? Why do private enterprises supply some sport activities while government supplies others? Who has power within the sport industry and why? Why can some sport organizations operate as monopolists to sell their television rights while others cannot? Why does a pair of basketball shoes cost $150? How is it that a baseball player is paid $10 million a year? Or, generally speaking, why are decisions about how sports is conducted made as they are? These are only samples of the questions that people may have and which we hope to begin to answer.

There are books available related to the economics of sport. We will cite many of them in the following chapters. However, most of them only focus on "big-time" sports in North America in such sports as professional football, baseball, basketball, and hockey, as well as in U.S. intercollegiate sports, especially football and basketball. We will also discuss these segments in the following chapters. However, there are many other parts of the sport industry where a knowledge of economics can help us to understand what is happening and why it's happening. So, we will talk about youth sports, recreational sports, the sporting goods industry, and many more other segments of the sport industry as well. Our goal is to demonstrate to readers that economics of sport includes more than just "big-time" sports. In addition, we want to clarify that the economics of sport is not just about sport in the United States. Many of the questions and issues raised about how and why sport operates apply to many countries. For this purpose, we have included examples and discussion of sport outside the boundaries of the U.S.

The primary target for the text is upper level, undergraduate students studying in sport management programs. Much of the material has been used in undergraduate sport economics taught by the authors. We have written the text at a level that anticipates students having had some exposure to economics concepts and analysis, perhaps through an introductory course in economics. However, there are several points at which we review basic economics concepts before discussing their application to the sport industry. The text could also be used either for a lower division elective course for economics majors or for masters' students studying sport management. In the last two cases, we would assume students have had more preparation in economics and will have less need for the basic review material. Finally, the text may serve as resource material for economics professors who are in the process of learning more about the sport industry.

The book has twelve chapters. In Chapter 1, the sport industry is defined, followed by an in-depth overview of the sport industry in the United States. It is intended that this chapter provide the student with a clear understanding of what the sport industry is even though this has never been unanimously agreed upon by professionals in sport management. Without such an understanding, it would be difficult for the students in sport management to comprehend those economic issues raised in the text.

Chapter 2 reviews economic concepts, including some basic definitions of economics and of benefits and costs. The theory of the firm and what motivates firms to act as they do is discussed. Throughout the book we will talk about profit maximization as a major motivator, however alternative models are also presented. We recognize that not all sport firms are organized to make a profit, so we also review motivators for nonprofit organizations.

Chapter 3 applies the concepts of demand, supply, pricing, and revenue to the sport industry. The basic concepts of demand and supply, including what determines demand and supply, are presented and then related to pricing of goods and services. Elasticity of demand and supply are discussed in terms of the decisions that sport managers must make. The importance of forecasting demand is also suggested.

In Chapter 4, we look at several basic market structures, from perfect competition to monopolies, and the distinguishing features associated to each of them. Organizations and the decision making of their executives are affected by the market structure in which they operate.

Sport and recreation is provided via several different delivery systems. Chapter 5 looks at government-provided sport, community sport, and private enterprise and examines the reasons each might be used. The discussion of sport delivered through private enterprise includes public versus private ownership of firms and the reasons for mergers and acquisitions.

A detailed review of issues related to how to determine and measure the size of the sport industry in the United States is provided in Chapter 6. It is intended to provide the student with a better understanding of how critical the sport industry is to the national economy. This chapter will also assess the contribution of the sport industry to the U.S. economy in terms of the number of jobs it creates each year.

Spending on sport activities and facilities is often supported with references to the economic impact they will have on a community. Chapter 7 reviews the concept of economic impact and demonstrates how economic impact studies are conducted and used to justify spending. Difficulties in conducting accurate impact studies are addressed.

Chapter 8 deals with labor-related issues in the sport industry. Labor is believed to be the most important factor of production in any form of economic activity. Professional athletes, public relations directors, and sales representatives in various types of sport firms and organizations are examples of labor. This chapter first provides an overview of the general labor market and then discusses specific labor issues in the sport industry.

In Chapter 9, economic theories related to both government and industry self-regulation are applied to the sport industry. How and why regulation occurs is reviewed and the impact how sport is provided is also discussed.

A fundamental argument for government regulation is to ensure fairness in business competition. In Chapter 10, antitrust laws and their applications in the sport industry are examined to provide the students with a clear understanding of how government uses the laws to promote competition in the sport marketplace.

In Chapter 11, we look at how economic systems affect sport governance in the world. In addition, reasons for international expansion as well as sport club systems used in nations all over are also discussed. With the increased internationalization of sport business activities, sport managers need an understanding of sport as a global activity.

To conclude the book, we look to the future to determine what economic issues will be in Chapter 12. Whether it is technological advancements or demographic changes influencing demand or changing labor markets, one of the goals of having an understanding of economics is to allow the sport manager to make decisions that will help the firm survive into that future.

Chapter One

INTRODUCTION

What is the sport industry? This question has never been answered clearly, either by scholars in sport management or by practitioners in the industry that we call "sport." In the past, numerous attempts were made, but no indisputable answer to the question was found. In other words, concerned scholars in sport management have not yet reached a consensus in terms of how to define the industry. Accordingly, people in the industry have literally used the term at their own discretion. For example, *organized sports* has been used as an equivalent term when calculating the size of the sport industry (Broughton, Lee, & Nethery, 1999). The authors believe that finding a new way to define the sport industry in North America has become an imperative task for sport management professionals. An understanding of the sport industry in North America will provide the student with an analytical foundation for further examinations of various economic issues in sport.

Definition of an Industry

An industry can be defined according to one of the two criteria: similarity of products and similarity of economic activities. Defined with the first criterion, an industry refers to a group of firms that provide similar, well-defined products and services (Lipsey, Coutant, & Ragan, 1999; Shim & Siegel, 1995). Most of the industries in the United States are labeled in this way, such as the automobile industry. An industry can also be defined by the similarities of firms in economic activities/production. The U.S. Census Bureau used this method in the development of the North American Industrial Classification System (NAICS). NAICS was developed jointly by the three nations in North America to provide new comparability in statistics about business activity across the United States, Canada, and Mexico. Based on a production-oriented conceptual framework, NAICS groups industries according to their similarities in the process of goods or service production (Office of Management and Budget, 1997).

An Overview of the Sport Industry in North America

XYZ International is an international firm specializing in sport marketing and facility management. The company was recently hired by the Sports Bureau of the People's Republic of China to provide consultation services to the Chinese sport leadership in terms of how to possibly model the sport industry in China after the U.S. model. At the first meeting between the Chief of the Sports Bureau and the general manager of the firm, the former asked the latter this question: "Can you give me a detailed description of the sport industry in the United States?" Assume that you were the general manager. What is your answer?

As mentioned above, NAICS defines an industry as a grouping of economic activities. So, industries are grouped by the similarity of their economic activities, not by their products. The producing units within a particular industry share a basic production process and use a similar technology in production (Office of Management and Budget, 1997). Using this definition as a guideline, NAICS groups all economic activities into a 20-sector structure, and it uses a six-digit coding system to identify particular industries and their placement in this hierarchical structure of the classifi-

Table 1-1. The 20 Sectors or Major Economic Activities That Are Categorized by NAICS

Two-digit Code	Industry Categories
11	Agriculture, forestry, fishing and hunting
21	Mining
22	Utilities
23	Construction
31-33	Manufacturing
41-43	Wholesale trade
44–46	Retail trade
48–49	Transportation and warehousing
51	Information
52	Finance and insurance
53	Real estate and rental and leasing
54	Professional, scientific and technical services
55	Management of companies and enterprises
56	Administration and support and waste management and remediation services
61	Education services
62	Health care and social assistance
71	Arts, entertainment and recreation
72	Accommodation and food services
81	Other services (except public administration)
91-91	Public administration

Source: Office of Management and Budget (1997). *North American Industry Classification System (NAICS), 1997.* US Department of Commerce, Washington DC..

cation system. The first two digits of the code designate the sector, the third designates the subsector, the fourth designates the industry group, the fifth designates the NAICS industry, and the sixth digit designates the national industry (Office of Management and Budget, 1997). Table 1-1 shows the 20 sectors or major economic activities categorized by NAICS. NAICS does not consider sport as a major economic activity and, therefore, does not treat the sport industry as a stand-alone industrial sector or industry. The industrial activities related to sport are placed into several of the major sectors, such as manufacturing, arts, entertainment, and recreation (see Table 1-2 for details).

The Sport Industry in North America

The contents of NAICS provide sport management professionals with a useful reference in terms of determining what activities are considered by the government as sport-related ones. Nevertheless, because NAICS groups the economic activities based on their similarity in production, the sport-producing units are scattered across eight NAICS sectors. It is very difficult, if not impossible, to conceptualize the industry we call "sport." In addition, many traditional sport-producing units, such as sport television and radio networks, are

Table 1-2. The 20 NAICS Sectors or Major Economic Activities and Placement of Sport-related Economic Activities

Two-digit Code	Industry Categories and Sport-related Economic Activities	
11	Agriculture, forestry, fishing and hunting	
21	Mining	
22	Utilities	
23	Construction	
	234990	Athletic field construction
31–33	Manufacturing	
315	Sport/athletic apparel, sports clothing	
	316219	Athletic footwear manufacturing
	33992	Sporting goods manufacturing
41–43	Wholesale trade	
	42191	Sporting and recreational goods and suppliers, and wholesalers
44–46	Retail trade	
	451110	Sporting goods stores, sports gear stores
	453310	Sporting goods stores, used
48–49	Transportation and warehousing	
51	Information	
52	Finance and insurance	
53	Real estate and rental and leasing	
	532292	Sporting goods rental
54	Professional, scientific and technical services	
55	Management of companies and enterprises	
56	Administration and support and waste management and remediation services	
61	Education services	
	61162	Sports and recreation instructions
62	Health care and social assistance	
71	Arts, entertainment and recreation	
	71121	Spectator sports
	711211	Professional or semiprofessional sports teams and clubs
	711212	Racetracks
	711219	Independent professional or semiprofessional athletes (race car drivers, golfers, boxers), owners of racing participants (e.g., cars), and independent trainers
	71131	Promoters of sports events
	711310	Sports arena and stadium operators, sports event managers, organizers, and promoters
	71132	Promoters of sports events without facilities
	711320	Sports event managers, organizers and promoters without facilities
	712110	Sports halls of fame
	71391	Golf courses and country clubs
	71392	Skiing facilities
	71394	Fitness and recreational sports centers
	71395	Bowling centers
	713990	Recreational or youth sports teams and leagues
	711410	Sports figures' agents or managers
72	Accommodation and food services	
81	Other services (except public administration)	
	81149	Sport equipment repair and maintenance
	81391	Municipal sports authorities and councils
	81399	Administrative or regulatory athletic associations (e.g., leagues)
91–91	Public administration	

Source: Office of Management and Budget (1997). *North American Industry Classification System (NAICS)—1997.* US Department of Commerce, Washington, D.C.

not specifically classified. Thus, a conceptual framework that includes and links all the sport-producing units in a systematic matter must be constructed. As mentioned earlier, attempts have been previously made to define and outline the sport industry.

Meek (1997) uses a three-sector model to describe the sport industry in North America:

1. sports entertainments and recreation,
2. sports products and services, and
3. sports support organizations.

The first sector, sports entertainment and recreation, includes professional and amateur sport teams, sport events, sport media, and sport tourism-related businesses. The sport-producing units related to sporting goods design, manufacturing and distribution, and related to provision of sport services are included in the second sector, the sports products and services sector. The sport support organizations, the third sector of the sport industry, includes all professional and amateur organizations, such as leagues, marketing organizations, and law firms (see Figure 1-1 for details). Meek's model presents a broad operational definition of the sport industry because it "includes not only the economy activity of sports teams and recreational sports but also the spending of participants, spectators, and sponsors in connection with sports events" (Meek, p. 16). So, the foundation of his model is spending, not just the eco-

Learning Activities

1. Assume the role as the general manager of XYZ International to describe the sport industry in the United States.
2. Identify a sport business or organization that has been discussed explicitly in the chapter in terms of its sector association in the model and argue where it should go.
3. Review the North American Industry Classification System (NAICS).

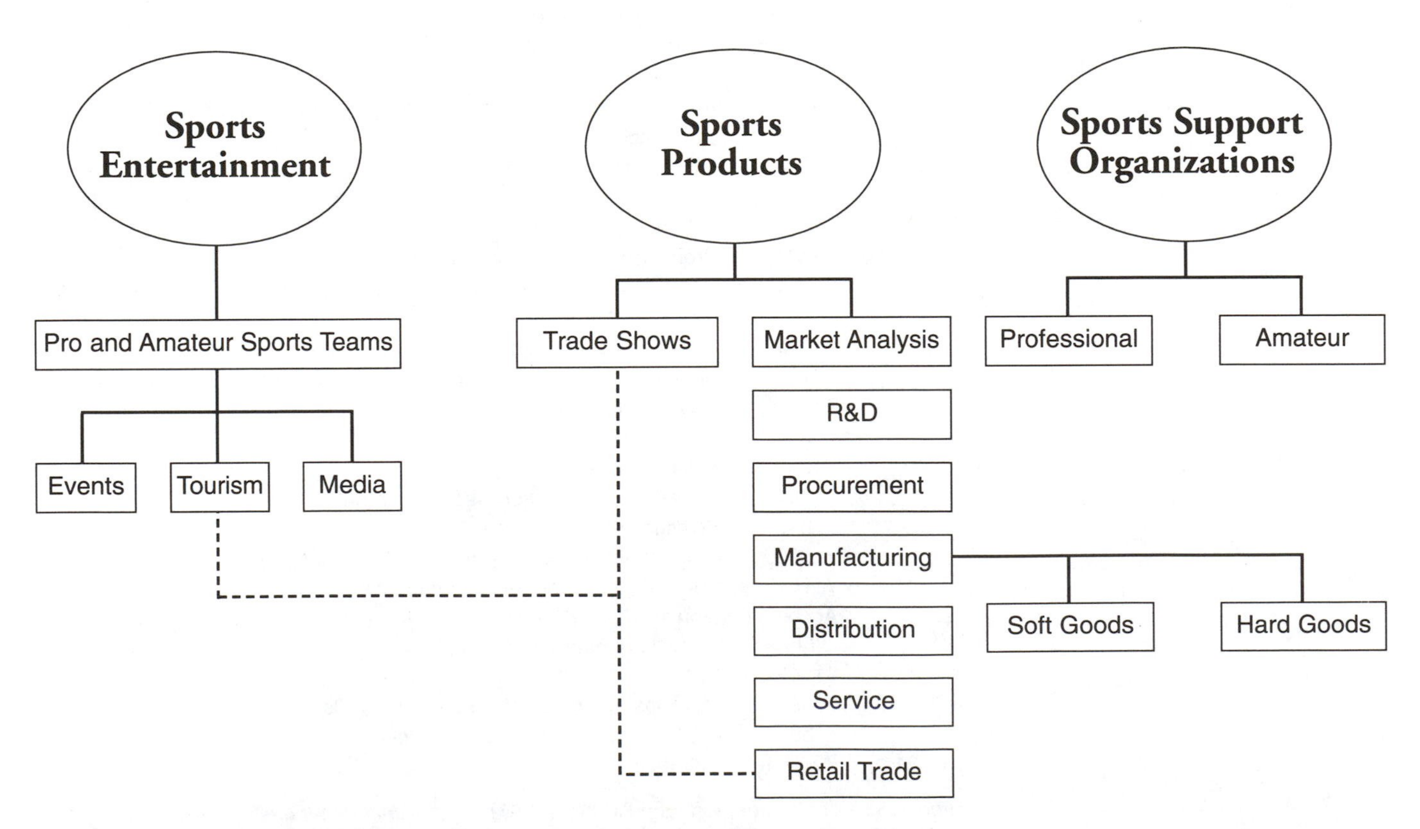

Figure 1-1. Meek's Model of the Sport Industry

Source: Meek, A. (1997). An estimate of the size and supported economic activity of the sports industry in the United States. *Sport Marketing Quarterly, 6*(4), 15–21.

nomic activity in which sport-related firms and organizations engage. This may be a limitation of his model. In addition, the three sectors are parallel, and they are not entirely separated from and independent of each other. Such a structure has caused some confusion as it does not clearly delineate the defined products or services of the sport industry.

Pitts, Fielding, and Miller (1994) also attempted to depict the sport industry with another three-sector model. In their model, the sport industry is defined as "a market in which the products offered to its buyers are sport, fitness, recreation, or leisure-related and may be activities, goods, services, people, places, or ideas" (p. 3). The industry is divided into three segments:

1. the sport performance industry segment,
2. the sport production industry segment, and
3. the sport promotion industry segment.

The sport performance industry segment refers to those sports firms that offer sport performance to the consumer either as a participatory or spectatorial product. The sport production industry segment includes those firms whose products are needed or desired for the production of or to influence the quality of sport performance, such as sporting goods manufacturers. The sport promotion industry segment includes those firms whose products offered as tools used to promote the sport product. Figure 1-2 shows the three segments and their respective descriptions. The separation of these three industry segments is based on the benefits of a product to a consumer. As Pitts and Stotlar (1996) maintain, "this type of categorization, called industry segmentation, is helpful to the sport market

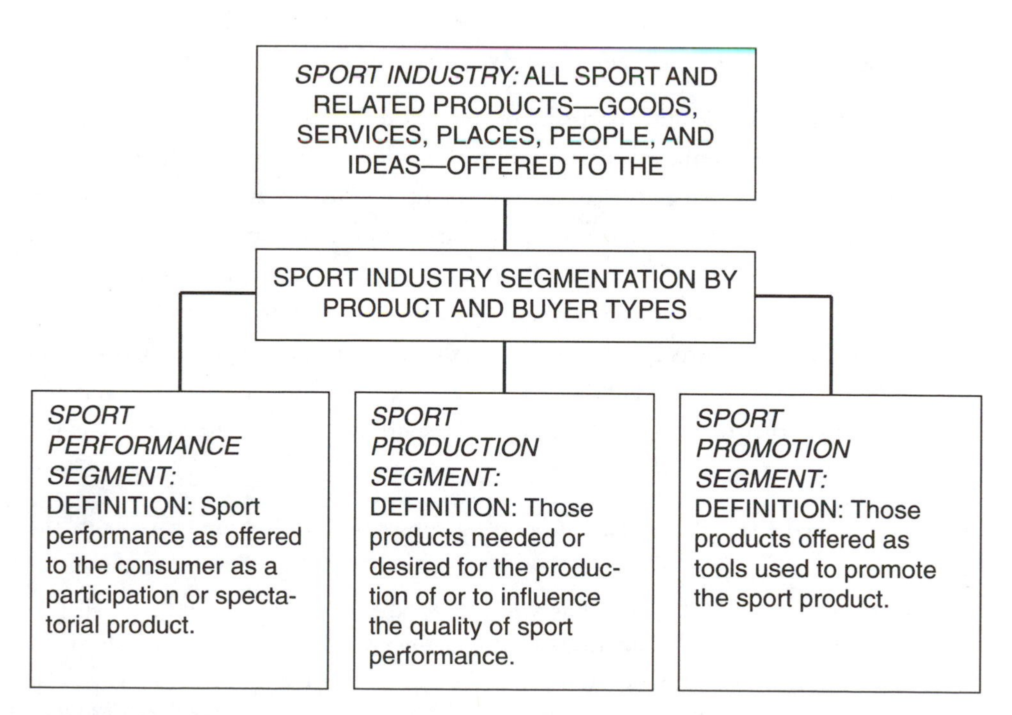

Figure 1-2. The Sport Industry Segment Model Proposed by Pitts, Fielding, and Miller

Source: From Pitts, B. G., Fielding, L. W., & Miller, L. K. (1994). Industry segmentation theory and the sport industry: Developing a sport industry segment model. *Sport Marketing Quarterly, 3*(1), 15–24.

ing professional in planning marketing strategies" (p. 19). This model does not, however, outline the relationship among sport-producing units of the sport industry. In addition, the separation of the three segments seems to imply that sport firms and organizations included in one segment are not related to those in another segment.

The authors of this book believe that sport activities (i.e., games and events) are one thing that all the firms and organizations in the sport industry can relate to. In other words, sport activities are the center around which many other products and services are produced in the sport industry. It is the sport activities that make this industry different from other entertainment counterparts. With this perception in mind, the authors of the book define the sport industry as the cluster of

1. the firms and organizations that produce sport activities,
2. the firms and organizations that provide products and services to support the production of sport activities, and
3. the firms and organizations that sell and trade products related to sport activities.

Conceptualized under this definition, a sport industry model is constructed.

The model has two main sectors. The first sector is the sport activity-producing sector. The firms and organizations that produce sport games, events, and services are included in this sector. Professional and semiprofessional teams, intercollegiate and interscholastic athletic departments, municipal and county recreation departments, sports and fitness clubs, and independent professional athletes, sports trainers and instructors, and owners of racing participants (e.g., race cars and horses) are examples of the sport activity producers. The sport activity-producing sector is the core of the sport industry. Sport activities are the main line of operations of all the firms and organizations in this sector. They can distinguish their line of operations clearly from those of other industries.

The second sector is labeled the sport-supporting sector. The firms and organizations that make up this sector are in the role of either providing products and services to support the production of sport activities or selling and trading products that are related to sport activities. There are six sport-supporting subsectors: administrative and regulatory athletic associations (e.g., USOC, NCAA, and NFL), sporting goods manufacturers, wholesalers and retailers, sports facilities and buildings, sport media, sport management firms, and municipal and county sports councils and authorities. Detailed descriptions on firms and organizations that are composed of these two sectors are given later in the section, and Figure 1-3 illustrates the conceptual framework of the sport industry and the relationship between these two sectors.

It must be noted that all the sport-supporting subsectors overlap somewhat with the sport activity-producing sector because sometimes firms and organizations in the sport-supporting sector also sponsor and organize sport events. This is indicated by the shaped areas between the big circle and the six smaller ones shown in Figure 1-3. However, because the primary role of firms and organizations in the sport-supporting sector is to facilitate the production of sport activities or to sell sport-related products, it would be appropriate to label them as sport-supporting subsectors. For example, sporting goods manufacturers, through their various wholesale channels, furnish athletic and sport equipment, such as baseball helmets, balls, and bats, to the municipal park and recreation

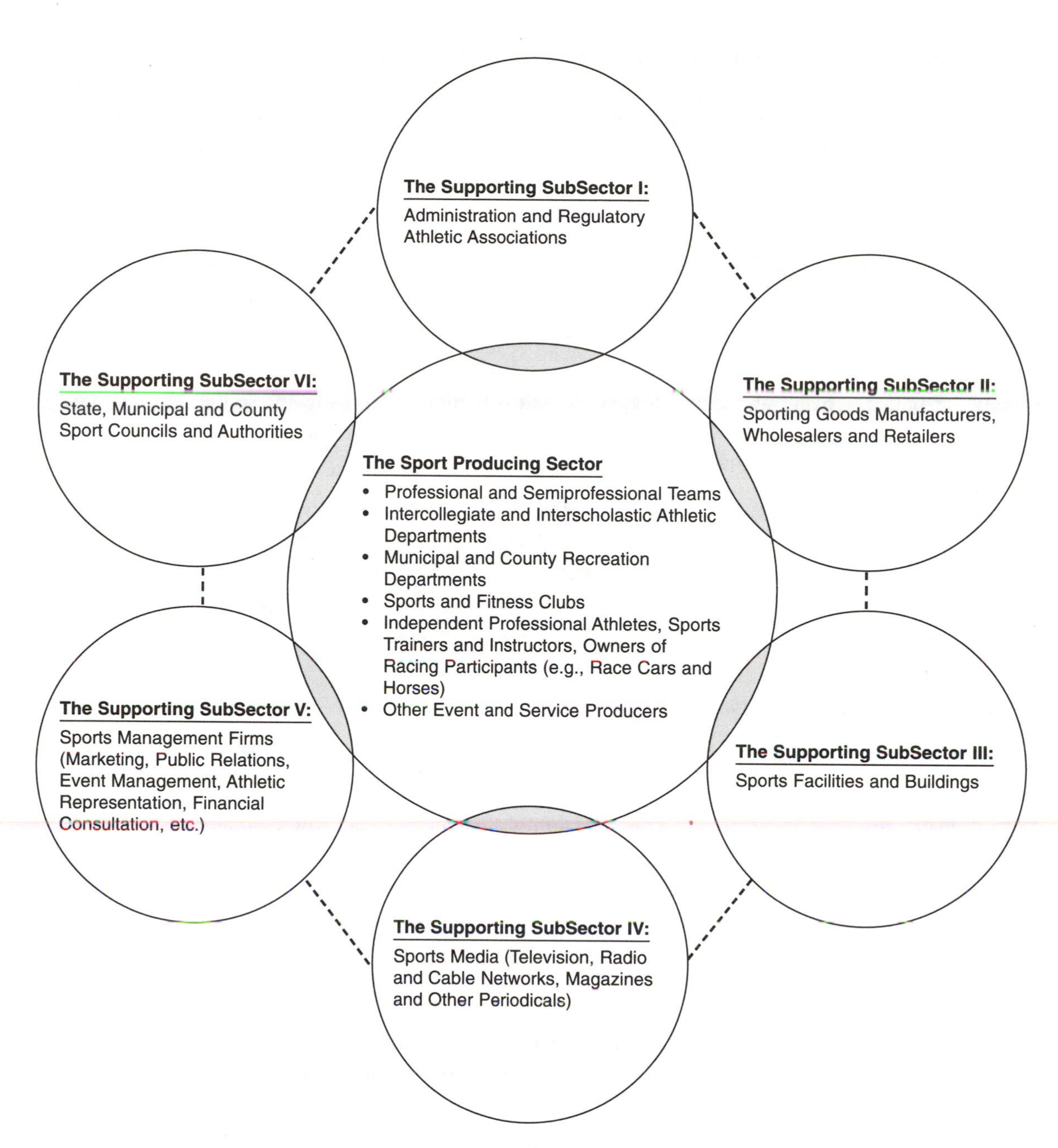

Figure 1-3. The Two-Sector Model of the Sport Industry

departments all over the country. They are not in the position to produce sport activities but to supply athletic and sport equipment and other sporting goods (e.g., athletic shoes and apparels) to firms and organizations in the sport activity-producing sector. This explains why sporting goods manufacturers, wholesalers, and retailers are classified as a sport-supporting subsector. The relationship between firms and organizations in the sport activity-producing sector and sport media is another good example to explain why the latter is a sport-supporting subsector. The games produced by and existence of professional sports teams provide the sport media with sources of information, such as news, statistics, and stories of players. This is what the sport media depend on and what they try to sell to the general public. It is logical, therefore, to regard the sport media as one of the important constituents of the sport-supporting sector.

The Sport Activity-Producing Sector

As mentioned above, the sport activity-producing sector comprises several types of firms and organizations that are primarily engaged in producing sport activities, events, programs, and services. They represent what the industry that we call "sport" is about.

Professional and Semiprofessional Sport Teams

Professional sport teams refers to those firms that are "primarily engaged in participating in live sporting events . . . before a paying audience" (Office of Management and Budget, 1997, pp. 659–660). According to the U. S. 1997 Economic Census (U.S. Census Bureau, 1999), there were about 462 professional sport teams or clubs affiliated with various leagues at both the major and minor league levels at that time. As firms in the sport-producing sector, individual sports teams or "franchises" are responsible for producing games to satisfy the needs and interest of consumers for sport entertainment. Each team usually has an exclusive right to market and operate in a designated area. Gate receipts, sales of premier seats and luxury suites, parking and concession, corporate sponsorships, and sales of local broadcast and telecast rights are the sources of revenues the teams receive to sustain their operations. More detailed discussion can be found in the section pertaining to administrative or regulatory associations in professional sport.

Intercollegiate and Interscholastic Athletic Departments

Intercollegiate sports is one of the unique aspects of both the higher education system and the sport industry in the United States. More than 4,000 colleges and universities play intercollegiate sports and compete under the sanction of three national governing bodies: the National Collegiate Athletic Association (NCAA), the National Association for Intercollegiate Athletics (NAIA), and the National Junior Collegiate Athletic Association (NJCAA). As of 2000, more than 1,000 institutions were affiliated with the NCAA, and approximately 350 small colleges are associates of the NAIA. The NJCAA has about 550 member institutions.

Each institution that holds membership with a national collegiate athletic association usually competes in a geographically determined conference at a competition level that matches its operating philosophy and financial resource. For example, member institutions of the NCAA are divided into three divisions (i.e., Division I, Division II, and Division III). The institutions with Division I football programs are further classified into two competition levels (i.e., Division I-A and Division I-AA). Although the mission and scope of operations of the athletic programs in the universities and colleges in the United States vary considerably, these programs have one thing in common: They all provide an athletic entertainment product (i.e., games) to their students, faculty, staff, and other constituents, such as their alumni and local communities. Again, more detailed information about athletic departments in colleges and universities can be found in the section discussing the administrative and regulatory athletic associations.

Municipal and County Recreation Departments

A recreation department is a government unit funded by local tax appropriation. Its mission is to provide opportunities for local residents to participate in various leisure and sports activities regardless of the residents' age, skill, and ability. The municipal and county recreation departments as a whole are the largest producer of sport-related events and activities in the United States. They sponsor a variety of adult and youth organized athletic programs all year.

Sports, Athletic, and Fitness Clubs

Golf courses, country clubs, and fitness and recreational sports centers are firms and organizations included in this crucial component of the sport activity-producing sector. They are primarily engaged in operating facilities featuring various fitness, athletic, and recreational sports activities (Office of Management and Budget, 1997). In 1997, more than 31,000 business establishments were classified by the U.S. Census Bureau as sports, athletic and fitness clubs (U.S. Census Bureau, 1999). Most of these types of business establishments rely primarily on membership dues or fees paid by users as a main source of income. Food and beverage, equipment rental, and instruction are other common types of services provided by those clubs. The distinction between a sports club that is included in the sport-producing sector and a sport facility that is listed under the sport-supporting sector is that the former is operated to provide services, in most cases, to their members, whereas the latter is used as a facility by clients who are not affiliated with it. Sports and fitness activities are the main line of operations of sports clubs. On the contrary, sports facilities, especially stadiums and arenas, are often used to hold many nonsport events. Detailed discussion on sport facilities and buildings is provided later in this chapter.

Independent Professional Athletes and Other Independent Activity Producers

Independent professional athletes are those individuals who perform and participate in live sporting events for the sake of their own financial well-being (U.S. Census Bureau, 1999). They make decisions independently on various matters, such as competition schedules and endorsements. Independent professional athletes are commonly seen in tennis, golf, track and field, bowling, and race car driving. Other independent activity producers include the owners of race participants, such as race cars, horses, and dogs. They enter the race participants into events and competitions for prizes and endorsements. Sport trainers and instructors are the third group of people who are independently engaged in providing specialized services to athletes and the general public. Sport medicine clinics and tennis schools are examples of this type of independent sport-activity producer. According to the 1997 U.S. Economic Census (U.S. Census Bureau, 1997), there were 2,591 independent professional athletes and other sport activity producers.

The Sport-Supporting Sector

All the firms and organizations other than those included in the sport activity producing sector make up the sport-supporting sector of the sport industry due to their special role in supporting the production of sport activities. Based upon their distinct purpose and functions, these firms and organization are placed into six sport-supporting subsectors.

Supporting Subsector I: Administrative or Regulatory Athletic Associations

The *administrative and regulatory athletic associations* refer to those organizations formed specifically to perform administrative or regulatory duties for and promote the interest of their members. Examples of administrative athletic association include the American Association for Professional Athletics (AAPA) and the National Football League Players Association (NFLPA). On the other hand, the National Basketball Association (NBA) and the United States of America (USA) Volleyball are examples of the regulatory athletic associations. They make and interpret rules of competition for their members and reinforce the policies set by the organization among members. Four types of administrative or regulatory athletic associations are discussed in the following section.

Administrative or regulatory associations in professional sport. Facilitating the presentation of professional sport as a business and entertainment product to consumers is the main goal of the administrative and regulatory organizations in professional sport. So, it is the primary responsibility for a professional sports league to create and maintain a constructive environment in which its players can compete. Their activities include, but are not limited to, setting up competition schedules, negotiating collective bargaining agreements with players' unions, making various rules (e.g., determining order of amateur draft) and regulatory policies to enforce its management rights, and negotiating national TV agreements.

A professional sport league in team sports is categorized as either a major or a minor league. The authors of this book define a major league as one that has a scope of operations nationwide, competes for media coverage from national television networks, attracts consumer dollars across the nation, and fills affiliated teams with the best available players. Using this definition, five men's professional sports leagues and one women's league in the United States qualify as major leagues: Major League Baseball (MLB), the National Basketball Association (NBA), the National Football League (NFL), the National Hockey League (NHL), and the Women's National Basketball Association (WNBA). To a certain extent, the Arena Football League (AFL) meets some of the criteria mentioned above; however, it is still perceived by the public as an entity with a semi-major league status because, in many aspects, it remains secondary to the NFL. The Canadian Football League is the only major league exclusively in Canada.

A professional sport league would be labeled as a minor league under two basic conditions. If a professional sport league voluntarily takes a secondary stance not to compete economically against the existing major league in the same sport even through its operations are national in scope, the league is a minor league. A league of this type does not try to compete with its major league counterpart for the same caliber of players or for the same financial resources, such as national television revenues and consumer dollars. The Continental Basketball League (CBA) is an example of this type of minor league. The second condition for a professional sport league to be considered as a minor league exists if it operates in a designated geographical region and it becomes inherently noncompetitive in both the sporting and economic senses to the league playing at the major level. There are usually more than one minor league in the same sport across the nation because of such geographical separation. Minor leagues and their affiliated teams often have agreements with teams in major leagues that make the minor league function as a farm system for teams in those major leagues. All major sports leagues in North America, except the WNBA, have minor league systems. The NFL has its minor systems in both North America and Europe (i.e., the Arena Football League and the NFL Europe).

In general, the minor league teams in North America compete against teams at their own level. For example, both minor league baseball and minor league soccer have a pyramid-like delivery system to supply talented players to their respective major leagues. Based on the size of the market and level of competition, a league playing minor league baseball is classified as either a Pony league/Rookie League, or an *A*, *AA*, *AAA* league. The higher the classification, the higher its level of competition. The number of leagues and teams decreases as the level of competition goes up. Most of the minor league baseball teams are affiliated with a major league franchise. The latter usually assumes some operating costs of the affiliated club (e.g., player salaries, travel expenses).

The minor league system serves several critical economic roles for major league teams:

1. It is a reserve system for major league franchises. A replacement player is called up from AAA when a major league player is hurt.

2. It is a training ground for player development. For example, in baseball, players drafted by a major league franchise from college and high school are usually sent to its affiliated minor league teams for development and future use.

Another good example to illustrate the relationship between a major league and its minor leagues and how the former uses the latter as a farm system in North America is the United Soccer League. The mission of the organization is to provide systematic training and opportunities for soccer players to work through the pipeline toward Major League Soccer, the top level of the pyramid. An agreement was reached by MLS and USL in 1996 to allow the USL to act as a farm system for MLS. There are also four levels beneath it. The immediate level is the A-League. It had 28 teams in 1998, including three in Canada. Under an agreement with MLS, one of the teams in the league is stocked entirely with players identified and supported by MLS, and other teams are affiliated with individual MLS teams. The next tier in the pyramid is called Division III Professional League. Forty teams played in the 1998 season. Again, all of the teams are associated with teams in MLS. The Division III Professional [Soccer] League is the lowest level of professional soccer in the system. The next two levels, the Premier Development Soccer League and National Youth League, are composed of amateur soccer teams. In addition to the four leagues mentioned above, a women's amateur soccer league, W-League, and an men's indoor soccer league, I-League, are also affiliated with the USL (United Soccer League, 1999).

There was not a minor league in professional football until the creation of American Football Association (AFA) in 1980. The goal of the organization is to advance and promote professional football at the minor league level. The AFA is an umbrella organization that consists of several semiprofessional/minor leagues in professional football. The Association and its member leagues produce a national play-off series, in which the league champions and wild-card teams participate. Two major differences exist between minor league football and other sports that also have minor league operations. First, the American Football Association has no backing or support from its major league counterpart, the NFL and its major league affiliates. In other words, those minor leagues are not recognized as development leagues or a farm system for the NFL. Second, the Association takes care not only of minor league professional football teams, but also of all levels of nonprofessional football leagues.

The National Lacrosse League (NLL) is the only professional lacrosse league in the world. Due to its limited scope of operations (mainly the northeastern part of the United States and southeastern region of Canada), NLL is still perceived as a minor league. The league was founded in 1997 as a result of the merger of two indoor lacrosse leagues, the Major Indoor Lacrosse League and the professional Indoor Lacrosse Leagues. Currently, it has seven franchises.

There are also some administrative or regulatory associations in professional sport that are mainly developed for individual sports, such as the National Association for Stock Cars (NASCAR), the Professional Golf Association (PGA), the Ladies Professional Golf Association (LPGA), the Senior Professional Golf Association (Senior PGA), and the Dupont World Team Tennis (the only professional tennis league in the United States of America). The following is brief description of the three associations in professional golf.

The most preeminent professional golf association in North America is the Professional Golf Association of America, or the so-called PGA Tour. The PGA of America was founded in 1916. Through its 80 years of evolution, the Tour has grown tremendously. To provide effective, direct communication with its members and amateur golfers, the PGA of America divides the country into 41 geographical regions and designates a PGA Section Office for each region. Section office have the responsibility for conducting regional qualifying tournaments for amateur events; sponsoring junior clinics and the Nike Tour; and offering educational programs, workshops, and seminars to local PGA members and their apprentices. The PGA has taken the full advantage of the increased popularity in golf in recent years. The Senior PGA Tour was founded by PGA in 1980 to accommodate professional golfers who are over 50 years old and no longer as competitive as the younger players on the PGA Tour. The major event in the Senior PGA Tour is the PGA Seniors' Championship.

The Ladies Professional Golf Association (LPGA) is another distinct professional golf organization in North America. Formed and chartered in 1951, the LPGA Tour organized only a handful of 7 to 8 events in its first year of operation, and little or no financial reward was given to the pioneering women players. In 1997, after more than 46 years of existence, the LPGA Tour was able to manage 41 events with over $30 million in prize money. Thirty-one of those events were televised on ABC, CBS, or ESPN. Currently, the Tour sponsors four major events: the Nabisco Dinah Shore, the McDonald's LPGA Championship, the U.S. Women's Open Championship, and the de Maurier Classic. Sprint, Merrill Lynch, Mercury, 7UP, and *Golf Magazine*, together with another 28 companies, are the official sponsors of the LPGA Tour in 1998.

Administrative or regulatory sport associations in college. The National Collegiate Athletic Association (NCAA) is the largest of the three national governing bodies in intercollegiate athletics. To a great extent, it represents how collegiate sports are governed in the United States. With this in mind, discussion of administrative or regulatory sport associations in college will mainly use the NCAA as an example.

In 1996–1997, the NCAA sponsored and administered 81 championships in 22 sports for its member institutions in three divisions. More than 24,000 men and women student-athletes annually compete in these events for national titles. Specifically, there currently are 10 national collegiate championships for which all divisions are eligible—three for men, four for women, and three men's and women's events. There are 23 national collegiate Division I championships (13 men, 11 women), 23 national collegiate Division II championships (13 men, 10 women) and 24 national collegiate Division III championships (13 men, 11 women) (National Collegiate Athletic Association, 1996). Several major sports sponsored by the NCAA are described in the following section.

All three divisions of the NCAA sponsor football, but not all member institutions play football. Again, due to differences in size and financial resources, two levels of competition also exist among the institutions that play football in Division I, commonly known as Division I-A and Division I-AA. There are 104 institutions playing in 10 Division I-A football conferences. Eight schools that do not hold membership in any Division I-A conference, such as Notre Dame, also compete at Division I-A level as so-called "independents." Another 120 schools are affiliated with Division I-AA football; 105 of these schools play in 13 athletic conferences, and the rest are independents ("College Football," 1997).

In the 1995–1996 academic year, the NCAA brought in $221 million, derived primarily from a contract with CBS Sports for television rights for a number of NCAA championship events, foremost of which was the Division I Men's Basketball Championship. Total television rights fees represent 82% of the NCAA's operating revenue. Additional revenue sources include six percent from royalties, nine percent from championship events, and three percent from other, miscellaneous sources. The NCAA also receives a $12 million grant from the federal government for the National Youth Sports Program. Of the approved operation budget, it is projected that a total of $130.7 million (59.1% of the NCAA's total expenditure budget) was distributed to the NCAA membership during the 1995–1996 fiscal year. This amount was distributed in the form of direct payments consistent with the revenue-distribution plan approved by the NCAA Executive Committee. Championship expenses, including transportation guarantees, per diem allowances, and game expenses, were projected at $40.3 million (18.2%). Almost $20.7 million, or 9.4% of the budget, was to be spent on program services and activities that benefit the membership such as drug testing, drug education, promotions, legal fees, publications, research, sports sciences, seminars, conventions, student and youth benefits, scholarships and catastrophic injury insurance. Committee and program administration accounted for the remaining $29.9 million, or 13.3% of the budget (NCAA, 1996).

Administrative or regulatory sport associations in high school. In the United States, high school athletics as a whole is administered at the state level, and little or no national high school athletic competition is held. The National Federation of State High School Associations (NFHS), which consists of high school athletic/activity associations in the 50 states plus the District of Columbia, is an umbrella organization of state associations. According to its mission statement (NFHS, 2000), the NFHS provides leadership and national coordination for the administration of interscholastic activities, including sports. However, its leadership is provided only through the publication of competition rules in 16 sports for both boys and girls, and the NFHS does not organize any national championships in all sports under its purview. The high school associations of individual states are the main sponsors and organizers of athletic competitions among high schools within a state. The competition is usually held at multiple levels, such as AAAA, AAA, AA, and A, based on the type and size of participating schools. Also, many associations across the nation have been created for the sake of organizing competition in certain sports at the high school level, such as the Interscholastic Sailing Association (ISSA), which governs secondary school sailing in the United States, in both independent and public high schools.

Administrative or regulatory associations in other amateur sport. In addition to the administrative and regulatory athletic associations mentioned above that operate mainly to provide support for the presentation of sports competition at professional, intercollegiate, and interscholastic levels, many other administrative and regulatory sport bodies are also involved in, and contribute considerably to, the economic activities of the sport industry.

Examples of this type of administrative and regulatory athletic associations include the United States Olympic Committee (USOC), some 50 individual sports federations, the Amateur Athletic Union (AAU), and the Women's Sports Foundation. Many other administrative and regulatory sport-governing bodies have been developed to serve specific demographic markets, such as people with disabilities and gay/lesbian athletes. In addition, many amateur sport organizations function as administrative and regulatory governing bodies at the state or local level. Georgia State Games Commission, one of some 40 state-games organizing agencies around the country, is an example. The following section briefly describes the USOC, the AAU, and the Women's Sports Foundations. It is hoped that the description will provide hints as to what the administrative and regulatory associations in amateur sport do to contribute to the advancement of sport in the United States.

The USOC is one of the biggest nonprofit sports organizations in the United States in terms of its budget and scope of operations. The mission of this organization is to assist and facilitate the participation of every American in sport and provide "leadership and guidance for the Olympic Movement" in the United States (USOC, 1998). Specifically, the USOC is responsible for

1. Supporting Olympic and/or Pan American sports in the United States,
2. Sponsoring U.S. teams and underwriting their expenses in the Olympic and Pan American Games,
3. Endorsing the bid of an American city for the hosting right of the Winter and Summer Olympic Games as well as the Pan American Games.

Public Law 95-606, the Amateur Sports Act (ASA) of 1978 (USOC, 2000), empowered the USOC to be the coordinating body of all Olympic-related athletic activities in the United States. In other words, the law gave the USOC the rights (a) to control Olympics-related phraseologies and logos and (b) to control more than 72 national governing bodies (NGB) and amateur sports in the United States. These NGB are responsible for organizing and sanctioning various national competitions in their jurisdiction. If the sport is a worldwide one, the international federation of the sport recognizes its NGB in the United States as the official U.S. representative.

The revenues and funds that the USOC receives mainly come from several major sources:

1. A portion of the revenues generated from the sales of American television rights for the Summer and Winter Olympic Games,
2. The sponsorship and advertising revenues from corporations using the Olympic rings in the United States;
3. Royalty fees from the sales of Olympic merchandise or goods that bear Olympic symbols;
4. Private donations.

In 1997, the USOC raised approximately $400 million to support its various operations.

Founded as a not-for-profit organization in 1888, the Amateur Athletic Union (AAU) is basically an alliance of national and district associations, amateur athletic groups, and educational institutions in the United States. Its mission is to promote the development of amateur sports and physical fitness programs in the country. Prior to the passage of the

Amateur Sports Act in 1978, the AAU served as a main representative of the United States to international sport organizations and was responsible for the preparation of athletes for the Olympic Games. After 1978, the AAU refocused its operations. By embracing the "Sports for All" philosophy, it has become a leader in domestic affairs pertaining to amateur sport. The AAU currently has 58 distinct associations, which annually sanction more than 32 sports programs, 200 national championships, and over 5,000 local events, which may include the AAU Junior Olympic Games, the AAU Sullivan Youth Excel Program, and the AAU Complete Athlete Program. A significant event took place in 1996, when the AAU joined forces with Walt Disney World and later relocated its national headquarters to Orlando, Florida (AAU, 2000). As a result of this partnership, the AAU is able to hold more than 40 of its national events at the new Disney's Wide World of Sports Complex.

Established as a national nonprofit organization in 1974, the Women's Sports Foundation has the clear mission of improving the physical, mental, and emotional well-being of all females through sports and fitness participation. Four programs exist for achieving this mission: education, opportunity, advocacy, and recognition. The educational program seeks to improve public understanding of the benefits of sports and fitness participation for females. This is done through several channels, such as publications and research, as well as events, like the National Girls & Women in Sports Day (NGWSD), to promote sports opportunities for girls and women. Through forming partnerships with various corporations, the Women's Sports Foundation offers grants to support girls and women who want to actualize their potential in athletic and leadership skills. Examples of these grants include the Ocean Spray Travel and Training Fund, the Leadership Development Grant, and the Tampax Grants for girls (Women's Sports Foundation, 2000). The advocacy function of the Foundation attempts to change the policies, laws, and social patterns to encourage more female involvement in sports and fitness. Advocacy activities include, but are not limited to, (a) organizing annual events in Washington to educate and inform legislators of the needs and achievements of as well as the issues related to girls and women, (b) monitoring any legislation that may affect girls and women in sports and fitness, and (c) establishing a network with politicians. The Women's Sports Foundation acknowledges outstanding individuals in sports and fitness in several different ways. The Community Awards Program recognizes girls and women with distinguished athletic achievements and contributions at the grass-roots level. The foundation also honors the more prominent achievers at an annual event, "A Salute to Women in Sports." The Women's Sports Foundation operates with funds that come from various sources, such as private donations, corporate sponsorships and partnerships, and membership.

Supporting Subsector II: Sporting Goods Manufacturers, Wholesalers, and Retailers

The sporting goods manufacturers, wholesalers, and retailers include companies that either manufacture sporting goods or distribute and sell those products in the sports and recreation market. As of 1999, close to 900 companies in the United States are categorized in this sector (Patino, 1999). *Sporting goods* is an umbrella term including equipment and gears for various sporting and recreational purposes. The U.S. Census Bureau (1997) divides sporting goods into four basic categories:

1. athletic and sport clothing,
2. athletic and sport footwear,

3. athletic and sport equipment (e.g., exercise equipment, golf equipment, team sports equipment, and related accessories), and
4. recreational transport (e.g., bicycles and snowmobiles).

Sporting goods are sold through a comprehensive distribution and sales system. Sporting goods manufacturers traditionally rely on various sporting goods wholesalers and retailers to distribute and sell their products. Although continuously using the external distribution channels, many companies today have formed their own wholesale and retail networks. For example, Nike has extensively used three of its own retail structures to sell its products directly, including the Nike towns, the Nike stores, and the Nike factory outlets. As a new marketing strategy, the in-house retail system can help sporting goods companies achieve greater consumer loyalty and strengthen their competitiveness, ultimately leading to greater market shares.

Supporting Subsector III: Sports Facilities and Buildings

Sports facilities and buildings refer to those public assembly facilities that are primarily used to host sport-related events. In general, sports facilities and buildings include stadiums, arenas, sports complexes, sports halls of fame, racetracks, and a facility used only by a single sport, such as bowling alleys, skiing facilities, and ice/roller-skating rinks. Many public assembly facilities (e.g., convention centers) that usually have large and spacious exhibit halls also can be utilized for various sports programming. Nevertheless, because sport is not the main line of operations of those facilities, they are not considered sport facilities. For example, the Savannah Civic Center is not viewed as a sport facility because it was built as a multipurpose facility and sports are not the main tenant of the facility.

The mission of sports facilities and buildings varies depending on size. Large stadiums and arenas are used for two basic objectives: (a) to provide a competition venue for a local professional sports team or teams or for the owners of race participants and (b) to support local economic development through contracting international, national, and regional sporting events to the facility. For example, the mission of the Georgia Dome is to provide a state-of-the-art home venue for the NFL Atlanta Falcons and to bring in events that can generate economic benefits to the state of Georgia and the city of Atlanta. For many small sport facilities, such as ice/roller-skating rinks and bowling alleys, maximization of their use is a main goal pursued persistently by owners of these facilities.

The scope of operations of the facilities varies also depending on the type of the facility ownership. There are two types of sports facilities in terms of ownership: publicly owned facilities and privately owned facilities. A large number of sport facilities today are owned by government. The Georgia Dome in Atlanta, Georgia, is owned by the State of Georgia, which has specifically created a facility management entity called the Georgia World Congress Center Authority to manage it.

Supporting Subsector IV: Sport Media

The term *sports media* encompasses a large segment of the sport industry that entertains consumers with special forms of sport-related products. These products range from electronic news and reports about sports events on television, cable, and radio networks to players' stories and team statistics in print sources like magazines and newspapers. The existence of the sports media signifies a unique relationship with the media and what the media intends to distribute and sell, the sporting activities (e.g., games and events). The following two points delineate this unique relationship (Coakley, 1994; Eitzen & Sage, 1997):

1. The success of sports as commercial entertainment depends on the media. This is because the discussions on statistics, records and standings, overall performance of players and teams, and upcoming games or matches help to promote and popularize a particular sport. It is also because the financial support (i.e., the rights fee) provides a sports organization with a critical source of revenues. In many cases, the revenues that a sports organization generates from the sale of media rights fee are greater than gate receipts.

2. The mass media take advantage of the public's vast interest in sports and use sport programming to enhance their program quality. It is believed that the marriage between a particular media network and sport will not only help the former enhance its image, but will also increase its revenues from sales of advertisements. Other perceived benefits that the media may receive due to such an alliance include the enhancement of its competitive position in the market, improvement of viewers' loyalty, and cross-promotion of other programming.

In general, the sports media consists of three major segments: the sport broadcast media, the sport print media, and the Internet sport media. The sport broadcast media refers to the media segment that delivers sports-related messages to the public through various electronic channels, such as television and radio broadcasting and cable networks. The sport print media communicate with the readership through various printed materials, which include magazines and newspapers. The Internet sport media are a newly expanded media segment that delivers sport-related information to the viewer or reader via the Internet.

Sport broadcast media. The sports broadcast system and the presentation of the broadcast media in the United States are configured in a relatively complicated, three-tier structure. At the national level, several media conglomerates, such as the American Broadcasting Company (ABC), the National Broadcasting Company (NBC), the Columbia Broadcasting System (CBS), and the FOX Broadcasting Company and their sports programming divisions together present extensive coverage of sports events, ranging from professional sports games to amateur college athletic competitions, and from the Super Bowl to the Indy 500 race. Nevertheless, because the sports events covered by these media giants account for a relatively small portion of their total programming, they are not considered part of the sport industry. In addition to the sport programming delivered by these national television networks, the sports-only cable channels at the national level, such as the Entertainment and Sports Programming Network (ESPN), the Golf Channel, and the Fox Sports Net, a subsidiary of the FOX Broadcasting Company, also produce sports programming for the national audience. Because these media companies are primarily engaged in producing sports-related media programs, they are regarded as one of the important components of the sport-supporting sector.

It must be pointed out that some entertainment cable networks, such as the Home Box Office (HBO), a Division of the Time Warner Entertainment Company, also provide sports programming on a pay-per-view basis. Professional boxing is the most common sport on these channels. Again, because their main line of operations is not sport oriented, these cable networks do not qualify for inclusion under the umbrella of the sport industry.

The second tier of sports presentations through the broadcast media is contributed by the so-called "superstations" and other regional networks. WGN-TV based in Chicago and the Turner Broadcast System (TBS) are examples of superstations that have signals available to a national audience, but do not have the same status as other national networks. The same argument used above in the discussion of whether or not HBO is a sport company holds true here. WGN-TV and TBS are not sport entities. There are some real sport-oriented regional networks, such as the nine regional cable sports channels owned by FOX Sports (e.g., the Fox Sports Midwest, the Sunshine Network).

Local television and radio stations constitute the third tier of sports programming. These stations are locally owned and run, and they have some sort of affiliation with the national networks. In addition to carrying signals of those sports events that are broadcast nationally by the networks the local stations are affiliated with, these stations often provide news and live coverage of games played by local teams at both professional and collegiate levels and of sports activities held in the community. Programming of this type of local stations is predominantly in news and other shows, and in no way can they be called "sport stations."

Sport print media. Sport print media refers to publications that are devoted primarily to sport, ranging from sports almanacs to sport magazines. Sport print media are a traditional source of information sought by consumers. There are mainly two types of sport print media: the one for the general population and the one for professionals. *Sports Illustrated* and *ESPN Magazine* are examples of sport publications for the general population that satisfy the needs of consumers for information in sport. Stories about players and teams and special commentaries on sport-related issues are their common themes and ingredients. On the other hand, the readership of the sport publications for professionals, such as the *Athletic Business*, the *Sports Business Journal*, and the *Sport Marketing Quarterly*, is primarily professionals in the field of sport. The contents of those publications are, therefore, technically oriented. For example, the *Sport Marketing Quarterly* is a publication that mainly targets sports marketing educators at colleges and universities as well as marketing practitioners and advertising agencies dealing with sports marketing.

Sport Internet media. Thanks to the development in communication technology, the sport Internet media have been gradually become a pervasive form of influence over many people's daily lives. Together with the two traditional forms (i.e., the sport broadcast and print media), the sport Internet media have shown a promising future. According to Intille (1996), more than 2,500 sport-related Web sites were identified, ranging from the CNN/SI.com to the ESPN SportsZone and from the SportLine.com to the GolfWeb. The sport Internet media may eventually rival the other two traditional forms of media.

The sport Internet media use sport online in several ways (Intille, 1996):

1. Information sources. Online sport provides updated, timely information to sport fans or sport enthusiasts with no distribution cost and hassle. Graphical illustrations of some sport actions can be replayed second-by-second by the enthusiastic fans with the help of advanced Internet technology. The amount of sport-related information that can be accessed by consumers is considerable.

2. Communication channels. Sport Internet media provide linkage among sport fans through email, mailing lists, and Internet chat services. Sport fans can share opinions on topics and issues that concern them.

3. Competitive systems. Fantasy games, online gambling, and online video games are three services that sport Internet media provide to sport enthusiasts so they can compete against each other on the Internet. A fee is usually charged to the fan who uses one of these competitive systems available online. For example, Nintendo has developed some games that can be simultaneously played by several people from different locations through the linkage of the Internet.

Supporting Subsector V: Sport Management Firms

Sport management firms refers to those companies and corporations that are primarily engaged in

1. organizing, promoting, and/or managing sports events,
2. representing and managing professional athletes, and
3. providing legal and financial consultant services to sport firms and organizations, and to individual athletes.

Not all sport management firms offer the same services to their clients. Some may specialize only in one or more of the above-mentioned areas. For example, Baker and Hostetler is a law firm that mainly handles various legal issues for clients in the sport industry, such as intellectual property, licensing, and labor matters (Patino, 1999). Approximately 367 firms in the United States are involved in event marketing and management, consumer promotion, public relations, and corporate sponsorships (Patino, 1999). The International Management Group (IMG), Advantage International, and the SFX Sports Group are the three largest sport management firms in the nation. As one of the subsidiaries of SFX Entertainment that was founded in 1998, the SFX Sports Group has emerged as one of the leading sport management firms in the sport industry. It provides unparalleled services in corporation consultation, talented athlete representation and marketing, stadium representation and marketing, stadium and arena naming rights, online services, event management, sponsorship sales, property marketing, television production and programming, and public relations (SFX Entertainment, Inc, 1999).

Supporting Subsector VI: State, Municipal, and County Sports Commissions and Authorities

In North America, sport has been widely recognized by community leaders as an essential instrument in the economic development of their communities. Thus, many states, municipalities, and counties have formed quasi-governmental sport organizations to facilitate and coordinate sport development. Sport commissions and sport authorities are two basic types of those structures. They usually have distinct operating functions. However, in some cases, a sport entity is created to take on all the responsibilities that are assumed by both structures.

Sport commissions. There are two levels of sport commissions, state and municipal. A sport commission at the state level is commonly set up as a private entity primarily for the sake of (a) promoting and developing the sport industry in a certain state, (b) serving the needs and interests of residents in the state for sports, and (c) using sports to boost economic development in that state. For example, the Florida Sports Foundation, Inc. is the official sports promotion and development organization for the State of Florida. The Foundation is a private, nonprofit corporation operating under contract with the Office of Tourism, Trade and Economic Development under the Executive Office of the Governor. The Foundation functions as a private entity and is overseen by a board of directors, with 15 members appointed by the governor and 15 appointed from the private sector (Florida Sports Foundation, 1998).

Sport commissions at the municipal level, sometimes called sport councils (e.g., the Greater Savannah Sports Council), are commonly affiliated with the chambers of commerce of their cities. Local government is their primary funding source. The major functions of sport commissions are (a) to solicit, create, and secure sports events that will stimulate the local economy; (b) to promote and enhance the image of a particular community; and (c) to provide entertainment and participatory opportunities to local residents to improve their quality of life. The USA/Russia Olympic Boxing Exhibition, the Women's Sports Foundation Summit, and the USA Volleyball Junior Olympic Championships are just few examples of the events attracted to the central Florida area by the Orlando Area Sports Commission.

Sport authorities. Sport authorities are another type of quasi-governmental organization that is primarily responsible for

1. securing funds and investment to construct sports facilities,

2. managing the sports facilities funded and owned by local government, and

3. obtaining a sports franchise or franchises.

The responsibility in fund security includes borrowing money, issuing debt, and collecting fees and charges for events held in the facility. For example, the main purpose of the New Jersey Sports & Exposition Authority was to secure $300 million in financing to construct the Meadowlands Arena complex (Deckard, 1990). The facility management function of a sport authority is exemplified by the responsibilities of the Tampa Sports Authority. The Tampa Sports Authority is responsible for planning, developing, and maintaining sports and recreational facilities for residents of Tampa and Hillsborough County. The Authority currently owns and operates three sports facilities, the new Raymond James Stadium, the Legends Field, and the Ice Palace Arena, and manages three public golf courses.

In many cases, a sport authority is empowered either by specific state legislation or by a local ordinance dealing with matters related to sports facility financing. For instance, in Florida, specific state legislation was enacted that provided each county with absolute discretion to create its own form of sports, entertainment, or cultural authority. In case of the Tampa Sports Authority, it was created by the Florida Legislature in 1965.

Chapter Questions

1. Explain how the North American Industry Classification System defines an industry.
2. Compare and contrast the three models constructed to depict the sport industry in the United States of America: the two 3-sector models proposed by Meek and by Pitts et al., and the two-sector model by Li, Hofacre, and Mahony.
3. Describe the two-sector model in terms of its components, and explain the rationale for the model.
4. Provide a brief overall description of the types of companies and organizations included in the sport-producing sector.
5. Briefly describe the sport organizations included in the "administrative and regulatory athletic associations" supporting sector.
6. Briefly describe the sport organizations included in the "sporting goods manufacturers, wholesalers and retailers" supporting sector.
7. Briefly describe the sport organizations included in the "sport facilities and buildings" supporting sector.
8. Briefly describe the sport organizations included in the "sport media" supporting sector.
9. Briefly describe the sport organizations included in the "sport management firms" supporting sector.
10. Briefly describe the sport organizations included in the "municipal and county sport councils and authorities" supporting sector.

Summary

This chapter has presented an overview of the sport industry. The overview and discussion are based on a model that groups all sport-producing industrial units into two major sectors: the sport-producing sector and the sport-supporting sector. On the one hand, the sport-producing sector consists of companies and organizations that produce sport activities (e.g., games and events) and services. The sport-supporting sector, on the other hand, includes companies and organizations that help the firms, organizations, and individuals in the sport-producing sector produce quality sport activities. There are six subsectors: administrative or regulatory athletic associations, sporting goods manufacturers, wholesalers and retailers, sports facilities and buildings, sport media, sport management firms, and sport commissions and authorities.

Chapter Two

Basics of Economic Analysis

What Is Economics?

Before beginning our discussion of the basic economic principles related to organizational motives, supply and demand, and market structures, it is important to first discuss the meaning of economics. To begin, we must make a distinction between finances and economics. Webster defines finances as the "management of money affairs." Although much of what we talk about in this book includes money affairs, the terms *finances* and *economics* are not synonymous. Economics is not just talking about income statements and balance sheets; it also is a way of viewing human behavior and decision making.

There are many definitions of economics. Samuelson and Nordhaus (1995) define it as "the study of how societies use scarce resources to produce valuable commodities and distribute them among different people." Lipsey, Courant, and Ragan (1999) simply say economics is the "use of scarce resources to satisfy unlimited human wants" (p. 4). A third definition, from Colander (1998), describes economics as the "study of institutional structure through which individuals in a society coordinate their diverse wants and desires" (p. 6). Two similar elements run throughout these definitions: (a) scarce resources and (b) human wants and desires. Economics addresses the question of how people make decisions about allocating scarce resources to satisfy human wants and desires. The economics of sport includes the study of two questions:

1. Why are scarce resources in a society distributed to sports?

2. How are scarce resources within the sport industry distributed?

For example, a city collects revenues via taxes and fees. It budgets those revenues to support a variety of public services. In a perfect world (from a city manager's perspective), the amount of money raised equals (or exceeds) the amount of money the manager would like to spend. Unfortunately, that does not frequently happen. It is generally the case that there are more places to spend the money than there is money to be spent. Economics examines the process by which city officials decide how many taxes to collect, how much to spend, and how much to spend on specific items. For example, if voters are willing to pass an increase of 1% in the sales tax,

Economic Motives of Sport Organizations

The Florida Marlins have just finished their 2002 season. Although GM Rich Goddard had high hopes for the season, the team only finished with a 75–87 record. In addition, ticket sales were low, and there is talk that the team may move to another city. Rich believes that part of the reason for the team's poor performance was that the pitching staff did not live up to expectations.

During the off-season, Rich discovers that San Francisco ace pitcher John Crowder may be available in a trade that would cost the Marlins their first pick in the upcoming 2003 draft and one of their best outfielders. Crowder, who is one of the league's most popular players and a definite gate attraction, is agreeable to the trade; he has said he will sign a long-term contract as long as the team is willing to meet his asking price of $20 million per year over 8 years. Rich decides to make the trade and to sign Crowder to a long-term contract for the $160-million asking price. Did GM Rich Goddard make a rational decision?

how will that money be allocated? Will it go to new stadiums for professional teams, new community ball fields, street repairs, or enhanced education? Knowledge of economic principles can help us understand this decision-making process.

Macroeconomics and Microeconomics

The general field of economics is divided into two areas of study. *Macroeconomics* views an economy as a whole, focusing on economic aggregates, such as inflation rates, total investment, business cycles, and growth. The aggregates are a result of the activity of many units and markets. *Microeconomics* examines the behavior of individual elements or markets of an economy (such as the sport industry) and how those elements interact. It focuses on individual decisions such as pricing policies of organizations (why ticket prices go up or down) or people's purchasing decisions (how they decide to buy an athletic club membership or a piece of exercise equipment). The focus of this book is a microeconomic one. We are not ignoring the fact that macroeconomic issues affect the sport industry, but the immediate decisions that most citizens and sport managers deal with arise from microeconomic issues, so that will be our focus.

The study of economics, particularly the study of economic decision making, is often based on the use of economic models. *Economic models* are "methods of analyzing and explaining circumstances in the economic environment. [They are] simplified views of reality, stated verbally, mathematically, and often graphically" (McCarty, 1986, p. 9). Although some students in sport management may not understand how studying these abstract models will provide them with a better understanding of the sport industry, the goal of this book is not only to explain these basic economic principles and models but also to demonstrate how sport

Learning Activities

1. Return to the beginning of the chapter and reread the story about the Florida Marlins. After reading this chapter, do you believe that GM Rich Goddard made a rational decision? Which models discussed in this chapter could be used to explain Rich's decision? Is there any additional information you would need before making a similar decision?

2. Roberta Sheets and Greg Reid are partners in the Lubbock Bowling Alley. During the past year, the business earned $200,000 in business profits. The profits are split 60/40, so Roberta's share of the profits was $120,000, whereas Greg's share was $80,000. Although they are both happy with the profitability of the bowling alley, they are open to other options. Roberta figures that with the money she has invested in the business, she could earn about $75,000. In addition, she has a job opportunity with a salary of $75,000. Greg figures that he could earn $40,000 investing his money elsewhere and that he could get a job earning $35,000 if he sold the bowling alley. What are the economic profits for each owner? Given these conditions, would you expect both owners to maintain their investment in the Lubbock Bowling Alley? Why or why not?

3. Spencer Sporting Goods is trying to decide between producing baseballs and producing soccer balls. It can efficiently produce only one type of ball, and whatever decision the company makes will commit them to one of the two options for the next 5 years. Company President Anita Spencer determines that if the company produces baseballs, it will earn profits of $1 million, $2 million, $2 million, $3 million, and $4 million in years 1 through 5 respectively. If she decides to produce soccer balls, the company will earn $5 million, $4 million, $1 million, $1 million, and $500,000 in years 1 through 5 respectively. Assuming there is no inflation and the value of the dollar does not change over time, which option would Anita choose according to the update theory of the firm? Would Anita's decision be likely to change if the country was going through a period of high inflation and a rapid decline in the value of the dollar?

4. Lakisha Baskin is the local director of the Special Olympics. She is going over three options for this year's big track meet. Under Option A, the organization would produce net profits of $10,000 and 200 participants. Under Option B, the organization would produce net profits of $5,000 and 600 participants. Under Option C, the organization would produce net profits of $-0- and 650 participants. Using the efficiency objective, which option do you think Lakisha will choose? Would her choice be likely to change if her compensation was based entirely on participation? Why or why not?

management professionals can use these principles and models to make better decisions about key managerial problems, such as the allocation of resources, the price to charge, and the quantity to produce.

Economic Models

It is also important that students learn how to use these economic principles and models to better understand the decisions made by sport managers and hopefully to be able to predict some of the decisions before they are made. This is particularly critical for sport managers when the organization under examination is a competitor. Understanding how competitors will react to changes in the organizational environment and to changes made by your organization can have a major impact on the decisions you make on behalf of your organization.

The goal of this chapter is to begin the discussion of basic economic principles that will continue in chapters 3 and 4. The chapter will provide sport-related examples to help explain the models under discussion and to show their application in sport settings. In particular, this chapter will examine the factors motivating managerial decision making. This will be important in helping us to better explain and predict the decisions made by management. Depending on the model being used, managers are seeking to either maximize or satisfy some goal (e.g., profits, sales, growth). The key, therefore, is identifying management's primary goal. Once the primary goal is identified, the theory underlying each of these models is that managers act in a rational manner in pursuit of their goal and will make the decisions they believe give them the best chance to reach this goal. In other words, managers will use rational decision making to determine how they should act in each situation. Because their decisions are rational, they can be both explained and predicted. For example, if the goal of the WNBA's New York Liberty is to win the most games possible and they believe most of their losses last season were related to a weak backcourt, we would predict that they will focus on improving their backcourt through trades, the college draft, and/or free agency. This strategy is rational because it is the best method to help them achieve their primary goal.

Economic Benefits and Costs

However, determining whether the decision by the Liberty is appropriate or not will involve an analysis of both the potential benefits of improving the backcourt (e.g., more wins, increased ticket sales) *and* the potential costs (e.g., increased salary costs). Economists focus on rational decision making as a function of weighing benefits and costs. All choices have benefits and costs, and although some of them can be objectively evaluated (e.g., increased sales revenue), others are more subjective (e.g., increased morale in the city because of a successful team). Using the example discussed earlier, what are the benefits and costs of spending the additional 1% on new stadiums versus the benefits and costs of spending it on street repairs? In a rational model, "if relevant benefits exceed relevant costs, do it; if relevant costs exceed relevant benefits, don't do it" (Colander, 1998, p. 11). Throughout this book, we will use the concepts of benefits and costs to explain decision making in the sport industry.

What Is a Firm?

The theory of the firm is the basic model of business (Hirschey & Pappas, 1995) developed by early economists to explain the behavior of firms (McGuigan & Moyer, 1986). A firm "is an organization that combines or organizes resources for the purpose of producing goods and/or services for sale" (Salvatore, 1993, p. 9). Firms include sole proprietorships, partnerships, and corporations (Salvatore). Firms in the sport industry range from producers of products, such as Nike and Callaway Golf Company, to those organizations that sell products and services directly to the public, such as Foot Locker and Gold's Gym. It should be noted that although firms produce more than 80% of the goods and services in the United States, there are many organizations that are not considered firms, such as government and private nonprofit agencies (Salvatore, 1993). Many sport organizations, such as the Special Olympics and a high school athletic department, are also not firms. Their motives are quite different. Detailed discussion on these organizations will be given in a separate section.

The Basic Theory of the Firm

Essentially, the basic theory of the firm states that the primary goal of the firm is profit maximization. The early versions of the theory of the firm, or *the profit maximization model*, suggested that owners/managers make decisions they believe will lead to the maximization of short-term profits (Seo, 1984). However, later versions of the model took into account that organizations are not simply focused on short-term profits, so the goal has been expanded to maximizing the owner's wealth and the long-term profits of the firm (Hirschey & Pappas, 1995; Seo, 1984). In other words, owners/managers make decisions they believe will result in the highest present value of future profits.

Present value profits is the value of profits based on the current value of the dollar. For example, we know that $100,000 earned today is worth more than $100,000 earned 10 years from now. Inflation causes the dollar value to decrease over time. Moreover, money earned today can be reinvested in the company to earn additional profits. The present value of profits takes into account that $100,000 earned today is worth $100,000, whereas $100,000 earned 10 years from now may only be worth $50,000 in present value profits for the organization.

The original and revised profit maximization models can be better understood using a sport industry example. Converse may be deciding between producing Sneaker A and Sneaker B. Sneaker A will produce $200,000 in profits this year and $500,000 in total present value profits, whereas Sneaker B will produce only $100,000 in profits this year, but $800,000 in total present value profits. Although the original profit maximization model would have suggested that Converse would have chosen to produce Sneaker A in order to maximize short-term profits, the revised model suggests that Converse will produce Sneaker B because that will maximize the owner's wealth and will add the most to the long-term value of the firm.

Obviously the revised model makes more sense for the organization and, therefore, should do a better job of predicting managerial decisions. For example, if the goal was only to maximize short-term profits, there would be no incentive for an organization, such as

Louisville Slugger, to spend money on research and development in order to produce better baseball bats. Research and development costs generally decrease short-term profits because the benefits of these activities do not occur in the short term. However, we know that Louisville Slugger and other companies do spend a lot of money on research and development in order to produce better sport products, which owners and managers know will allow the company to produce a better product in the future and thereby maximize long-term profits.

Economic Profits vs. Business Profits

Business Profits

It is important at this point to distinguish between economic profits and business profits. Each year, the firm will issue an income statement that will indicate the net profit (loss) at the bottom of the statement. The profit in this case is the "residual of sales revenue minus the explicit accounting costs of doing business" (Hirschey & Pappas, 1995, p. 10), or more simply put, profit is equal to revenue minus expenses, expressed in the following equation:

Business Profits = Revenue - Expenses

This accountant's determination of organizational profits is referred to as the organization's business profits. For most people, business profits is how they traditionally define profitability.

Economic Profits

When determining economic profits, economists also try to determine the difference between organizational revenues and cost. However, economists define costs more comprehensively. They recognize that the costs of producing the revenue extend beyond the costs recognized on the income statement because the owners had the option of investing their money and effort elsewhere. The return that could have been obtained from the next best investment alternative is defined as opportunity costs. Therefore, economic profits are equal to the business profits minus the opportunity costs. The relationship among economic profits, business profits, and opportunity costs is expressed in the following equation:

Economic Profits = Business Profits - Opportunity Costs

To continue investing their resources into the business, the owners must earn business profits that are at least equal to the opportunity costs. When business profits equal opportunity costs, the condition is defined as a *normal rate of return* (Hirschey & Pappas, 1995). This suggests that a firm earning zero economic profits is not actually losing money. In fact, owners earning a normal rate of return are likely to continue their investment in the firm because there is no investment available that would result in a greater return. However, if the organization does not earn a normal rate of return over time, owners will remove their resources and invest them elsewhere.

For example, Laura Carbone is the sole proprietor of a sporting goods store into which she has invested $500,000 of her money. During 1999, Laura determines that her sporting goods store has earned a business profit of $100,000. If Laura believes that the most she could have earned from investing her $500,000 in the next best alternative would be

$100,000, she is likely to maintain her investment in the sporting goods store. Although she has earned zero economic profits, she has no incentive to invest her money elsewhere because the return would be the same or less, or

Economic Profits = $100,000 - $100,000 = $0

However, if Laura also works in the store full time, the opportunity cost is the amount of money she could have earned investing her $500,000 in the next best alternative *plus* the amount of salary she could have earned working for another organization. If Laura determines that she could earn $100,000 from investing her money in the next best investment and could earn $75,000 by working full time someplace else, the normal rate of return necessary for her to continue owning and operating the sporting goods store would be $175,000. If she consistently earns only $100,000 in business profits, we would predict that she would not continue as the owner of the store. Although accountants would say that Laura is earning a profit of $100,000 per year in this scenario, economists would suggest that Laura would have an economic loss of $75,000 per year, or

Economic Profits = $100,000 - $175,000 = ($75,000)

Constraints on the Theory of the Firm

When making decisions based on a desire to maximize the long-term value of the firm, managers face certain constraints that place limitations on these decisions. These constraints arise from both internal and external sources (Bridges & Roquemore, 1996). One of the major internal constraints faced by all organizations is the *limitation on the availability of resources* (Bridges & Roquemore). Organizations never have an unlimited supply of money or personnel available to accomplish everything they want. For example, the New York Mets may want to sign all of the popular players available in the free-agent market. They believe that if they can sign these players, more fans will attend their games and watch their games on television, thereby maximizing the value of the team. However, even a large-market franchise like the Mets does not have the resources available to outbid the other 29 Major League Baseball teams for all the available players.

Moreover, even if a company did have unlimited resources, it would be *limited by the availability of necessary inputs in the environment* (Salvatore, 1993). For example, if the Mets had an unlimited amount of money available and they wanted to sign five quality free-agent starting pitchers, they might find that there were not five quality starting pitchers available through free agency. The Mets can only try to put together the best pitching staff they can, given the constraints that they face.

Organizations also face *limitations placed on them by government laws and regulations* (Bridges & Roquemore, 1996). For example, the National Football League may want to prevent a new league from emerging as a competitor. To accomplish this goal, they could try to include a clause in the standard player contract stating that each player promises he will never play for a rival league and that if he does, the player will have to pay back all of his salary from the NFL team. Although this may appear to be an effective way to prevent a competitive football league from forming and thereby maximize the long-term value of the league, it is likely that the courts would deem such a clause in the standard player contract to be a violation of the antitrust laws (see chapter 10); therefore, such a clause could end up costing the league and its teams a large amount of money in a future legal case.

Sometimes the profit-related decisions of organizations are *limited by public demands* (Bridges & Roquemore, 1996). Another example can be seen in the recent actions of Nike and other sporting goods manufacturers. Many of these organizations realized that they could produce their products for less in developing countries and thereby maximize their wealth. They have been accused of paying their employees very low wages and having them work in poorly maintained facilities. However, when reports by journalists brought their actions to the public's attention, many Americans were outraged at the unethical treatment of the foreign employees of these sporting goods companies (Carr, 2000; Gilley, 1998). In order to prevent widespread boycotts of their products, Nike and other companies invested a lot of money to improve both working conditions and pay and to publicize their "humanitarian" efforts. Essentially, public opinion became a constraint that prevented these companies from acting in a manner that would have maximized the wealth of the firm.

It should be noted that the firm also faces a number of other constraints, which are imposed by *limited technology, contractual obligations, and the polices of governing bodies* (e.g., Bridges & Roquemore, 1996; Salvatore, 1993). For example, a sport organization may not be able to present its games in the manner it wants because the necessary technology is not available yet. In another example, a college football team wishing to schedule better opponents to increase game-related profits may be limited by prior contractual agreements with other universities. Finally, a college athletic department wishing to sign the best women's basketball player cannot offer her a signing bonus because this would violate NCAA rules.

Limitations of the Theory of the Firm

Although the theory of the firm has proven quite useful in explaining and predicting managerial decisions (McGuigan & Moyer, 1986), this model has limitations in its ability to explain all managerial decisions. For example, many decisions faced by managers have moral and/or ethical implications (Seo, 1984). Although some sporting goods companies changed their treatment of workers in developing countries as a result of public pressure, there were also some companies that treated their employees well before there was any public pressure. Managers in these organizations "did the right thing" even though they knew that they could maximize wealth and value of the firm by paying employees less.

Also, in a number of cases (e.g., NCAA Final Four, the Olympics), a sport organization charges a lower price than it could. We know that tickets in some of these cases have greater value because scalpers charge well above the face value. The stated reason for undervaluing the tickets is that by doing so these sport organizations can make their games affordable and accessible to the "common man." In addition, some companies donate large amounts of money to worthy causes. Although these donations often have the potential to create goodwill with the public and thereby increase profits from additional sales, many organizations donate so much money that they are most likely decreasing profits (Seo, 1984). In each of these cases, the actions of managers are based more on their ethical standards than their desire for profit.

Alternative Models of Firm Motivation

Although the theory of the firm, also known as the profit maximization model, is the most common model of firm motivation, the presence of goals other than profit maximization has led economists to develop a number of alternative models of firm motivation (Seo, 1984). Among the other theories that have been suggested are

1. management utility maximization model,
2. sales maximization model,
3. growth maximization model,
4. long-run survival model, and
5. satisficing behavior model (e.g., Hirschey & Pappas, 1995; McGuigan & Moyer, 1986; Salvatore, 1993; Seo, 1984).

Management Utility Maximization Model

The management utility maximization model suggests the decisions made by managers may be motivated more by their own self-interest than by a desire to maximize the firm's wealth (McGuigan & Moyer, 1986). A number of researchers have noted that many modern corporations have a separation of ownership and management (Berle & Means, 1932; Galbraith, 1952, 1958, 1967; Williamson, 1963). Although the owners/stockholders want to maximize the firm's profits in order to increase the amount of money available to pay them dividends, the stockholders may be far removed from the day-to-day decision making of the corporation; therefore, their desires may not have a large impact on managerial decisions (Seo, 1984). This theory suggests that most of the decisions are actually made by nonowner managers who are motivated by increasing their own benefits.

For example, a high-level executive with the Churchill Downs horse racing track, who has no stake in the ownership, may try to authorize a large salary increase for himself. Although the salary increase would have a negative impact on profits, it would improve his personal financial position so he has plenty of incentive to make this decision. In addition, he may make a number of other decisions regarding the use of organizational resources that will also negatively affect the profitability of the firm. He may give himself a number of perquisites (e.g., company car, bonus, large expense account) that are not necessary for the operation of the firm or may hire a large and expensive staff of employees to reduce his own workload and to make his job easier (McGuigan & Moyer, 1986). These nonessential expenses are often referred to as *organizational or management slack* (McGuigan & Moyer; Seo, 1984).

Although some studies have supported the management utility maximization model by showing that profits were lower in manager-controlled firms than in owner-controlled firms (e.g., Monsen, Chiu, & Cooley, 1968), many studies found no significant differences (e.g., Holl, 1997). Early support for the notion that managers often do not pursue profitability was based on research that indicated that managerial salaries were not closely linked to profitability (McGuire, Chiu, & Elbing, 1962). However, later studies found that total compensation, which often includes stock options and profit sharing, is more closely tied to the profitability of the firm (Mason, 1971). Because managers of successful organizations do tend to be better compensated (Seo, 1984), it could be argued that pursuing profits is both in the owner's best interest *and* in the manager's best interest. Therefore, the pursuit of profits may also maximize management utility over the long term. In our example, the Churchill Downs executive may recognize that his ability to get owner support for increasing his salary will improve if the organization is more profitable. However, this model does suggest that owners who fail to reward managers based on profitability are increasing the chances that managers may pursue personal benefits that conflict with the owner's profitability goals.

Sales Maximization Model

Baumol (1959) suggested that after managers earn enough profit to satisfy owners, they attempt to maximize sales. This theory was closely related to the management utility maximization model because early studies suggested that executive salaries were more closely related to sales than to profits (Salvatore, 1993). For example, an executive with Wilson may be more focused on selling a greater number of tennis rackets than Wilson's competitors (e.g., Penn), as opposed to maximizing profits. The executive may believe that selling more tennis rackets, and perhaps being the number one seller of tennis rackets, will please Wilson's owners and increase the executive's compensation.

Although this theory appealed to a number of early economists, rigorous testing has failed to support it (e.g., M. Hall, 1967). Moreover, although many organizations that focus on capturing a larger share of the market appear to be more concerned with maximizing sales over profit, economists now believe this behavior is actually consistent with the goal of long-term profit maximization (Seo, 1984). They suggest these firms are simply sacrificing some short-term profitability in order to enhance the long-term wealth of the firm. The larger market share will make it easier for the firm to earn additional profits in the future. For example, the executive with Wilson may believe that being the number one seller of tennis rackets will also help the firm increase its market share and ultimately become the most profitable tennis-racket producer over the long term.

Growth Maximization Model

Many firms focus on maximizing growth as a basis for organizational strategy (Seo, 1984). When using the profit maximization model, managers seek an optimal level of output at which profits are maximized. Once they find this output level, they produce and sell this amount of output, and there is no incentive to increase sales or production, as long as costs and demand remain constant (Seo). However, we know that many managers are not satisfied with the status quo and often seek to increase the size of their organization. Therefore, the manager may pursue organizational growth as a primary objective. The recent increase in mergers inside and outside of the sport industry would be consistent with the growth maximization model.

This model is also related to the management utility maximization model. Reid (1968) found that nonmerging firms have larger profits in relation to stockholder assets and that their stock increased in value more. Although this would suggest growth maximization may have a negative impact on the wealth and value of the firm, Penrose (1959) argued that managers would still pursue growth because they could "gain prestige, personal satisfaction in the successful growth of the firm with which they are connected, more responsibility and better positions, and wider scope for their ambitions and abilities" (p. 242). Growth maximization is also consistent with McGuire et al.'s (1962) finding that there was a close relation between size of the firm and executive salaries.

Moreover, it could be argued that some owners also may be willing to pursue growth over profit maximization. The acquisition decisions by "sport" owners, such as Ted Turner and Rupert Murdoch, may be driven more by their egos and their desire to have more power and control than by their desire to increase the wealth of their organizations. However, others have argued that pursuing growth will lead to long-run profits and, therefore, the growth maximization and profit maximization models are consistent and result in similar behavior. When pursuing growth, managers may again be simply sacrificing some short-term profitability for long-term wealth.

Long-Run Survival Model

Another goal that has been offered as an alternative to profit maximization is the long-run survival of the firm (McGuigan & Moyer, 1986). Based on this theory, decisions made by managers would be focused on ensuring that the firm would exist in the future. Once again, this theory is somewhat related to the management utility maximization theory. The incentive for managers to focus on survival over profit maximization is that "their present and future compensation depends on the firm's continued existence" (McGuigan & Moyer, p. 15). If the firm ceases to exist, the managers will not have jobs and will be without compensation. Often the long-run survival theory is used to explain why many managers make decisions that are more conservative and designed to avoid risk, even though riskier strategies could result in greater profits. For example, some sporting goods manufacturers may have hesitated to make a large investment in the production of in-line skates during the late 1980s. Although the product was very popular and short-term profits would have been available, managers may have been concerned that in-line skating was a fad and that maintaining their focus on more stable sporting goods items (e.g., sneakers) may have increased their chances for long-run survival.

It should be noted, however, that the long-run survival model is also not completely inconsistent with profit maximization. Avoiding risky decisions ensures the firm will survive, which will also generally result in greater long-term profitability. It only makes sense that a firm that exists for 50 years will generally earn more profits than one that is bankrupt after 10 years.

Satisficing Behavior Model

The satisficing behavior model, originally proposed by Simon (1959), challenges the very notion that managers put the effort into their jobs and their decisions that would be necessary in order to maximize profits. The theory suggests that most firms have some minimal standards for profits, sales, and/or growth (McGuigan & Moyer, 1986). The managers then make decisions based on their desire to meet these minimal standards, referred to by Simon (1959) as *satisficing* behavior, rather than based on a desire to optimize or maximize these goals (e.g., profits, sales, growth).

Like many of the other alternative models, this model has some relation to the management utility maximization model (McGuigan & Moyer, 1986). Proponents of the satisficing behavior model suggest that finding the best decision in order to maximize goals would require too much hard work for managers and would not be worth this level of effort. Moreover, managers face too many constraints and too much uncertainty and have to make too many decisions quickly to ever be able to actually determine all the decisions that will lead to the maximization of profits. Therefore, they look at the expectations of the owners and attempt to meet these expectations at a satisfactory level, which will ensure their continued employment and financial well-being. For example, the CEO of Reebok may be presented with profit-related goals by the organization's board of directors. In this case, the goal is $10 million in profits. According to the satisficing behavior model, we would expect the CEO to try to reach $10 million in profits, but not $20 million. In general, the effort and risks associated with trying to reach the $20-million level in profits would be too great for the CEO.

Again, it should be noted that this theory is not completely inconsistent with the traditional profit maximization model (Salvatore, 1993). The satisficing behavior model suggests the desire to satisfice is related to the unreasonable difficulty pertaining to finding the decision that will maximize profits, rather than general underachieving by managers. If the managers were provided with more information and were given more time to make their decisions, they would certainly choose to maximize rather than settle for a satisficing decision. In our example, if the CEO of Reebok were presented with information that led him or her to believe that the firm could reach the $20-million level of profits without considerable amount of effort and risk, we would expect the CEO to pursue this higher profit level even though the owners' goal was only $10 million.

Reasons for Continuing to Use the Profit Maximization Model

Despite the many alternative theories related to the underlying motivations for firm decisions, most economists still believe that the profit maximization model does the best job of explaining most managerial decisions (e.g., Salvatore, 1993; Seo, 1984). There are a number of reasons for maintaining profit-maximization as the primary model. First, there is little empirical support for any of the other models (Seo). Second, survival in competitive industries requires profits (Seo). High sales and/or growth without profits will generally lead to failure. Third, although managerial salaries are not always closely related to the profitability of the firm (McGuire et al., 1962), management compensation does tend to be closely related to profits (Mason, 1971). Fourth, the profit maximization model has been the most useful model over time for explaining and predicting behavior by firms (Seo). Fifth, the profit maximization model analyzes both benefits and costs. Some of the other models (e.g., sales maximization model) look only at the benefits. It is unrealistic to think that managers will completely ignore costs when making decisions (see discussion of cost/benefit analyses in chapter 1).

Although we will generally use the profit maximization model to predict and explain managerial decisions throughout the remainder of the book, the other models are still useful when examining managerial decisions in the real world. Managers may occasionally pursue goals, such as personal benefits, increased sales, and organizational growth, even when they do not believe that their efforts will increase profit. If we restrict ourselves to believing that profit maximization is the only goal managers ever pursue, we may inaccurately predict and explain certain decisions by management.

An Alternative Theory for Sports: The Winning Maximization Model

Although the models already discussed can be easily applied to both sport and nonsport industry settings, one theory of managerial motivation is unique to sport. Examinations of decision by sport managers suggests that they sometimes pursue winning as their primary objective. For example, professional sport executives often spend a large amount of money to sign a player who is considered to be a "difference maker" even if they do not believe that the economic profits will be enhanced by signing the player.

Applications in Professional Sport

In December 1998, the Los Angeles Dodgers signed pitcher Kevin Brown to the largest contract up to that point in league history (King, 1998b) because they believed that Brown would increase their chances of winning a championship. However, the winning maximization model is not completely inconsistent with the profit maximization model. If the team wins more games, attendance and television ratings for team games will likely increase, leading to increased profits. Still, the Dodgers made the decision to sign Kevin Brown to an expensive contract even though he has never been the type of marquee player who brings in significantly larger crowds or who attracts very large television audiences. Although there are certainly some financial benefits in signing a star player like Kevin Brown, it is hard to justify such a large contract using purely profitability goals. Most would agree that sport owners and managers want desperately to be associated with a winning franchise and that they are often willing to decrease profitability in order to win more games.

In fact, the desire of professional sport owners to institute salary caps is related to their inability to control their own spending. If they refused to sign a player to any contract that led to an economic loss, there would be no need for a salary cap. Owners would not pay excessive salaries unless they believed that the player would increase revenue by at least the amount that he or she cost. However, owners often pay salaries that exceed the economic benefits because they want to win; therefore, they need the salary caps to keep themselves from pushing their teams toward bankruptcy. In contrast, many of the major sneaker companies have recently dropped star players because they believed the endorsement deals were costing more than they were worth (A. Bernstein, 1998). With no focus on winning games, these corporations made their decision based purely on profit maximization.

Applications in Nonprofit Sport Organizations

The desire for winning in sport is not restricted to firms. The United States Olympic Committee (USOC) and the individual sport national governing bodies (e.g., USA Volleyball, USA Track & Field) often make many of their decisions based on a desire to increase the number of medals won by Americans in international events such as the Olympics. NCAA Division I athletic departments often sign coaches to huge contracts to increase their chances of winning, even though a cheaper coach may lead to greater profits. Moreover, it is likely that if the NCAA rules changed, these same athletic departments would offer large contracts to the top high school players as well. In fact, many colleges spend excessively on recruiting, their only means of obtaining the best players without violating NCAA rules. College athletic departments have often been accused of making poor economic decisions with regard to the amount of money that they pay in coaching contracts and recruiting expense (e.g., Sperber, 1990). However, if their goal is actually related more to wins than profits, then these decisions are easily explainable and predictable.

It is important to note, however, that the USOC, the national governing bodies, and the college athletic departments are nonprofit organizations. Therefore, profit maximization is not an appropriate goal for these organizations (McGuigan & Moyer, 1986). Economists have developed other goal-related models to explain and predict managerial decision making in both public and private sector nonprofit organizations.

Goals in Nonprofit Organizations

Nonprofit Sport Organizations

There are many public and private sector nonprofit organizations in the sport industry. The major difference between the two is that public-sector nonprofit organizations, such as high school athletic departments and local recreation departments, often receive much of their funding from government sources, whereas private-sector nonprofit organizations, such as the Special Olympics, YMCAs, and country clubs, rely more on donations and membership fees. Although it has been suggested that some nonprofit organizations in sport, such as YMCAs (Miller & Fielding, 1994) and university athletic departments (e.g., Sack, 1988), actually operate in a manner that is hard to distinguish from that of profit-oriented firms, it is inappropriate for nonprofit organizations to have profit maximization as their primary goal (McGuigan & Moyer, 1986). Although it is legal for a nonprofit organization to make a business profit, a primary focus on maximizing profits would clearly be a violation of their nonprofit status.

The questions then are

- What goals are appropriate for nonprofit organizations?
- What models have been useful in explaining and predicting the behavior of nonprofit executives?

A number of goal-oriented models currently exist for nonprofit enterprises. The objectives in the models used for nonprofit sport organizations include efficiency.

Efficiency Objective

One theory suggests that managers of nonprofit organizations attempt to maximize both the quantity and quality of their output while still maintaining a break-even budget (McGuigan & Moyer, 1986). For example, a recreation department may attempt to maximize the number of activities offered without exceeding its budget constraints. This is also sometimes referred to as the *efficiency objective*, which suggests nonprofit managers make decisions that maximize the ratio of benefits to costs (McGuigan & Moyer). They can accomplish this goal either by maximizing the benefits for a given level of costs or by minimizing costs for a fixed level of benefits.

For example, a local recreation director may be given a set budget, and the director will then try to offer as many participation opportunities as possible for the local community for this set level of costs. It is also possible that she will decide before receiving the budget which activities she wants to offer and will then try to minimize the costs of providing all of these opportunities.

The efficiency objective has proven useful in examining decision making in a variety of nonprofit organizations. However, it is still necessary, first, to define the benefits sought by the nonprofit organization before predicting the decisions that its managers will make. For example, the Special Olympics may focus on maximizing the number of participants and the positive experiences of the participants, while operating within a break-even budget constraint. These goals may also be priorities in many high school and small college athletic departments. However, we often find that because the number of participants is easier to quantify than positive experiences, participation numbers is the goal that has a greater impact on decision making.

Winning Maximization Model for Nonprofit Sport Organizations

As previously discussed, winning maximization is also a frequent goal for organizations such as the USOC, national governing bodies, NCAA Division I athletic departments, and even some high school athletic departments. Although Division I athletic departments frequently argue their main goal is to provide a positive experience for the student-athlete, their decisions often suggest that winning is a higher priority (e.g., Sperber, 1990). This again may be related to the fact that winning is easier to measure than positive experiences. However, other reasons than winning may be emphasized are closely related to other theories on management decision making in nonprofit organizations.

Satisfying Contributors Model

The satisfying contributors model suggests managers of nonprofit organizations attempt to maximize the satisfaction of the current and potential contributors. Therefore, managers in Division I athletic departments will be motivated by a desire to please their athletic department donor groups, as well as their other ticket holders. Because winning is often important to athletic department donors (e.g., Coughlin & Erekson, 1985; J. S. Hall & Mahony, 1997; Sigelman & Brookheimer, 1983), the pursuit of winning at Division I schools may be an attempt to please the donor groups.

Management Utility Maximization Model

Another model used when examining nonprofit decision making is the management utility maximization model. As was discussed in firms, managers want to maximize their own benefits. Division I administrators realize that it is in their best interest to keep the donors happy because that will generally maximize administrators' personal long-term benefits. Winning, therefore, becomes the goal for nonprofit administrators because they believe that the success of their athletic teams will maximize their own personal benefits.

Satisficing Behavior Model

Because objectives are often difficult to measure in many public and private nonprofit organizations, many of the other models discussed in relation to firms also apply for them. In fact, in some cases, these models work even better within nonprofit organizations. For example, managers with government agencies that are guaranteed resources may adopt the satisficing behavior model presented by Simon (1959). Because it will be difficult for their superiors to determine if they are maximizing or simply satisficing in their pursuit of goals that are difficult to measure, managers in nonprofit organizations can put less effort into their jobs and pursue minimal goals with less fear.

Long-Run Survival Model

Although managers of nonprofit organizations may have less need to be concerned about maximizing profits than have managers of firms, the former still must be concerned with the long-run survival of their organization in order to guarantee that they will continue to receive their compensation (McGuigan & Moyer, 1986). Some have suggested that this managerial focus on survival is the reason that many government agencies survive long after they have truly provided a useful contribution to society (McGuigan & Moyer, 1986).

For example, a local recreation program may have been started to offer participation opportunities for children from families with lower socioeconomic standing . If the local community becomes significantly more affluent over time, the need for this program may disappear. However, it is quite possible that the director of the program may continue to focus on maintaining this program despite the demographic change. He may start to recruit children from higher socioeconomic classes or from other nearby communities in order to maintain the participation levels necessary to convince government officials that the program is still needed. If no one examines the program closely, the director might be able to maintain the program and his related compensation for many years after the program has stopped being useful to the local community.

Growth Maximization Model

Finally, another model suggests that growth maximization is often the goal underlying managerial decision making in nonprofit organizations (McGuigan & Moyer, 1986). Because profitability cannot be used as a measure of organizational success, nonprofit managers must seek other methods for demonstrating to others how well they have performed and for gaining prestige for their organizations and themselves. As the organization grows, the managers gain more prestige, gain more power, become more important, control the distribution of more resources, and are often better compensated (McGuigan & Moyer, 1986).

For example, one could argue that the NCAA's growth from a small, basically insignificant organization prior to the 1950s to the dominant organization in college athletics was motivated by the desire of its executives for greater prestige, power, importance, control, and personal compensation. Although NCAA executives would certainly argue their decisions were motivated by other goals, all of these factors (e.g., power, personal compensation) have clearly increased during the NCAA's growth, and therefore, growth cannot be ignored as a motive underlying decision making.

Overall, when we examine the goals of nonprofit organizations in the sport industry, the efficiency objective may generally be the best fit. However, the other models are also effective at predicting and explaining managerial decision, in nonprofit organizations in certain situations; thus, they cannot be ignored.

Chapter Study Questions

1. Compare and contrast finance with economics.
2. Compare and contrast macroeconomics and microeconomics.
3. Compare and contrast the original theory of the firm with the updated theory of the firm.
4. Compare and contrast economic profits with business profits. Explain why economic profits are more meaningful to economic decision making.
5. Explain the various constraints and limitations on the theory of the firm.
6. Identify which of the models, other than the profit maximization model, you think are best for explaining decision making in sport and why.
7. Identify the various managerial motivations that have been used to explain decision making in firms and discuss which of these could also be used for nonprofit organizations and why.
8. Explain why salary caps would be less important if professional sport teams always used the profit maximization model when making decisions.

Summary

The main goal of this chapter was to introduce the reader to various economic models that can be useful for both explaining and predicting managerial decision making. When examining firms in general, we usually use the profit maximization model to analyze the choices that managers make. We assume, regardless of the market type, that the managers are motivated by a desire to maximize their firm's profits. However, other models, such as the sales maximization model and the management utility maximization model, have also been used by economists to explain and predict the actions of firms. Moreover, the profit maximization model is not appropriate for nonprofit organizations, so many of these other models can certainly be used for analyzing this type of organization. Although the efficiency objective may be most appropriate for the nonprofit organizations, other models may be better in certain situations.

Chapter Three

INTRODUCTION

As the scenario about pricing demonstrates, sport management professionals need a background in product demand and supply to make sound decisions. A good understanding of demand and supply concepts is also important in new product development, capital investment projects, and advertising. In this chapter, we discuss how demand and supply, two basic concepts in economics, are relevant in the sport industry.

Demand

Consumers in any society have needs and wants for a wide range of goods and services. Some of these, such as food, shelter, and health care, are necessities. Others like entertainment and athletic clothing are wants; that is, things that are desirable but not required for existence. To satisfy consumer needs and wants, businesses develop goods and services, but there will be many ways to satisfy any particular need or want. If people are hungry, they can go to the store and purchase food to prepare at home, or they can choose from a variety of restaurants, from fast food to fine dining, from Chinese to Mexican. If people want to be entertained, they can attend a movie, a concert, or an athletic event, or they can go to a sports bar. If they want to get in shape, they might join an athletic club, purchase home exercise equipment, or hire a personal trainer. Each of these options results in demand for a specific good or service. The choices people make about what to consume and how to consume it depend upon many factors. Suppliers of goods and services in the sport industry need to have an understanding of the consumer's decision-making process.

Demand, Pricing, and Revenue

The Midwest Marks is a team in the Women's Professional Softball League. Each year it plays 64 games, 32 at home. The Marks have a two-tier ticket price structure, with box seats costing $8 per game and all others $5. Average attendance for a game is 900, out of 1,500 available seats. The Marks owners met recently to discuss a possible price decrease, to $7 and $4. Advocates of the proposal argue that the decrease in ticket prices would increase the number of tickets sold and increase the revenue for the club.

At the meeting, the owners engaged in a heated debate over the proposal. It soon became evident that the board did not have enough information to make a sound decision. For instance, the concessions operator indicated that it planned to make substantial price increases at the beginning of the season. Would this increase affect the demand for tickets and, thus, the optimal pricing policy? Although customers might buy more tickets at lower prices, would total revenue or profits necessarily increase? Would it be better to attract additional customers by improving the quality of play or by lowering price? (Adapted from an example in Brickley, Smith, and Zimmerman, 1997)

A basic relationship of interest to producers of goods and services is that between demand and price. The *law of demand* states that if all things are equal, the lower the price of some item, the higher the quantity demanded; and the higher the price, the lower the quantity demanded. For example, if ticket prices for a sporting event were suddenly cut (say from $10 to $5), more people would want to buy them. If the ticket prices went up (from $10 to $15), fewer people would want to buy them. Figure 3-1 illustrates a *demand curve* for sporting event tickets.

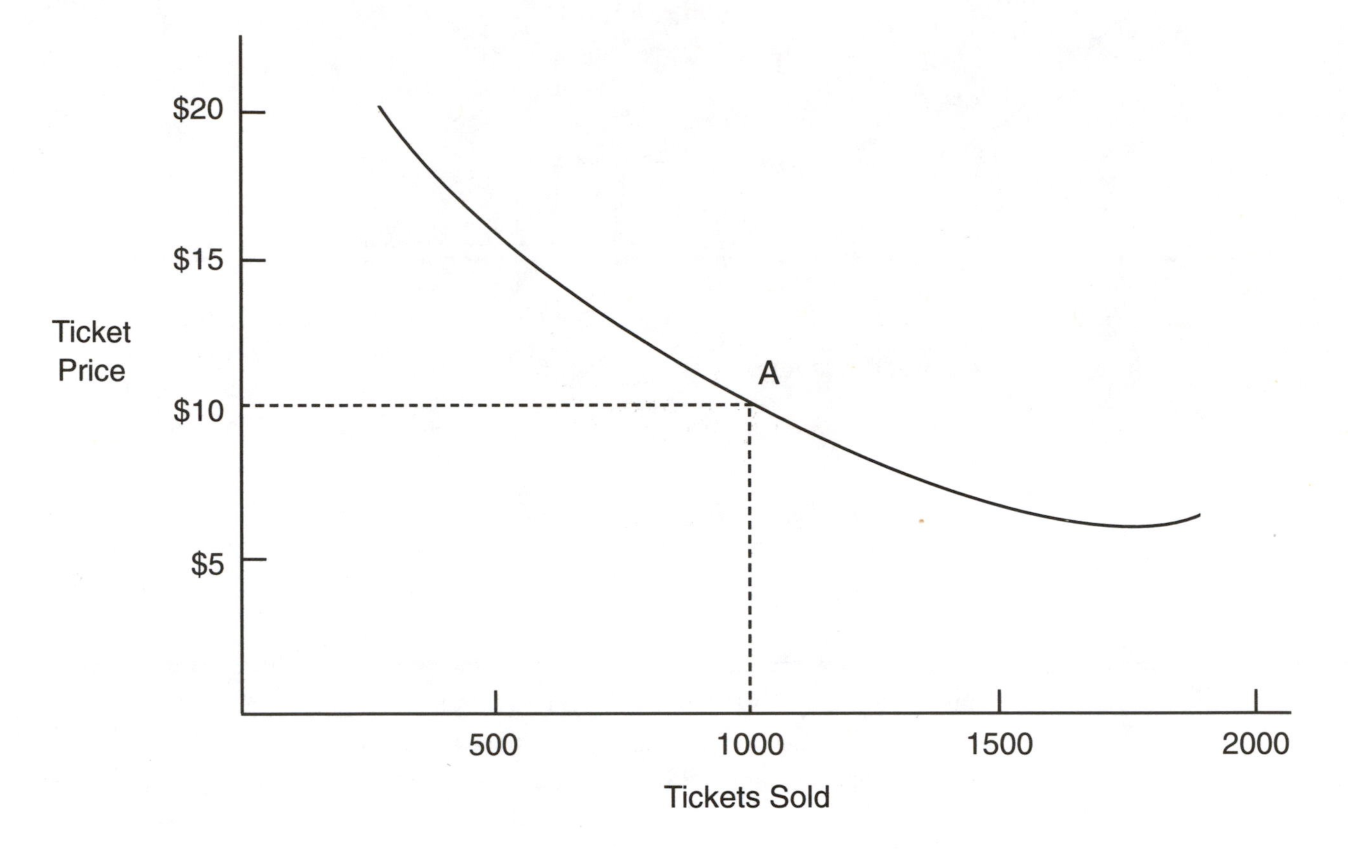

Figure 3-1. Demand Curve

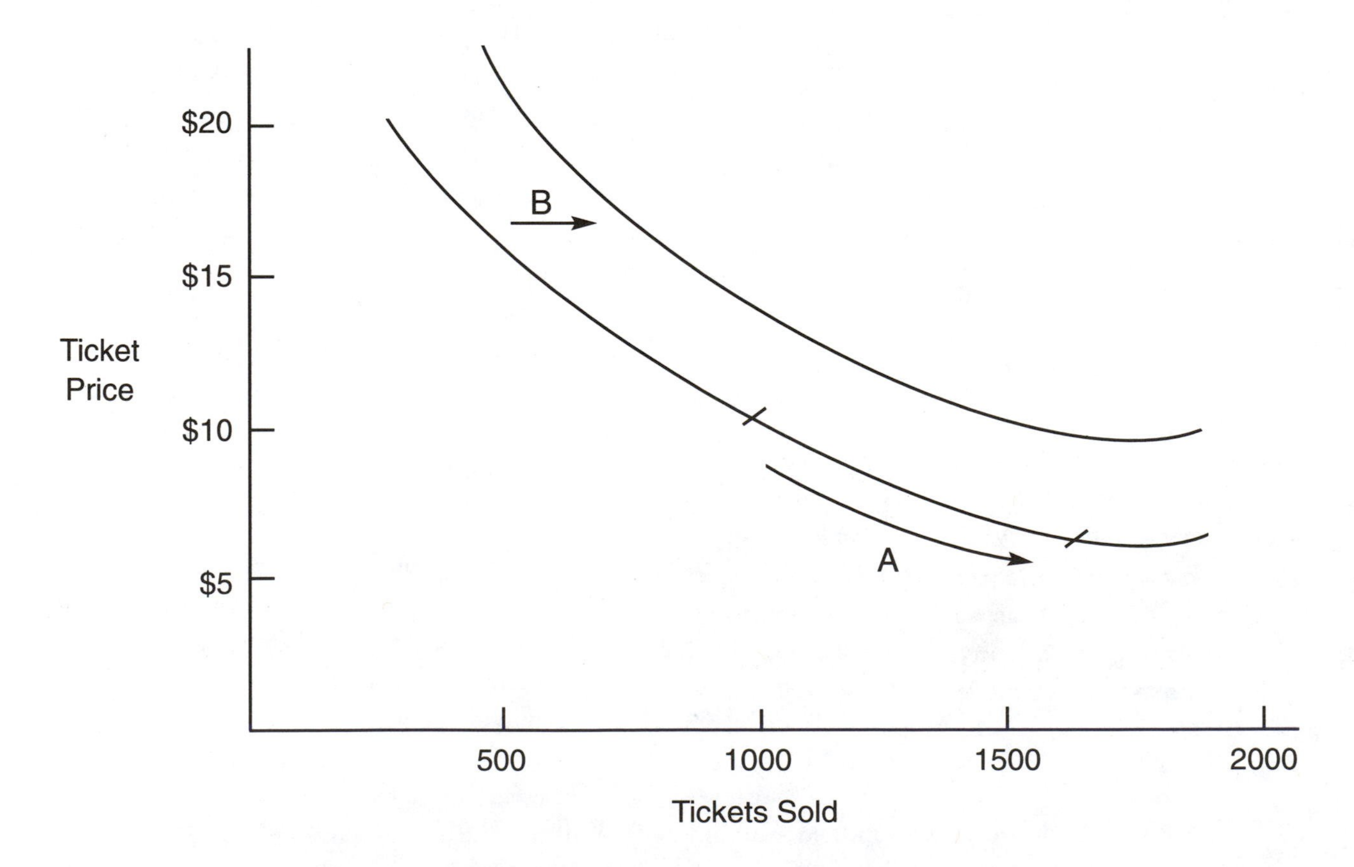

Figure 3-2. Quantity Demanded and Demand Curve

Demand includes all values along the entire range of the demand curve. It is the relationship between all the prices and all the quantities demanded for a good or service. In Figure 3-1, as the price of tickets rises, the number of tickets sold declines. *Quantity demanded* is the amount of specific goods or services that individuals (singly or as a group) will purchase at some specific period of time and at some specific set price. Point A in Figure 3-1 demonstrates that at $10, 1,000 people will purchase tickets. A *change in quantity demanded* refers to the effect of a change in price on the quantity demanded. If the price of a ticket decreases to $5, there will be a change in quantity demanded from 1,000 to 1,500. A *shift in demand* refers to nonprice factors that cause a shift of the entire demand curve. A shift in demand means that at each price, more (or fewer) units will be demanded. In Figure 3-2, Arrow A represents a change in quantity demanded, and Arrow B represents a shift in demand.

The demand curve represents the willingness of people to pay for additional units of products or services. The downward slope of the curve means that people are less willing to pay for additional units of some good or service. This is the concept of *marginal benefit*. If a baseball fan usually attends three games per season, he or she will not be willing to pay as much to attend 10, 15, or 20 games. A player in a softball league is willing to pay $50 for one pair of turf shoes but would probably not be willing to pay $50 per pair for 10 pairs of shoes. The (marginal) benefit received from the 10th pair is much less than that received from the first pair.

In discussing matters related to demand and supply, we should be cautious as it is often difficult to identify outcomes that result from specific changes. Economists use the phrases "all other things constant" or "other things being equal" to place a limit on conclusions that can be drawn. The law of demand tells us that, "all things being equal," an increase in the cost of basketball shoes should result in a decrease in the number of shoes purchased. However, for several years in the 1990s, shoe purchases and prices increased as basketball footwear became a clothing fad, especially among teenagers. In this case, "all things were not equal" because other considerations (fashion trends) entered into the equation. For the purposes of the remaining discussion, we will follow the economists' lead and assume all things are equal.

Determinants of Demand

Demand varies for different products and services. Sport managers should think about what influences the demand for their product or service. In general, the demand for an item is determined by a number of factors:

1. Price of the item itself
2. Price of other (related) goods
3. Expectations about the future
4. Consumer tastes
5. Consumer income

As previously discussed, the price of an item is a major determinant of demand. Most people want to know how much something costs before spending money for it. Price is also very visible. Increases or decreases in price result in changes in quantity demanded, or movement along the demand curve. This is the assumption behind store sales: Lower prices will encourage purchases. Some of the Midwest Marks owners believe in this philosophy, and that is why they want to lower ticket prices. In the sport industry, ticket discounting is an example of trying to increase demand by manipulating price. Two-for-one offers, senior citizen and family discounts, and season plan discounts are examples. When considering pricing decisions, sport managers have to take into account demand and the impact that a change in price might have. If the price of a round of golf at a course rises, some people will decide that playing at that course is no longer worth paying that price, and fewer rounds of golf will be sold. If the price of a round of golf declines, more people may be attracted to play.

Demand is affected by the price of other related goods. As mentioned previously, there are many goods and services produced. *Substitutes* are items that also satisfy consumers' wants and needs. If Javier is a golfer and a tennis player, both activities satisfy his desire for recreation. If the price of a round of golf rises (relative to the price of playing tennis), Javier may choose to play tennis instead. If the cost of playing tennis rises (relative to the price of playing golf), he will choose to play golf. Thus, the existence of alternatives and the price of those alternatives are important. *Complements* are products that are used jointly. Both tennis and golf require the use of a ball. If the price of tennis or golf balls suddenly changes, that change can affect Javier's choice of activity. If golf balls suddenly cost $20 and Javier generally loses one ball each time he plays, it will increase his cost to play golf. Accordingly, he may choose to play tennis. This is an issue for several segments of the sport industry because the price of the sport activity itself is often equaled or exceeded by ancillary costs (Mullin, Hardy, & Sutton, 1993). Even if the price of the core activity is constant, increases or decreases in other items will change the total cost of consumption. A family with children involved in ice skating will spend dollars on equipment, lessons, ice time, transportation, and food. A change in the prices of these other items creates shifts in the demand curve.

Expectations about future activity can influence current consumption and produce shifts in the demand curve. Many professional sports teams building new stadiums sell current season tickets by linking their purchase to seats at the future stadium. The argument is that fans should buy now because demand will be high when the new stadium opens. New athletic clubs attempt to increase sales by offering locked-in membership prices or suggesting that people should join now because demand will be high for a limited number of memberships.

Learning Activities

1. Choose a major sporting event happening this semester. What is the face value of tickets? How much are the tickets being sold for through alternative avenues? (You might check city newspapers or ticket brokers for this information.) What can you conclude about supply and demand for the event?

2. Select a sport organization in your area. How does it practice price discrimination? How much demand is there at each price level?

3. Conduct a survey of a class. How many athletic shoes would each student buy if the price of the shoe was $30, $60, $90, $120? Can you construct a demand curve for this information? (Caution: Using only a few students probably won't provide sufficient information.)

4. Locust Hill Golf Club is a private country club. It charges an initiation fee of $12,000. When members quit the club, they receive no refund on their initiation fees. They simply lose their membership. Salt Lake Country Club is also a private golf course. At this club, members join by buying a membership certificate from a member who is leaving the club. The price of the membership is determined by supply and demand. Suppose that both clubs are considering installing a watering system. In each case, the watering system is expected to enhance the quality of the golf course significantly. To finance these systems, members would pay a special assessment of $1,500 per year for the next 3 years. The proposals will be voted on by the memberships. Do you think that the membership is more likely to vote in favor of the proposal at Locust Hill or Salt Lake Country Club? Explain. (Brickley et al., 1997)

Changes in taste over time also affect demand. Injuries caused by aerobics led athletic clubs to offer low-impact aerobics, such as step aerobics, slide aerobics, water aerobics, and tap aerobics. Racquetball, a booming activity in the 1970s, drastically declined in appeal in the 1980s, leaving athletic club managers with empty courts. As the number of people participating in downhill skiing decreases, resorts are adding white-water rafting, mountain biking, and snowboarding. The more people desire an activity, the higher the demand for it. As the appeal of an activity declines, demand decreases. However, changes in taste are more difficult to quantify than are other impacts on demand.

Income levels are another factor that may cause shifts in the demand curve. Certainly, those who have more income are more able and likely to satisfy wants through purchases. In general, as household income rises in a society, consumption rises and the demand curve shifts to the right (at each price, more goods will be demanded). However, other income issues also influence demand. When economic conditions change (either positively or negatively), not all segments of the population are affected equally. If an economy is booming, some people may see their income rise considerably whereas others may notice little impact. Changes in government policies create different economic impacts for different income groups. For example, in 1994, the U.S. government passed a law eliminating the deductibility of country club membership fees as a business expense. Not all clubs were affected in the same way by the change. Many older, high-cost clubs that cater to a high-income personnel have experienced a decline in membership (Walker, 1999) whereas many clubs that appeal to a more medium-income audience are thriving. More of the high-cost clubs had members affected by the deductibility provision. A second issue in examining how income affects demand is that, as income rises, demand may either rise or fall. For some items, demand rises as income rises. These items, called *normal* goods, would include steaks, yachts, cellular phones, stadium luxury boxes, or resort vacations. For other items, demand declines as income rises. These items are called *inferior* goods. Commonly used examples are Spam and bologna. As people gain more income, they reduce their purchase of less desirable items in favor of more desirable ones. It is open to debate as to whether sport activities are normal or inferior goods. Even though most sport activities are considered as normal goods, some economists suggest baseball (Noll, 1974) or hiking and backpacking (Walsh, 1986) are inferior goods. Other economists (Siegfried & Eisenberg, 1980) do not support these assertions, stating that the evidence is not clear-cut.

Other Elements of Demand for Sport Activities

In addition to the factors listed above, which apply to many firms that supply goods and services, numerous studies have examined demand specifically for sport and recreation activities. These studies suggest several additional factors are relevant for the sport industry.

Table 3-1 shows several factors related to outdoor recreation demand (Walsh, 1986). Age, education, income, and gender are significant in discussing demand for activities. In addition, travel time to activities, quality of the attraction, and congestion are relevant.

A number of demand studies have centered on professional sports, especially on American baseball. The studies have focused particularly on price, uncertainty of outcome, and quality of the team. These studies measure demand by attendance at the game. Most of the North American professional sports leagues (and even U.S. colleges) rely heavily on attendance to generate revenue. This is truer for the National Hockey League, Canadian

Table 3-1. Socioeconomic Determinants of Adult Participation in Outdoor Recreation, United States

	Strength of the Relationship	
Socioeconomic Variables	All adults	Working adults
Age	-.51***	-.43***
Education	.09***	.09***
Income	.08***	.06*
Race	.07*	.10*
Sex	.08***	.09***
Size of city	-.06***	-.07*
Type of dwelling	-.04	-.02
Hours worked	.02	.01
Vacation time	NC	.08***
Have yard	.07***	.06**
Have park nearby	.09***	.08***
Coefficient of determination, *R*	.63	.51
Sample size	2,970	1,709

Significance:*=.05; **=.01; ***=.001
NC = Not calculated because vacation time data were not available for those not employed in a paid job.
Source: Walsh (1986) p. 159, taken from Heritage, Conservation, and Recreation Service.

Football League, and Major League Soccer than for the National Football League or National Basketball Association. The latter two leagues, with their reliance on lucrative television packages, are less dependent on attendance.

Siegfried and Eisenberg (1980) found price, quality of excitement of play (not necessarily winning), and promotional efforts are determinants of attendance in minor league baseball; however, price was not as important as other studies have suggested. The authors proposed that minor league teams tended to be located in smaller cities, with fewer available substitutes. In addition, they suggested that profit maximization was not the only objective of the clubs and that the clubs engaged in creating a general atmosphere that attracted fans. Although Cairns, Jennett, and Sloane (1986) had limited success in estimating professional sports attendance using price and income variables, Gruen (1976) found betting at the horse tracks to be influenced by both price and income. This may be because there are many substitutes for betting, particularly at the horse tracks.

Several studies have explored the impact of the uncertainty of outcomes on attendance. This issue is of particular interest in the sport field, especially because one of the characteristics often used to define sport is that the outcome of an event is uncertain (Leonard, 1998). Many individuals make (and lose) large amounts of money by betting on that uncertainty of outcome. Knowles, Sherony, and Haupert (1992) suggest that uncertainty is a significant determinant of Major League Baseball attendance, especially when the home team is slightly favored. Attendance (demand) is higher when the game is likely to be a close one. The authors argue that a league is best served, in terms of profit maximization for the league, when competitive balance exists across the league. Competitive balance enhances the uncertainty of outcome.

Supply

The sport industry produced $152 billion of goods and services in 1996 (Meek, 1997). Who determines what and how much to produce? Why have some firms been successful whereas others have failed? Why do firms produce athletic shoes rather than dress shoes? Why do they produce more basketball shoes and fewer aerobics shoes? These are questions related to supply. Sports organizations have an inventory (supply) of events, apparel, and information that they are willing to trade for cash from someone who wants to attend an event, wear apparel, or read a sports magazine (demand). Figure 3-3 is a supply curve that illustrates the relationship between price and supply for basketball shoes.

Supply is the various quantities of a product offered at a range of prices or the entire range of the demand curve. The supply curve shows the relationship between all the prices and all the quantities of a good or service that is available. In Figure 3-3, as the price of basketball shoes rises, more shoes are produced. *Quantity supplied* is the number of specific goods or services supplied at some specific period of time and at some specific price. At Point A in Figure 3-3, if basketball shoes sell for $50, 1,000 shoes will be produced. A

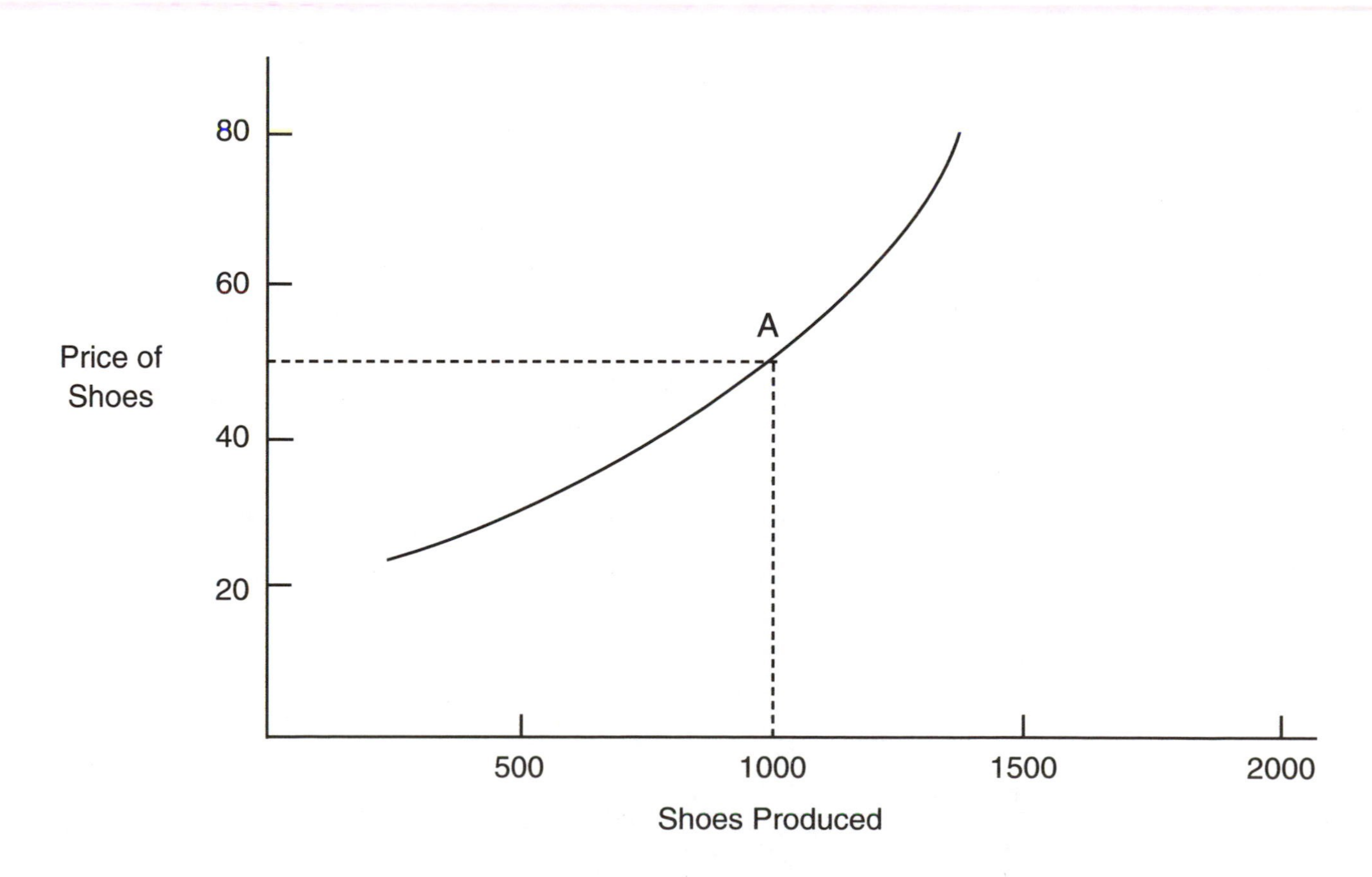

Figure 3-3. Supply Curve

change in quantity supplied refers to the effect of a change in price on the quantity supplied. If the price of shoes decreases to $30, 500 shoes will be supplied. A *shift in supply* refers to nonprice factors that cause a shift of the entire supply curve. If the entire supply curve shifts, more units are produced at each price. In Figure 3-4, Arrow A represents a change in quantity supplied, and Arrow B represents a shift in supply.

The supply curve represents the effect of prices on quantity produced. It slopes upward, from left to right, because the relationship is generally a positive one. The corollary to the law of demand is the *law of supply*. With all other things being equal, the higher the price of a good offered, the more will be supplied. On the other hand, the lower the price of a good, the less of it will be supplied. As the price of a product increases, producers can make more profit and will want to maximize that by producing more. They may also shift from making a lower-priced item to a higher-priced one (as long as production costs are similar). In addition, because there are profits to be made, additional producers will enter the market.

As with demand, sport products and services vary in the amount available. Factors that affect supply include

1. Price of the product
2. Prices of inputs needed to make the product
3. Technology

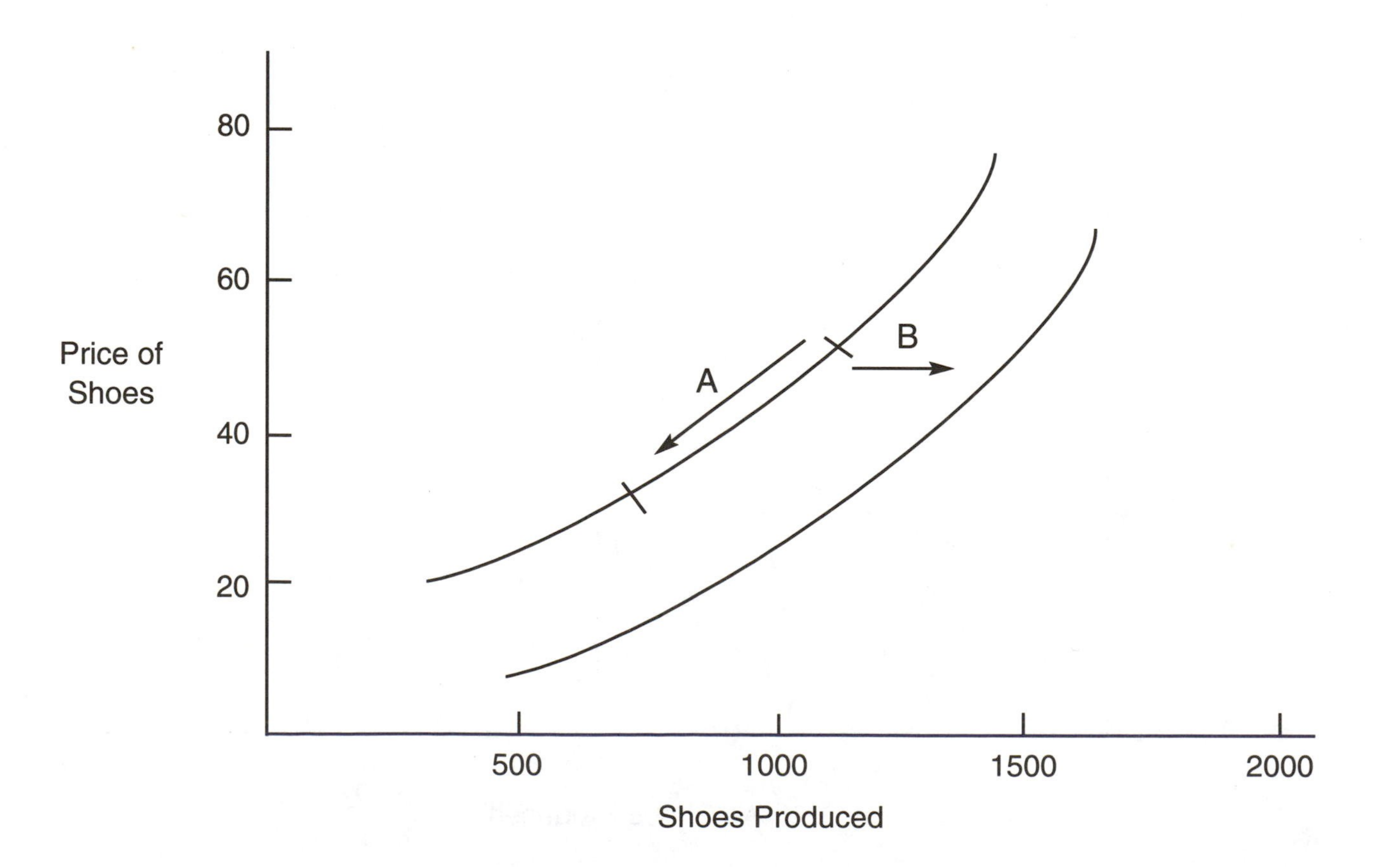

Figure 3-4. Supply Curve

4. Suppliers

5. Taxes and subsidies

Changes in product price result in movements along the supply curve. We have already discussed some of the ways in which product price determines supply, so we will go on to other factors.

All the elements a firm uses to make products, including materials, labor, and machines, are called *inputs*. Generally, the higher the cost of inputs, the lower the profit realized, and the fewer the number of items that will be supplied at each price (shift in supply curve to the left). If the cost of inputs declines, profit increases, and the greater the number of items that will be supplied (shift in supply curve to the right). For example, when sport industry manufacturers use foreign labor, the result is much lower-cost labor inputs than would be possible in the United States. Shoe manufacturers make more profit and produce more shoes. What would happen if shoe manufacturers were suddenly forced to increase the wages they pay in other countries?

Technological improvements that act to lower costs also increase profits and result in shifts in the supply curve to the right. Over the years, improvements in production processes and in materials have made many goods more plentiful at lower prices. Today, avid sports fans are purchasing foot-wide satellite disks to put on their roofs and, in some cases, paying nothing for the disks as long as they purchase programming. Compare that to a few years ago when a six-foot-wide disk might cost several thousand dollars. The growth of cable television, including pay-for-view, and direct broadcast services have increased the number of sporting events available to the viewer (Hugh-Jones, 1992).

The number and expectations of suppliers influence supply. As firms make more profits, new firms enter the market hoping to also profit. Over time, more products are offered at every price along the supply curve. The sport industry has seen tremendous increases in supply in recent years. Existing sports leagues have expanded their schedules, and new professional sport leagues (e.g., WNBA, ABL, MLS, Arena Football) have provided more events. Additional sports (e.g., Extreme Games) are now available for consumers to watch, either in person or on television. The supply of recreational ice and dek hockey rinks in many Northeastern cities, such as metropolitan Pittsburgh, PA, has doubled, responding to the growth in hockey and roller blades. The increase in supply will eventually result in a decrease in prices, but in the short term, supply will increase at a given price. The growth in supply provides for increased competition. On the other side, as firms leave a market, perhaps because of too much competition and less opportunity for profit, supply decreases.

Taxes and subsidies also affect profits and supply and shift supply curves. Many cities have imposed an amusement tax on sporting events as a way of generating revenue. Sport organizers claim that the tax decreases profits, and they would prefer to take their inventory of events to a place where there is no tax. In contrast, subsidies lead to an increase in supply. Municipalities routinely subsidize recreational programs and facilities and, increasingly, subsidize corporate sport in the guise of stadiums and arenas.

Demand and Supply and Price

The relationship between demand and supply is important in determining the price of a product. In an *equilibrium state*, the amount that consumers demand and the amount that producers supply is in balance, and prices remain constant. For example, in a state of equilibrium, the number of athletic shoes available for sale is equal to the number of shoes desired by buyers. What happens when demand exceeds supply or when supply exceeds demand? Figure 3-5 graphically represents such a situation.

If there is more demand for a product than there is product available, a state of excess demand exists. When excess demand occurs, prices will rise. As prices rise, producers create more product until demand is satisfied and prices stabilize. In the late 1980s through the 1990s, ice hockey was experiencing growth not just at the professional level but also at the recreational level. The number of participants and teams wanting to play was increasing. However, there were not enough ice rinks to accommodate the demand. Because of the excess demand, ice time became very costly, and recreational teams often practiced or played as late as midnight or 2:00 A.M. New ice rinks were created, and the cost of ice time stopped increasing.

Demand and supply and price are related in other ways. For example, each year the NCAA conducts a lottery for available Final Four basketball tickets. The lottery is necessary because there are many more people who want tickets than there are tickets available (in 2000, 174,000 people applied for 10,250 tickets available to the general public) (Finalfourseats.com, 2000). The price of an NCAA Final Four package (three games) has risen from $50 in 1988 to $100 in 2000, in spite of an increase in supply (the size of the arenas in which the event is played has increased). The NCAA could raise the package price even more because of excess demand. We should note that one of the reasons there is so much excess demand is that the NCAA has intentionally kept prices lower than it

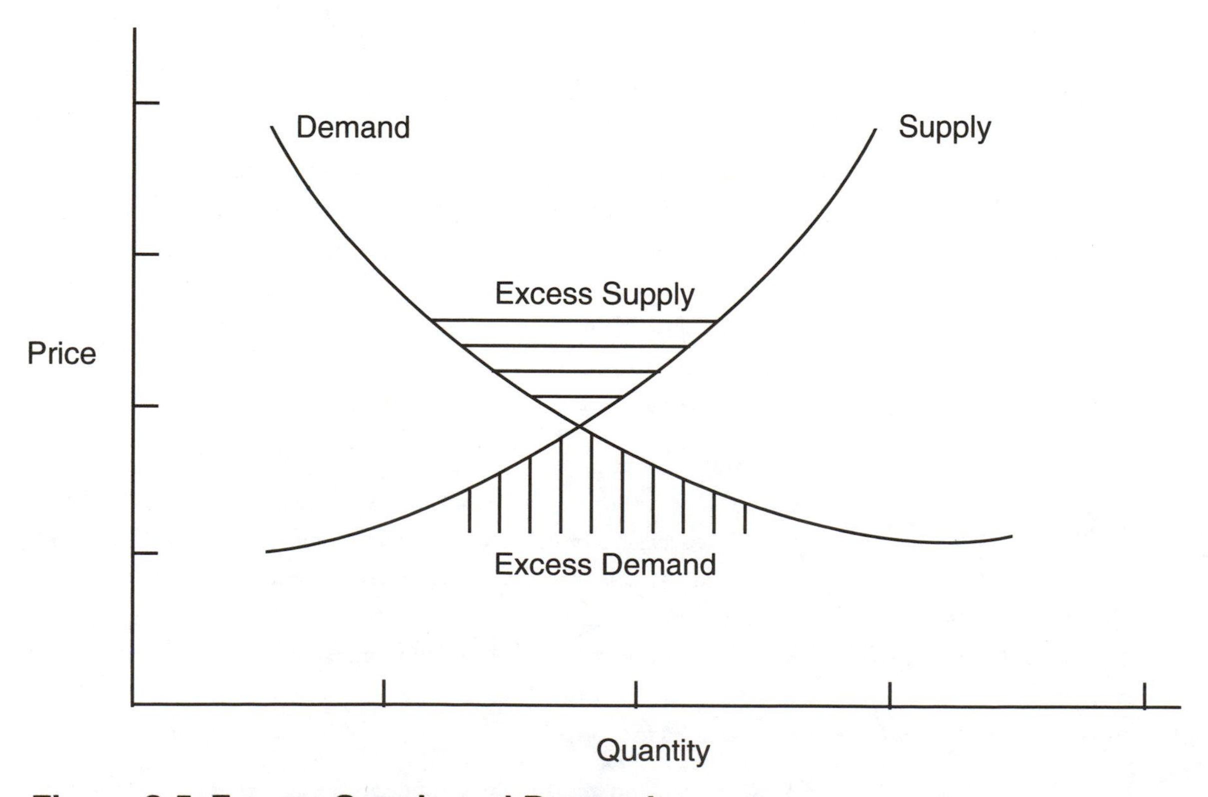

Figure 3-5. Excess Supply and Demand

could charge.[1] If it allowed prices to freely adjust on the open market, as the package price increased, demand would decrease until equilibrium was reached.

If there is more supply of a product than there is demand, a state of excess supply exists. Some producers will not be able to sell all the goods or services they have. In such a state, producers reduce prices, hoping to capture a larger market share. However, all producers will likely do the same, a strategy that leads to reduced profits for everyone. Ultimately, as prices come down, consumers will be more willing to purchase, and equilibrium is reached. In 1999, a hot golf equipment market cooled, as consumer demand for $400 clubs was filled. The result was lower sales and excess inventories and, ultimately, lower prices (Spanberg, 1999).

The sport industry has its own term for the demand and supply relationship. *Scalping* is buying tickets at a low price and reselling them to consumers who have not been able to satisfy their demand for tickets through a ticket office. Many high-level sporting events experience ticket scalping. A few years ago, Florida State and Notre Dame were scheduled to play in football. Ticket prices were $27 in preseason and sold out. Halfway through the season, both teams were unbeaten, and tickets could be obtained from scalpers for $200. One week before the game, both teams were still unbeaten, and tickets could be obtained from scalpers for $600. Two days before the game, the scalpers' price fell to $400 (Colander, 1998). What happened at each step?

The above situations are covered by the *laws of supply and demand*:

1. If the quantity demanded is greater than the quantity supplied, prices tend to rise. When quantity supplied is greater than quantity demanded, prices tend to fall. With ice rinks, demand for time resulted in hourly rates increasing from approximately $80 to as much as $200. The opposite was true with golf clubs. The demand for a $400 club turned into a demand for $100 substitutes.

2. The larger the difference between quantity demanded and quantity supplied, the greater is the pressure for prices to rise (if there is excess demand) or fall (if there is excess supply). If the waiting list for Final Four tickets is 10,000 people, prices can rise more than if the waiting list is 100 people.

3. When quantity demanded equals quantity supplied, prices will tend to remain the same.

Elasticity of Demand and Supply

The above discussion sets the stage for talking about an economic concept called *elasticity*, something in which the owners of the Midwest Marks are interested. Elasticity is a measure of what happens to a variable when another variable is changed. For example, if an organization changes its pricing structure, what happens to sales and revenues? If a team or event raises ticket prices, what happens to ticket sales and/or revenue? If the price of joining a bowling league increases, what impact does it have on participation? Price elasticity of demand and price elasticity of supply are two concepts that we will talk about in the following section.

---

[1]The lowest price package available from one ticket broker for the 2000 Final Four was $650 <www.finalfourseats.com/finalfour.html>.

Price elasticity of demand is a measure of the amount of change in demand that occurs as a result of change in price. The relationship can be expressed below:

Price elasticity of demand = Percentage change in quantity demanded/
Percentage change in price

Demand elasticity is usually a negative number, although many economists drop the negative sign (a convention we will follow). Its value can vary from zero to infinity; a zero value represents price inelasticity, or little relationship between demand and price. For example, an elasticity of 0.4 means that a one-percent increase in the price of a good or service results in a 0.4% decrease in number of units consumed. For example, for minor league baseball, Siegfried and Eisenberg (1980) found elasticity of demand of 0.25. A one-percent increase in the price resulted in a 0.25% decline in attendance. They concluded that changes in price did not result in major changes in attendance.

Note that elasticity measures percentage, not absolute, changes. We compare percentage changes in price to percentage changes in demand and supply. Using percentages allows us to compare change without having to remember the exact unit being used. It also makes it possible to compare elasticities of different goods (tickets, athletic shoes, memberships).

Table 3-2 represents estimated elasticities of demand for several recreational activities. Although these elasticities are generally low, for some activities, such as belonging to a golf club (0.70), demand is more affected by changes in price than is true for other activities, such as golf in general (0.12).

What happens to supply if price is changed? *Price elasticity of supply* is a measure of the amount of change in quantity supplied that occurs relative to change in price. The relationship is expressed below:

Price elasticity of supply = Percentage change in quantity supplied/
Percentage change in price

For example, if the price of a golf club declines from $400 to $300 (a 25% decrease), producers start to reduce their production of the clubs, perhaps by 10%. The supply elastic-

Table 3-2. Estimated Elasticity of Demand of Selected Recreation Activities, United States

Activity	Demand
Golf (general)	0.12
Golf (club members)	0.70
Tennis	0.20
Outdoor pool	0.23
Attending sports event	0.33
Skiing	0.40
Visiting fairs, amusement parks	0.20
Camping	0.15

Source: Walsh (1986), p. 259.

ity would be 0.40. If the price of tennis balls declines by 10% and 10% fewer tennis balls are produced, the supply elasticity would be 1.0. When we compare the two figures, it is clear that the supply of tennis balls would be more responsive to changes in price than would be the supply of golf clubs.

Sport managers need to be aware of this relationship because they are often changing prices. Ticket prices are an example, not just for team sports, but for ski resorts, golf courses, and major events. Athletic clubs and country clubs adjust membership prices. Sellers of sponsorship, advertising, and signage should consider the impact of pricing changes on their sales.

Economists generally classify the relationship between price and demand as being elastic, inelastic, or unit elastic:

Elastic demand refers to a state in which the proportional change in quantity is greater than the proportional change in price (E > 1). *Inelastic demand*, on the other hand, means the proportional change in quantity is less than the proportional change in price (E < 1). *Unit elastic demand* indicates the proportional change in quantity is equal to the proportional change in price (E = 1).

Let us compare a baseball and a football team to illustrate how elasticity works. In 1998, approximately 1.4 million fans paid an average ticket price of $7.50 to attend a professional baseball team's games. For the upcoming year, the team management is discussing whether to raise ticket prices. Prices of concessions, parking, and merchandise will remain the same. The team management has to make some judgments about what the change will do to attendance. Table 3-3 presents options.

For the baseball team, would the demand be elastic or inelastic?

$$\text{Elasticity of baseball} = \frac{.121}{.10} = 1.21$$

The answer is elastic (E > 1): A 10% ($.75) increase in the price of the average ticket has a corresponding decrease of 12.1% in sales (remember the negative relationship).

As another example, consider a football team in the same town, subject to the same economic environment. Last year they sold out each of their games, for an average attendance

Table 3-3. Sample Price Elasticity of Demand for a Baseball Team

Price	% P	Quantity	% Q	Elasticity
$7.50		1.40 million		
$7.75	.033	1.35	.036	1.09
$8.00	.067	1.29	.079	1.18
$8.25	.100	1.23	.121	1.21

Table 3-4. Sample Price Elasticity of Demand for a Football Team

Price	% P	Quantity	% Q	Elasticity
$30		58,000		
$31	.033	58,000	.00	.00
$32	.067	58.000	.00	.00
$33	.100	57,900	.002	.02

of 58,000, at an average ticket price of $30. What would happen if they raise their ticket prices by the same amount as the baseball team? Again, all other prices remain the same (see Table 3-4)

How would you describe the demand for football tickets?

$$\text{Elasticity of baseball} = \frac{.002}{.100} = .02$$

Here the demand is inelastic (E < 1): The change in price has virtually no impact on the change in attendance.

By now you may be thinking: Wait. What about team performance and other such trivial factors? Keep in mind, economists look at relationships "all things being equal." In these cases, we assume that the team's performance on the field and other factors are consistent from year to year.

Factors that make demand for goods and services more elastic include

1. More substitutes for that good or service. If a team or athletic club or shoe manufacturer raises its prices, what are the alternatives to spend money? The more alternatives, the more elastic the good or service is.
2. The longer the time interval considered. More substitutes are available in the long run. The growth of ice and dek hockey rinks during the 1990s is an example. In addition, over time, consumers adjust their purchasing habits and develop substitutes. This is the reason economists develop short-run versus long-run demand curves.
3. The less a good is a necessity. Necessities (e.g., prescription drugs, utilities) have fewer substitutes. As previously mentioned, recreation and sport are not considered necessities.
4. The more specifically a good is defined. Sports or recreation taken as a whole has more elastic demand than do individual sports or recreation activities. There are many substitutes for sports as entertainment; there are fewer substitutes for a round of golf or a baseball game.
5. The larger the expenditure for a good relative to one's total income. To buy tennis balls at $3.00 a can does not result in much impact on one's total income. To be asked to

pay a $10,000 initiation fee to join a golf club will result in many people looking at other alternatives.

Elasticity of supply is also affected by available substitutes, but the influence is felt most when considering time factors:

1. The longer the time period being considered, the more elastic is supply. Over a longer time period, producers have more opportunities to adjust production and supply.

2. Ease and cost of adding supply. How easy is it to add new supply? To add more rounds of golf may require building a new course whereas increasing the number of available spots in a 10K race requires little in costs. The former is more difficult and costly in time and money.

What does this mean to an administrator with a sport organization? If you are making decisions for the previously described baseball team, you have less flexibility in your options, at least in ticket prices. Your sales are responsive to changes in ticket prices. If you are making decisions for the football team, you have more flexibility. You can change prices without having to worry as much about the impact on demand. For almost any sport organization like an athletic club, event, or resort, a sport administrator must attempt to determine what the impact of price changes will be in order to make smart pricing decisions.

Demand, Supply, and Revenue

The issues above are not just questions of demand and supply and price but also of the impact on total revenue for an organization. *Total revenue* is the price charged per unit of some item times the number of units sold (TR = P x Q). What happens to total revenue if price changes? Keep in mind that if price changes, demand is likely to change.

1. If demand is elastic, the relationship is inverse; that is, an increase in prices results in a reduction in total revenue.

2. If demand is inelastic, the relationship is positive. It means an increase in prices results in an increase in total revenue.

3. If demand is unit elastic, a rise in prices has no impact on total revenue.

Tables 3-5 and 3-6 illustrate what happens to total revenue for various price changes with the baseball and football teams. For the baseball team, the jump from $7.50 to $8.25 (an increase of 10%) results in a decline in demand and a loss in total revenue of $350,000. However, for a smaller price increase—from $7.50 to $7.75—although demand declines by 40,000 people, revenue actually increases by $40,000. It may be beneficial from a ticket revenue standpoint for the baseball team to accept some decline in attendance to maximize revenues. Of course, this is with all things being equal. In practice, the sport manager needs to consider impacts on ancillary revenue such as concessions and parking.

Table 3-6 shows that for the football team, the impact of the rise in prices is clear: Revenue increases. A 10% rise in ticket prices, from $30 to $33, results in a 9.7% rise in revenue, or an addition $1.71 million. In this case, maximizing revenue does not necessarily involve a decline in attendance.

Table 3-5. Total Revenues for Sample Baseball Team

Price	% P	Quantity	% Q	Elasticity	Total Revenue (P x Q)
$7.50		1.40 million		$10.50 million	
$7.75	.033	1.36	.029	.88	$10.54
$8.00	.067	1.29	.079	1.18	$10.32
$8.25	.100	1.23	.121	1.21	$10.15

Table 3-6. Total Revenues for Sample Football Team

Price	% P	Quantity	% Q	Elasticity	Total Revenue (P x Q)
$30		58,000			$1.74 million
$31	.033	58,000	.00	.00	$1.80
$32	.067	58.000	.00	.00	$1.86
$33	.100	57,900	.002	.02	$1.91

Price Discrimination

One last element enters our discussion of supply and demand. In using the baseball team as an example, we used a single ticket price. However, rarely when we go to a baseball game is there just one price for tickets. Rather, there is a range, giving consumers an option of how much they will spend. This is true for many sports venues. Ski resorts vary prices by weekend/weekday or half-day use; athletic clubs have family, single, social memberships; and weekend 10K events have different prices for early and late registration and/or for walkers. This concept, called *price discrimination*, recognizes that different segments of consumers have different price elasticities.

Table 3-7 illustrates this concept for visitors to a ski resort. The elasticity for day skiers, who are likely to live close to the resort, is 0.30 whereas for skiers on vacation trips, the elasticity is almost 0.09. For the latter, demand is more inelastic. People going to ski on vacation are not as concerned about changes in price as are those who ski on a day pass, perhaps because the lift ticket price itself is a smaller portion of the overall cost of the vacation or because they have a higher income level. Using the concept of price discrimination, sport managers may have more flexibility in changing prices for certain consumer segments and less flexibility for others. As another example, prime behind-the-plate seats in baseball are more likely to be inelastic whereas bleacher seats are more likely to be elastic. Businesses and high-income attendees are more likely to purchase prime seats. For them, the cost of tickets is likely to be a small percentage of their total income, or they may write off the tickets as a business expense. Either way, they are less concerned about price.

Table 3-7. Price Elasticity of Demand for Ski Lift Tickets

Day tickets	0.35
Weekend use	0.22
Vacation trips	0.087

Source: Walsh (1986), p. 279.

Forecasting Demand and Supply

Sport managers can use their knowledge of demand and supply to forecast events or conditions. Forecasts are basically predictions. For example, a sports apparel company may want to project demand for its clothing over the next 3 to 5 years to determine whether or not it should open a new production line or new stores. Before developing new slopes, a ski resort manager might want to estimate the future demand for ski days. One of the goals of forecasting is to reduce uncertainty on the part of the sport manager in making decisions. With good estimates of what would happen, given changes in price, demand, and supply, better decisions are possible. However, forecasting does not eliminate uncertainty. It only provides a tool to the manager to assist in making decisions.

Forecasting, or *demand estimation*, is a complicated topic and is the content of entire academic courses. However, sport managers should be aware of some basic considerations. People looking at doing forecasts need to consider several relevant factors. An important beginning point is to determine what a forecast is intended to accomplish. Who will use the predictions? How will they be used? What format is most useful? What is the relevant time period? After answering these questions, the forecaster considers general factors: (a) general economic conditions, such as GNP or population distributions, and (b) industry conditions, in either the sport industry or specific segments of it (e.g., clubs, sporting goods). Specific demand factors involved in forecasting might include (a) income levels of the population, (b) consumer habits and tastes, and (c) market potential for various groups. From a supply side, the forecaster might want to examine related regulations and laws. These might include enacted laws, agency regulations, and court decisions. For example, many ski resorts use Forest Service land for slopes. Are changes in regulations governing the use of that land imminent?

Although important to do, forecasting is not an easy task. It requires thorough analysis of what has happened as well as assumptions about what will happen. Economists have developed elaborate models in many industries; however, sports is not one where models have been frequently applied. The following description is a brief summary of techniques used in developing economic forecasts that have been used in the sport industry. It is not designed to be a comprehensive explanation.

Opinion polls, market research, and spending plan surveys are commonly used to identify changes in people's activities. These techniques can help determine who consumers are, why and how they make the purchases they do, and what future plans consumers have for spending. Such surveys are done by individual businesses, industry groups (for example, the National Sporting Goods Association provides extensive information on sporting goods consumers), and research centers (the Survey Research center at the University of Michigan is one example). Doing market research and polls has many advantages and disadvantages. A course in research methods provides a useful background.

Expert opinion is another tool. These experts may be corporate executives in an industry or salespeople for a business. *Street & Smith's Sports Business Journal* (1999) provided an example of the former when it brought together six of what it deemed the "masters of their various disciplines" to describe what they see happening in the sport industry in the 21st century (Schoenfeld, 1999). Business can also look within the organization. A resource often overlooked is a business's own sales staff. Who else is in continual contact with consumers, talking with them, asking them what they are going to want? Although this technique may be useful, it also has disadvantages, not the least of which is that using a selected group of people does not necessarily give a representative view.

Another way to make projections is to look at past demand and use it to determine how supply might be adjusted. This can be a useful technique, especially if the manager is trying to predict what is going to happen in the very near term. However, using such a method does present difficulties, one of which is that conditions under which a company operates change, especially over a longer period. For example, the sport apparel business is one that is subject to fads. What has been a hot item over the past 3 years may very well be out-of-date in the next year. As a result, using past information can provide a very misleading picture of the future. A variety of statistical techniques have been developed, including time series analysis and constant compound growth rates, to improve the use of past data. A knowledge of statistics and econometrics is helpful.

Even though each of these techniques has disadvantages, those disadvantages should not dissuade the sport manager from using them. A bad scenario occurs when the manager does not attempt to determine what the future holds and how to position the organization to meet future demands.

Summary

Supply and demand are basic economic concepts. In fact, they can be used to answer many of the questions we have about why industries and individuals make the decisions they do. The general law of demand states that, all things being equal, the lower (higher) the price of some item, the higher (lower) the quantity demanded. The general law of supply states that, all things being equal, the higher (lower) the price of a good offered, the more (less) of a product will be supplied. Many factors influence supply and demand; the major one is price. In making decisions, sport managers need to consider elasticity of demand and supply, or the responsiveness of demand and supply to changes in prices. Sport managers can use their knowledge of supply and demand in making forecasts and decisions for their organizations.

Chapter Study Questions

1. As an expert in the area of pricing decisions, what do you think are the issues the owners of the Midwest Marks need to consider? What would your advice be? What would you consider?
2. What is the difference between demand and quantity demanded? What is the difference between change in quantity demanded and a shift in the demand curve?
3. What is the difference between supply and quantity supplied? What is the difference between change in quantity supplied and a shift in the supply curve?
4. You are a ski resort operator. In the next 5 years, what factors might affect your business in terms of supply and demand?
5. The U.S. women's soccer team won the World Cup in 1999. If you're in the soccer business, how might that influence your decision making?
6. What is elasticity? Elasticity of demand? Elasticity of supply? Distinguish between elastic and inelastic demand and supply.
7. What makes demand for some goods and services more elastic? What makes supply of some goods and services more elastic?
8. If you're the CEO for the baseball and football teams that are considering raising their prices, what would your decision be? How much would you raise the prices? Why?
9. Many professional athletes make millions of dollars each year whereas the salaries of elementary school teachers are a fraction of that. We pay huge amounts to some people to "play" whereas others, responsible for shaping the abilities and attitudes of children, make so much less. How would you argue this makes economic sense, using the concepts of supply and demand?
10. Why do organizations use price discrimination?
11. What methods are available for managers to forecast demand and supply?

Chapter Four

INTRODUCTION

The purpose of this chapter is to continue our discussion of the basic economic principles that can be useful in explaining and predicting managerial decision making. In particular, this chapter will focus on the basic market structures. A *market structure* "describes the competitive environment in the market for any good or service" (Hirschey & Pappas, 1995, p. 495). Although each is based on the assumption that the organization or firm is seeking to maximize its profits, classifying organizations into one of these markets will further enhance our ability to explain and predict managerial decision making. Table 4-1 presents the four basic market structures—perfect competition, monopoly, oligopoly, and monopolistic competition—along with the distinguishing features of each. When discussing each of the market structures, we will examine a number of factors to determine the optimal output for the firm. Although demand was discussed in detail in chapter 3, it is important to discuss the other factors before discussing the market types.

Market Structures in the Sport Industry

Ellen Thompson, Rob DiRocco, and Laurie Roberti are owners of the three health clubs in the town of Aaronville, Colorado. The clubs offer comparable services and are seen by members of the community as being fairly similar. During the past year, Ellen, Rob, and Laurie have been lowering their prices in order to acquire new members. This price war has led to a decrease in profitability for all three. Unless something changes soon, all three health clubs are in danger of going out of business. Is there anything that Ellen, Rob, and/or Laurie can do to turn around their current financial situation? Do any of these options have legal implications? What is the best option available?

Table 4-1. Market Structures

Market Structure	No. of Producers	Type of Product	Power over Price	Barriers to Entry	Non-price Competition
Perfect Competition	Many	Standardized	None	Low	None
Monopoly	One	Unique	Much	Very High	Advertising & Product Differentiation
Oligopoly	Few	Standardized or Differentiated	Some	High	Advertising & Product Differentiation
Monopolistic Competition	Many	Differentiated	Some	Low	Advertising & Product Differentiation

Marginal Revenue and Marginal Cost

Perhaps the most important factors are the marginal revenue (MR) and the marginal cost (MC). *Marginal revenue* is the additional revenue the firm will earn if it produces one more unit of output, whereas the *marginal cost* is the cost to the firm of producing that additional unit of output. A firm will continue to produce more when the marginal revenue exceeds marginal cost and will decrease production if marginal cost exceeds marginal revenue. Therefore, firms will generally stop producing units at the point at which the marginal cost is equal to marginal revenue because there is no incentive to produce any more; this is frequently referred to as the *equilibrium point.*

For example, Reebok may determine that the marginal revenue of producing one additional pair of sneakers is $50. If the marginal cost is only $40, managers would be expected to produce more units, but would decrease production if marginal cost is equal to $60. In contrast, if the marginal revenue and marginal costs are both equal to $50, Reebok would stop producing more.

Average Total Cost

Other factors to examine when determining the number of units to supply to the marketplace include average variable cost (AVC), fixed costs, and average total cost (ATC). *Average total cost* is the average amount it costs to produce a certain number of units. Although average total cost may look to be the same as marginal cost, the two terms are different. For example, the STS Corporation may be producing race cars. When producing three cars, the marginal costs for Car 1, Car 2, and Car 3 may be $52,000, $53,000, and $60,000 respectively. Therefore, although the marginal cost of producing Car 3 is $60,000, the average total cost of producing the three cars is $55,000.

Average Total Cost = ($52,000 + $53,000 + $60,000)/3 = $55,000

Fixed Costs

Included in the total cost of producing the three cars are certain costs (e.g., building maintenance) that will exist even if no output is produced. The costs of these items are defined as *fixed costs,* and they will exist regardless of the level of output.

Learning Activity

1. Siegfreid Golf Clubs is looking at a definite loss. However, the owner, Ken Siegfreid, believes that he may be able to lose less money if he stays open. Given the following information, what would you recommend that Ken do in each case?

Scenario 1

Fixed Costs = $100,000
Marginal revenue for each set of golf clubs = $150
Total Variable Costs for the first 100 set of clubs = $20,000
Total Variable Costs for the second 100 set of clubs = $15,000
Total Variable Costs for the third 100 set of clubs = $10,000
Total Variable Costs for the fourth 100 set of clubs = $5,000
Total Variable Costs for the fifth 100 set of clubs = $10,000
Total Variable Costs for the sixth 100 set of clubs = $20,000
Total Variable Costs for the seventh 100 set of clubs = $30,000

Scenario 2

Fixed Costs = $100,000
Marginal revenue for each set of golf clubs = $100
Total Variable Costs for the first 100 set of clubs = $20,000
Total Variable Costs for the second 100 set of clubs = $15,000
Total Variable Costs for the third 100 set of clubs = $10,000
Total Variable Costs for the fourth 100 set of clubs = $5,000
Total Variable Costs for the fifth 100 set of clubs = $10,000
Total Variable Costs for the sixth 100 set of clubs = $20,000
Total Variable Costs for the seventh 100 set of clubs = $30,000

Average Variable Cost

The *average variable cost* is the average total costs minus these fixed costs. In the STS example, if the fixed costs were $15,000, the average variable costs for the three cars would be $50,000.

Average Variable Cost = ($52,000 + $53,000 + $60,000 - $15,000)/3 = $50,000

Overall, the examination of all of these factors will help the manager determine the optimal level of output for the firm.

Perfect Competition

Distinguishing Features

Although there may be no industry that is a "perfect" example of perfect competition, this market type is among the most frequently discussed and has proven to be quite useful for examining and predicting corporate decisions (Mansfield, 1992). Advocates for capitalism often promoted perfect competition as the "ideal" model for economic activity in a capitalist society and suggested that perfect competition would result in the optimal price and level of output for society (Mansfield). Certain conditions distinguish perfect competition from other market types. First, there are *a large number of buyers and sellers in the market.* Therefore, the firm's output in a perfectly competitive industry is very small relative to market volume, and its output decisions will have no major impact. In other words, the firm could increase its output or completely stop producing its output, and no one would notice any substantial change in this industry.

Second, the firm has *no power over the price charged for the product.* Because the impact of the decision to increase or decrease production by one firm is so small, the firm does not have the ability to influence the price; therefore, a firm in perfect competition is said to be a *price taker*. The price is set by the marketplace, and the firms have no choice but to accept this price. Third, *the products or services in the industry are standardized and homogenous.* Essentially, consumers perceive the products produced by firms in the industry as all being the same. Because all products are believed to be the same, firms cannot engage in nonprice competition related to product quality.

Fourth, there *are few, if any, barriers to entry into or exit from* the perfectly competitive industry. Firms can easily enter the industry or leave the industry, and their resources are mobile enough to make these moves easily. Fifth, *there is widespread information available*, such that the players in the marketplace (i.e., buyers and sellers) have all of the information (e.g., cost, price, product quality) they need to make the best decisions. Therefore, firms would be unsuccessful if they tried to convince consumers the price of their product is lower or the quality of their product is better.

Finding examples of firms in perfectly competitive markets outside of sport is very difficult, and the task becomes even harder inside of sport. The best examples usually given of perfectly competitive industries are parts of the agriculture industry (Mansfield, 1992). Most consumers do not distinguish milk at one farm as being different from milk at another, and no one farm is large enough to have a major impact on the industry. Within the sport industry, there is no good example of a perfectly competitive industry. However, although no perfectly competitive industries may exist, it is not uncommon for society to try to push industries towards perfect competition because of the perceived societal benefits of perfect competition. Therefore, examining perfect competition is still useful for understanding the economic environment in the sport industry.

Determining Market Price

The first piece of information needed by firms in a perfectly competitive industry in order to make their output decisions is the market price. As discussed earlier, individual firms produce a small portion of the total supply, and individual consumers purchase only a small portion of the total amount of the product available, so neither group has any impact on the price. The price, therefore, is determined by the aggregate supply from all producers and the aggregate demand from all consumers. As the price increases, the amount the producers are willing to supply will increase, whereas the amount of the product demanded by the consumers decreases with price increases. Figure 4-1 demonstrates how the aggregate supply and aggregate demand are combined to determine the equilibrium market price. The point at which the supply curve intersects with the demand curve (E1) determines the market price (P1) and the quantity of the product that will be produced and sold at this price (Q1).

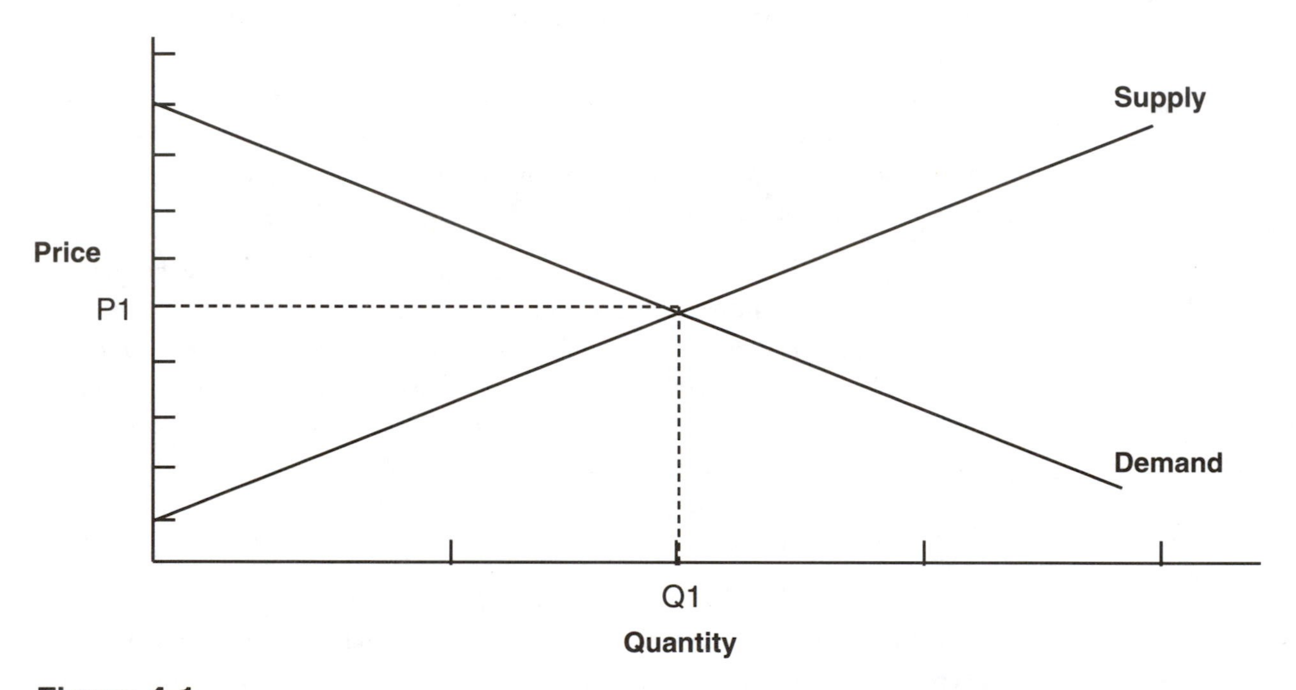

Figure 4-1

Graphic Representation of a Firm in Perfect Competition

Once the market price is determined, each firm also knows the marginal revenue curve. Because the price remains the same regardless of the output of the firm, marginal revenue will be the same for each unit produced. Moreover, the small firm can sell as much as it produces at this set price. Therefore, the demand curve is equal to the marginal revenue curve, and as shown in Figure 4-2, the curve is a horizontal line. To maximize profits, the firm will then produce an output level at which marginal revenue is equal to marginal cost.

As shown in Figure 4-2, MCR Athletic Footwear will produce 1,000 pairs of sneakers because this is the point at which the marginal cost curve intersects the marginal revenue curve. For every pair of sneakers before the 1,000th pair, marginal revenue exceeded marginal cost, so MCR would be motivated to produce more. In contrast, for each pair after the 1,000th pair, the marginal costs exceed the marginal revenue, so producing these sneakers would decrease profitability; essentially, MCR would lose money on each pair of sneakers after the 1,000th pair, so there is no incentive to produce more. As long as the price of the sneakers and marginal costs remain the same, MCR will continue to produce 1,000 pairs of sneakers to maximize their profits. However, if either curve shifts, the output level will also change. For example, if the price of the sneakers goes from $50 to $75, MCR will increase its production from 1,000 pairs of sneakers to 1,500 pairs of sneakers, as shown in Figure 4-2.

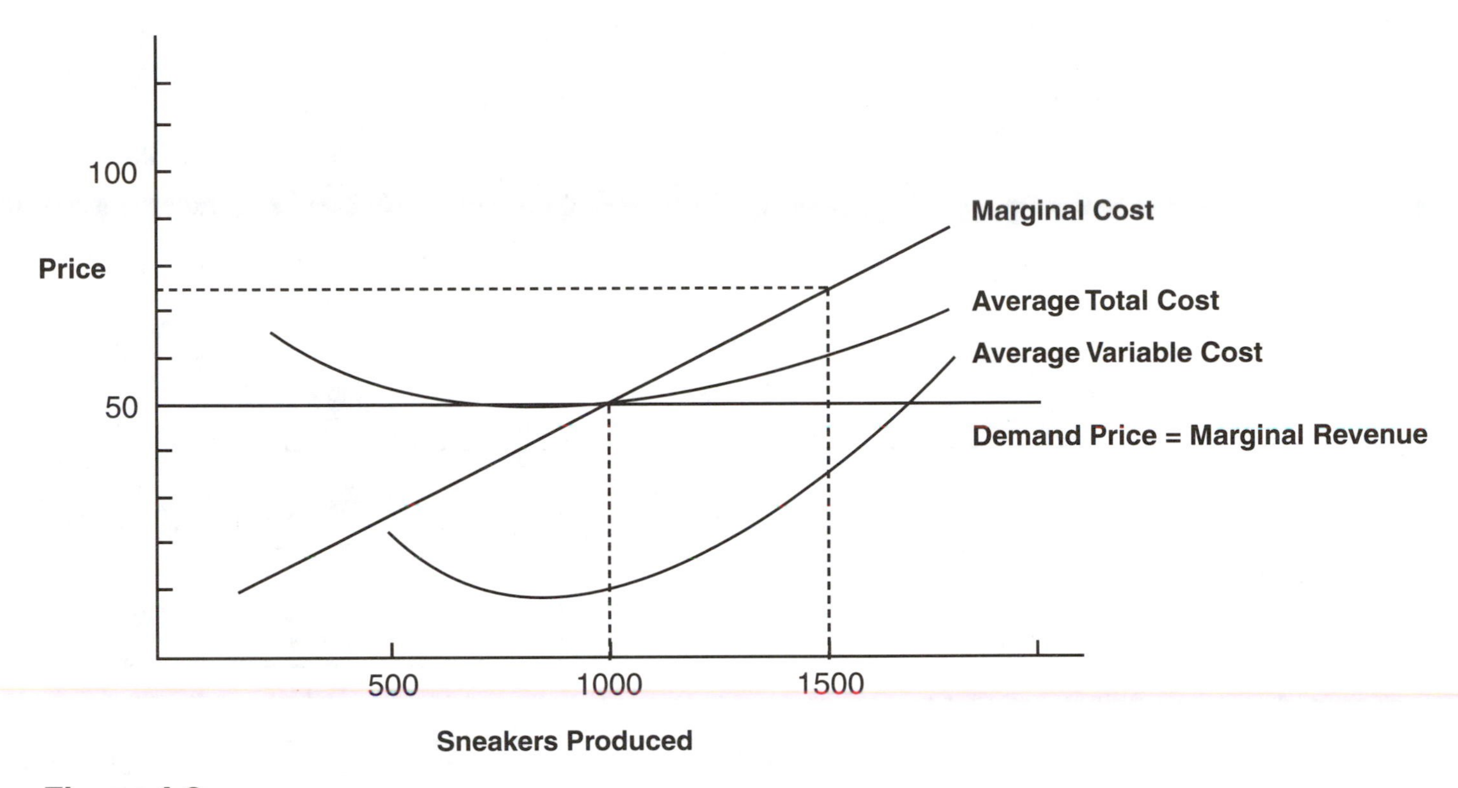

Figure 4-2

Short-Term Economic Losses in Perfect Competition

It is important to note that it is possible over the short term for MCR's marginal costs to be high enough that there is no point at which the firm can earn an economic profit, as shown in Figure 4-3. In this case, the managers would then examine the average variable cost curve and the average total cost curve. Although MCR would still be losing money, the firm would be willing to produce units in the short term if there is a point at which price exceeds average variable costs, even though the average total costs will still exceed the price. Because MCR will have to pay the fixed costs even if they produce nothing, they will produce 500 pairs of sneakers in order to reduce its losses on those fixed costs.

In Figure 4-3, MCR will lose $5,000 if they produce and sell the 500 pairs of sneakers, instead of the $10,000 it would have lost if it produced nothing. However, if the average variable costs had always exceeded the price, MCR would have produced nothing and simply lost $10,000. In this second case, producing any additional sneakers would have increased MCR's losses to an amount greater than $10,000 (see Table 4-2). It is important to understand that this scenario would only occur over the short term. If managers of MCR believed that marginal revenue would never again exceed marginal cost, they would drop out of this industry and invest their money elsewhere.

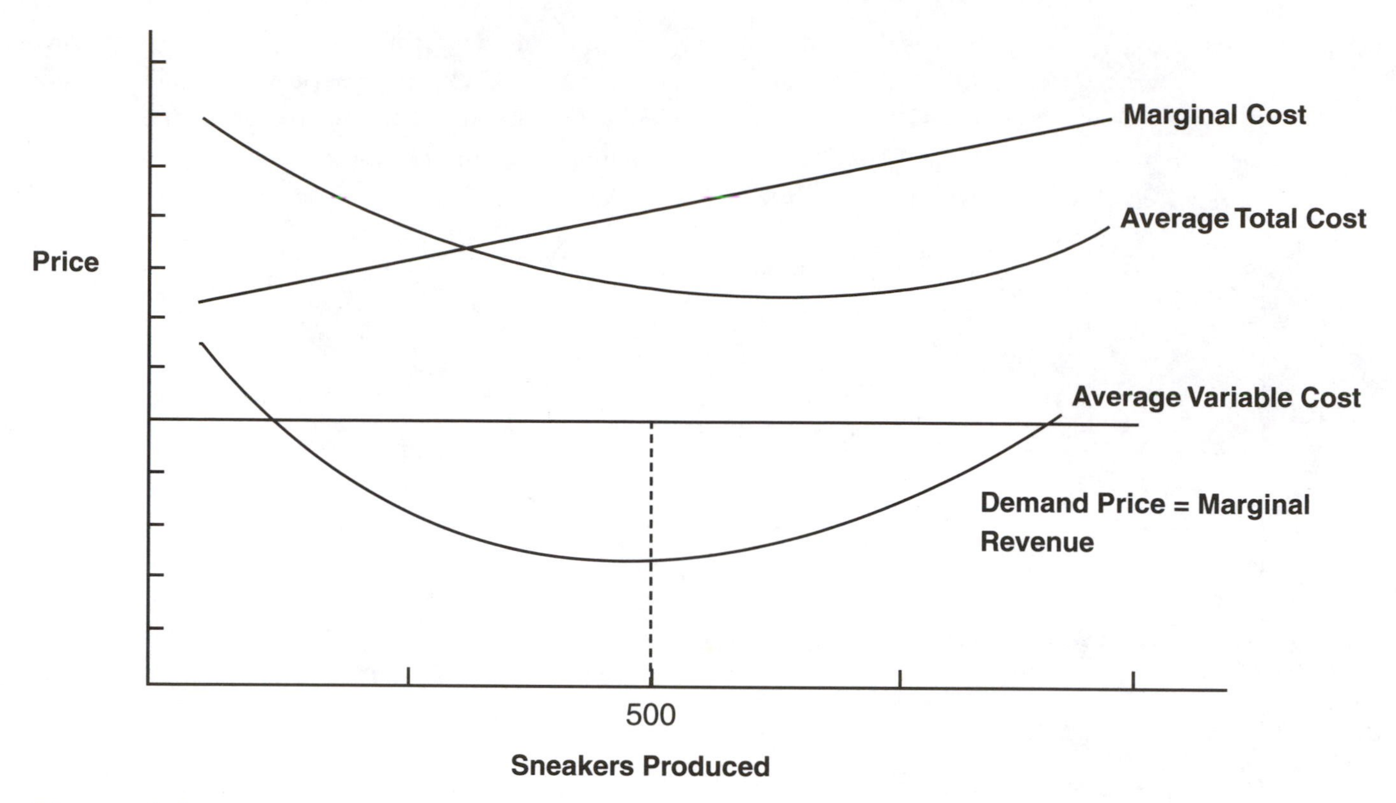

Figure 4-3

Table 4-2. Losses for MCR Athletic Footwear

Quantity	Revenue	Total Variable Costs	Fixed Costs	Total Loss
0	$ 0	$ 0	$10000	$10000
100	$ 3000	$ 3000	$10000	$10000
200	$ 6000	$ 5500	$10000	$ 9500
300	$ 9000	$ 7500	$10000	$ 8500
400	$12000	$ 9000	$10000	$ 7000
500	$15000	$10000	$10000	$ 5000
600	$18000	$13500	$10000	$ 5500
700	$21000	$18000	$10000	$ 7000

Monopoly

Distinguishing Features

In contrast to perfect competition, which has a large number of sellers, a monopoly is a market in which there is *only one* seller. Other factors also distinguish monopolies from the other market types. First, the product being sold in a monopoly is *highly differentiated.* It would not be easy for another firm to copy this product or service. Second, the firm in a monopoly has *considerable control over price*, and in contrast to firms in perfect competition, a firm in a monopoly is referred to as a price *maker* instead of a price *taker*. Third, even though there are no competitors, monopolists do *engage in nonprice competition.* Monopolists advertise to maximize the use of their product or service, rather than to take sales away from another company (Mansfield, 1992).

Monopolies also have high barriers to entry. If there were no such barriers, competitors would be attracted to and would enter the marketplace due to the high profits that monopolists traditionally earn. For example, the large amount of money made by the National Football League (NFL) would appear to make starting a rival league a popular idea, and in fact, a few rival leagues have started during the last 30 years (e.g., the World Football League, the United States Football League). However, a number of barriers to entry, such as the cost of stadium construction, the limited number of major television contracts available, the limited number of large communities without a team, and strong loyalty fans have toward their current favorite NFL team, have combined to prevent many new leagues from forming and have damaged the efforts of the rival leagues that have started.

In general, there are a number of other reasons that the barriers to entry may be high for a particular monopoly. For example, the U.S. government grants companies patents on their inventions for 17 years (Salvatore, 1993). This has allowed firms to be the sole supplier for that period. Meanwhile, other firms have become monopolists by controlling all of the input. In some cases, the government may grant an organization the right to be a monopoly if this will lead to an increase in efficiency *and* benefit society. Finally, in some cases, demand for the product or service is so low that the industry cannot support more than one firm. For example, a local health club in a small town may have a local monopoly simply because the population is not large enough to support two health clubs. This type of market situation is called natural monopoly and is also frequently subject to government regulations (Mansfield, 1992; Salvatore).

Graphic Representation of a Firm in Perfect Competition

Because monopolists are the sole producers and have considerable control over the price charged, the marginal revenue and demand curves appear much different from those of perfect competition. As shown in Figure 4-4, neither the marginal revenue curve nor the

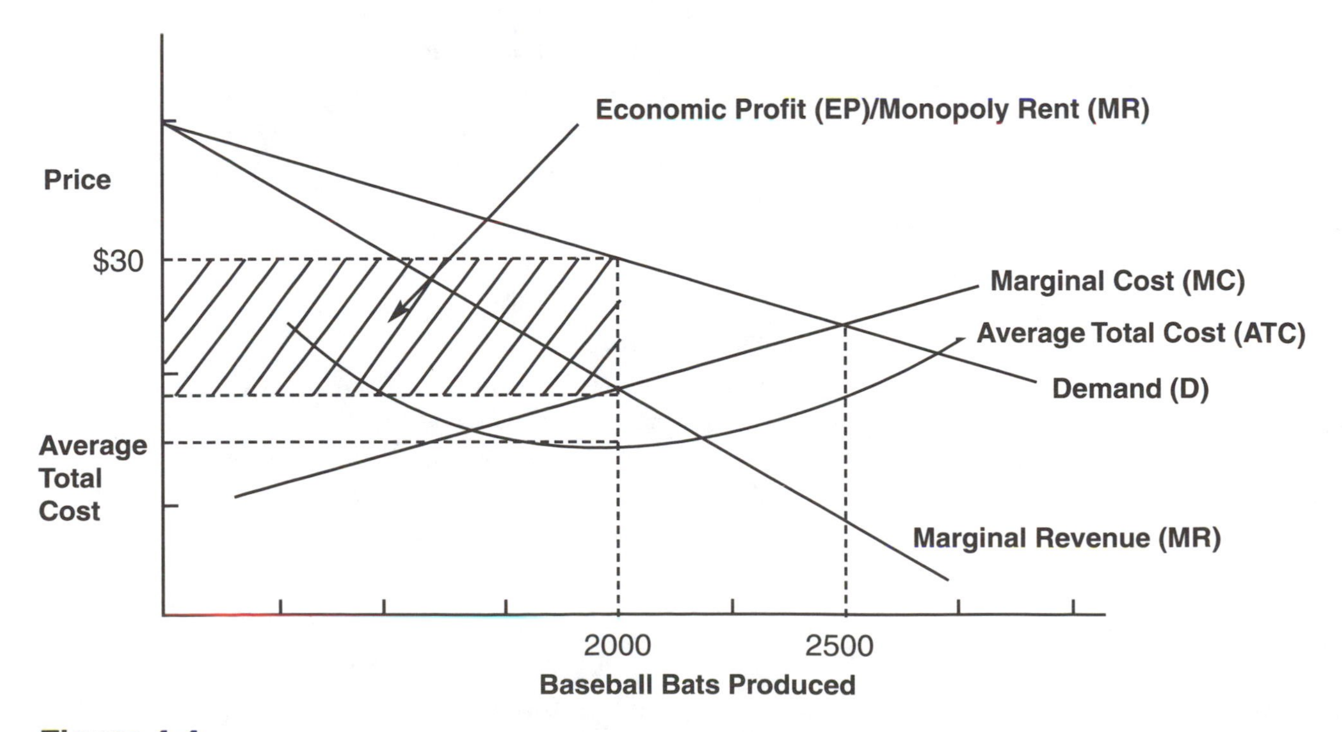

Figure 4-4

Table 4-3. Marginal Revenue and Demand Price for a Monopoly

Quantity	Demand Price	Total Revenue	Marginal Revenue
1	$100	$100	$100
2	$ 95	$190	$ 90
3	$ 92	$276	$ 86
4	$ 90	$360	$ 84
5	$ 88	$440	$ 80
6	$ 85	$510	$ 70
7	$ 82	$574	$ 64

demand curve is horizontal, and they are no longer equal to each other. The downward sloping demand curve indicates that consumers are willing to pay the most for the product or service when the output is the lowest (see chapter 3). Because the consumer will be willing to spend the most for the product when only one unit is produced, the marginal revenue for each additional unit will be less than the amount of revenue from the first, and the marginal revenue curve will also be downward sloping. In fact, as Table 4-3 indicates, the marginal revenue will be less than the demand (price) curve for each item after the first.

Although the demand and marginal revenue curves appear differently for the monopoly firm than for the firm operating in a perfectly competitive industry, the goal is still profit maximization. Therefore, if Louisville Slugger were a monopolist and had monopoly power over the production of and sales of baseball bats, they would produce units of output only until marginal revenue is equal to marginal cost. In Figure 4-4, the number of bats produced would be 2,000 at a price of $30 each. There are two aspects related to monopolies that are important to note. First, Louisville Slugger can earn an economic profit over the long term, the shaded area in Figure 4-4. Second, there is an optimal production point for society (i.e., 2,500 bats) at which the marginal cost of producing the bats is equal to the demand price.

This failure to produce the quantity demanded at the point that marginal cost is equal to demand is the reason that monopolies are seen as being socially inefficient and underproductive (Hirschey & Pappas, 1995; Mankiw, 1998). Although Louisville Slugger still could earn a normal rate of return (economic profits = 0) while producing 2,500 bats, they can earn greater economic profits while producing 2,000 bats. Therefore, they have no incentive to meet the consumers' demand for an additional 500 bats. This underproduction in monopolies is the main reason that Adam Smith and others believed that monopolies would have a detrimental effect on the operation of a capitalist system (Mansfield, 1992). More discussions related to this topic will be provided in chapters 9 and 10.

Difficulty in Maintaining Monopoly Status

Although production decisions by monopolists are frequently discussed, it should be noted that few monopolies actually exist. As will be discussed in chapter 10, the antitrust laws are designed to prevent monopolies from occurring. For example, the firms with patents lose their ability to use their patent as a barrier to entry after 17 years. Moreover, because of the antitrust laws, firms that have patents have been required by the courts in some cases to license their patents so that they cannot retain their monopoly status (Mansfield, 1992). The courts have also broken up monopolies that result from control over the entire supply (Mansfield). Finally, government-sanctioned monopolies and natural monopolies must deal with government regulations that often prevent them from setting a high price that would allow them to maximize economic profits. Natural monopolies refer to a market situation in which efficiency will be the greatest if only one firm produces a product or renders a service in an industry (Shim & Siegel, 1995).

Criticisms of Monopolies

There are also other common criticisms of monopolies, some of which are more accurate than others. First, monopolies are often accused of being inefficient in their operations. Because they are price makers, they do not have to control costs the same way a firm in a perfectly competitive industry would. Even if somewhat inefficient, they can nevertheless make an economic profit. Although there may be some truth to this, there are still rewards (i.e., higher economic profits) for being efficient in a monopoly, so even executives in monopolies will generally focus on reducing inefficiency.

Second, some argue that monopolists can charge whatever they want for their product. Although they certainly could charge whatever they want, they would be foolish to do so. Much like a firm in a perfectly competitive industry, there is an optimal price at which the monopoly will maximize profits (e.g., $30 for the Louisville Slugger bats in Figure 4-4). The monopoly will not charge more than this price because to do so would reduce profits. Moreover, if the monopoly increases its prices too much, it is increasing the chance that a competitor will enter the market. As long as the price remains reasonable, the monopoly can avoid competition and maintain monopoly profits.

Third, prices are higher in an industry with one producer than in a perfectly competitive industry. This is true because the absence of competition increases the price that the firm can charge. Fourth, monopolies are guaranteed profits. Although competition is not present, it is possible there will not be a point at which marginal revenue exceeds marginal cost. The cost of production might be quite high, whereas the demand for the product or service in society is low. The decision to either continue producing or to drop out under these conditions is the same as the decision would be for a firm in a perfectly competitive industry, which was discussed earlier (see Figure 4-3).

Monopolies in the Sport Industry

It has been suggested that the sport world is filled with monopolies. Many of the professional sport leagues in the United States (e.g., the NFL, Major League Baseball, the WNBA) have frequently been accused of being monopolists because of their ability to control their respective professional sports. Similarly, the National Collegiate Athletic Association (NCAA) was cited by one group of economists as the greatest monopoly in the United States (Barro, 1991). Although these sport organizations do act similarly to monopolists, they are probably more accurately labeled *cartels*, a term that will be explained in more detail later in this chapter. Similar to larger society, the sport world has few true monopolies on a national level. However, it is not uncommon for a sport organization, such as professional sport teams, health club, or sporting goods store, to create a local monopoly. As discussed, these organizations will probably charge a higher price and supply less of their product or service to the market than would a firm with competition; therefore, their local monopoly status is not in the best interest of society.

Monopsony

Because many professional sports leagues operate as sole producers of a certain entertainment product (e.g., professional football), they are often accused of being monopolists. However, if examined from the purchase end, these professional sports leagues can also be considered as monopsonists because they are the sole purchasers of a specific supply, talented players, and therefore can control the price they pay for that supply. A *monopsony* is a firm that is the sole purchaser of a product or service. Similar to situations in monopolies, monopsonists also have a great deal of control over price because the firms selling to them have no other buyers. Although the actions of a monopsony are also subject to antitrust legislation, they are more likely to be left alone than are monopolies (Hirschey & Pappas, 1995). The ability to keep the costs of critical inputs low allows the organization to produce a product or service for less and then sell it to consumers for less. Therefore, some have argued that monopsonies, in contrast to monopolies, actually keep prices lower and thereby benefit larger society.

Monopsonies in Professional Sports

The owners of professional sport leagues had significant control over professional athletes prior to the end of the reserve clause in the mid-1970s (see chapter 10). Because players generally had only one league in the United States to which they could sell their services and the reserve clause took away any opportunity to negotiate with more than one team in that particular league, the leagues were able to keep salaries well below what the players were actually worth to the teams. Salaries in these leagues did occasionally increase when a competitor league (e.g., the American Basketball Association, the World Football League) emerged to take away their monopsony power. The leagues generally reacted either by merging with the rival league (e.g., the American Basketball Association with the National Basketball Association) or by driving the rival league out of business (e.g., the World Football League). Their ability to keep player costs low allowed professional sport teams to keep ticket prices lower, while earning a large profit. A more detailed discussion about monopsonies in professional sport will be provided in chapter 8, "Labor Market Issues."

Monopsonies in Intercollegiate Athletics

The NCAA could also be considered a monopsony with regard to student-athletes. High school athletes in certain sports (e.g., football, women's basketball) who want to continue playing their sport do not have many options. Becoming a professional athlete may not be a viable option in these sports, so the NCAA institutions are the only place that these athletes can "sell" their services. This relationship between buyer and seller has allowed the NCAA to make rules that significantly restrict the compensation of these athletes and the power of the athletes to earn money from other sources (e.g., endorsement contracts). In fact, the NCAA still compensates college athletes well below what some are worth

(Brown, 1993, 1994). The recent decision to allow student-athletes to work during the school year to earn more money was passed only after a number of basketball players started to leave for the professional leagues before they completed their collegiate eligibility. Although the NCAA lost complete monopsony power and was forced to react by increasing compensation opportunities slightly, the organization continues to maintain tight controls over athlete compensation. Although this certainly allows the NCAA to keep costs low, a similar attempt to control assistant coaches' compensation made the NCAA liable under the antitrust laws (Drowatzky, 1997; see chapter 10 for more detailed information), and many economists believe that the controls on athlete compensation also violate antitrust laws (Barro, 1991).

Oligopoly

With perfect competition and a monopoly as the two extreme forms of market structure, in the middle are two structures, oligopoly and monopolistic competition, which are referred to by economists as imperfect competition (Mankiw, 1998). Economists suggest that oligopolies exist in many industries in the United States (McGuigan & Moyer, 1986).

Features of Oligopolies

In an oligopolistic market, there are only a *few producers of the product or service.* Two examples of oligopolies in sport are the tennis ball industry and the athletic footwear industry. The tennis ball industry is dominated by four firms: Wilson, Penn, Dunlop, and Spalding (Mankiw, 1998). Likewise, most of the sneakers purchased are produced by one of the few major athletic footwear companies, such as Nike, Reebok, Adidas, Fila, New Balance, and Puma. If you go to the store to buy tennis balls or sneakers, you are most likely going to come home with an item produced by one of these companies.

The reason for the limited number of firms in the industry is generally related to the *relatively high barriers* to entry. Although there are a number of possible barriers to entry, as was discussed related to monopolies, a significant barrier in the tennis ball and athletic footwear industries is the name recognition and loyalty to current product. To challenge these producers, a new firm would have to invest a significant amount of money in advertising, which may ensure an economic loss.

In addition to having a limited number of producers and relatively high barriers to entry, an oligopoly has a number of other features. Although the products are sometimes standardized, called a *pure oligopoly*, sometimes the products are seen as differentiated; this is called a *differentiated oligopoly* (Mansfield, 1992; Salvatore, 1993). Although a sophisticated tennis player can tell the difference between the different types of tennis balls, most consumers see them as basically the same. In a pure oligopoly such as this, the decision to buy one brand over the others will probably be affected by price. In contrast, many consumers believe there are differences in the brands of sneakers. Many of the sneaker companies have invested a lot of money in advertising to convince consumers their sneakers are better. Because this would be a differentiated oligopoly, the decision regarding which sneaker to buy will probably be affected by perceptions of both product quality and price.

Although the producers in an oligopoly have *some control over price*, they must recognize any decision they make to change their price will cause a reaction by both the consumer and by the competitors. If the four major producers of tennis balls all are selling their product at $3 per can and Wilson decides to lower its price to $2 per can, consumers will react by buying more Wilson tennis balls. However, Wilson should anticipate that Penn, Dunlop, and Spalding will react by lowering their prices as well. Therefore, Wilson's decision to lower prices may increase their sales in the very short term, but it is also likely to decrease the profitability of all four firms over the long term. This close interrelationship between the firms and the monitoring of and reacting to decisions made by the other firms is a common feature of an oligopolistic market. The question becomes: how do oligopolistic industries avoid driving each other out of business?

Cartels and Collusion

One way to avoid the negative impact of competition on profitability is for firms to engage in collusion. *Collusion* occurs when the firms in an industry come to an agreement on the quantities to be produced by each firm and the price to be charged (Mankiw, 1998). Essentially, the firms form a *cartel*, which is a group of firms in the same industry working together to maximize the profits of all of the firms in the market. By working together, the cartel has price-making power similar to that of a monopoly. One of the most famous cartels in history is the Organization of Petroleum Exporting Countries (OPEC). OPEC was the means by which the oil-producing countries were able to control the world marketplace and to increase prices. Some have suggested that the NCAA and many of the professional leagues are also cartels (Berry & Wong, 1986; DeSchriver & Stotlar, 1996; Fleisher, Goff, & Tollison, 1992). By working together, these groups can limit production (e.g., number of teams in an area, number of games televised) and thereby increase the prices charged. For example, the large amount of money the NFL received in its most recent television deal probably would not have been possible if the teams engaged in open competition and each tried to sell its games to the television stations separately.

Factors affecting the success of a cartel. The economic success and failure of a cartel depend on its ability to control and manipulate the following six areas (J. Koch, 1984):

1. Number of firms. To effectively regulate the behavior of the affiliated members through policing to prevent opportunism, a cartel usually sets a limit on the numbers of firms that can obtain membership with it. For example, many of the professional sport leagues strictly control the number of teams in their respective leagues.

2. Number of points of initiative. "A point of initiative is a place where one buys, sells, exchanges, or otherwise utilizes the property rights to a resource" (Koch, 1984, p. 363). The more points of initiative, the harder it will be for a cartel to monitor its members for violations. For example, a cartel is easier to monitor in professional sports than it would be in the sporting goods industry because there are far fewer points of selling in professional sports (i.e., there are considerably more sporting goods and athletic footwear stores).

3. Knowledge of cartel transactions. One way for a cartel to exert regulatory power is to keep the affiliated members informed about activities and transactions that will be beneficial only to the cartel membership and about action to be taken against those members who have breached the cartel agreement. For example, the NCAA makes a clear effort to publicize when a university athletic department has violated the rules of their cartel.

4. Barriers to entry. It will not be economical if a cartel has a free entry policy. The fewer the associates, the more the economic rent will be. Successful cartels always tend to set barriers to entry to prevent others from sharing their profits. For example, professional sport leagues have generally been successful at limiting entry into their respective leagues *and* making entry into their market very difficult (e.g. professional football in the United States).

5. Similarities of interests. Homogeneity in terms of membership's interest seems to be a critical determinant for a cartel to be successful. It would be disastrous if there were too much internal friction and conflict among the members due to their diverse interests. For example, one could argue that much of the NCAA's trouble related to enforcing their cartel agreement is related to the diversity of interests among members (e.g., education vs. entertainment emphasis; for one team to earn increased money from winning, others must lose).

6. Demand conditions and price fixing. "It is a basic principle of cartel theory that the economic success of a cartel is enhanced when that cartel purchased its inputs from sellers who are small and unorganized" (p. 367). For example, the NCAA's ability to act like a cartel related to student-athletes is enhanced because the student-athletes lack the organization necessary to oppose the rules of the NCAA.

Barriers to collusion. Although forming a cartel may appear to be a great idea for firms in an oligopoly, there are several barriers to collusion. First, although an explicit agreement among firms in an oligopoly is legal in some parts of the world (Hirschey & Pappas, 1995), such an agreement violates the antitrust laws of the United States (Mankiw, 1998). Cartels result in social inefficiency because they begin to take on the characteristics of a monopoly and earn monopoly profits, and therefore, society benefits by outlawing cartel behavior.

Second, collusion becomes more difficult as the number of firms becomes greater. As in other aspects of life, it is much easier to get two people to agree on a decision and stick to that decision than it is to achieve the same result with three or more people. It is very common, as the number of members increases, that at least one member of the cartel will believe its best interests are not being served by the agreement. For example, Dallas Cowboys owner Jerry Jones decided a few years ago that he could earn more money by negotiating his own sponsorship agreements rather than by letting the NFL negotiate sponsorship agreements for the entire league (Masteralexis, 1997). Likewise, the University of Oklahoma and the University of Georgia sued the NCAA in the early 1980s because they believed that the NCAA's association-wide television contract for football was not in their best interests (Drowatzky, 1997).

Third, there is often a lot of incentive to cheat on the agreement reached by the cartel (Mansfield, 1992). Although the profitability of all members of the cartel combined is greatest when they all follow the agreement, additional profits are often available for firms that violate the agreement. Each firm realizes that if it lowers its price slightly from the agreed-upon price, it can sell more than the other firms in the cartel and thereby capture more of the total profits available. Members of the cartel also know that because the first one to make the price change will have an advantage until the other firms have time to react, it is not in their best interest to let someone else make the first move (Maurice & Smithson, 1988). Finally, once the other firms learn that one firm is cheating on the agreement, they will also start to cheat, and the agreement essentially falls apart (Mansfield). Widespread violations of the agreement are most common when the penalties for violating the agreement are light (DeSchriver & Stotlar, 1996; Koepp, 1986).

Failure of the NCAA's cartel agreement. The NCAA provides a good example of the breakdown of an agreement among firms in a cartel. The NCAA sets the amount that can be given to a student-athlete as compensation (e.g., tuition, room, board). If all schools do not violate the agreement, they can keep player costs low and thereby increase profitability. However, these schools also know that if they violate the agreement whereas others follow the agreement, they can offer a small number of additional incentives to the best athletes available and significantly improve the quality of their team and their profitability. As is typical with cartels, institutions following the agreement soon hear rumors that others are violating the agreements, and so they, too, start to offer additional incentives. The facts that NCAA penalties generally have little impact on the teams (Mahony, Fink, & Pastore, 1998) and most of the violators are probably not caught (Sperber, 1990) combine to increase violations of the agreed-upon rules.

Price Leadership

Because of the difficulties, both legal and otherwise, of outright collusion and because of the potentially devastating effect of intense competition among firms in an oligopolistic market, price leadership is often used to coordinate the behavior of the firms (Hirschey & Pappas, 1995; Mansfield, 1992). *Price leadership* means that one firm sets the market price, and the other firms follow. In contrast to collusion, this is legal. Although there is no actual agreement among the firms, they recognize that charging the same price helps them to avoid the negative impact of price competition.

There are generally two types of price leaders. The dominant firm model occurs when there is one dominant firm in the industry and a number of smaller firms (e.g., McCarty, 1986). In this case, the dominant firm sets the price, and the smaller firms follow. The barometric firm model occurs when one firm traditionally changes its prices first, and this price is generally accepted by the other firms (e.g., Hirschey & Pappas, 1995; Salvatore, 1993). Although the barometric firm is not necessarily the largest, it becomes the price leader because of its ability to understand the basic cost and demand conditions in the market (e.g., McGuigan & Moyer, 1986). This model often occurs when all of the firms are seeking stability after periods of heavy price fluctuations (Mansfield, 1992). Although price leadership has the potential to break down over the long term in the same manner as the cartels, during the short term, it can be quite effective in helping the industry and the member firms to achieve some stability without risking legal action.

Graphic Representation of an Oligopoly

Because there is such a strong interrelationship among firms in an oligopoly, the demand curve for a given firm in this market structure is unique. Sweezy (1939) introduced the concept of a kinked demand curve to help explain decision making in an oligopoly. As shown in Figure 4-5, firms in an oligopoly react differently to price increases as opposed to pricing cuts by rival firms, resulting in a kink at the optimal price. The general assumption is that rivals will ignore price increases above the optimal price because consumers will simply substitute the product of a given firm, in this case Donohue Skis, with

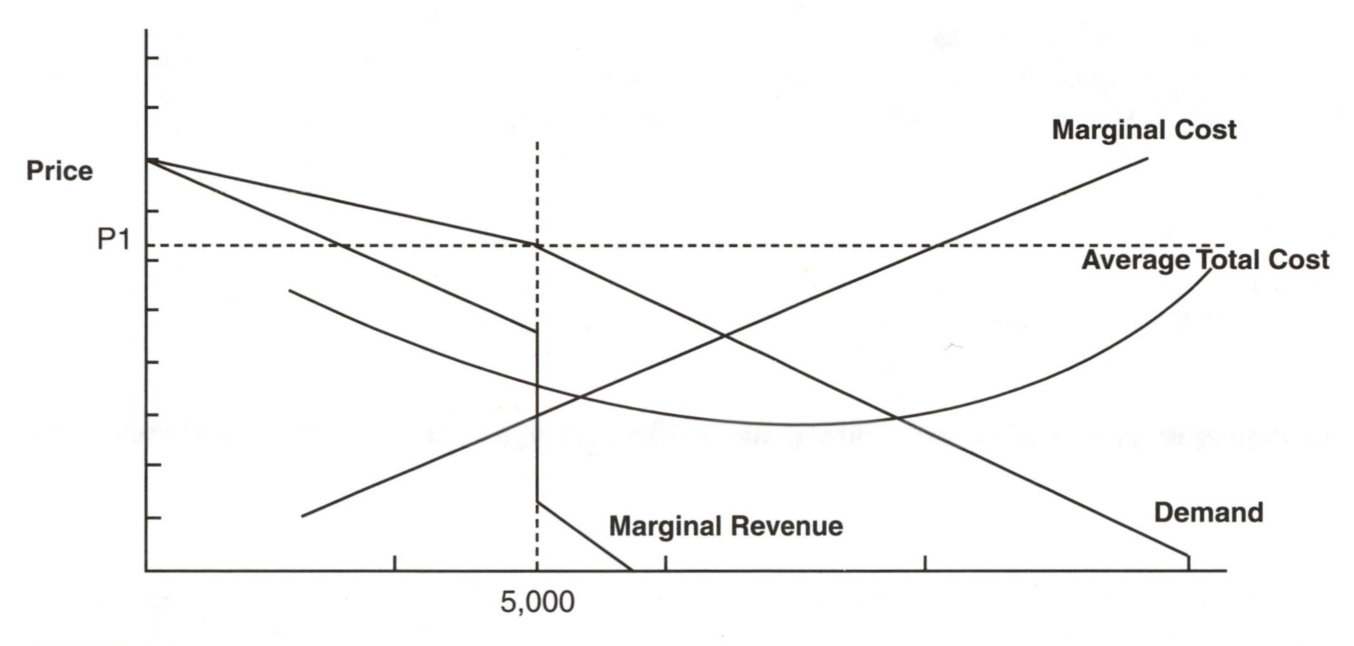

Figure 4-5

the product of a rival firm. Therefore, even a small increase in the price will lead to a large decrease in the quantity sold. As shown in Figure 4-5, an increase in the price of the skis over $200 results in a large decrease in the quantity sold.

In contrast, rival firms will follow any price cuts made by Donohue Skis to prevent Donohue Skis from capturing more of the market. Therefore, a price reduction will not have much of an impact on demand because all of the firms will be reducing their price at about the same time. The price reductions also will cause a dramatic reduction in the marginal revenue leading to a vertical marginal revenue curve for many of the possible prices below the optimal price of $200. For example, Donohue Skis would still only sell 5,000 pairs of skis even if they received only $100 in marginal revenue. When looking at this curve it is easy to see why there is so much incentive for rival firms in an oligopoly to come to an agreed-upon price, either through collusion or price leadership.

Nonprice Competition in Oligopolies

Although price competition among firms in an oligopoly may be foolish, these firms are likely to compete in other ways. Although monopolists have some incentive to promote their product through advertising, firms in oligopolistic industries have even more incentive to advertise their product (Mansfield, 1992). Both when there is little and when there is a great amount of difference in products, advertising allows a firm to increase its name recognition and to perhaps increase the consumer's perception of the quality of their product. The fact that most of us believe that Titlelist golf balls are better than a generic brand is as much related to the fact that we recognize the name Titlelist as to any actual quality difference that we notice when we play.

However, some firms in oligopolistic markets do try to develop better products and improve their profitability through product development (Mansfield, 1992; McCarty, 1986). Some of Nike's early success was related to innovations in developing running shoes. Many serious runners began to buy Nike running shoes because they believed the product was better than the other running shoes available in the market at that time. Likewise, professional sport teams that sign star players are basically attempting to improve the quality of their product in order to increase profits. Although both advertising and product improvements can be expensive, it is a sound economic decision for the firm to spend the money if the additional revenue produced by the advertisements or product improvement exceeds the additional costs.

Overall, oligopolistic markets fall somewhere between perfect competition and a monopoly. For example, they generally make greater economic profits than those of firms in perfect competition, but less than those of monopolies. However, they will move closer to one of the two extremes when factors change. For example, when the firms in an oligopoly engage in heavy competition and there is little product differentiation they move closer to perfect competition, whereas they become more like a monopoly when collusion occurs or price leadership works.

Monopolistic Competition

Features of Monopolistic Competition

The other example of imperfect competition, which also falls somewhere between perfect competition and a monopoly, is monopolistic competition. First identified by Chamberlin (1933), monopolistic competition, like perfect competition, occurs when there are *many producers* and *barriers to entry are low*. However, firms in monopolistic competition produce *products that are differentiated*. As the product or service becomes more differentiated, it becomes less likely that consumers will be able to substitute another product or service, and the firm will *have more control over price*. Because of product differentiation, firms in monopolistic competition *are not price takers* and face a downward sloping demand curve, as shown in Figure 4-6. Although the firm may produce economic profits in the short term, over the long term, competition causes *economic profits to be equal to zero*, similar to a firm in a perfectly competitive market.

Graphic Representation of Monopolistic Competition

However, there are two important differences between long-run equilibrium under monopolistic competition and perfect competition. Although firms in perfect competition will produce the socially efficient output (i.e., the point at which average total costs are minimized), a firm in monopolistic competition will produce below this level (Mankiw, 1998). Therefore, the firms in monopolistic competition are said to have excess capacity (Mankiw, 1998). In Figure 4-6, Krisko Racing Tires will produce 1,500 tires because that is the point at which marginal costs are equal to marginal revenues. However, an output of 2,000 tires is the point at which average total costs are minimized and is the optimal output for society (i.e., the efficient output).

The second major difference is that for a firm in perfect competition, the demand curve and the marginal revenue curve are the same, so that price is equal to marginal cost at the optimal level of production (see Figure 4-2). However, for a firm in monopolistic competition, the demand curve is greater than the marginal revenue curve. Therefore, as shown in Figure 4-6, the price is greater than marginal cost at the point where marginal revenue is equal to marginal cost. The difference between the marginal cost and the price is called the *markup* (Mankiw, 1998).

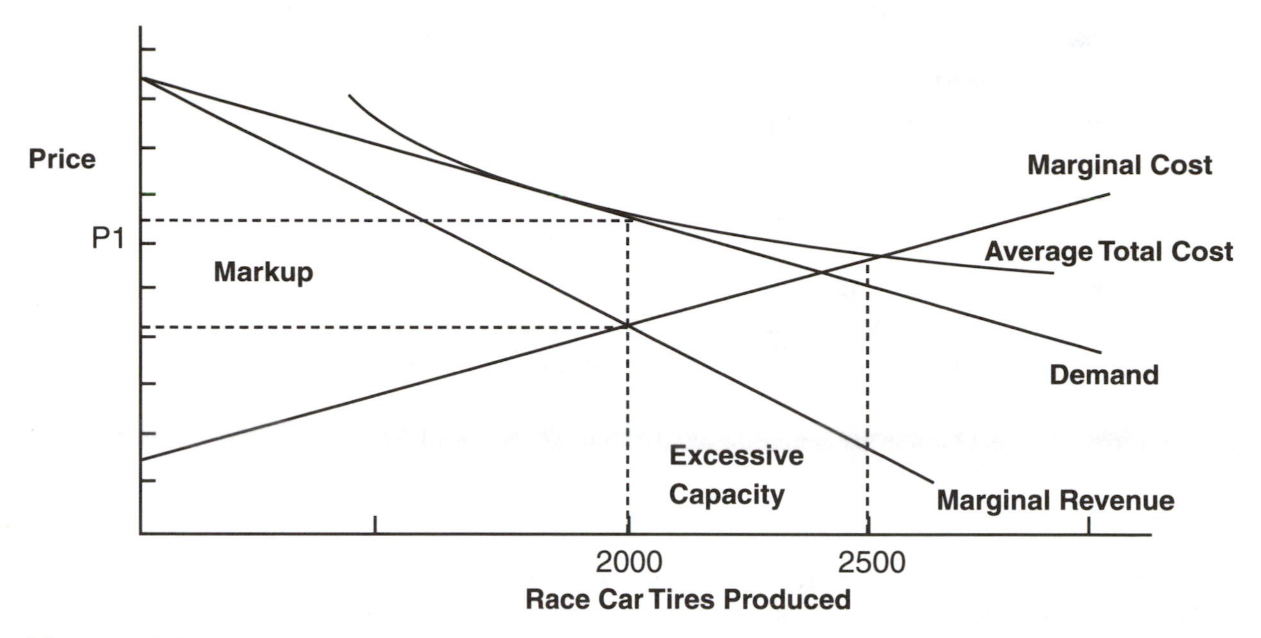

Figure 4-6

However, it should be noted that the price at this point is equal to the average total cost so the economic profits, as discussed before, are equal to zero. Because of the markup, the major difference is that a firm in a monopolistically competitive industry has more incentive to sell additional output. If Krisko Racing Tires were to sell one more tire, the price would be greater than the marginal cost. This difference in motivation will certainly affect decision making in the two types of markets.

A good example of monopolistic competition is the book industry (Mankiw, 1998). There are always a number of books available at the book store, so competition between book publishers is intense. However, an autobiography by Ken Griffey, Jr. is no substitute for a book by William Shakespeare. Most consumers would see these books as very different and would choose the book to buy based on their personal preferences. Although book prices are generally comparable, many bookstores discount less popular books. Therefore, price competition does occur in monopolistic competition. However, much of the competition is related to product differentiation. Publishing companies try to get the rights to sell the best books in order to increase sales and profits. They also spend a significant amount of money on advertising to increase interest and the consumer's evaluation of the perceived quality of their books. They hope that through advertising they will be able to shift the demand curve upwards to sell more books at the same price (McCarty, 1986). They also try to maximize sales and profits by positioning different books in different markets (e.g., children, young adult).

Sport also offers good examples of monopolistic competition. For example, one could define the sport participation industry as one large monopolistically competitive industry. In this case, the consumer is generally looking for a specific type of participation experience (e.g., noncompetitive aerobics, a recreational bowling league, a competitive adult basketball league). In most cases, a given consumer of the recreational bowling league would be unlikely to try out for the competitive adult basketball league. Consumers see these activities considerably different and, therefore, not substitutes. However, in some cases, activities that are similar may be somewhat substitutable. The consumer interested in the competitive basketball league may substitute participation in a recreational league if no competitive league is available, the cost of the competitive league is too great, or playing in the competitive league simply stops being enjoyable.

Monopolistic Competition vs. Oligopoly

The distinction between monopolistic competition and oligopoly is not always very clear. One main difference is that for some oligopolies the product is standardized, whereas the product is always differentiated in monopolistic competition. When the product is differentiated, the main difference between these two market types is the size of the market. In an oligopoly, a few firms dominate the marketplace, whereas there are many firms in monopolistic competition. One way to examine the number of firms in the market is to compute the concentration ratios (Hirschey & Pappas, 1995).

Concentration ratios measure the percentage of total market share concentrated in the top four or top eight firms in a given industry; these ratios are used to determine the amount of competition in a given industry (Hirschey & Pappas, 1995). Industries in which the concentration ratio for four firms is less than 20% are believed to be highly competitive and are examples of monopolistic competition (Hirschey & Pappas). In contrast, when concentration ratios are above 80%, the industry is seen as highly concentrated, and it offers an example of an oligopoly (Hirschey & Pappas). However, few industries have concentration ratios either greater than 80% or less than 20%; about 75% of all industries are between 20% and 80% (Hirschey & Pappas), so many industries lie somewhere between monopolistic competition and oligopoly and exhibit some characteristics of both. Although there are no clear benchmark numbers, as the industry moves closer to a concentration ratio of 20%, it will function more like a monopolistically competitive industry, whereas those approaching 80% will function more like an oligopoly.

Defining the Market

Moreover, sometimes the definition of the market determines its classification. If we define professional football as a market, the NFL could be described as a monopoly because it is the sole provider of professional football in the United States. However, one could also suggest that the NFL is an oligopolistic market with 31 firms acting together as a cartel (Berry & Wong, 1986). One could also combine all sport spectator events together into one large industry, which would include multiple sports (e.g., football, soccer, basketball) at multiple levels (e.g., professional, college, high school). Defined this way, the market would appear similar to the monopolistically competitive book industry described earlier. We have a number of spectator options, but most fans will clearly see a distinction between watching the New York Islanders against the New York Rangers in hockey and watching Indiana University play the University of North Carolina in women's soccer.

In general, both models may be useful when examining decision making by organizations. Although decisions regarding ticket prices at University of Cincinnati men's basketball games will be most affected by prices charged for men's basketball games at cross-town rival Xavier University (oligopoly), the managers at the University of Cincinnati also recognize that they are competing with other sporting events, such as Cincinnati Reds baseball games, Cincinnati Bengals football games, a variety of local high school games in a variety of sports, and a number of sport events on television (monopolistic competition).

Summary

The main goal of this chapter was to continue to introduce the reader to various economic models that can be useful for both explaining and predicting managerial decision making. This chapter focused on the concept that the firms and the decision making of their executives are affected by the market in which they operate. Four market types—perfect competition, monopoly, oligopoly, monopolistic competition—have been identified by economists and have proven useful for analyzing the decisions of firms.

Chapter Study Questions

1. It was suggested in the chapter that perfect competition rarely exists in the real world. Briefly discuss reasons why perfect competition rarely exists and is particularly unlikely to exist in the sport industry.
2. Explain the differences and similarities between a monopoly and a cartel. Cite examples of both within the sport industry.
3. Explain the differences between a monopoly and a monopsony. Which is more likely to be acceptable to society and why?
4. Explain why oligopolies are often reluctant to engage in price competition.
5. Explain what concentration ratios are and how they help to distinguish between monopolistic competition and an oligopoly. Provide examples of both types of industries within sport.
6. Explain how the Minnesota Vikings may be defined as being part of more than one type of industry.

Chapter Five

INTRODUCTION

Sports are provided to consumers through three main suppliers (see Table 5-1). Although there is some overlap, each type of supplier has differences in philosophy, objectives, financing, leadership, and membership. In any city or town, examples of each of these delivery systems can be found.

In fact, these suppliers can be viewed as complements rather than competitors, although there are instances where competition does occur. Taken together, they increase the likelihood that consumers' desire for sport and recreation will be satisfied.

Sport Industry Delivery

Western City is a medium-sized city in the western part of the United States that is experiencing explosive population growth. Several new corporations have relocated to Western; housing starts are skyrocketing; and traffic congestion and crime have increased. There are numerous opportunities for recreation and sports in the city; however, there is not enough supply to accommodate demand. Waiting lists have developed for fields and leagues. Current facilities are a mix of city owned—parks, swimming pools, softball and baseball fields, soccer fields, tennis courts, a golf course, recreation centers—and privately owned—athletic clubs and golf courses. Professional sports in the city include a Triple A baseball club and an A-League soccer franchise. The city allocates approximately one percent of the general operating budget for the recreation department, but it is feeling financial pressures to deal with the population growth. A member of the city council has floated the idea of a .25% increase in the city sales tax to be used for expanding sport and recreation opportunities. A second council member agrees with the tax increase but wants to use it to obtain an expansion franchise in one of the major league sports. A third member strongly disagrees with any tax increase for sports, arguing that if the need truly exists, private enterprise can and should fill it. He would use the increase to improve the city's infrastructure.

From an economic perspective, Western City presents many interesting issues. Why are the sports offerings structured the way they are? Why are some sports and recreation being supplied by the city? Why are others, of the same nature, being supplied by private entities? To whom do benefits accrue? What is public choice theory, and does it help us understand how scarce resources might be allocated?

Government-Provided Sport

Many economists believe that private enterprise operating in an open market is the most efficient means of providing goods and services to consumers. Why, then, do we find government and community organizations in the business of providing sports services? What constitutes government's proper economic role in providing services and goods to its citizens? Certainly, we are accustomed to government, at all levels, providing a variety of services. Moreover, although there is general agreement that government should provide some services, there is not agreement as to what kind of, and how many, services. At one end of the continuum are those who believe government should regulate a variety of economic activities; at the other end are those who would assign only minimal responsibilities to government.

One economic viewpoint is that private business, operating in a free market, will always provide services and goods more effectively than will government. In a free market system, private enterprise will recognize and produce goods to satisfy demand. Parties will trade, and both will be better off. If one or both parties do not benefit, trade will not occur. Thus, both sides have incentive for effective trade. In addition, costs of a

Table 5-1. Suppliers of Sport

	Government	Community	Private
Philosophy	Sport for all	Sport for members	Satisfy public demand and make profit
Goals	Contribute to well-being of citizens and area, nonprofit	More limited in membership, people with similar philosophies, generally nonprofit	Profit maximization
Finance	Primarily taxes, user fees	Membership fees, donations, fundraising	Private investment, admissions/user fees, memberships, media
Leadership	Professional, often civil service, and some volunteer	Professional and volunteer	Professional
Membership	Open to all	Organizational restrictions, often on age, residence	Open to those who can pay
Examples	City parks and recreation	Little League, local soccer associations, YMCAs	Private athletic clubs, professional sports teams, bowling alleys, sporting goods

product will be assumed by those who benefit from the service or good. Because the benefits of sport accrue to those who use sport, they should also bear the costs. When government intervenes in an economy, even more problems are created.

Why, then, has government been a major provider of recreational and sport services? Since the late 1800s, government intervention in markets has been viewed as important to correct problems coming from a reliance on the market mechanism. This perspective is represented by the statement that

> A public recreation program can increase the welfare of society if the resources given up by the private sector (via taxes, opportunity costs) are used to produce greater benefits than they would produce in the absence of the government programs. (Walsh, 1986, p. 558)

Essentially, government redistributes resources for the benefit of the general public.

Government is viewed as an appropriate supplier of services, including sports, for many reasons. First, a primary function of government is to service human needs, among which is recreation. Recreation contributes to the social, physical, and mental well-being of citizens. Second, government can provide services regardless of citizens' ability to pay. Not all residents can afford private services, which are frequently focused on profit maximization.

Through its power to collect revenues, government can afford to subsidize services for those who would not otherwise have access to them because of financial restrictions. Third, governments are long-standing bodies, as opposed to private businesses, which may come and go. Continuity and reliability of services are viewed as desirable. Fourth, government has the power to regulate land for use. Government has or can acquire land (e.g., for fields, arenas), and it can create zoning regulations (e.g., requiring open or green space in real estate developments). Fifth, government can bring together diverse groups within the community to maximize benefits. Creating a recreation program may require input and assistance from parks and recreation departments, school districts, public safety, and private entities. Finally, without government regulation, private enterprise can conspire to restrain trade, which does not benefit the public.

Learning Activities

1. Determine what sport and recreation services are provided in your home community. Who provides them? Why has this delivery system arisen? How well does it work? Does everyone get served?

2. You are a news reporter, covering a debate in the local community. Arguing that the community provides other children with summer leagues in which to participate, a group of parents who have children with disabilities has demanded that the mayor and supervisors offer a summer Challenger Baseball League for their children. The mayor and supervisors say there isn't enough money in the budget to support such a program. Write an article that reviews the debate and the economic issues that underlie it.

3. Wong Company is a major builder of recreational soccer complexes throughout the South. The company has been very successful and has a lot of cash available for growth. Company president Rosanne Wong wants to expand operations and needs advice as to what might benefit the company. She has come to you as a consultant on mergers and acquisitions. Write a memo to her suggesting the direction she might consider. What might be good targets for a merger or acquisition? Why would this be logical for Wong Co.?

Economists explain government provision of sport and recreation using the concept of *externalities*. Externalities exist when "actions of one party affect the utility or production possibilities of another party outside an exchange relationship" (Brickley et al., 1997, p. 46). Another perspective is that "Some benefits or costs associated with the production or consumption of a particular product accrue to parties other than the buyers or sellers [or users] of the product" (Keat & Young, 1992, p. 583). Externalities are relevant when talking about government provision of roads, education, parks, and recreation. For example, if a person has no children, why should this person pay for the provision of education? Why not let the private market provide education to those who need it? If education were provided solely as a private enterprise, this person would probably not purchase it. However, does this person (and society) benefit from having educated children? Most would argue the answer is yes. So, even through the person is not a buyer or seller or user of the education services, this person does benefit from them. If the person accrues benefits, then this person should also accrue costs. In the case of education, government collects monies from the person (i.e., property taxes, income taxes) to support schools. Education has *positive* externalities.

How about sport and recreation? If a person never uses the city's parks or soccer fields or never attends a professional sporting event, why should this person support those facilities and programs? This argument has been heard frequently throughout the 1990s as taxpayers have been asked to bear the costs of new stadiums and arenas for professional sports teams. A positive externalities argument would suggest that the person does benefit, perhaps from "preservation values," including (a) the option of future use, (b) the value of just knowing a facility or program exists, and (c) the satisfaction from knowing a program or facility will be available to future generations (Walsh, 1986). Many governments use the argument that such facilities and programs enhance the general quality of life and make the area more desirable for growth.

Specific arguments have been offered for government's providing sport and recreation services:

1. Sport and recreation help to create an appealing community. Ratings of most desirable places to live routinely evaluate the recreation environment. Cities increase their visibility and enhance their image when they provide such opportunities. This can pay off in direct financial benefits, by attracting businesses to locate in the city and attracting more convention and tourism business (Howard & Crompton, 1995)
2. Sport and recreation enhance the health of the community: "A community of physically active people will ultimately be a community with reduced traffic congestion, air pollution, and health care costs" (Seeley, 1997, p. 72).
3. Sport and recreation keep youth occupied and out of trouble and lessen costs related to youth crime. Since the late 1800s, one of the perceived roles of sports and recreation has been to give youth a constructive way to occupy their time. A recent example is midnight basketball leagues for inner-city youth (Gratton & Taylor, 1992; Sailes, 1999).

Negative externalities also exist. A municipal golf course built with taxpayer dollars may provide positive benefits to the entire community, not just to the golfers who use it. However, the golf course may also displace wildlife habitat, result in contamination from use of chemicals, and divert dollars that could be used for other purposes. These negative impacts exist for all city residents. For the city, it is necessary to look at all costs and all benefits to arrive at a decision. Residents of Colorado rejected a proposal to host the 1976 Winter Olympics on the grounds that the harm to the environment and disruption of lifestyle (negative externalities) were too great to justify using tax dollars.

Economists make a distinction between *private* and *public* goods. Private goods provide benefits to those who use (pay for) them, and public goods are available for anyone to enjoy. Athletic shoes are an example of private goods because the benefits of wearing them go only to the people who have purchased them. Championship teams are often cited as examples of public goods. When a university football team ends the season ranked number one in the country, its fans receive many benefits, even though they may not have contributed in any way to the success of the team. This concept is called *nonexcludability*. Anyone can share in the benefits of a winning team. A second feature of a public good is that it is *nonrival*. Many people can enjoy a product or service at the same time. Many people can call themselves fans of the number one team. The same is not true of a private good. Only one person at a time can benefit from wearing the athletic shoes. The concepts of externalities and of public and private goods go hand in hand. When we talk about externalities, we are generally talking about public goods. Thus, education and many sport activities are public goods.

Consider that producers of public goods with either positive or negative externalities may not take into account the impact on nonpurchasers. Their decision to produce (in a free market situation) does not represent the optimal amount for the market system. Government becomes involved in order to remedy this failure.

Government Spending

When we look at spending by government, a strong commitment to recreational expenditures is clear. All levels of government in the United States spent over $20 billion on parks and recreation programs in 1995 (U.S. Census Bureau, 1998). Of that, $2.2 billion, $2.97 billion, and $14.92 billion were spent by federal, state, and local governments, respectively. In Canada, the 1996–1997 budget had expenditures of $9,142 million on recreation and culture (Statistics Canada, 2000).

Local government is the level closest to the consumer and provides the most services. For most people, the governing body oversees the city or town in which they live. Depending upon the size of local government, a variety of services are provided. Table 5-2 gives two examples of what a local area might provide. Local governments will generally allocate from one to two percent of an annual operating budget on recreation services. That does not include special requests, such as a new stadium or arena. County government is the next level up, or for unincorporated areas, it may even be local government. Here, the most common participation involves making facilities available.

Table 5-2. Sample Sport and Recreation Provided by Governments of Two Cities

	City A	City B
Facilities:		
	Golf course	Playground
	Boat launch	Tennis courts
	Recreation centers	Parks
	Swimming pools	
	Tennis courts	
	Playgrounds	
	Parks	
Athletic Programs:		
	Baseball contests	Basketball clinics
	Basketball camp	Tennis lessons
	Youth bowling	5K Race
	Fishing lessons	
	5K and 10K Race	
	Ultimate frisbee	
	Junior golf clinic	
	Golf tournaments	
	Roller skating	
	Soccer leagues	
	Swimming lessons	
	Tennis clinics	
	Tennis leagues	
	Special Olympics	
Special Events:		
	Regatta	Community festival
	Vintage grand prix	
	Community festivals	

A special district provides services that cross city and county lines. Perhaps the most common services provider in this category would be public schools. Although schools provide facilities and programming primarily for the students in the district schools, the general population also benefits. People in the community may attend sports contests, use the track for jogging, or play in a summer basketball league in the gym. In some locations, special parks or recreation districts cross city and/or county lines.

State or provincial government provides services in a variety of settings, including state parks and correctional facilities. States also provide subsidies for local provision of sports and recreation. An example of state support includes subsidies to state and local sports commissions, state games, and sporting events.

The U.S. government consists of more than 90 federal agencies, bureaus, commissions, and/or councils that provide park, recreation, and leisure services (Kraus, 1984). The federal government supports national parks and the recreational programming provided through the U.S. Armed Forces, correctional institutions, and the Park Service. The federal government also develops programs and policies that encourage health and fitness through the President's Council on Fitness. In Canada, the government subsidizes sports training centers, bids for sporting events, national teams and agencies, such as the Fitness and Amateur Sport Branch, which provides a variety of services to recreation and fitness programs.

Recent Issues With Government Support

Issues related to government spending on sport and recreation exist in virtually every community. Most recently, professional sports teams have been very visible in their demands for publicly built stadiums and arenas, along with the threat that the team will leave town if it does not get a new facility. An indication of the extent to which municipal governments have agreed to those demands is shown in Table 5-3.

Table 5-3. Taxpayer Share of New Professional Sports Facilities

City	Team	Cost (millions $)	Taxpayer %
Cincinnati	Bengals (NFL)	404	100.0
Raleigh	Hurricanes (NHL)	158	87.3
Miami	Heat (NBA)	228	78.1
Pittsburgh	Steelers (NFL)	233	67.6
Dallas	Mavericks (NBA)/ Stars (NHL)	300	41.7
Detroit	Tigers (MLB)	295	39.0
San Francisco	Giants (MLB)	306	8.5
Los Angeles	Kings (NHL)/ Lakers, Clippers (NBA)	350	3.4
Columbus	Blue Jackets (NHL)	150	0

Source: Street & Smith's SportsBusiness Journal (May 10–16, 1999), p. 5

In Canada, the national government is being pressured to provide subsidies, in the form of tax breaks, for NHL teams (Aubrey, 1999). The Canadian teams argue that they cannot compete in the same market with subsidized (in the form of new arenas) U.S. teams when the Canadian clubs face heavy tax burdens, bad dollar exchange rates, and no subsidies. However, critics of the proposed breaks argue that it is "unconscionable for the government to continue contemplating tax adjustments for the NHL while rejecting schemes to help out Canada's 1.3 million disadvantaged children to play sports" (Aubry, p. 2). The debate about how government should spend its limited resources on elite level and/or general participation sports is an ongoing one.

Professional sports is not the only area where issues of who will pay for sports facilities and programs exist. Many cities experiencing population growth face increasing demands for public services from a population that has come to expect government to supply those services. An example of those issues currently under debate is the availability of playing fields for recreational soccer. Organized soccer participation among youth in the United States has increased from 890,000 in 1980 to 3.57 million in 1998 (El Nasser, 1999). With the addition of adult participants, that number increases to more than 17 million. The boom in participation has resulted in a shortage of fields. Who should provide the fields? In November 1998, local communities across the United States approved 200 bond issues for the development of park spaces. Two-thirds of the funds approved were earmarked for recreation facilities, including soccer fields (El Nasser, 1999). Additional funds are coming from sales tax increases, fees charged to real estate developers, donations, and fees assessed to soccer participants.

Although the national visibility obtained from professional sports teams and facilities is often heard as a justification for spending taxpayer dollars, the same cannot be said of youth soccer leagues. Such leagues do not attract national attention. However, the arguments for public support remain similar. Organizers of the 2000 Midwest Regional soccer tournament to be held in Lawrence, Indiana, claim a $35-million economic impact for the city as a result of the tournament (El Nasser, 1999). More detailed discussion on economic impact studies is provided in chapter 7.

Public Choice Theory and Privatization

The historic perspective of government taking on responsibility for a variety of public services began to change in the 1960s as a result of changing economic times and a new economic theory. In the 1960s, a concept called *public choice theory* emerged in economics. Public choice theory suggests that if public officials monopolize service delivery, the result is oversupply and inefficiency (Boyne, 1998). If government is the only entity responsible for providing roads, maintenance, transportation, education, and recreation, then a monopoly exists, and there is no incentive to operate services in an efficient manner. In fact, as noted in the management utility maximization model in chapter 2, there is incentive for government officials to operate in their own self-interest. However, if services are provided in a competitive market, the result will be a more efficient service.

In the 1970s, many local and state governments began to experience two trends. The first was a demand for more services, and the second was budgetary constraints that made it difficult to maintain existing levels of services, much less to provide more. Government officials looking for a way to deal with the difficult economic environment found that public choice theory justified the idea of turning some government services over to private enterprise.

Privatization is "an array of techniques designed to promote greater involvement on the part of the private sector in the administration or financing of traditional government services" (Auger, 1999, p. 2). Cities are using privatization for diverse services, such as airports, waste management, education, corrections, and recreation. Why is government willing to privatize services and take on some of the risks and rewards of the free market system? Officials cite two basic reasons:

1. Reducing costs and increasing revenues are motivators. However, there is much disagreement on the financial impact of privatization.

2. There is a belief that private enterprise can operate more efficiently, via enhanced flexibility to adjust services and increased ability to quickly obtain materials and staff. By specializing, private enterprise has more expertise.

Privatization can take many forms. Frequently, private enterprises are contracted to supply services. Waste collection is often handled this way, and a few cities have tried privatizing educational services. Second, some cities and states have suggested use of vouchers, whereby residents are given vouchers to purchase private services. For example, a great deal of discussion is occurring over the use of vouchers in education. Partnerships with voluntary and quasi-voluntary organizations are a third option. In the most extreme case, cities will sell assets to a private firm, thus eliminating the responsibility for the service.

In the United States, certain sport services are targets for privatization. For many years, governments have contracted with private management companies to operate stadiums and arenas. City and county officials believe that private management companies can bring certain managerial and entrepreneurial skills that government does not necessarily have to managing their facilities. One of the largest facility management companies in the world is Spectator Management Group, with annual revenues in excess of $125 million from assisting cities and counties with their public facilities (Macnow, 1989).

The operations of many municipal golf courses are gradually being turned over to private companies (Mahtesian, 1997). One of the largest such companies in the United States is American Golf Corporation, which operates over 145 public golf courses in 20 states. Founded in 1968, "[Its] approach involves initial investment, improving the course and related infrastructure, dramatically increasing rounds of play . . . and reducing costs largely through more flexible and cost-effective utilization of personnel" (Howard & Crompton, 1995, p. 121). The corporation collects revenues from greens fees, concessions, and equipment and cart rentals in exchange for the right to operate. Interestingly enough, when American Golf Corporation signed an agreement to operate courses for Detroit, city government excluded two courses from the deal, preferring to maintain some level of competition between course managers. The city recognized the difficulty that might arise from providing American Golf Corporation with exclusivity in city-provided golf. The U.S. Forest Service and state parks departments have contracted with private companies to provide many services, including concessions, housing, and dock management. These can be high-price agreements: The Forest Service's contract with Delaware North Companies for Yosemite Park is worth approximately $1.5 billion a year (Clifford, 1993).

The struggle over obtaining public support for new sports facilities has resulted in public-private partnerships in some cities. Numerous facilities have been financed jointly between public and private entities, including the Bradley Center Arena in Indianapolis, Coors Stadium in Denver, and Jacobs Field in Cleveland (Regan, 1996). In Lawrence, Indiana, new soccer fields are being built with city-donated land, a bond issue, and investment from private company Motorsports, Inc. (El Nasser, 1999). Because these providers have differences in philosophy, such joint agreements contain a future risk that goals and objectives of the participating partners may be difficult to reconcile.

Aside from private entities, government has also teamed with community-based organizations to supply facilities and programs. The U.S. Tennis Association spent $10 million to build the Louis Armstrong tennis center in New York (Howard & Crompton, 1995) on ground leased by New York City to the USTA. The facility is available to the city for 305 days per year and to the USTA for no more than 60 days. In another instance, both the Los Angeles Olympic Organizing Committee and the Atlanta Olympic Organizing Committee built facilities and turned them over to their respective cities.

The move to privatization has had mixed results, both in general services and in recreation. Many golfers have been complimentary about the improvements in golf courses taken over by private firms whereas other golfers are dissatisfied (Lieberman, 1994; Vitullo-Martin, 1998). At most privatized courses, greens fees increase, especially for those who are not residents of the local government unit. Access to courses for individual golfers is also lessened because of increased use of courses for revenue-maximizing golf tournaments. The goal for private enterprise in providing services is not necessarily the same as that of the government. In the extreme case, the private enterprise does not provide the same stability as government does. In 1998, the company contracted to operate the reservation services for California's state parks declared bankruptcy ("A Tighter Rein on Privatization," 1998). Although the private marketplace may indeed produce more efficient operation and provide more revenues to cities, this outcome is not guaranteed.

The move toward privatization is not a fad. Over 70% of state agency and recreation department heads have predicted expansion in privatization efforts in their area (Auger, 1999). As cities continue to face increased demand for services without a corresponding increase in resources to supply the demand, alternatives to direct government supply of services will grow.

Community Provision

North America has a history of sports being provided by community-based organizations, sometimes also called voluntary associations. These include groups such as the Boy Scouts, YMCAs, Little League Baseball, and Rotary and Lions clubs. Although some associations, such as Little League or U.S. Youth Soccer Association, are organized around sport(s), others, such as Boy Scouts and Lions, provide sports as one of a variety of activities. Many of these organizations focused on youth sports; however there are also those that operate for adult participants. Revenue to operate community organizations comes from a number of different sources: membership dues, donations and sponsorships, sales, and government subsidies (because such organizations operate as tax-exempt, nonprofit entities).

Table 5-4. Selected Community-Based, Non-Profit Sport Organizations

	Year Founded	# Members
YMCA	1851	14,000,000
U.S. Youth Soccer Assn.	1973	2,500,000
Little League Baseball	1939	2,500,000
American Bowling Congress	1895	2,250,000
U. S. Tennis Assn.	1881	500,000
Canadian Soccer Assn.	1912	430,000
Canadian Curling Assn.	1990	352,000
Canadian Lacrosse Assn.	1867	150,000
USA Volleyball	1928	125,000
U.S. Slo-Pitch Softball Assn.	1968	125,000
USA Track & Field	1979	120,000
Swimming/Nation Canada	1970	71,000
Disabled Sport USA	1967	60,000
Athletics Canada	1884	20,000
Canadian Amateur Wrestling	1932	15,000
U.S. Luge Assn.	1978	650

Source: Myers, K. J. (1998). *Sports Market Place* (Ed.). Mesa, Arizona: Custom Publishing Inc.

Weisbrod (1977) provides economic rationales for community rather than government provision of sport. First, government may not have adequate information about what citizens really want. Thus, decisions are made on the basis of what officials think citizens want. A decentralized entity may have more local knowledge and a better grasp of what people want. This can be especially true in larger cities where demand is likely to be diverse. It is also true when examining demands of minority interests. A second rationale is that government officials often act in their own self-interest rather than according to concepts of efficiency.

Government has an incentive to provide subsidies to these organizations. This is because government will not have to provide services if they are already provided by those organizations. Although the organizations often have restrictions on who may participate (generally based upon age or residence), they also often serve segments of the community who could not afford to purchase the services on the private market. Thus, community organizations are remedying failures of both the private and government systems. Government subsidies are generally in the form of a tax-exempt status but may also include use of public facilities or grants.

A distinguishing element of community organizations is their reliance on volunteers. As opposed to the private and government sector, community sports have a free labor resource. Such labor may be provided by participants themselves (main beneficiaries), former participants (former beneficiaries), parents and families of participants (indirect beneficiaries) or nonparticipant-related volunteers (who receive positive benefits from volunteering; Gratton & Taylor, 1992). The use of volunteers means that community organizations can operate at a lower cost than can government or private enterprise.

Generally, people participate (directly or indirectly) in community organizations for reasons of self-interest. They receive some benefit that exceeds their costs. People make a choice about how they are to incur costs of sport participation. If they purchase services from a private enterprise, there is a cash cost. If they obtain services from a government entity, there may be costs related to restrictions on who may participate or how many or when activities are offered. If they participate in community organizations, the cash outlay is smaller than for private enterprise, but there is an opportunity cost. What else could people do with their time if they were not being a coach, chaperone, booster club member, or event organizer? As evidenced by the large number of community organizations that exist, many people believe that benefits exceed costs in evaluating their decision to use community sport suppliers.

We need to note that forms of community organizations can range from local, small scale (Moon Area Soccer Association) to national (U.S. Youth Soccer Association) ones. Chapter 2 discusses some of the goals that exist in nonprofit organizations. However, at the most highly organized level, organizations act in some ways as quasi-private enterprises, with large paid staff, and major revenue flows from television and sponsors. They operate closer to a profit-maximization model. For example, private athletic clubs have argued that some YMCAs should lose their tax-exempt status because they are acting more as private clubs, with upscale services, higher membership prices, and few community services. The dispute between metropolitan YMCAs and private athletic clubs illustrates the blurred line that sometimes exists between community and private enterprises.

Sport as Private Enterprise

By far, the majority of organizations delivering sport in the United States are private enterprises. These enterprises take a variety of forms—local to national, small to large, privately owned to publicly held companies. Private enterprise emerges because someone sees the opportunity to make a profit by providing a service that is in demand. An entrepreneur is "an individual who sees an opportunity to sell an item at a price higher than the average cost of producing it" (Colander, 1998, p. 578). By allowing entrepreneurs to earn profit, market economies encourage people to supply goods and services. Entrepreneurs create supply to meet demand.

There are many forms of private enterprise. Businesses may be organized in three basic forms: sole proprietorships, partnerships, or corporations. Of the 18 million businesses in the United States, approximately 69% are sole proprietorships, 8% are partnerships, and 23% are corporations (Colander, 1998). However, in terms of total receipts, corporations conduct the vast majority of business. The following discussion focuses on forms of enterprise most often seen in the sport industry.

Specific regulations, especially those taxes-related, affect the operations and decision making of each of these business forms. If I decide my community has an unfilled need for sporting goods, I can decide to set up my own sporting goods store. Because I am a sole proprietor, starting a business is fairly easy from a legal standpoint, and I have control over how the business operates. Of course, I might persuade my best friend to be my partner, an action that divides the responsibilities, creates liabilities for each partner, and can dilute control.

Many sport organizations are corporations. Corporations are legal entities, independent of the ownership of the firm. An important reason for choosing a corporate structure is that it limits the liability of owners. As a sole proprietor or partner, I am personally liable for any judgment if someone sues my sporting goods store. If someone sues my firm that is a corporation, I have no personal liability as an owner. Owners in a corporation purchase shares and vote for a board of directors that sets policies of the corporation. Some corporations have very limited ownership and are not available in an open market (privately held), whereas many sell shares to the general public (publicly held).

Sport organizations may be corporations themselves, such as Nike, American Skiing, and the Boston Celtics, or they may be one part of the overall holdings of a corporation such as the Colorado Avalanche and Denver Nuggets (Ascent Entertainment Group). Table 5-5 lists several sports teams owned as part of a parent corporation.

It is important to understand that ownership structure affects the firm's objectives and operations. As discussed in chapter 2, a profit maximization model is frequently used to explain managerial decision making. If I start my own sporting goods store, I certainly want to make a profit. If I don't, I won't be in business long. However, the larger the firm and the more owners there are, the more likely that managers will be hired to run the firm. Managers of firms, who may or may not be owners, do not necessarily have the same incentive to maximize profit. They may operate on a different model, perhaps emphasizing

Table 5-5. Selected Professional Sports Teams Owned by a Parent Corporation

Team	Parent Company
Anaheim Angels (MLB)	Walt Disney Co.
Atlanta Braves (MLB)	Time Warner Inc.
Atlanta Thrashers (NHL)	Time Warner Inc.
Buffalo Sabres (NHL)	Adelphia Communications
Chicago Cubs (MLB)	Tribune Co.
Los Angeles Dodgers (MLB)	News Corp.
New York Knicks (NBA)	Cablevision Systems Corp.
Philadelphia Flyers (NHL)	Comcast Corp.
Philadelphia 76ers (NBA)	Comcast Corp.
Vancouver Canucks (NHL)	Northwest Sports Enterprise
Vancouver Grizzlies (NBA)	Northwest Sports Enterprise

management utility, sales maximization, or satisficing behavior. When managers and owners have different perspectives, the potential exists for *agency* problems.

Corporate Ownership

Corporate ownership of sport entities is an old concept. In 1869, the Cincinnati Red Stockings were financed through a joint stock association that raised $15,000 in capital. That year, the club earned a profit of $1,700, a return-on-equity of 11.3% (Gorman & Calhoun, 1994). In 1876, Spalding began operations with $800 in capital on its way to becoming the first national sporting goods manufacturer (Spalding Sports Worldwide, Inc., 1999). The company remains a privately held corporation.

Professional sports has experienced a mix of individual and corporate ownership. Throughout the late 1800s and into the 1900s, there were publicly held baseball teams, but they soon died away, affected by economic conditions and poor performances. Today, although five Major League Baseball clubs are owned by corporations, just one, the Cleveland Indians, is traded publicly on its own. In 1923, the Green Bay Packers sold $200 shares in the team to people in the community. As recently as 1998, they sold additional shares. The Packers remain the only publicly held football club because the NFL has a rule forbidding corporate or public ownership of teams. The intent of such prohibition is to have owners focused on football and to avoid having corporate ownership change the way NFL owners operate. In the NHL, seven teams are owned by corporations, and two, the Florida Panthers and Vancouver Canucks, are publicly traded. In 1986, the Boston Celtics raised $48 million by selling 40% of the team to the public, and it remains the only publicly held franchise in the NBA. Five NBA teams are owned by corporations. At league levels below the four major leagues, many teams are held by corporations, but they are not publicly traded. An exception is the Orlando Predators of the Arena Football League, which made a public offering in 1997.

It is not only North America where the concept of public ownership of professional sports exists. In the 1990s, there was much discussion among European football clubs of making public stock offerings in an effort to produce additional revenue. Formula One car racing has also discussed going public (Anonymous, 1998; Brandman, 1999).

Outside team sports, publicly held companies are common. From sports apparel/footwear (Nike, Rawlings) to sport products (Callaway, Huffy) to resorts (American Skiing Company, Vail) to motor sports (CART, Speedway Motorsports) to facilities (Family Golf Centers, Hollywood Park), there are many companies in which the public can purchase shares. Table 5-6 lists several sports corporations and their market capitalization. *Capitalization* equals price of a share multiplied by the number of shares outstanding.

Why make shares in a company available to the general public? For corporations, there is a desire or need to create revenue with which to operate the firm. In 1999, Churchill Downs announced plans for a secondary stock offering, which could raise as much as $75.3 million (Mullen, 1999). The 1998 initial stock offering for Championship Auto Racing Teams resulted in $80 million. The Cleveland Indians raised $60 million in its 1998 stock sale. SportsLine USA, Inc. went public in 1997 and collected $28 million. Proceeds from public offerings pay down debt, finance acquisitions, and engage in capital construction.

Table 5-6. Market Capitalization for Selected Publicly-Held Sport Corporations

Corporation	Capitalization (000,000)
Nike	$17,174
International Speedway	2,024
Speedway Motorsports	1,695
Callaway	1,052
Reebok	1,001
SportsLine	771
Vail Resorts	645
Hollywood Park	413
Panthers	431
Family Golf Centers	171
Huffy	155
K2	150
Cleveland Indians	115
American Skiing	113
Rawlings	74
Boston Celtics	32
Orlando Predators	22

Although public offerings are common in the general business world, professional sports has been slower to adopt that model. In the professional sport examples, franchises have been able to raise a substantial amount of money to maintain a quality product. Why don't more clubs take this approach, especially for what are termed "small-market" teams? It would seem the benefits would outweigh the costs. It could be a way to raise revenue for the team. By so doing, the team could also lessen its reliance on government subsidies or on ticket or media revenue.

Although selling stock has advantages, it also has disadvantages. One is a potential loss of control over the firm. If unhappy shareholders can gather enough votes (shares), they have the power to make change. Even a minority of shareholders can make operations difficult. Ascent Entertainment Group Inc. agreed in 1999 to sell its sports teams (the Colorado Avalanche and Denver Nuggets) and Pepsi Center for $400 million. Angry shareholders filed suit claiming that the sale price was too low (Kaplan & Mullen, 1999) and that an officer of Ascent would excessively benefit. Florida Panthers Holdings Inc. was sued by several investors upset about the company's diversification into real estate (Kaplan, 1999). Nike has faced criticism from shareholders as well as the general public over its southeast Asia manufacturing operations.

A second disadvantage for a firm to go public is that public ownership requires financial information be made available to the public and to potential competitors. Many companies are reluctant to allow such information become public. Competitors can use the information to their own advantage. In the case of professional sports teams, arguments that the team is losing money may not be supported by financial statements. As a privately held corporation, a company is not required to disclose its financial information.

Generally, publicly held companies make their stock available without restrictions. Professional sports teams have been more careful in selling their stock. In most of the cases where professional teams have publicly sold shares, the percentage available for sale is limited. The Celtics' sale of 40% ownership is an example. Franchises sell only a limited percentage of shares in the club, thus retaining majority ownership. The Packers placed many restrictions on their community ownership, including no payment of dividends, no trading of the stock on an exchange, no stock appreciation, and limited voting rights. Cleveland Indians stockholders were restricted in their ability to share in the appreciation if the club was sold.[1]

For most publicly held stocks, there is an economic incentive to purchase. The goal is that, either through stock appreciation or dividends, the stockholder will obtain income that exceeds the possible income from any other use of the money invested. This is the concept of opportunity cost. If there are few financial benefits to be obtained from the purchase of professional team stocks, why does the public still buy them? It does not seem to make financial sense. However, from an economic perspective, people still obtain benefits from being a shareholder of such stocks, even if the benefits are not financial ones. These benefits might include demonstrating team loyalty and the uniqueness of being an owner (albeit on a small scale).[2] For a relatively small cost, the benefits are high.

Single Entity Ownership

Yet another variation in ownership structure has emerged in professional team sports as a result of the labor environment. In the major professional sports, individual players sign contracts with individual clubs. However, labor costs for any individual club are not independent of labor costs for another club. What one owner pays a player affects what other owners will have to pay. This environment is a result of free agency and arbitration. When one owner is willing to pay a player far beyond what has been typical, other owners become upset. (More in-depth discussion on labor issues will be provided in chapter 8.)

An attempt to overcome this problem is a structure called single entity ownership. Rather than have one owner(s) for one club in a league, a group of owners jointly owns all clubs in the league. Today, this structure appears in Major League Soccer and in the Texas-Louisiana Baseball League.

In MLS, investors participate in the league as a whole but receive the right to operate one of the 12 franchises. Players sign contracts with the league, which then allocates them to

[1]Proposals have been presented to delete this provision.

[2]Remember from chapter 2 that benefits and costs are sometimes difficult to measure.

specified teams. Although a franchise operator can request certain players, there is no assurance that such a request will be honored. The league allocates players for the benefit of the league rather than the benefit of an individual club. In this case, profit maximization of the league as a whole is the goal. The franchise operator makes decisions about marketing and operation of the club but does not have unlimited authority. The Texas-Louisiana League (independent baseball) contains seven franchises, six of which are owned by the league.[3] Each franchise has a general manager hired by the league, and the players sign contracts with the league. Again, the league controls allocation of players, but in this case, the league also controls much of the marketing and business operation.

Such a structure eliminates the possibility of owners driving up labor prices by competing for players. It has dispensed with a free market for players and has centralized control, essentially moving from an oligopoly to a monopoly. Leagues can plan their labor costs, which contributes to long-term survival. However, single entity ownership also has disadvantages. One is a legal threat. Major League Soccer players are currently suing the MLS and arguing that their ability to obtain jobs is being unfairly restricted (restraint of trade). A second problem is *free riders*. If revenues and expenses are handled through a central office, there is less incentive for any individual club to maximize profit. The advantage of a free market is that owners who make profits keep profits. Under a centralized operation, an individual operator may be able to gain a "free ride" on the success of other operators.

Single entity ownership also has disadvantages for its investors. For most investors in professional sports, a reward for investing is the ability to operate a team—to make decisions about player acquisition, marketing strategies, and operations. MLS restricts investors' ability to conduct business. In addition, under ordinary circumstances, the MLS might also be a good candidate for a public stock offering. League officials currently want to expand, which will be expensive. A public offering could raise the capital necessary to undertake growth. However, until the MLS resolves issues regarding player allocations, it is unlikely the league would be willing to make a public offering, which would require opening up the books. There will be more discussions related to this topic in chapter 9.

Mergers, Acquisitions, and Integration

The past two decades have seen a flurry of activity among corporations in terms of acquiring and merging with other companies. Many well-known companies have been part of such behavior, including Westinghouse and CBS, Daimler-Benz and Chrysler, Amoco and British Petroleum, Norwest and Wells Fargo banks, and U.S. West and Qwest. The sport industry has echoed this general business activity. Why do companies engage in such behavior? If we assume that firms analyze the benefits and costs of mergers and acquisitions before engaging in them, what are the benefits and costs?

Consumer goods and services are generally provided through a series of steps described as the *chain of production*. Figure 5-1 shows two chains of production, one for a consumer good, such as an athletic shoe, the other for a service, such as a round of golf. Each point in the chain represents some activity by a firm to move the product or service toward the

[3]As of 1999, one club was privately owned. It entered the League when its previous league folded.

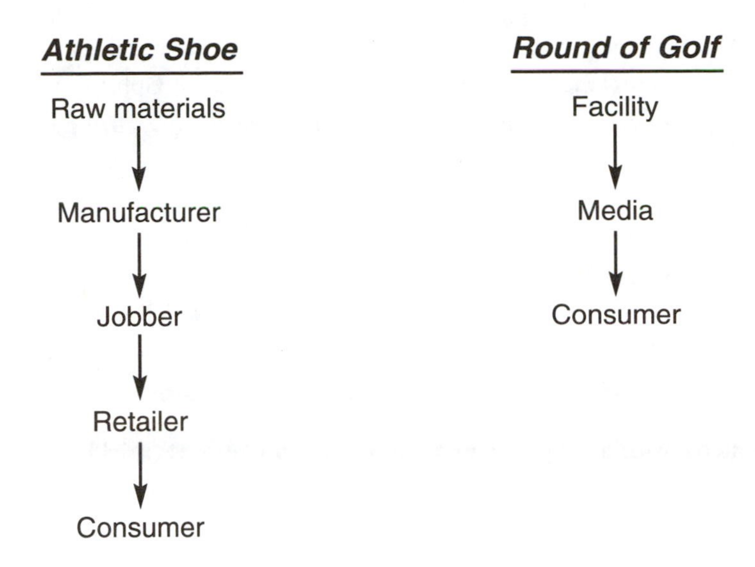

Figure 5-1: Chain of Production

end consumer. The chain for a consumer good is more involved than that for a service. This is especially relevant in sport industry where much of what organizations provide is represented by the shorter chain.

Given their own operating environment and including competition from other firms, firms have to continually make decisions about how to move products and services along the chain in a way that will best satisfy consumers. Strategic decisions that firms can make to accomplish this include mergers and acquisitions. Mergers and acquisitions result in firms' being integrated along the chain of production. *Horizontal integration* is "the combining of two companies [at the same level] in the same industry" (Colander, 1998, p. 760). In 1996, American Skiing, an operator of several ski resorts in the Northeast, acquired SKI Ltd., another operator of Northeast ski resorts. The result was a single company that owned seven resorts (Gilpin, 1996). For American Skiing, benefits came from more integrated marketing and advertising and the ability to offer more options to consumers. In 1990, sporting goods manufacturer Spalding acquired Dudley, the premier manufacturer of softballs (Spalding Sports Worldwide, Inc., 1999). Spalding, which considers itself a premier sporting goods company, was now able to offer one additional product to its business consumers and keep them within the Spalding sphere of influence.

Vertical integration is "a combination of two companies that are involved in different phases of producing a product, one company being a buyer of products the other company supplies" (Colander, 1998, p. 760). A firm will then operate at more than one point on the chain of production. Vertical integration may be either *backward*, where a firm moves closer to the supply of inputs, or *forward*, when a firm moves closer to the ultimate consumer. In the sport industry, many media companies have engaged in vertical integration. An example is Cablevision Systems Corp., which acquired the New York Knicks and New York Rangers in 1997, giving them control over the product as well as the delivery system (Burgi, 1997). Media company acquisitions of sports franchises have been common occurrences in North America and Europe. In most cases, media companies have found it cheaper to buy their product (teams) rather than pay escalating rights fees.

Some firms practice both horizontal and vertical integration. During 1998 and 1999, SportsLine, a global Internet sports media company, acquired International Golf Outlet (a retailer of fine golf equipment), Golf Club Trader (an Internet retailer specializing in used pro-line golf equipment), and Infosis Group Limited's Sports Division (a provider of sports information for SportsLine; CBS SportLine, 1999). The first two acquisitions allowed SportsLine to diversify horizontally, providing a wider range of items to offer through its Internet delivery system. The last acquisition is an example of vertical integration in that SportsLine acquired one of its information suppliers. In addition, SportsLine and CBS have combined. CBS gained enhanced access to Internet delivery whereas SportsLine gained the visibility that comes with the CBS name, as well as cash.

A firm might want to merge with or acquire another firm for many reasons (Brickley et al., 1997, p. 356). One is to increase power and influence. Generally, the larger the company, the more power it tends to have. One of the concerns with mergers and acquisitions is that firms can develop too much power and influence. At the extreme, such consolidation would result in monopoly power. That is why the government occasionally reviews, and even disallows, a merger or acquisition. There was discussion about American Skiing's gathering too much power in the Northeast ski resort industry although no antitrust investigation occurred (Gilpin, 1996).

A second reason relates to *transaction costs*. Going outside the company for inputs and outputs involves costs, including searching out partners. Escalating rights costs for sporting events are a major cost for media companies. Measuring the quality of a supplier's production also involves costs. At every point along the chain of production there are costs. The necessity of coordinating such activities as production, transportation, and pricing decreases the opportunity for profit. Additionally, a company's reputation depends on its suppliers because poor suppliers or retailers can cost reputations.

Third, companies want to ensure the supply and quality of important inputs. Quality reflects on reputation. For example, makers of wooden bats depend on growers of wood to supply a good product. No matter how good the bat maker, if the wood is not good, baseball players will be unhappy. In addition, shortages occur in the marketplace. A sporting goods retailer who also controls the manufacture of items to be sold has much more control over the amount produced and has more assurance of consistency of supply. A cable television company depends on programming. If the cable company owns a baseball or basketball or hockey team, it has consistent supply and does not have to compete on the open market.

Mergers and acquisitions have both costs and benefits. They also raise many issues, not the least of which is government interest in maintaining competition. Several of the firms mentioned above have faced antitrust concerns. Chapter 10 will talk more about antitrust issues.

Summary

Sport is supplied via several delivery structures, each of which has implications for how it ultimately reaches the consumer. Government-supplied sport reallocates resources collected from all citizens to provide sport to all citizens. There are many arguments for and against government's providing sport services, including the concept of positive and negative externalities. In some cases, government has sought means by which it can turn over its responsibilities, perhaps through privatization or through subsidies to community organizations.

Community-based organizations supply a variety of sport experiences to people. These are nonprofit organizations that seek to fill need not met by either government or private enterprise. The goals for such organizations can vary, as discussed in chapter 2. Much sport is provided through private enterprise, where the goal is generally profit maximization. Corporate ownership is responsible for much of the business activity in the sport industry. Benefits and costs exist for both public and private ownership of firms. Merger and acquisition activity also has benefits and costs that must be considered before a firm participates in such behavior

Western City (at the beginning of this chapter) is an illustration of the issues involved in choosing how to supply sport. Each of the options presented by council members has costs and benefits that must be considered in making decisions.

Chapter Study Questions

1. What are externalities?
2. What are two arguments in favor of government's supplying sport? What are two arguments against?
3. Why do people participate (directly or indirectly) in community-based sport organizations?
4. How does a firm's ownership structure affect the firm's objectives and operations?
5. Why would a municipal government consider privatizing its sport services?
6. Chris Branvold is the General Manager of the Colorado Rockies. The Assistant Director of Baseball Operations has come to him and informed him that three of the club's minor league affiliates are up for sale. Chris has been thinking that there might be advantages to buying the minor league clubs but worries that the disadvantages might be too great. What are the advantages and disadvantages? Would it work?

Chapter Six

INTRODUCTION

The sport industry has been viewed as a critical center in the United States economy. Using the Gross National Sports Product (GNSP) to determine the size of the sport industry in the United States, *Sports, Inc.* reported in 1987 that sport was a $50-billion industry (Sandomir, 1987). Using 1995 data, Meek conducted a similar study in 1997, which indicated that the sum of the output and services of the sport industry, measured by the Gross Domestic Sports Product (GDSP), was approximately $152 billion. The same study also found that the sport industry was ranked 11th in size when compared to other industries in the United States (see Table 6-1 for details). A recent special report, compiled by the *Street & Smith's SportsBusiness Journal,* entitled "The Sports Business at the End of the Millennium," substantially increased the figure to $212.53 billion based on the 1997 data (Broughton, Lee, & Nethery, 1999b). The report considered the sport industry as one of economic behemoths, and it is bigger than the automobile industry, bigger than all the public utilities put together, and bigger than agriculture. Is the sport industry really that big? How did those studies estimate the size of the sport industry? This chapter will provide students with a detailed review of the issues related to determining and measuring the size of the sport industry so that they will gain a better understanding of how critical the sport industry is to the national economy. This chapter will also assess the contribution of the sport industry to the U.S. economy in terms of the annual number of jobs the industry creates.

The Sport Industry: A Critical Center of Economy

Devon Lee, chief executive officer of the Jacksonville Footswear Corporation, was recently invited to give a speech at a meeting sponsored by the Chamber of Commerce for the Greater Jacksonville Area. In his presentation, he pointed out that the sport industry is a $213-billion industry, and its impact is even greater than some conventional industries, such as the public utility industry. At the Q & A section, he was asked to explain how he came up with the number. Do you know how he did that?

Determining the Size of the Sport Industry

The value of the output of all final goods and services produced by any industry in a given economy is expressed as either the Gross National Product (GNP) or the Gross Domestic Product (GDP). GNP is the total value of output owned by residents of a particular nation in a certain year. GDP, however, is the total value of output (i.e., the final goods and services) produced in the nation during a single year. It uses market prices because they are the values that people place on goods and services, and measures all the goods produced over some time period, usually a year, whether they are sold or not. Final goods and services are those goods and services purchased for final use. The difference between GNP and GDP is the net investment income that the country's residents receive from other parts of the world. For example, Nike has overseas factories in many foreign countries, and the value of goods produced by those factories is included in the calculation of GNP, but

Table 6-1. Top 25 U.S. Industry Ranking (Estimated 1995 Industry GDP; billions of $)

Rank Industry	Size
Real estate	850.0
Retail trade	639.9
Wholesale trade	491.0
Health service	443.4
Construction	227.6
Business service	275.3
Depository institutions	223.9
Utilities	205.3
Other service	194.9
Telephone and telegraph communication	155.7
Sports	**152.0**
Chemicals and allied products	141.0
Electronic and electrical equipment	138.5
Industrial machinery and equipment	123.3
Insurance carries	115.4
Food and kindred products	113.3
Trucking and warehousing	100.6
Legal services	100.5
Printing and publishing	89.7
Motor vehicle and equipment	88.7
Fabricated metal products	86.0
Farms	85.0
Security and commodity brokers	75.6
Oil and gas extraction	62.7
Auto repair, services and parking	60.5

Source: Meek, A. (1997). An estimate of the size and supported economic activity of the sport industry in the United States. *Sport Marketing Quarterly, 6*(4), 15–21.

not GDP. After 1991, the U.S. Department of Commerce decided to use GDP to measure the aggregate economic activity, instead of GNP.

Measurement of GDP: The Expenditure Approach

The U.S. Department of Commerce uses several approaches to measure GDP. The one that has been widely adopted is the expenditure approach, or the final sales method (Auerbach & Kotlikoff, 1995). The expenditure approach includes four components in the estimation of GDP: personal consumption expenditures (C), gross private domestic investment (I), government purchase of goods and services (G), and net exports of goods and services (NX). Each of these components will be discussed in detail later in this chapter. The following is an expressive equation that reveals the relationship between GDP and its four components:

$$GDP = C + I + G + NX$$

Personal Consumption Expenditures (C)

Personal consumption expenditures are household expenditures on goods and services produced by firms, such as beverages, exercise and sport shoes, athletic club memberships, and bikes. Personal consumption expenditures exclude purchases of households on real property (e.g., house, land). Because house and land purchases are counted as a type of private investment, they are calculated in a separate category. Personal consumption expenditures are the largest and relatively stable component of GDP.

Gross Private Domestic Investment

The expenditures of business firms on purchasing new capital equipment, newly produced physical structures (e.g., a new plant), and inventories are included in this category. The money that individual households spend on acquisition of new residential houses is also part of the gross private domestic investment. Specifically, gross private domestic investment analyzes two basic items: (a) net private domestic investment and (b) consumption of fixed capital. The net private domestic investment is the part of gross investment that adds to the existing stock of physical structures and equipment. The consumption of fixed capital consists of depreciation and an allowance for accidental damage to the physical structures and equipment.

Learning Activities

1. Return to the beginning of the chapter and reread the scenario. Assume you are Devon Lee and explain to the class (the audience of the meeting) how to calculate the Gross National Sports Product.
2. Calculate the GDSP of your state.
3. Visit the Web sites of the Bureau of Economic Analysis (www.bea.doc.gov), the U.S. Census Bureau (www.census.gov), and the Sporting Goods Manufacturers Association (www.sportlink.com/press_room/index.html) to get some information on consumer expending on sports activities. Using the data obtained, calculate the personal sport consumption in a certain year.

Government Purchases of Goods and Services

The goods and services purchased by all levels of government, from the federal government to local municipalities, are calculated in this area. They may include the costs and expenditures of providing services and law enforcement. Transfer payments are not included in the calculation of this particular GDP component because they do not involve the production of goods and services. Transfer payments are payments by government to persons for the service they do not render. For example, federal and state governments each year spend money to subsidize interest payments on higher education loans.

Net Exports of Goods and Services

The difference between the value of exports and the value of imports is the net export of goods and services. Exports are produced in a country and purchased by foreigners. The value of a pair of baseball gloves produced in the United States and sold in Hong Kong is part of the U.S. exports. On the other hand, imports are produced abroad and are purchased by U.S. citizens in that country. When an American buys a warm-up outfit made in Italy, what he or she pays is calculated as part of the U.S. imports. In recent years, the net exports of goods and services have been a negative component of GDP. That means Americans have imported more goods from other nations than they have sold to the rest of the world.

Table 6-2 shows the GDP of the United States in 1998 and how much each of these four

Table 6-2. Real Gross Domestic Product (1998)

GDP and Its Components	Symbol	Amount (billions of dollars)	Percentage of GDP
Personal consumption expenditures	C	5,805.6	68.2
Gross private domestic investment	I	1,368.7	16.1
Government purchase of goods and services	G	1,487.5	17.5
Net exports of goods and services	NX	-151.2	-1.8
Gross domestic product	GDP	8,510.6	100.00

Source: U.S. Department of Commerce, National Account Data (February 1999). Available: www.bea.doc.gov/bea/dn/niptbl-d.htm

categories of expenditures contributes to it. Personal consumption expenditure is the biggest source of GDP (approximately 68%), followed by government purchases of goods and services.

There are basic rules that need to be rigidly followed in measuring the value of the output of a particular economy. The most important is that a single dollar cannot be counted twice (Sandomir, 1988). It is extremely important to remember that when calculating GDP, the value of intermediate goods and services and of goods purchased for resale or for use in producing other goods should not be included. Only the final goods and services produced count toward GDP. For example, when someone buys a new fishing boat from a local marine shop, the value of the boat is counted as part of GDP. However, the amount of money the marine shop pays to the manufacturer for the boat is not included in the calculation of GDP because doing so would cause the value of the boat to be double-counted.

Measurement of GDP: The Factor Income Approach

The factor income approach is the second method used by the U.S. Department of Commerce in its estimation of GDP. This approach measures GDP by adding all of the incomes paid by firms to households for the services of the factors of production that they use, including labor hired, interest paid for borrowed capital, rent paid for land use, and profit. The result of measurement is approximately the same as that of measurement using the expenditure approach. According to the National Income and Product Accounts for the United States, published by the Bureau of Economic Analysis of the Department of Commerce, factor incomes are split into five components:

1. compensation of employees,
2. rental income,
3. corporate profits,
4. net income, and
5. proprietors' income (Auerbach & Kotlikoff, 1995; Parkin, 1993).

Compensation of Employees

Compensation of employees refers to the total payments by business firms for labor services. These payments include the wages and salaries that employees receive in a certain period (e.g., weekly, biweekly, and monthly), the portion of income withheld for tax purposes, and all fringe benefits paid by the employer. Social Security, health insurance, and retirement are examples of the fringe benefits that employees usually obtain as part of their compensation. For example, as athletic director of the Southern Athletic Club in Decatur, Georgia, Karen Smith receives a salary of $35,000 from the club.

Rental Income

Rental income is the payment received by the owner of an asset (e.g., land, building, other rented structures) as he or she gives the right to other people to use that asset. The monthly payment that a landlord receives from tenants is a major component of rental income. The imputed rental income for an owner-occupied house is another major component of rental income. The imputed income is the implicit benefits received by a homeowner who has used the house as a business office. By considering the rental payment for the house as a cost to the business, the owner, in fact, saves an equivalent amount of money as a result of using the house as an office. Thus, the saving should be calculated as part of the owner's income.

Corporate Profits

Corporate profits are the total net income or profit that all business firms make in a given economy over a certain time. The period could be a month, a quarter, 6 months, or a year. For example, the annual profit of Gallaway Golf in 1997 was $132.7 million.

Net Interest

Net interest is the difference between the interest payments received by households on loans made by them and the interest payments made by households on their own borrowing. The interest that households receive from their investments in bonds and the interest payments that households owe to financial institutions on their credit card balances are examples of various types of interest with which households commonly deal. For example, if a person receives an interest payment of $200 annually from an investment in a 20-year municipal bond, but pays $300 interest each year to a bank for a car loan, the net interest in this case is negative $100.

Proprietors' Income

Personal income is a mixed index. A proprietor is an individual who owns and operates a business and who supplies labor, capital, land, and buildings to his or her own business. Proprietors' income is a category that mixes all four of the above elements because it is difficult to divide the income earned by a proprietor into such elements as compensation for use of labor, payment for use of capital, rental payment for use of land and buildings, and profit.

Measurement of Gross Domestic Sports Product

Using the framework about how GDP is measured, we can determine GDP in the sport industry, which is labeled the Gross Domestic Sports Product (GDSP). GDSP is the sum of the output and service produced domestically by the sport industry. There are five categories included in the measurement of GDSP. The first four are directly derived from the four basic corresponding elements of GDP; that is, personal sport consumption (PSC), gross sport investment (GSI), government sport purchases (GSP), and net sport exports (NSE). The fifth category of GDSP is the advertising expenditures of nonsport businesses (ENB) in the sport industry. The conceptual relationship between GDSP and the five categories of sport expenditures is expressed as follows:

$$GDSP = PSC + GSI + GSP + NSE + ENB$$

The measurement of GDSP is far more complex than that of GDP for two reasons. First, the scope of the phenomenon, what we call "sport," can be very limited or inclusive depending on how we define the concept "sport." For example, should we consider rock climbing, hunting, and skin diving as sport activities? If yes, the magnitude of GDSP would be much higher than when these activities are excluded. Second, no sole category of expenditures in sport is defined by government economic statistics. The economic significance of sport has been counted only as part of the contributions rendered by many other industries, such as the recreation and entertainment industry.

Personal Sport Consumption

Personal sport consumption refers to consumer expenditures on goods produced by companies in the sport industry and on services rendered by service-oriented sport businesses. The goods include sporting goods and other such items as souvenirs and novelties. From the discussion in chapter 1, we know that sporting goods, as defined by the U.S. Census Bureau, include sports and athletic apparels, sports and athletic shoes, sports and athletic equipment, and recreational transport. The money paid for a round of golf and for the admission to a minor league hockey game exemplifies the spending by consumers for sport services. Personal sports consumption is highly inclusive as it covers the money that people spend on a variety of things. According to Meek (1997), the consumer expenditures on sports can be classified into three main categories: entertainment and recreation; products and services; and nonsport-related advertising expenditures. (The authors believe that this last category is a stand-alone element of GDSP that should be discussed in a separate section.) In 1995, sports consumers spent $144,848 million on sport. This is the largest component of GDSP.

Entertainment and recreation. The expenditures on entertainment and recreation cover the money that consumers spend on sports as both participants and spectators. Whatever consumers pay for participating in a sport activity like an entry fee or whatever consumers spend as spectators at a sport event is included in this category. This category of expenditures can be further subdivided into several types of spending activities:

1. Participating in sport activities. The registration fee paid for participating in the Savannah (Georgia) Great Bridge Run and the money spent playing a sports video game are examples of expenditures that consumers may incur as a result of being participants in sport activities. Overall, in 1996, 88.8 million Americans participated in sports and fitness activities on a frequent basis (Sporting Goods Manufacturers Association, 1998).

2. Attending sport events. There are many costs associated with attending sports events. Monies spent on tickets, parking, transportation, and concessions fall under this cate-

Table 6-3. Personal Consumption Expenditures on Spectator Sports[1] (1985–1995) (in million current dollars)

Sport	1985	1986	1987	1988	1989	1990	1991	1992	993	1994	1995
Professional Baseball	325	350	385	426	469	489	562	592	781	648	691
Professional Football	263	259	263	293	323	348	373	398	408	414	443
Professional Basketball	217	248	286	192	240	268	281	299	310	332	365
Professional Soccer	4	5	9	3	7	10	10	11	24	25	25
Professional Hockey	188	204	226	138	151	162	171	185	207	197	194
Dog and Horse Racing	312	316	327	345	398	381	391	346	335	300	281
College Football	139	149	160	165	182	196	206	206	206	226	230
College Basketball (men & women)	123	131	141	151	164	180	191	196	189	182	216
High School Athletics	1,222	1,157	1,123	1,387	1,670	1,684	1,803	1,948	2,176	2,404	2,575
Other Sports	487	464	445	470	543	520	534	473	457	478	518
Total	3,279	3,284	3,366	3,569	4,147	4,238	4,522	4,656	5,093	5,206	5,537

Source: Statistical Abstract of the United States, 1997.

gory. The expenditure of consumers on spectator sports over the last decade is summarized in Table 6-3. The figures in Table 6-3 indicate that consumers have gradually spent more money on attending various spectator-oriented sporting events. They include the traditional athletic events like professional and collegiate football, basketball, and baseball games, as well as the nontraditional events, such as auto, horse, and dog racing.

Table 6-4 shows that privately owned sport establishments received more than $33.4 billion from their users in 1997 (U.S. Census Bureau, 1997). In other words, in 1997, American consumers spent that amount of money to attend various sports events, to purchase memberships in various fitness and sports clubs, or to use recreational sports facilities like roller-skating rinks and golf courses.

1. Watching pay-per-view sports events. In addition to attending spectator sports events, consumers also spend millions of dollars to receive pay-per-view sports events at home. Pay-per-view is a $1-billion-a-year business. A variety of sports programming is available for viewers, ranging from pro sports to college basketball March Madness. Although approximately 60 million U.S. households have cable TV connections, 35 million pay for converter boxes that enable them to watch pay-per-view events. Although the cost for viewing an event averages about $29.95 (Smith, 1995), it is estimated that more than a million viewers subscribed to the Holyfield-Lewis fight, at a cost of about $50 each (Crowe, 1999).

2. Visiting sports halls of fame, touring sports facilities, and attending special banquets with sports celebrities. For fulfilling their desire to meet sports celebrities, many sports fans are willing to pay a relatively large entry fee to attend various organized banquets that may have some sports celebrities in attendance.

3. Partaking in legal sports gambling. Gambling costs are the last category of personal sports consumption. Money that consumers spend on various gambling activities,

[1] The spending figure consists of admission to all professional and amateur spectator sports events.

Table 6-4. Contributions of Sports Establishments[2] to the Economy of the United States of America (1997)

Types of Sports Establishments	Number	Receipts[3]	Employment[4]
Professional Baseball Clubs	194	2,296,558	14,410
Professional Football Clubs	45	2,503,399	4,107
Other Professional Sports Clubs	244	3,008,787	14,813
Bowling Centers	5,590	2,820,685	88,044
Fitness & Recreational Sports Centers	16,604	7,944,954	256,397
Golf Courses & Country Clubs	8,546	8,636,921	160,118
Auto Racetracks	590	897,600	22,215
Horse Racetracks	161	2,448,351	144,331
Dog Racetracks	56	796,069	36,997
Roller Skating Rinks	1,611	416,339	19,416
Ice Skating Rinks	381	298,737	8,870
Skiing Facilities	379	1,340,813	58,513
Total	34,401	33,409,213	828,231

Source: 1997 Economic Census, U.S. Census Bureau, U.S. Department of Commerce.

including wages paid for betting on the results of sports competitions, such as horse racing, and money spent on sport-related lotteries or lotteries that are sold and earmarked specifically for the sake of sports development are included here. Many Americans are deeply obsessed with gambling, and they spend millions of dollars each year on gambling activities. A recent report on sports gambling reveals that Americans spent $18.55 billion on legal gambling in 1997 (Broughton et al., 1999b).

Purchasing sporting goods and services. The expenditures on sporting goods include spending on sports and athletic equipment, outfits, souvenirs, and novelties. Table 6-5 shows various figures in sporting goods sales from year 1987 to 1996. According to the Recreation Executive Report presented by the Sporting Goods Manufacturers Association (SGMA), the sales of sports and athletic equipment, apparel, and footwear hit $44.8 billion in 1997, and the wholesale amount for camping, hiking, backpacking, and other outdoor equipment totaled $1.58 billion in the same year. It is estimated that the sales of sports footwear, including both branded and unbranded shoes, grew to $9.86 billion in 1998 (Sporting Goods Manufacturers Association, 1998). The same report also indicated that from 1986 to 1997, the sales of golf equipment grew from $740 million to $2.4 billion. In 1998, this number was estimated to increase to around $2.6 billion. The sales of golf clubs that combine advanced design and spaceage materials grew 13% between 1992 and 1997 (Recreation Executive Report, 1997). The U.S. Census Bureau in its *Statistical Abstract of the United States, 1998* reports that Americans overall spent $57,168 billion in sporting goods in 1996.

[2] An establishment is a single physical location at which business is conducted. The list does not include sports organizations related collegiate athletics, such as individual athletic departments and conferences, and other non-profit sports organizations.
[3] Receipts refer to what customers pay for receiving the services rendered by those sports establishments. The number is in thousands.
[4] Employment refers to the number of people who are on the payroll of those sports establishments.

Table 6-5. Sporting Goods Sales, by Product Category: 1987 to 1996 (In millions of dollars, except percent)

Selected Product Category	1987	1988	1989	1990	1991	1992	1993	1994	1995	1996
Sales, all products	36,791	43,937	48,585	48,250	47,104	47,110	49,129	53,453	55,452	57,168
Percent of retail sales (%)	2.4	2.7	2.8	2.6	2.5	2.4	2.4	2.4	2.4	2.3
Athletic and sport clothing	4,645	9,555	10,286	10,130	10,731	8,990	9,096	9,521	9,699	10,030
Athletic and sport footwear	6,373	6,797	10,435	11,654	11,787	11,733	11,084	11,120	11,420	11,835
Walking shoes	996	1,471	2,419	2,950	2,689	2,688	2,673	2,543	2,841	2,955
Gym shoes, sneakers	1,537	1,602	2,303	2,536	2,545	2,397	2,016	1,869	1,741	1,758
Jogging and running shoes	1,023	987	1,106	1,110	1,192	1,232	1,231	1,069	1,043	1,106
Tennis shoes	467	448	645	740	759	748	599	556	480	489
Aerobic shoes	634	514	667	611	600	590	500	356	372	380
Basketball shoes	364	493	631	918	974	984	874	867	999	1,049
Golf shoes	186	183	186	226	249	260	275	238	225	234
Athletic and sport equipment	9,900	10,705	11,504	11,964	12,062	12,846	13,880	15,257	15,060	15,691
Firearms and hunting	1,804	1,894	2,139	2,202	2,091	2,533	2,722	3,490	2,955	3,015
Exercise equipment	1,191	1,452	1,748	1,824	2,106	2,050	2,602	2,449	2,857	3,000
Golf	946	1,111	1,167	1,219	1,149	1,338	1,248	1,342	1,366	1,434
Camping	858	945	996	1,072	1,006	903	906	1,017	1,208	1,305
Bicycles	930	819	906	1,092	(NA)	(NA)	(NA)	(NA)	(NA)	(NA)
Fishing tackle	830	766	769	776	711	678	716	717	737	751
Snow skiing	661	710	606	606	577	627	611	652	607	644
Tennis	238	264	315	287	295	296	267	257	241	248
Archery	224	235	261	265	270	334	285	306	302	296
Baseball and softball	173	174	206	217	214	245	323	295	249	254
Water skis	148	160	96	88	63	55	51	51	54	55
Bowling accessories	129	129	143	155	155	164	159	157	160	165
Recreational transport	15,873	16,880	16,360	14,502	12,524	13,541	15,069	17,555	19,273	19,612
Pleasure boats	8,906	9,637	9,319	7,644	5,862	5,765	6,246	7,679	9,064	9,518
Recreational vehicles	4,507	4,839	4,481	4,113	3,615	4,412	4,775	5,690	5,894	5,768
Bicycles and supplies	2,272	2,131	2,259	2,423	2,686	2,973	3,534	3,470	3,390	3,356
Snowmobiles	188	273	301	322	362	391	515	715	924	970

Source: Statistical Abstract of the United States, 1998.

Purchasing sports-related publications and video games is another category of sport consumer purchases. Magazines, newspapers, and trading cards are publications that are commonly purchased by sport consumers. According to *Sports Collectors Digest*, the sales of new sports trading cards in 1999 were around $400 million (Zuckerman, 1999). "NFL GameDay 2000," "NBA Live 99," and "1080 Snowboarding," just to list a few, are examples of sports videos available for consumers.

Gross Sport Investment

Gross sport investment refers to (a) the expenditures of sport businesses on purchasing durable/capital equipment and on restocking inventories and (b) the expenditures of individuals on acquiring big-ticket items in sports. Sail boats and luxury race cars are examples of big-ticket items. Like their counterparts in other industries, sport businesses also constantly invest a large sum of their operating revenue on purchasing needed durable/capital equipment, on inventorying, and on building new facilities.

Sport equipment is the first category of expenditures of sport businesses. Sport equipment refers to the equipment essential for participants to play a sport or to engage in a physical activity. Each year, American sports businesses and organizations spend millions of dollars on various kinds of equipment. These expenditures range from buying a scoreboard for a minor league baseball team to paying for a treadmill for a sports club. The expenditures of sport businesses on business inventories, the second category of gross sport investment, are usually determined by focusing on those segments of the sport industry that involve production, distribution, and sales of goods. These include sporting goods manufacturers (e.g., NIKE, Reebok, New Balance, and Wilson), distribution warehouses (including those affiliated with the producers and independent ones), and retail sporting goods stores (e.g., Foot Locker, the world's largest retail source for athletic footwear and apparel).

Private participation in sport facility construction has been a growing trend in the last two decades. There are two methods of private participation: (a) Private dollars are used exclusively to build a sports facility, and (b) private dollars are joined with monies from the public sector to share the construction cost of a sports facility. The first means is commonly seen in golf course and athletic club construction. The amount of funding involved usually is relatively small, and the owners of those facilities can raise the construction funds through their own contributions or a bank loan. It is estimated in 1997, "more golf courses have been built in the United States in the past eight years than have been opened in England in the past four hundred," and about eight percent of them are privately built and operated (Golf Research Group, 1997). The boom in golf courses in this country is attributed to the strong public demand for recreation. The number of people who play golf increased from 13 million in 1975 to 25 million in 1995 (U.S. Census Bureau, 1998). The second method of private participation in sports facility construction involves sharing the development cost between the public and private sectors. In many cases, in order for a professional sports franchise to have the public support for either renovating an existing facility or building a new one, the team ownership has been asked to provide a portion of the needed construction fund.

There are two basic types of individual sports investment: (a) money spent on long-term big-ticket items and (b) funds used to buy sports-related stocks. The sport-related long-term big-ticket items include the individuals' purchase of luxury race cars and sailboats, which usually have a relatively long useful life.

Gross sport investment in 1997 was estimated around $11,815.6 million (Meek, 1997). It counted for 7.8% of the total GDSP in that year.

Government Sport Purchases

Government sport purchases refers to the goods and services purchased by all levels of government (mainly the state and local governments) for sport development and for provision of services to fulfill the needs of citizens for sport activities. Government spending on sport is mainly done through one of three areas: (a) construction and maintenance of publicly owned sports facilities, (b) purchases and maintenance of sports equipment for local parks and recreation departments, and (c) bidding for organization of various sports events.

Category (a), construction and maintenance of publicly owned sports, includes the money spent by all levels of government, from federal to local, on constructing public assembly facilities that may be used for various sports functions (e.g., arenas, civic centers, stadiums, recreational sports complexes) and on remodeling or renovating existing sports facilities. In the past decade alone, it is estimated that 30 new public assembly facilities have been built for the use of professional sports teams at a cost of more than $4 billion (M. F. Bernstein, 1998). In addition, 40 more facilities are currently planned, which may add another $7 billion to the price tag. The construction of almost all these facilities is funded in large part by the government. According to an estimate by *USA Today*, four of every five dollars in stadium construction costs now come from public sources (M. F. Bernstein, 1998). Even though public funding for new facilities has become a controversial issue, many government officials still strongly embrace the argument that new stadiums will create jobs and attract professional sports teams to their communities and that the presence of a professional sports team will significantly boost the economy of the involved community. Accordingly, officials have done many desperate things to lure a professional sports team or to keep it in their community. Using public funds to build and maintain sports facilities has become a common practice among those politicians. For example, in November 1996, voters in Houston, Miami, and Detroit approved bond issues worth almost $1 billion to construct new stadiums that would either keep their pro teams or lure new ones (Laing, 1996). In addition to spending a certain portion of its funds appropriated by local governments (i.e., the city council or county commission) on sports facilities, local public sports agencies, such as park and recreation departments, also use part of their budgets on purchasing and maintaining sports equipment (e.g., football and baseball helmets, basketball goals).

Sports events have been viewed as an economic catalyst that can generate a considerable amount of economic impact on the economy of a region, whether it is a metropolitan area or a relatively small community (see chapter 7 on how to determine the magnitude of economic benefits brought about by a sports activity to a particular locale). All levels of government in the United States spend a portion of their tax revenues each year on bidding for sports events through a conduit like a sports commission or authority. For example, the County Commission of Palm Beach in Florida in 1999 allocated 5% of the first three pennies raised from the 4% bed tax, or so-called hotel occupancy tax, to a tourism development fund. This equals $172,000 a year used exclusively for supporting various local organizations in their efforts in bidding for sports events (P. Gerig [executive director of Palm Beach County Sports Commission], personal communication, May 10, 1999).

Net Sport Exports

Net sport exports are the difference between sport exports and sport imports of a nation in a particular year. Due to the strong value of the dollar against that of foreign currencies, U.S. net sport exports have been negative in recent years. Sport exports refer to the amount of sales in foreign nations of sporting goods that are manufactured in the United States. The categories of such goods may include sportswear, footwear, fishing gear, bicycles, gym and exercise equipment, equipment and accessories for winter sports, water sports, track and field, camping, hunting guns, race cars, and so on. The world demand for certain American sporting goods has been in a state of constant growth because U.S. brands have an appealing image, especially among the younger population. Table 6-6 demonstrates this growth trend. According to the Sporting Goods Manufacturers Association (1997b), American sporting companies exported approximately $960 million worth of goods in 1989. In 1997, less than 10 years, the value of sporting goods exported jumped to $2.43 billion, a 250% increase from 1987. This estimate did not include the number of exports in sports apparels and other recreational sports equipment. The actual number of exports would have been higher if sports apparel and recreational sport equipment had been included in the calculation. More than one-third of the sporting goods exported by American companies were sold in Mexico and Canada in 1996. Asia bought about 25% of sporting goods manufactured in the United States in the same year (Sporting Goods Manufacturers Association, 1998). The increase in exports in American-made sporting goods is mostly due to the international expansion effort of U.S. sporting goods companies. They have been very aggressive in expanding into international markets and have fought for greater market shares. In addition to receiving revenues from sales of exported sporting goods, the American sport industry also takes in licensing fees from foreign companies that use the trademarks of American professional sports teams and leagues. According to Meek (1997), the United States obtained about $1 billion from licensing fees internationally.

Table 6-6. U.S. Sporting Goods Exports[5] (1989–1997)

Year	Value of Export (in billions)	% Change from Prior Year
1989	0.96	38.1%
1990	1.10	14.4%
1991	1.19	8.1%
1992	1.36	14.4%
1993	1.54	12.9%
1994	1.78	15.5%
1995	2.16	21.4%
1996	2.27	5.3%
1997	2.43	6.8%

Source: Press Release, Sporting Goods Manufacturers Association (SGMA), 1997.

[5]The statistics excluded the amount of exports in sports apparel, camping equipment, and other recreational equipment.

Table 6-7. U.S. Sporting Goods Imports[6] (1989–1997)

Year	Total Imports (in billions)	% Change from Prior Year
1989	4.988	+ 2.4%
1990	5.745	+15.2%
1991	5.953	+ 3.6%
1992	6.621	+11.2%
1993	6.881	+ 4.6%
1994	6.516	- 5.3%
1995	6.803	+ 4.4%
1996	7.220	+ 6.1%

Source: Press Release, Sporting Goods Manufacturers Association, 1997.

Sport imports refer to the number of sales in the United States of sporting goods that are manufactured in other nations. Table 6-7 shows U.S. sport imports from 1989 to 1996. As the table indicates, American companies bought about $4.988 billion and $7.22 billion worth of foreign-made sporting goods in 1989 and 1996, respectively. China, Taiwan, and South Korea are the three top contributors or import leaders. Together, they provide about 54% of U.S. sport imports.

As mentioned earlier, the difference between sport exports and sport imports is net sport exports. According to data provided by SGMA, sport imports in the United States outnumber sport exports. For example, from Table 6-6, we can see that the value of sport exports in 1989 was $0.96 billion. This translates into a $4.028 billion difference between sport imports and sport exports in this country in that particular year. On average, the difference between them was $4.775 in the period from1989 to1996. The economic crises experienced by many countries in Asia, Europe, and South America have contributed greatly to the increase in sport imports in the United States in this decade. As long as the value of U.S. dollar is comparatively strong, the momentum of the sport imports will be high. Accordingly, net sport exports will continue to be on the negative side.

Expenditures of Nonsport Businesses

Each year, many American businesses spend a portion of their budgets to advertise in sports-related events and to sponsor sports teams, events, and facilities. According to Burton, Quester, and Farrelly (1998), the spending of corporations in the world on sponsorship was about $15.3 billion. In North America alone, $2.84 billion was spent in sports sponsorship, and it is ranked higher than all other major categories, such as entertainment tours and attractions, and festivals, fairs, and annual events (International Event Group, 1997). In North America, global business giants like Coke, Kodak, Gillette, Anheuser-Busch, UPS, and Visa have continued their efforts to develop further bonds with sports, and to "create corporate power bases that derive their strength from the continuing popularity of sports as big business" (Burton et al., p. 8). Other than spending millions of

[6]The statistics excluded the amount of imports in sports apparel, camping equipment, and other recreational equipment.

dollars on sport-related advertising and sponsorships, some American nonsport businesses invest part of their wealth to purchase personal seat licenses (PSL) and luxury suites in various sports facilities. This is another way that the nonsport business spends on sport.

Jobs in the Sport Industry

The sport industry, to a certain extent, is a labor-intensive one. In 1997, more than three-quarters of a million people, 828,231 to be exact, were employed by privately owned sports establishments (see Table 6-6 for details). This figure indicates only a small portion of the jobs created in the sport industry. If we assume that every $40,000 in consumer spending creates a job, $152 billion in GDSP then translates into 3.8 million jobs.

Summary

Because it was ranked 11th among the biggest industries in the nation in terms of the number of sales, the sport industry is clearly a critical component in the U.S. economy. The Gross National Product (GNP) and the Gross Domestic Product (GDP) are two concepts that measure the economic status of a nation. GDP consists of four components: personal consumption expenditures, gross private domestic investment, government purchases of goods and services, and net exports. Gross Domestic Sport Product (GDSP) is an industrial category of GDP, and it has five components: personal sports consumption, gross sport investment, government sport purchases, net sport exports, and expenditures of nonsport businesses on sport. In addition to analyzing the number of sales in the sport industry to determine its significance to the U.S. economy, to truly appreciate the economic importance of the sport industry, we should look closely at the number of jobs it creates for the nation.

Chapter Study Questions

1. Why is the sport industry viewed as a critical center of the economy?
2. Define both GDP and GNP and explain what is different between them.
3. Elaborate on each of the four components of GDP.
4. What is the basic rule that must be used in measuring GDP?
5. Discuss how to measure GDP using the so-called Factor Income Approach.
6. Explain why it is more complicated to estimate GDSP than GDP.
7. How many components comprise GDSP?
8. What factors of personal expenditures must be considered in order to accurately estimate the amount of personal sports consumption?
9. What are the elements that contribute to the estimate of gross sport investment?
10. Explain what costs the government incurs in providing sport services that are included in the calculation of government sport purchases.
11. Using statistical data, explain why sport imports outnumber sport exports in the United States.
12. Why are the expenditures of nonsport businesses on sport part of the GDSP calculation formula? Explain.
13. Discuss how economically critical the sport industry is in terms of the number of people it employs.
14. Explain the importance and significance of globalization of sport to the growth of the sport industry in the United States.

Chapter Seven

INTRODUCTION

Economic impact of sport refers to "the net change in regional output, earnings and employment that is due to new dollars flowing into the region from outside the region" (Humphreys & Plummer, 1995) as a result of hosting a sport tourism event or providing a sport or leisure activity (Turco, 1995). It is one of the topics extensively debated by sport economists in the last two decades. The debate focuses on whether or not a community will benefit economically (i.e., the net change in the economy of the region will be positive) through hosting a sport event or through subsidizing the construction of sports facilities to be used later by professional sports franchises. To understand the arguments of both sides of this debate, the sport management student must develop a working knowledge of what economic impact is and how such impact is measured. The following sections provide information about the theoretical foundation of economic impact research and the procedural steps in conducting an economic impact study in the sport industry.

Theoretical Foundation of Economic Impact Studies

The question of how to accurately measure the size of economic impact of an event or facility on a community is one that economists have examined for more than 200 years (Yeh, 1997). Examinations have included attempts to use various mathematical models to quantify the size of effect, one of which was the famous input-output model developed by Leontief in the 1930s (Leontief, 1985).

Economic Impact of Sport

The Grand Prix at XYZ Harbor will be held in Tybee Island on March 26. This will be the first time since 1920 that another race event comes back to the City of XYZ. Before the City decided to endorse and sponsor the event, local media debated heavily whether the City should spend taxpayers' money to renovate the long-abandoned race track. Proponents believe that the event can attract a large number of visitors and bring a considerable number of tourism dollars to the community. Although the city council finally decided to endorse the event and spend $1 million to upgrade the facility, most council members were not sure if it was a worthwhile endeavor. Accordingly, a sport management professor from a local university was asked to head a research team that would conduct an economic impact study on the event to provide City government with some justifications of the City's investment. What kind of information should the research team collect in order to make a proper estimate of the magnitude of the economic impact caused by the event?

The Input-Output Technique

The input-output model (I-O model) is a mathematical model used to estimate money flows between industrial sectors (e.g., the sporting goods manufacturers purchase all kinds of fabrics from the mills and factories in the same region that produce those fabrics to make sports and athletic apparels) in quantitative terms (Slesinger, 1972) and measure the "interdependence among economic activities within a region"(Pomery, Uysal, & Lamberte, 1988, p. 282). This model is based on the notion that the production of output requires inputs. The inputs can be semi-manufactured goods, raw materials, or inputs of services supplied by the households or government. Having acquired inputs from other sectors, households, and government, a sector produces output and sells this either to the other producing sectors, to the final users such as households or government, to the residents of the other regions, or to other firms for investment purposes (Leontief, 1985). Let's use an example to illustrate this economic notion. The City of Savannah wants to build a new baseball stadium for the Savannah Sand Gnats, and a construction company is hired to do the project. To build the facility, the company needs to purchase a variety of semi-manufactured goods and raw materials, such as bricks, sands, steel, and cement from suppliers. It also needs to hire skilled workers (i.e., to purchase their services). If the company fails to acquire the needed construction materials and skilled workers from Chatham County, where Savannah is located, it has to seek them from other regions.

The essence of the I-O model is the double accounting principle. This means that the gross regional production can be accounted for by adding up the costs of raw materials (e.g., number of logs used to make baseball bats; number of tons of cement used in the stadium construction), intermediary inputs (e.g., strings purchased and used in assembling badminton racquets), as well as the labor and capital costs (e.g., salaries and wages paid to workers involved in producing those sporting goods and money invested by the owner of the sporting goods manufactory in machines and buildings). The gross regional production can also be accounted for by tracking the flows of output from sectoral sources to the destination of intermediary and final use (Leontief, 1966). In other words, the number of baseball bats and badminton racquets purchased by consumers or final users can also be used in calculating the gross regional production.

The application of the I-O model involves the use of a so-called I-O table that records various transactions among industrial sectors in a particular region. The table shows data collected from the sales and purchases of these sectors over a designated period, usually a calendar year. Table 7-1 is a simplified example of the I-O table (Yeh, 1997).

The interindustrial purchases of the agricultural industry, the manufacturing industry, and the service industry, as Table 7-1 shows, compose both the intermediate inputs and

Table 7-1. Simplified Input-output Table

	Output						
	Intermediate Output			Final Output			Total Output
	Agriculture	Manufacturing	Service	Household Consumption	Government Expenditure	Expert	
Input							
Intermediate Inputs		[I]			[II]		
Agriculture	X_{11}	X_{12}	X_{13}	C_1	G_1	E_1	X_1
Manufacturing	X_{21}	X_{22}	X_{23}	C_2	G_2	E_2	X_2
Service	X_{31}	X_{32}	X_{33}	C_3	G_3	E_3	X_3
Primary Inputs							
P	P_1	P_2	P_3	PC	PG	PE	P
T	T_1	T_2	T_3	TC	TG	TE	T
I	I_1	I_2	I_3	IC	IG	IE	I
Total Inputs	X_1	X_2	X_3	C	G	E	X

outputs. The intermediate inputs are provided by various sectors within each of these three industries that sell intermediate products to other sectors within the same industries in a defined economy. On the other hand, the intermediate outputs are produced when interindustrial purchases of intermediate or final products occur among sectors across these three industries. The primary inputs also include three components. The first one involves the resources provided by household (e.g., the services rendered by workers) and the payments (i.e., salaries and wages) in return given back to them (P). The next component relates to the resources provided by government sectors and the payments received by them accordingly (T). For example, the City of XYZ built a multipurpose convention/sport facility, which, in return, generates revenues (i.e., the payment received the government) for the City. Import of intermediate and final products is the third type of primary inputs to a defined economy. The primary inputs provide resources for intermediate or final demand in a defined economy. Consumption of households (C), government expenditures (G), and exports (E) make up the final outputs. A portion of the table shows the purchasing activities of these three sectors of the intermediate or final inputs (products) for final outputs (consumption) in a defined economy.

Learning Activities

1. Return to the beginning of the chapter, and reread the scenario. Assume you are the professor who is in charge of the research project. What kind of information would you collect?
2. Conduct an economic impact study on one local sports event that may have "nonresident" participants and/or spectators to determine the magnitude of its economic impact on the local community.
3. Compile several economic impact studies done for sports facilities and events, and make comparisons in methods, sources of information, and multipliers used in their studies.

The information presented by an I-O table can be interpreted in three ways:

1. Exactly where an industrial sector obtains its inputs and where its product or output goes,
2. How the particular industrial sector links to others in the same region through its purchasing and sales activities
3. How the resources from the input side flow to the output side and the payments flow from the output side to the input side.

The total inputs should always be equal to the total output; that is,

$$P + T + M = C + G + E$$

or

$$P + T = C + G + E - M$$

Where

P + T = Gross regional income

C + G + E - M = Gross regional product .

The I-O table is constructed in such a way that the rows record the output or sales distribution of an industrial sector and the columns show the purchases for each industrial sector of the regional economy. As a whole, the table highlights the relationships among industrial sectors in the region. Thus, the table includes information about all sales revenues, costs, and residual balancing items of profit, and it provides details about all the economic activities that have occurred in a region and the complete structure of its economy. The interdependence of all the industrial sectors can be expressed with a set of linear equations, the solution to which forms a matrix. Each element included in the matrix shows the direct, indirect, and induced changes in the output of a particular industry as a result of a change in the final demand of that industry (Pomeroy, Uysal, & Lamberte, 1988).

The solution of the I-O table can be expressed in a mathematical matrix notation

$$X = [I-A]^{-1} Y$$

Where X = total output necessary to support the final demand Y

Y = final demand

$[I-A]^{-1}$ = a matrix of interdependency coefficients .

An I-O model usually consists of several of these matrices. From the matrices, multipliers are generated and used to measure the net change of economy in a given locale in three basic types of economic variables: output, earning, and employment.

Multiplier and Multiplier Effect

As discussed above about the I-O model, industrial sectors in an economy are interdependent for inputs and resources. So any initial-round spending will stir up further rounds of respending of these initial dollars among industrial sectors within that economy. The initial round of spending in the context of sport generally comes from the spending of visitors to a sport event on such areas as lodging, food and beverage, and miscellaneous retails. Detailed discussion on how to measure the spending of visitors will be provided later in this chapter.

As Turco (1995) maintains,

> Visitors spending into an area does not stop as soon as the dollar has been spent . . . A portion of the dollar then re-circulates through the local economy before slowly leaking out to pay for basic purchases and supplies elsewhere. That portion of the respending that stays in the community is the multiplier effect and that portion that is lost to respending elsewhere is termed "leakage" (p.1).

A multiplier can be understood as a "ratio of the total economic effect on a regional economy to the initial change" (Coughlin & Mandelbaum, 1991, p. 19), and it helps to trace the flows of respending of the money initially injected into the economy until its complete leakage out of the economy and to determine the interdependency among industrial sectors within the economy (Stynes, 1999a). In other words, a multiplier helps capture the secondary effect of the initial monetary injection. The larger a defined economy is, the more interindustrial purchases among industrial sectors will be made within the economy, and therefore, the larger the multiplier will be. The multiplier is higher in a self-sufficient economy than in a small and specialized economy.

Types of Multipliers

Three types of multipliers are used to estimate the magnitude of economic benefits as a result of a dollar injected from outside of a defined economy. They are the output multiplier, the earning multiplier, and the employment multiplier. The output multiplier is also called the sales multiplier. An output multiplier estimates the total change in output of all industrial sectors in a defined economy by the addition of a dollar of final demand. The higher the interdependency among industrial sectors, the higher the multiplier will be. In other words, the degree to which the industrial sectors in an economy can satisfy each other's needs for intermediate or final products without relying on the industrial sectors outside this economy to furnish those intermediate or final products determines the size of the multiplier effect. An output multiplier of 2 means that an addition of $1 million in final demand will increase the total value of production or output in all industrial sectors of that particular economy by $2 million. The earning multiplier is sometimes referred to as the income multiplier. It indicates how much has changed in salaries and wages of households of a defined economy as a result of an additional dollar spent. The magnitude of this type of multiplier also depends on the degree of interdependency among industrial sectors in the given economy. The more self-sufficient it is, the higher the multiplier will be for the economy. An earning multiplier of 2.5 implies that $1 million spent may lead to the increase in wages and salaries of households in a defined economy by $2.5 million. The employment multiplier is used to estimate the change in employment (number of jobs created) in a defined economy due to the addition of new wealth. The interpretation of the employment multiplier differs in various I-O models. An employment multiplier of 12 could mean that for every $1 million spent, 12 full-time equivalent jobs are expected to be created in a defined economy. It could also mean that an increase in employment by one person in a particular industrial sector may create 12 full-time equivalent jobs in that economy overall.

Figure 7-1 illustrates the multiplier effect. As shown in Figure 7-1, for every dollar spent in a defined economy, 40 cents remain in it and 60 cents leak out of that economy

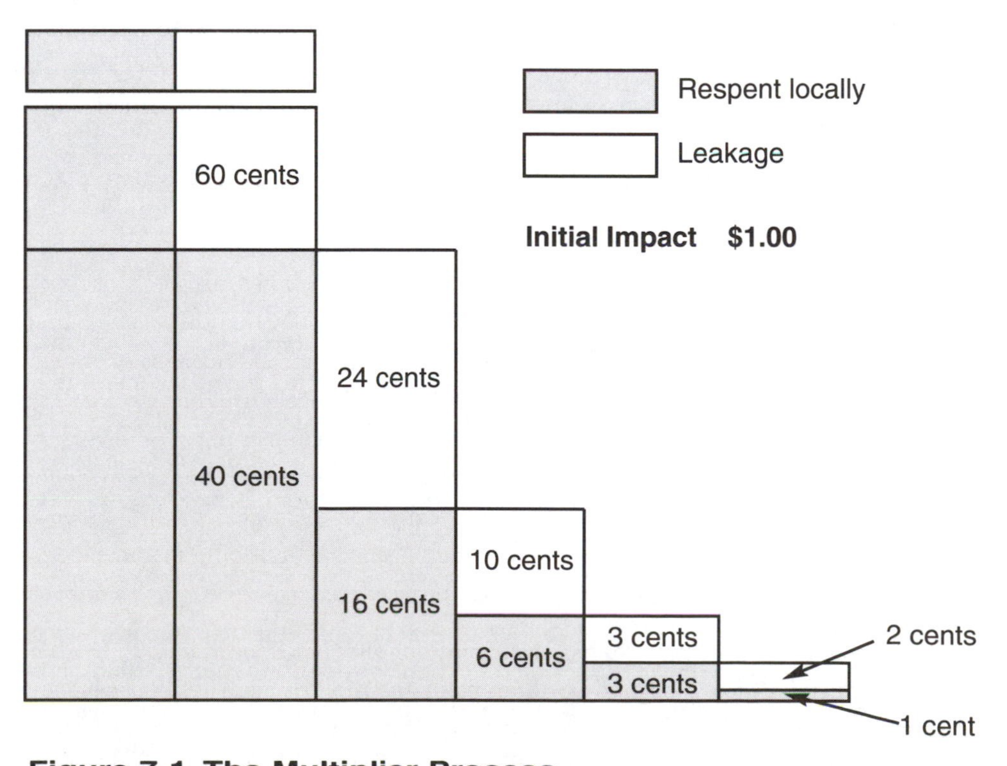

Figure 7-1. The Multiplier Process

through nonlocal taxes, nonlocal purchases, and income transfers. In the next round of re-spending, only 16 cents stay, and 24 cents go elsewhere. In the subsequent rounds of re-spending, the portion that remains in the economy becomes smaller and smaller until the money has completely left the economy. The change in total economic activity as a result of an additional dollar to the economy, thus, can be calculated as

$$\$1 + \$0.40 + \$0.16 + \$0.06 + \$0.03 + \$0.01 = \$1.66$$

The 1.66 is the multiplier. It means that $1.66 of total economic activity is created in that economy for each dollar of external input.

As far as whether households are included as part of the industrial system is concerned, two kinds of multipliers are respectively used. Type I multipliers exclude households in the interaction process among industrial sectors, and this type of multiplier considers households as part of the final demand. Type I multipliers treat the income or earning received by households as a leakage. If households become an integral part of the industrial system and their spending will be added to the total effect, the multiplier used is the Type II multiplier. The Type III multiplier is another type of multiplier that has been used in many economic impact studies. As a matter of fact, technically, the Type III multiplier is very similar to the Type II multiplier. The only difference is that the former treats households as exogenous and the latter considers households as a sector of the local economy. For example, Types I, II, and III output multipliers are calculated with the following formulas, respectively:

$$\underline{\text{Type I Output Multiplier} = \textit{Direct Sales} + \textit{Indirect Sales}}$$
$$\text{Direct Sales}$$

$$\underline{\text{Type II Output Multiplier} = \textit{Direct Sales} + \textit{Indirect Sales} + \textit{Induced Sales}}$$
$$\text{Direct Sales}$$

$$\underline{\text{Type III Output Multiplier} = \textit{Total Direct Sales} + \textit{Indirect Sales} + \textit{Induced Sales}}$$
$$\text{Direct Sales}$$

The concepts of direct sales, indirect sales, and induced sales will be discussed in the following section.

Economic Impact Models

Derived from the input-output method, several economic impact models have been commonly used in measuring the size of economic impact of an event. The most common ones include the impact analysis for planning (IMPLAN), the regional input-output model system (RIMS II), and the travel economic impact model (TEIM). These models provide the researcher conducting economic impact study with multipliers to be used to understand the effect on local output, earning, and employment. Researchers, however, must realize that some differences exist among these models and should exercise caution when trying to compare the results of impact studies that have used different models.

IMPLAN. The Forest Service of the U.S. Department of Agriculture has been instrumental in the construction of the IMPLAN model (Minnesota IMPLAN Group, 2000). Economic data from 528 intermediate industrial sectors, 12 final demand sectors, and six primary supply sectors are assimilated in the model in all U.S. counties. Accordingly, this model can be used to generate economic data for regions (e.g., single counties, groups of counties, single state or group of states, and entire United States) and compute input-output multipliers. The model was later extended by the Minnesota IMPLAN Group, Inc.

RIMS II. Developed by the Bureau of Economic Analysis of the U.S. Department of Commerce, this model "contains a set of industry and area specific multipliers which allows one to determine the total impact of an exogenous change in spending on the local economy" (Division of Research, 1990, p. 4). Many economic impact studies conducted in the sport industry, including the one done to estimate the induced economic impact of the 1996 Atlanta Summer Olympic Games, have used this model to generate multipliers. According to the Bureau of Economic Analysis (1997), "the RIM II multipliers can be estimated for any given region composed of one or more counties and for any industry, or group of industries, in the national I-O table" (p. 2). Two series of multipliers are provided by RIM II. Series 1 multipliers are for 490 detailed industries, and Series 2 includes aggregated multipliers for 38 industries. Four tables are included in each series: Table 1 for final-demand output multipliers, Table 2 for final-demand earning multipliers, Table 3 for final-demand employment multipliers, and Table 4 for the summary of final-demand multipliers for output, earnings, and employment and direct-effect multipliers for earning and employment (Bureau of Economic Analysis, 1999).

REIM. The REIM model, developed by Regional Economic Models, Inc. of Amherst in Massachusetts, specifies commodity-trade and personal-income flows between regions. Forty-nine nonfarm private industrial sectors, three government sectors, and the farm sector are categories included in the model. REIM is constructed with the combination of an industry-based input-output component with an econometric component. Because of this feature, the model is relatively dynamic and can be used not only as an impact model, but also as a model for economic forecasting (Rickman & Schwer, 1993).

Estimates of Economic Impact of Sport

Before attempting to estimate the magnitude of economic impact of a sport activity or service (e.g., a sport event) on a region, the researcher must develop a thorough grasp of the important concepts, issues, and procedures pertaining to how to properly conduct an economic impact study. Without such an understanding, it is impossible for him or her to render an accurate estimate. The following section will present these important concepts, issues, and procedures.

We can measure and examine the economic impact of a sport activity or service in two ways: the short-term impact and the long-term impact. All economic impact studies analyze the short-term effect, but only a few of them also consider the long-term benefits.

The Short-Term Economic Impact

The short-term economic impact mainly analyzes the expenditures of several groups of people associated with an activity, which may include the spending of the activity organizer and the spending of the activity participants, who include athletes, officials, media personnel, spectators, and other visitors. For some hallmark events (e.g., the Olympic Games), the short-term impact may also include the spending of various corporations in their promotion and marketing activities. The short-term impact is calculated through the determination of three subcategories of impacts: the direct impact, the indirect impact, and the induced impact. The sum of the direct, indirect, and induced impacts is the total short-term impact of a sport activity.

The *direct impact* is the change in economic activity during the first round of spending by visitors. The direct impact is also referred to as "final demand"—the amount of direct economic activity generated by a sport activity or service. For example, money spent by the visitors to a regional golf tournament or the business sales to visitors by the involved industrial sectors signifies this type of impact. The *indirect* impact is the changes in output, earning and employment in other industrial sectors within the region due to their supplying of goods and services to the industrial sectors that receive money from visitors' initial round of spending. The industrial sectors usually affected by visitors' initial round of spending are hotels, restaurants, retail stores, and other entertainment-related businesses. During and/or after the event, these sectors restock themselves through some interindustrial purchases from other industrial sectors in the same region. For example, the hotel sector needs to restock its inventory in alcoholic products from various breweries. In short, the indirect impact examines the spending of the economic benefits felt by local businesses as an indirect result of the sport activity or event.

The *induced* impact is the change in economic activity caused by local households who spend their income earned directly or indirectly from visitors as they purchase goods and services during a sport activity or event. For example, the employees of a local restaurant patronized by visitors during a golf tournament spend their income locally to buy groceries. The sum of the indirect and induced impacts is sometimes collectively called the *secondary* or *ripple effect* of the sport activity or service. The sum of the direct impact, indirect impact, and the induced impact is the total impact of the sport activity or service on a given region or community.

When estimating the magnitude of the short-term economic impact for a hallmark event like the Olympic Games, the researcher should take account of the displacement or disturbance effect while calculating the total impact. The *displacement effect* refers to the reduction in tourism spending as a result of economic recession, strong and highly valued currency, negative publicity related to the travel and accommodation conditions of the host region, and altered vacation plans by visitors. For example, researchers examining the Los Angeles Summer Olympic Games subtracted some $331 million as displacement caused by the Games from the total economic impact.

The Long-Term Economic Impact

The long-term economic impact refers to the long-term benefits (catalytic effects) that the host region would enjoy after a sport activity or event. Such an effect includes

1. The creation and development of new facilities,
2. The national and international recognition of the host city, state, and the nation due to extensive media exposure, and
3. The community benefits including local volunteerism, job creation and training, youth education programs, and funding for community economic development projects and cultural programs.

Table 7-2. Legacy of Olympic Venues (amounts in million dollars)

Facility	Total Investment	ACOG Share
Olympic Stadium	189	189
Georgia International Horse Park	90	28
Wolf Creek Shooting Complex	17	17
Stone Mountain Tennis Center	18	18
Lake Lanier Rowing Center	10	10
Georgia Institute of Technology		
Dormitories	194	47
Natatorium	24	21
Alexander Memorial Coliseum	1.5	1.5
Atlanta University Center	51	51
Stadiums—Morris Brown College/Clarke Atlantic Univ	37	37
Basketball Arena—Morehouse College	11	11
Tennis Facility—Spelman College	1	1
Drug Testing Center—Morehouse School of Medicine	1	1
Interdenominational Theological Center	0.8	0.8
Georgia State University		
Gymnasium Renovation	2	2
Clayton County International Park	3	0
TOTAL	**599.3**	**384.3**

Note: Values shown only include portion of project budget dedicated to construction/renovation of permanent facilities.

Source: Atlanta Committee for the Olympic Games, HE Advisors and The Selig Center for Economic Growth, Terry College of Business, The University of Georgia (June, 1995).

Table 7-2 shows the long-term economic impact of the 1996 Atlanta Summer Olympic Games on the City of Atlanta.

Steps in Conducting Economic Impact Studies

Economic impact studies, like many other forms of research inquiry, require the researcher to follow a systematic and ordered sequence of activities. These steps include

Step 1: Determination of the purpose and scope of the impact study

Step 2: Selection of data collection methods

Step 3: Collection and analysis of data

Step 4: Interpretation and report of the results.

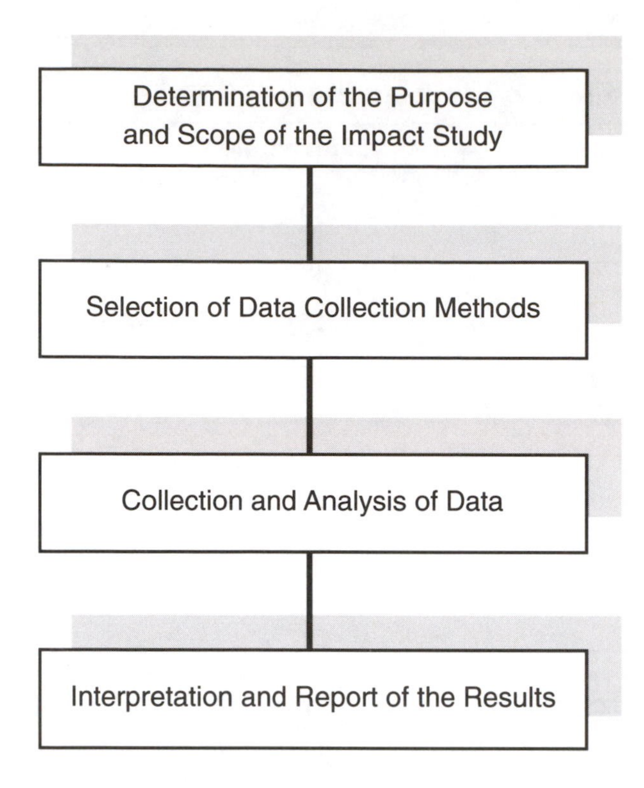

Figure 7-2. Steps in Conducting Economic Impact Studies

Figure 7-2 portrays these four steps.

Determination of the purpose and scope of the impact study. The determination of the purpose and scope of the impact study is the most important step in conducting a sport economic impact study. This step involves three tasks: (a) determination of a cause of impact, (b) definition of a source or sources of impact, and (c) determination of an impact region.

The researcher first needs to determine what causes the net economic changes to the region. In some economic impact study in recreation and tourism, "action" is used as the interchangeable term as the activity that cause economic changes (Stynes, 1999b). Without clearly delineating the cause of the impact, it is impossible to properly collect the necessary information. The impact could be caused by a short-term sport activity or event, lasting from a day to a week. It could also be caused by a sport activity or event that lasts longer than a year. The Super Bowl, the NCAA Basketball Final Four, and the Indianapolis 500 are examples of short-term sports activities or events. On the other hand, the Summer and Winter Olympic Games are examples of sport activities or events that take longer than a year for the organizer to prepare and produce. The preparation usually includes the formation of various functional departments and units, intensive promotion of the event, and massive construction of facilities and infrastructures. The impact of this type of long-term activities or events may last a number of years.

An economic impact study can also be used to determine the magnitude of the net change in the local economy of a community caused by a sport-related establishment, such as a business enterprise, a facility, or an institution. Professional sports franchises have been considered instrumental in stimulating economic development in their host communities (Office of Business and Economic Research, 1995). A facility, such as a sports stadium, an

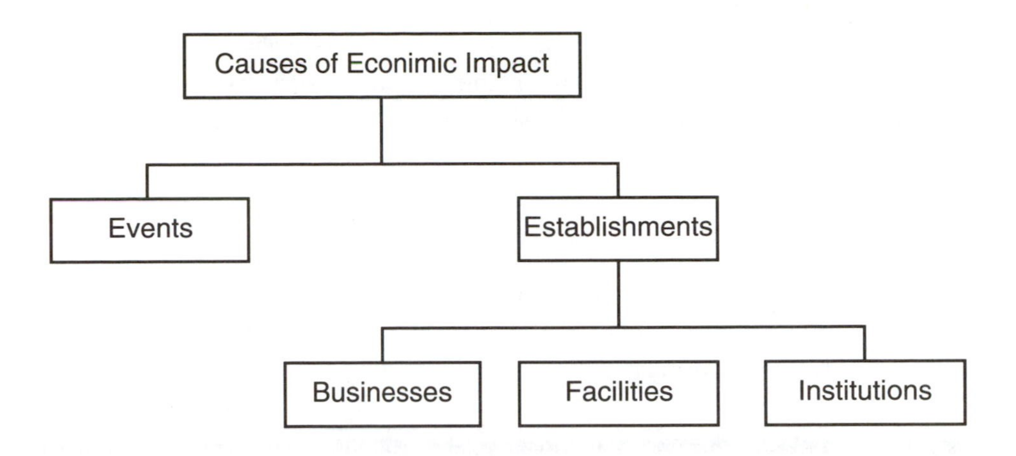

Figure 7-3. Causes of Economic Impact

arena, and a convention center, can also be an economic energizer for the local community within which it resides. Both types of establishments affect the net economic changes of a community by attracting tourist dollars. In addition, an athletic department as part of an educational institution can bring economic benefits to its host district. For example, it was estimated that the economic impact of the athletic programs at the University of Georgia on the economy of the Athens metropolitan statistical area (MSA) was about $44.6 million in 1998. Figure 7-3 helps to illustrate the various causes of economic impact.

As discussed previously, to actually determine the magnitude of the economic benefits brought about by an activity or event, researchers must collect information pertaining to the kinds of spending by various parties involved in the activity (Stynes, 1999b), for example, the amount spent by visitors before, during, and after the event in the region where the activity is held and the amount of money spent by the government of the host community on the activity. In general, the information is listed in two categories: the primary source and the secondary source. Due to the difference in cause of impact, the information needed in making impact estimation varies from study to study. Nevertheless, some items, such as number of visitors, visitors' expenditures, length of visit, size of each visitor group, their demographic, and expenditures of organizers, seem to be generic and sought for in almost all impact research.

An impact region refers to a geographic area over which the economic impact will be measured. As mentioned previously, the impact brought about by the provision of a sport activity refers to the total economic change in a local community as a result of the activity. Therefore, the determination of the size of the community, or the so-called impact region, is considered one of the critical steps in designing appropriate economic impact research because the magnitude of the economic impact varies with the breadth of the region (Beck, Elliott, Meisel & Wagner, 1995). The size of the impact region may have a considerable impact on the accuracy of calculation of the total economic change caused by the injection of "new money" by visitors in that particular community.

An estimate of the overall impact can be accomplished by using various multipliers (e.g., output, earning, employment) derived from an input-output model. The application of such a model requires a clear definition of the geographic area or region. The greater the area, the more economic interactions and interrelationships among involved industries will exist; therefore, the output and earning multipliers will be higher, and subsequently, the impact will be greater. Studies examining the economic benefits of activities in recreation and tourism usually use a 30- to 60-mile radius to define the impact region (Stynes, 1999b). The U.S. Travel Data Center defines a visitor as "one who travels a minimum of 100 miles away from home within the United States or stays one or more nights in paid accommodations regardless of the distance away from home" (Frechtling, 1994).

Selection of data collection methods. Once the purpose and scope of an economic impact study (i.e., the cause and source of impact and the impact region are determined) is clearly defined, the next step in the planning process of the study is to determine the most appropriate and comprehensive method or approach for data collection. As indicated previously, the investigator may wish to investigate several important sources of impact. Nevertheless, the decision regarding which data to collect and how to collect them should be based on what the researcher wants to accomplish in a particular impact study as well as on the availability of resources (Delpy & Li, 1998). The methodology adopted by the researcher dictates the kind of information to be collected. In general, there are two ways to estimate the magnitude of the economic impact: the survey methods and nonsurvey method (Behavior Research Center, 1993; Datapol, Inc., 1988; Division of Research, 1990; Fleming & Toepper, 1990; Murphy & Carmicheal, 1991; Schaffer & Davidson, 1976; Turco, 1993, 1995; Wang & Irwin, 1993).

The survey method is commonly used in the economic impact studies in sport. It is a research technique in which data are collected from a sample of visitors, such as spectators and participants, by using a questionnaire. From the responses, researchers usually obtain information about visitors' expenditures and their demographic characteristics. Visitors' expenditures are considered the basic components in estimating the total economic wealth injected by the visitors into a particular community or region. In practice, the survey method consists of four data-collection approaches: on-site interview, telephone interview, self-administered survey, and expenditure logs. Table 7-3 summarizes the merits and shortcomings of various survey methods.

On-site interviews are conducted in some high-traffic areas (e.g., entrances and exits, spectator seating areas, concession stands). There, interviewers intercept visitors to collect the needed research data. Telephone interviews are often conducted after an activity or event. Based on the information obtained from registration, such as the home address and phone number, the interviewer randomly identifies some visitors and interviews them on the phone. The interviewees are asked to recall and provide information about their spending associated with the activity. Self-administered survey is implemented by placing questionnaires in several high-traffic areas, including the entrances and exits, concession stands, and information booths around the event site. A certain incentive is used to encourage visitors to complete the survey instruments. Expenditure logs and diaries are also utilized by researchers in various economic impact studies. Prior to the activity, the surveyor identifies and contacts a number of visitors to determine their willingness to participate in an economic impact survey. Again, an incentive is generally offered. Those who agree to cooperate are asked to keep track of their expenditures with a diary over the period of their visit to the region where the activity is held and to mail the diary back to the surveyor after returning home (Delpy & Li, 1998).

Table 7-3. Summary of the Merits and Shortcomings of Various Survey Methodologies

Methods	Merits	Shortcomings
Survey		
On-site interview	Opportunity for feedback	Cost
	High participation	Labor intensive
	High completion of survey	Projection bias
Telephone interview	Opportunity for feedback	Cost
	Absence of face-to-face contact	Sample bias
Self-administered survey	Recall and response bias	
On-site self drop-off survey	Low labor intensity	Low return rate
	No interviewer bias	Response and projection bias
Mail survey	Low labor intensity	Low return rate
	No interviewer bias	Recall and response rate
	A representative sample	Cost
Expenditure logs or diaries	Most reliable and accurate	High mortality rate
		Low response rate
Non-survey method		
Interview with event/facility	Pre-event	Attribution error
or business managers/owners	Low cost	Accessibility to private records
Public tax records	Low cost	Time delay
		Limited information

Notes: This table is modified from the one developed by Turco (Turco, D. W. (1995) 'Measuring the Economic Impact of a Sporting Event', paper presented at the 1995 North American Society for Sport Management Annual Conference, Athens, GA).

Although the nonsurvey method, sometimes also referred as the *eco-metric* method, is adopted to determine the impact figure, various means are utilized to obtain data to use in estimating the generated benefits that accrue to economic areas in the form of payroll, employment, and taxes (Fleming & Toepper, 1990; Pomeroy, Uysal & Lamberte, 1988; Stynes, 1999b). No surveys are needed. Instead, the data are mainly obtained from secondary sources of information (e.g., government sources and similar studies). One example of the nonsurvey method is the so-called LOCI model or the Local Area Impact Model developed by the Georgia Tech Economic Development Institute. The LOCI model incorporates two sets of secondary local data into impact calculation: community-related data and project-related data. The community related data include

1. Taxes (sales, personal and real property, business, alcohol, income);
2. Utility information water, wastewater, solid waste removal, electric, natural gas);
3. Retail activity (effective buying income);
4. Demographic information (disposable income, number of household, employment);

5. Economic base information (discount rate, total personal income); and
6. Tourism-related information (lodging excise tax rate, revenue and value added for tourism-related industries). (Kanters, 1999, p.6)

The following are project-related data:

1. Information on the construction of the facility (materials, labor, percentage local purchases, development subsidies);
2. Operation of the facility (sales, percentage of sales subject to sales taxes);
3. Specific multipliers for income and employment calculated for the industry in question and the county under investigation (input-output model);
4. Utilities rates and consumption;
5. Employee characteristics; and
6. Tourism information (number of visitors, duration of stay, average of daily expenditures). (Kanters, 1999, p. 7)

The tourism-related information is estimated through comparisons of the facility studies with those of similar facilities. The major advantage of the nonsurvey method is that it eases the difficulty in estimating the economic impact of hallmark events, such as the Olympic Games, on the host region. Due to the scale of those events in terms of the number of participants, spectators, and other types of visitors, it is uneconomical and difficult, if not impossible, to use the survey methods for obtaining the needed expenditure data. Nevertheless, using the nonsurvey method requires the provision of detailed input information for accuracy in estimation (Wang & Irwin, 1993). Table 7-4 provides brief descriptions of four basic methods or approaches of data collection in economic impact analysis in terms of how to collect needed expenditure information and how to derive multipliers for analysis and estimation.

Table 7-4. Methods/Approaches to Economic Impact Assessment

Level	Activity	Spending	Multiplier
1—Judgement	Expert judgement to estimate activity	Expert judgement	Expert judgement to estimate multipliers
2	Existing counts for the area or total estimates from a similar area or facility	Use or adjust spending averages from studies of a similar area	Use or adjust aggregate spending multipliers from a similar region/study
3	Estimate activity by segment or revise estimates by segment from another area	Adjust spending that is disaggregated within particular spending categories	Use sector-specific multipliers from published sources
4—Primary Data	Visitor survey to estimate number of visitors by segment or a demand model	Survey random sample of visitors to estimate average spending by segment and spending category	Use an input-output model of the region's economy

Source: Stynes, D. J. (1999). Economic impacts of tourism. Bulletins on Concepts and Methods, Department of Parks, Recreation, and Tourism Resources, Michigan State University, Lansing, Michigan

Collection and analysis of data. Because the survey method is the most frequently used in the economic impact research in sport, we will mainly discuss how to use this method in the data collection and analysis section. Information regarding the number of visitors to the region, the size of each visitor group, and on average, the amount each visitor group has spent in such categories as lodging, food and beverage, local transportation, entertainment, admission to the event, and miscellaneous retails must be collected through a survey. Once the needed data have been collected, a series of computations are followed. First, the total expenditure of visitors in each spending category needs to be determine using the two formulas shown below (Turco, 1996):

Total Categorical Expenditure = *ADS* x *Number of Groups* x *Average Number of Days*

Where:

Average Daily Spending = The average daily spending of all visitor groups in each concerned category, such as lodging, food and beverage, etc.

Number of Groups = The number of groups of visitors

Average Number of Days = The average number of days of all visitor groups stayed in the impact region

Dividing the total number of visitors by the average group size, we can obtain the number of visitor groups. The average number of days that all visitor groups stayed in the impact region is determined by dividing the total number of days they stayed by the number of visitor groups. The sum of the total categorical expenditure of all concerned spending categories is the total direct impact.

Determining the secondary effects is the next step if the researcher is interested in the ripple effects of visitor spending, or the effects of the sum of the indirect and induced impacts. The ripple effects are determined by multiplying the total categorical expenditures with respective multipliers obtained either from an input-output model (e.g., IMPLAN) or from published studies done in the same region. As we know, the total economic impact is usually estimated in three areas: (a) total output, (b) total earning, and (c) total

Table 7-5. The Secondary Effects of the Spending of Visitors to the Savannah Open Golf Tournament

Expenditure Category	Total Spending	Indirect Effect[1]	Induced Effect[2]	Output Multiplier[3]	Total Output
Lodging	$4,000,000	$1,161,160	$1,623,452	1.699893	$ 6,799,572
Food & Beverage	$3,500,000	$1,029,102	$1,420,521	1.699893	$ 5,949,636
Retail Shopping	$1,500,000	$ 441,044	$ 608,795	1.699893	$ 2,549,840
Total	$9,000,000	$2,631,306	$3,652,768		$15,299,048

Note:
1. The indirect effect coefficient is 0.294029.
2. The induced effect coefficient is 0.405863.
3. It is a Type II output multiplier.

employment. The process may be understood better with an example. The calculation of the total visitor spending in a golf tournament held recently in Savannah yields a total spending of $4 million in lodging, $3.5 million in food and beverage, and $1.5 million in retail shopping. The secondary effects of visitor spending, or the sum of the indirect and induced impacts of the spending on total output, are shown in Table 7-5.

As Table 7-5 indicates, the total direct spending of visitors to the golf tournament is $9 million. As a result of considering the production changes resulting from various rounds of respending of the money by the affected industries (e.g., hotels, restaurants, and retail stores) and the changes in economic activity resulting from the spending of income by the employees of the affected industries, the total output or impact becomes over $15 million. The difference between the total direct spending and the total output, or approximately $6 million, is the secondary effect.

In addition to estimating the impact created by the spending of visitors in total output, total earning, total employment of the affected region, the researcher should look at the local sales tax impact to obtain a comprehensive view on the effect of a sport activity or event. The local sales tax impact can be felt from three main areas: retail, lodging, and gasoline. Due to the difference in tax rates, the local sales tax impact in each of these three areas must be calculated separately. Their sum is the total local sales tax impact. The calculation usually follows such a formula:

Tax Revenue = Total Spending of Visitors in One of the Three Areas x Local Tax Rate

For example, the visitors to the 1997 world series champions of the North American Gay Amateur Athletic Alliance held in San Francisco spent roughly $658,000 on lodging, and the tax rate for hotel accommodation is 16%. So the tax revenue from the visitors is $105,280.

Turco (1995) suggests using the "return on investment" (ROI) to examine the financial return of spending by the government of a community on a certain sport activity or event if it is organized by a unit of the government, such as the parks and recreation department. The return on investment is estimated with the following formula:

ROI = (ER + LTR)/EE

Where

ER = Event Revenue

LTR = Local Tax Revenue Generated

EE = Event Expenditures

For example, the parks and recreation department of the City of Statesboro/Bulloch County in July 1999 sponsored a state softball tournament from which the department generated $34,000 in operating revenue. Visitors from all over the state brought in $2,400 tax revenue. For preparing the tournament, the parks and recreation department spent $32,000. The ROI in this case is 114%, or add $34,000 and $2,400 and then divide the sum by $32,000. The return on investment has been used by many local sport organizations as a leverage for receiving discounted services from other local government units, such as police and emergency medical rescue (Turco, 1995).

Interpretation of the data or the total impact. After completing tedious calculations to determine the magnitude of the impact on output, earning, and employment, the researcher must present this information in language that concerned individuals, such as local politicians and the management of a sports event, can understand. Those people usually do not have adequate training and or background to comprehend the abstract impact numbers. Interpreting the results is an important task that the researcher should not overlook. The interpretation should focus on total output, total earning, and total employment and should explain what they mean. Table 7-6 shows the economic impact of the 1990 MCI Heritage Classic on the Hilton Head area (The Division of Research, 1990).

As Table 7-6 indicates, the direct spending of the two spending categories is $13,652,878. The total output, total earning, and total employment effects are $18,988,183, $6,029,097, and 616, respectively. That means, as a result of the approximately $13.7 million spent by visitors (both the out-of-town attendees and the event sponsors' patrons) in Hilton Head Island as final demand, the total value of production or output in all industrial sectors of that economy increased by about $19 million, or 1:1.39 ratio. That is, for every new dollar injected, the production of the industries in the island as a whole increased 39 cents in their output. The $6,029,097 is the change in wages and salaries of households in Hilton Head Island as a result of the spending of $13,652,878 by visitors. The $13.7 million is the new wealth injected into the area, which may have some impact on the earning of local residents. As the region gains more wealth, its residents may expect some increase in their income. The total employment effect implies that 616 jobs could be created in Hilton Head due to the addition of new money in amount of $13.7 million. These could be full-time, part-time or seasonal jobs.

Significance of Economic Impact Studies

When an economic impact study should be conducted and why it should be conducted are two questions have come to the attention of many concerned economists in the sport, tourism, and other related industries due to the growing in popularity of studies of this type. Commonly, economic impact studies in the sport industry are conducted for three reasons (Crompton, 1995; Delpy & Li, 1998; Turco, 1995):

1. To examine the cost and benefits of an economic endeavor or financial investment to determine if it is worthwhile. For example, the advocates in Tampa, Florida, who

Table 7-6. Economic Impact of the 1990 MCI Heritage Classic on Hilton Head Island[1]

Spending Category[2]	Spending Level	Output Effect	Earning Effect	Employment Effect
Classic Tournament Attendees	$12,267,778	$16,742,110	$5,306,373	544
Sponsors and Patrons	1,385,100	2,246,073	722,724	72
Total	$13,652,878	$18,988,183	$6,029,097	616

Note:
1. The results are obtained from the study entitled "The Economic Impact of the MCI Heritage Classic on the Economy of Hilton Head Island, South Carolina" conducted by the Division of Research, College of Business Administration at the University of South Carolina, Columbia, South Carolina.
2. This table includes only the spending of tournament attendees, and sponsors and patrons.

supported the use of public funds to build the Raymond James Stadium for the Tampa Buccaneers may conduct an economic impact study to justify their position. Through the study, they could find such information as the increased number of visitors to the area and the increased local business sales. On the other hand, the City of Tampa and surrounding counties can also use the study to justify their decision in public subsidies by showing the amount of "new dollars" injected into the community as a result of building the facility.

2. To use the results of an economic impact study to influence legislators and lobby for more legislative support. It is common for a local park and recreation department to use the results of an economic impact study to justify its request for increasing local budget appropriation. The impact study may provide the department with information in terms of how many out-of-town teams visited and used its facility, how long the visiting teams stayed on average, and how much the local businesses have been benefited from those visiting teams.

3. To raise public awareness of the importance of the sport industry. An economic impact study can help city or county government officials or the local business community develop an understanding pertaining to what the sport industry as a whole can do to the region's economy so that the government and the private sector can work together to use the sport industry to its full potential.

Common Errors in Sport Economic Impact Studies

Many errors have been found in sport economic impact studies. For example, in order to get the total output impact, some researchers simply multiply the total number of visitors by the output multiplier. The following section will specifically discuss several of the commonly detected errors (Crompton, 1995; Stynes, 1999b).

Not clearly defining a cause or action. The basic purpose of an economic impact study is to estimate the net change in the affected economy due to the injection of "new money." To properly attribute the change in economy, the cause of the injection should be first determined. In determining the reason for the change, the researcher must decide if the study only focuses on the spending by visitors or also on the spending of the event organizer for capital improvement and on the spending by government, etc. This is especially true when the impact study is done for a hallmark event like the Olympic Games. The organizer, such as the Atlanta Committee for Olympic Games (ACOG), usually spends a considerable amount of money on construction or renovation of sport facilities (capital improvement). Part of the funds used for that purpose might be obtained from outside the designated region (e.g., a bank loan or prepaid sponsorships).

Not clearly defining an impact region. One crucial step in conducting an economic impact study is to define the impact region. As we know, the major purpose of an economic impact study is to estimate the economic benefits that accrue to a host community by visitors. So the definition of a region would provide a researcher with clues to determine who are visitors and who are local residents so that the researcher can separate the spending by visitors from the spending by local residents. Without clearly defining the impact region, such a separation would become an impossible task. The inclusion of local spending inflates the impact attributed to a sport activity. Defining the size of a region is another related issue. The smaller the region, the more likely for some local residents to be regarded as visitors.

Using inappropriate multipliers. Multipliers have been used by various economic impact studies inappropriately in many ways. The most common error is to adapt a statewide multiplier to a local region, which may inflate the ripple or secondary effect because the statewide multiplier is always bigger (sometimes substantially bigger) than that of a particular locale within the state and the economy of a state is always larger than that of the locale. As mentioned earlier, the larger a defined economy is, the more interindustrial purchases will occur among industrial sectors within the economy. The more interactions among industrial sectors, the more self-sufficient the economy (less leaking of the injected money), consequently, the larger the multiplier. The multiplier is always higher in a self-sufficient economy than in a small and specialized economy.

Misinterpretating employment multipliers. Many economic impact studies attempt not only to estimate the total spending by visitors and its direct effect on the concerned region, but also to convert the estimate on total spending by visitors to income and employment. This conversion may yield such approximation in terms of how much income is generated and how many employment opportunities are created as a result of organizing a sport activity or providing a sport service. For example, the multiplication of the total spending by visitors with an aggregated employment multiplier suggests that an annual sport event may create 100 jobs in the economy. This number, however, needs to be interpreted very carefully. These jobs are not full-time equivalents, but seasonal and part-time. The demand for labor for an event of this type is usually met by the local existing labor force or by volunteers. Local residents may work overtime or use their vacation hours to work for the event. Exaggeration of the number of "full-time equivalent" jobs created by a sport activity has been seen as another common error.

Not isolating spending by visitors from spending by local residents. In estimating the impact magnitude of a sport activity or event to the economy of a host community, some studies have included the spending of local residents in their calculation. This inclusion inflates the economic benefits brought about by a sport activity because the money spent by local residents in the impact region is not "new dollars" to the region. If the residents had not spent the money on the activity, they would have used it in other ways or for other forms of entertainment in the region. If a study wants to determine the economic significance of a sport activity, the spending of local residents with the event can be obtained. The data, however, should be interpreted separately.

Including all spending by visitors in impact calculation. If an economic impact study includes the spending by visitors on purchases made outside the impact region, such as the spending on side-trips out of the designated region during an event, the impact figure would be incorrectly inflated. For example, a family of four from Michigan attended the MCI Classic –Heritage of Golf Tournament held in Hilton Head Island for a week. While staying in Hilton Head, they took a side-trip to Savannah and spent a day there. The expenditure incurred from the Savannah trip should be excluded from the calculation of the family's total spending attributed to the tournament. Another mistake often made related to the inclusion of all spending by visitors is including in the calculation some money that visitors pay for the trip to the region where the activity is held. The money in most cases will not be allocated back to the impact region. A good example is the package deal for an event that includes a round-trip airline ticket, a couple nights of hotel accommodation, and a ticket to the event. It is very difficult, if not impossible, to determine how much or what portion of the money will be paid by the travel agency to affected businesses in the designated region. Inclusion in entirety of the payment for the package again exaggerates the actual benefit received by the region. The error most commonly committed by researchers in economic impact studies is to include all retail spending without taking consideration of the price paid by the retailer to get the goods from outside the region. For instance, while attending the MCI Classic–Heritage of Golf Tournament, a visitor bought a T-shirt from a local retailer for $50. The retailer, in fact, only paid $20 to get the shirt from a wholesaler in Atlanta. So the actual injection of "new dollars" is the difference of the retail price and the wholesale cost, or $30. It is believed that only 60–70% of visitors' spending can be considered as final demand in a region (Stynes, 1999b).

Summary

In this chapter, we provided information about how to properly conduct an economic impact study. The theoretical foundation of economic impact studies—the input-output technique—was first discussed and examined, followed by a detailed description of the procedural steps in terms of how to execute an economic impact study. These steps include (a) determination of the purpose and scope of the impact study, (b) selection of data collection methods, (c) collection and analysis of data, and (d) interpretation and report of the results. In this chapter, we also explained why researchers conduct economic impact studies as well as the common errors committed in executing economic impact research.

Chapter Questions

1. Discuss the nature of the I-O Technique and explain why it is the theoretical foundation of economic impact research.
2. Discuss the multiplier effect.
3. List three types of multipliers that are commonly utilized in economic impact research and explain what each of them means.
4. List and define three components of the short-term economic impact.
5. Compare and contrast the merits and shortcomings of the four types of survey methods used in the economic impact studies in sport.
6. Explain how to determine the induced and total impacts.
7. Why conduct an economic impact study? Give at least three reasons.

Chapter Eight

An Overview of the Market for Labor

Labor, capital, and land are three factors of production. They are used as inputs into production activities, and they generate income for their owners. Labor is considered the most important factor of production in any form of economic activity (Parkin, 1993). Professional athletes, sales representatives of sporting goods retail stores, and employees of sports facilities are examples of labor, and they are critical contributors to the economy of the sport industry. This chapter mainly examines labor as a factor of production in the sport industry. First, an overview of the labor market and related important concepts will be provided. In the second half of the chapter, specific labor issues in the sport industry will be discussed.

The Demand for Labor

Labor is demanded as a factor of production to help produce goods and services. The demand for labor is, therefore, considered a *derived demand*, which means the demand for labor is, in fact, derived from the demand of consumers for the goods and services that the labor can produce. The amount that labor can produce is a critical determinant of demand. The amount of the demand for labor also depends on other factors such as technology and market condition as well as the objectives of a business firm. The more technology a firm uses in production, the less labor it will demand. For example, a computerized production line for athletic shoes may reduce the demand for labor who would otherwise be hired to manually assemble parts. The higher the demand from consumers for a certain product, the more labor the firm that produces the product needs. For example, after Mark McGwire shattered the home run record in 1998, the St. Louis Cardinals fans rushed to the souvenir stands and bought anything that might commemorate the record-breaking day. Such enthusiasm and high level of demand caused a shortage of the supply of McGwire-related merchandise. This sort of demand, in turn, puts high pressure on the firms that manufacture these products to hire more temporary workers and quickly expand their outputs.

> ***Labor Market Issues***
>
> *On February 24, 2000, the owners of the Arena Football League demanded that the players form a union and engage in collective bargaining on the terms and conditions of employment. The reason for the owners' action was obvious: to avoid the antitrust problem. Earlier, the owners as a group had decided to introduce a new system that would have substantially trimmed players' free agency rights. A group of players challenged the decision in the court, claiming that the owners had violated the antitrust law. To defend themselves against the lawsuit, the owners urge the players to form a union (M. Miller, 2000). Why would forming a player's union help the owners?*

Profit maximization, as discussed in chapter 2, is one of the major objectives of a firm. The pursuit of profit maximization requires the firm to constantly evaluate its economic strategies in production in terms of how to produce and what its demand is for labor. In general, a profit-maximizing firm, no matter whether it is in a perfectly competitive market or in a monopoly, always sets its output level at a point where marginal cost equals marginal revenue. On the other hand, as chapter 4 defines it, a monopoly is a market situation in which there is a single seller of a product with no close substitutes. So if the addition of labor affects more of the change in total revenue than total cost of production, the firm would maximize its profit at which the additional cost for producing one more unit of output equals the additional revenue as a result of producing this extra unit of output (Parkin, 1993).

When discussing the demand for labor, *marginal revenue product* is a concept that must be understood first. It is defined as "the net addition to total revenue attributable to the addition of one unit of the variable productive services or the dollar value of the marginal product of an input" (Shim & Siegel, 1995, p. 226). For example, employing another worker in the shoe assembly line of a sporting goods factory will result in more shoes produced per hour, and these shoes in turn will be sold to generate revenue. Therefore, how many employees a profit-maximizing firm will hire depends on when the marginal revenue product of the hired employees equals the marginal cost of them. In a competitive labor market, the marginal cost of labor is the same as the market wages that the firm pays to hire those employees. In a monopoly labor market, the monopoly firm faces a negatively sloped demand curve. However, in a perfectly competitive market, the same firm may face a horizontal demand curve for its product because regardless of what output level the firm chooses, it will face a fixed price for its product.

Learning Activities

1. As a group project, develop a research proposal on how to estimate the marginal revenue product of professional soccer players.
2. Return to the beginning of the chapter, and reread the scenario. Then debate the advantages and disadvantages of having a players' union in a professional sport league.

Table 8-1 shows how to calculate the marginal revenue product of labor. Assume the XYZ Sporting Goods Factory operates in a perfectly competitive market. Recently, the firm de-

Table 8-1. Marginal Revenue Product and Average Revenue Product at XYZ Sporting Goods Factory

Quantity of Labor (L) (number of workers)	Output (Q) (bicycles assembled per hour)	Marginal Product (MP) (bicycles assembled per worker)	Total Revenue (TR) (dollars)	Marginal Revenue Product (MRP) (dollars per worker)	Average Revenue Product (ARP) (dollars per worker)
0	0		0		
		 5		 400	
1	5		400		400
		 4		 320	
2	9		720		360
		 3		 240	
3	12		960		320
		 2		 160	
4	14		1120		280
		 1		 80	
5	15		1200		240

veloped a new line of bicycles called "Rock." A popular Olympic medalist in cycling soon endorses the product. Because of the endorsement, consumer demand for the bicycle is high, and the firm can sell as many as it makes to the sporting goods retail stores nationwide at a price of $80 a bicycle. The total revenue of the firm earned from the selling of the bicycles is the product of the number of bicycles sold multiplied by $80. For example, $1,200 dollars would be the total revenue if 15 bicycles were assembled and sold. The marginal revenue product of each worker in the bicycle assembly line is shown in the fifth column. As this column indicates, the marginal revenue product of labor decreases as more workers are hired. When there is only one worker, the marginal revenue product of labor is $400. It falls to $320 when a second worker is added to the assembly line. So, marginal revenue product is a measure of the economic value of hiring an additional unit of input (worker) in the production process that derives from the value of the final good or service being produced. In general, as more and more of a variable input is added to production, the marginal product of that input will decline. The decline in marginal product as more input is added will cause the decline in marginal revenue product.

The marginal revenue product can also be calculated by multiplying marginal product (MP), shown in the third column, by marginal revenue (MR), which equals the sales price in a perfectly competitive market. The marginal product of hiring a second worker is four bicycles, and $80 is the marginal revenue. The product of these two numbers is $320, the same as the result obtained by multiplying the output (Q) with the marginal revenue, a process shown by the following formula:

$$MRP(X) = MP(X) \times MR(Q)$$

The marginal revenue product of labor can be illustrated by a curve, shown in Figure 8-1. The curve shows the marginal revenue product of labor at each quantity of workers hired.

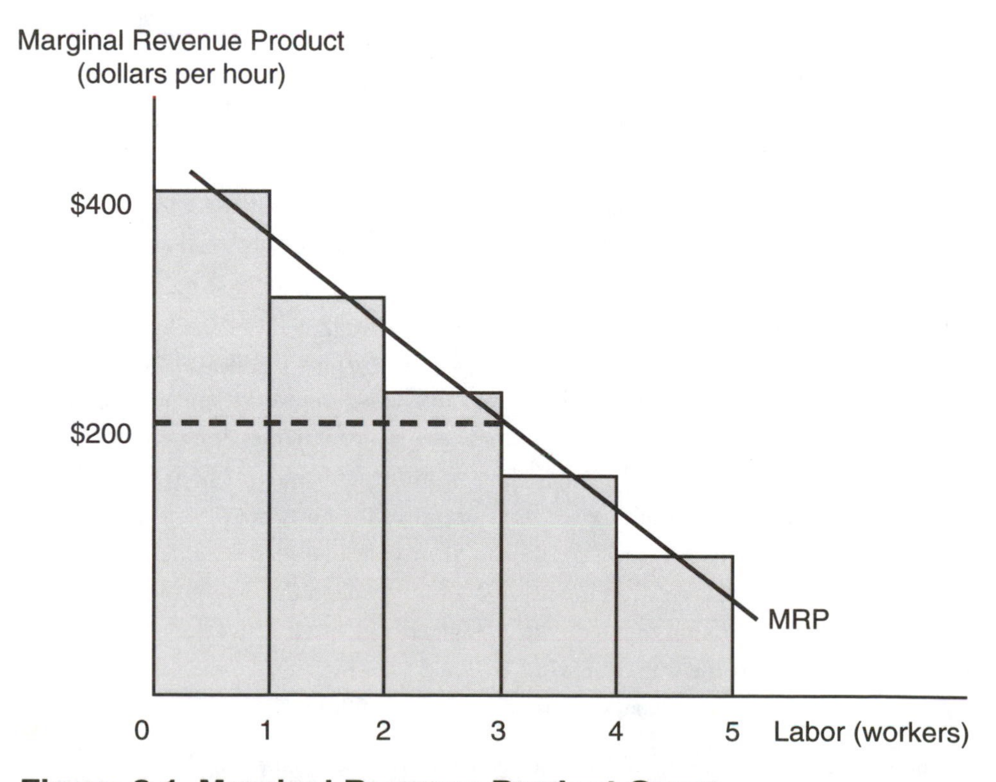

Figure 8-1. Marginal Revenue Product Curve

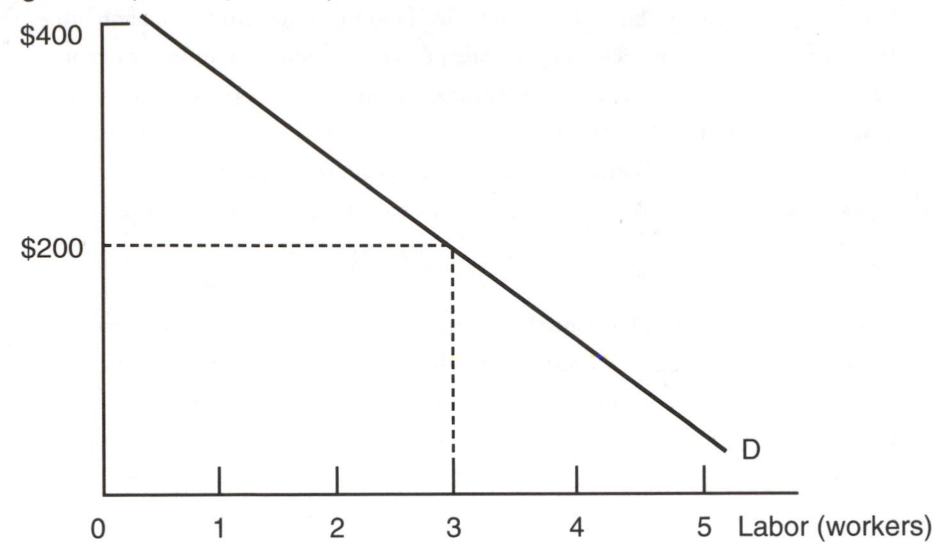

Figure 8-2. Demand for Labor Curve

The firm's demand for labor can also be shown in a graph (Figure 8-2). If we compare these two figures and look closely, we may find that they are identical. The explanation of this phenomenon is that because the firm hires the profit-maximizing quantity of labor, the firm will keep bringing in one more worker if the cost of the hiring (the wage rate) is less than the marginal revenue product of labor contributed by this additional worker. When the wage rate equals the marginal revenue of product of labor, the firm maximizes its profit potential, and it would be no incentive for the firm to hire one more worker. The quantity of labor demanded in a competitive market by all firms depends on several factors, including the market wage rate, the price of the product produced, and the prices of substitute workers.

The Supply of Labor

Let us reiterate this point. That is, labor is the single most important factor of production. There are two types of activities that a household is engaged in daily: market activity and nonmarket activities (Parkin, 1993). Market activity refers to the activity in which the household is engaged for a wage or the household's supplying of labor to the labor market for income. Nonmarket activities, on the other hand, are those committed by the household for leisure pursuit, education and training, and household works. The household decides how much time to devote to each of these two major activities, both of which have a certain value and can bring either immediate or future returns to the household. Participation in educational and training activities improves the household's skills in a certain occupation and, thus, its value in the labor market. Increased market value may mean a higher wage rate. In economic terms, leisure is a form of good that has its own value. For a household to provide labor to the market, a high enough or attractive wage rate must be offered. That is to say, the wage rate must be equal to or higher than the value perceived by the household for the nonmarket activities (Parkin, 1993).

As mentioned earlier, a household must often choose between supplying labor for market activities or pursuing nonmarket activities. In this section, we mainly examine the process used by the household in contemplating the choice between supplying labor and pursuing leisure. As Figure 8-3 shows, W_0 is the initial hourly wage for the household that supplies labor to the market, and at that point, the household is not engaged in any leisure activity at all. L is the point where the time of the household is completely devoted to leisure (24 hours a day), and no market activities are done and, of course, no wage is earned as well. The line W_0L symbolizes the budget constraints experienced by the household. Assume a is the point at which the household is happy about the income earned (the line OLa reveals the hours the household needs to work) and the time the household has for leisure (the line LaL). If the wage rate is increased from W_0 to W_1, the household's budget constraint line becomes W_1L. If Point c is chosen, it may imply that the household decides to devote more time to work and spend less time for leisure. On the contrary, if Point b is picked, it reveals that the household would rather work fewer hours at a higher wage rate, compared to point a.

To induce more households to supply labor, a higher and more attractive wage rate needs to be offered. A wage rate that is higher than the value perceived by the households on the last hour they spend in nonmarket activities would persuade some people to cut down their time for nonmarket activities and to enter the labor market. Nevertheless, two offsetting effects result from the increased wage rate: (a) the substitution effect and (b) the income effect. The substitution effect refers to "the effect of a change in price on the quantities consumed when the consumer remains indifferent between the original and the new combination of goods consumed" (Parkin, 1993, p. 1070). In other words, the substitution effect occurs when a household realizes that the return from engaging in a market activity is greater than the value generated from a nonmarket activity, so the household will

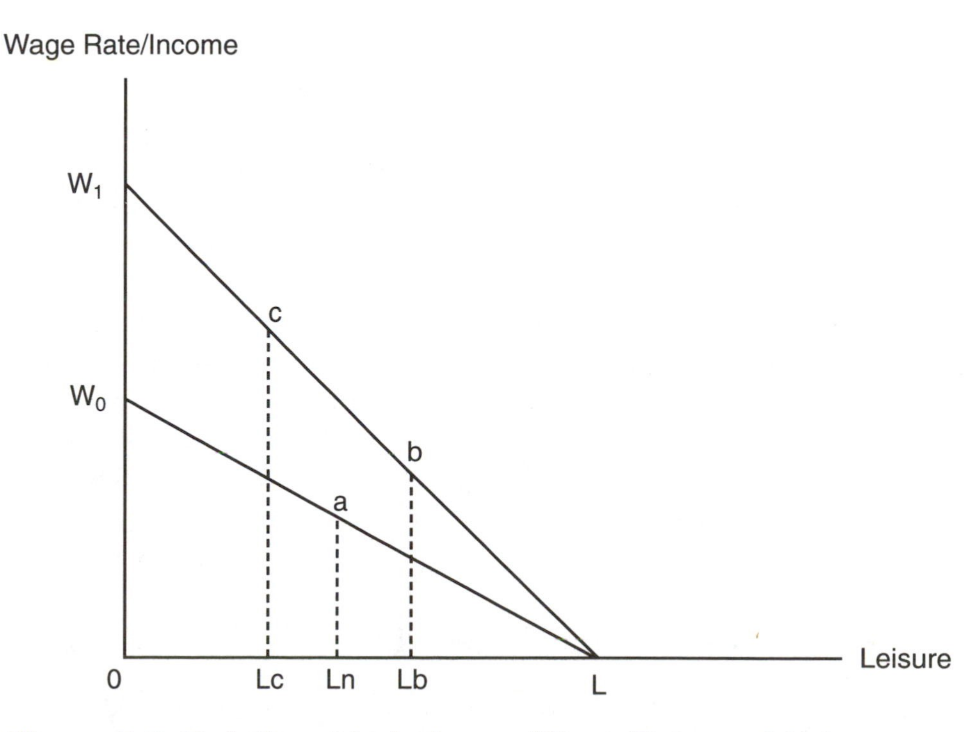

Figure 8-3. Relationship between Wage Rate and Leisure

Adapted from Southwick, L., Jr. (1985) *Managerial Economics*. Plano, TX: Business Publications, Inc.

commit more time to the market activity. For example, a stay-at-home parent who graduated from a college with an accounting degree used to take two sons to afternoon soccer practice. Recently, the demand in the local labor market for people with accounting skills has risen due to the drastic increase in the number of new businesses, and an accountant's hourly wage rate is $20. The parent believes that it would be to the family's best economic interest to go back to work. So the parent takes a job and hires a college student to take care of the two sons, including taking them to soccer practice.

The income effect is "the effect of a change in income on consumption" (Parkin, 1993, p. 1063). As mentioned above, a higher wage rate may attract a household to supply labor and to render more time to market activities. The direct consequence is an increase in household income. The increase in household income will lead to an increased household demand for goods, including leisure, which in economic terms is a form of good. The pursuit of leisure may force the household to trim down the time committed to market activities.

According to Southwick (1985), the increase in wages in a certain occupation will attract more households to move into the labor market or will motivate more people to acquire the needed education or training for that occupation. These two effects will ultimately change the shape of the demand back to the usual one in the long run.

Competitive Labor Markets

In chapter 4, we discussed important parameters under which organizations and firms operate in one of the four basic market structures (i.e., perfect competition, monopoly, oligopoly, and monopolistic competition) and how those parameters affect their managerial decisions. In the following section, we will discuss these market structures as well as those parameters pertaining to demand and supply of labor.

Perfectly competitive labor market. In a perfectly competitive labor market, both the demand for and supply of labor are high. Each firm faces a perfectly elastic supply of labor because each firm is just part of the total labor market and it has no influence on the wage rate (Parkin, 1993). If the supply of labor is perfectly elastic, it means that the percentage change in quantity of labor supplied is substantially greater than the percentage change in the wage rate received by labor. According to Boal and Ransom (1997), if labor supply in a market is perfectly elastic, individual firms have zero monopsony power (the concept of monopsony power will be discussed later). For example, imagine there are three rival professional football leagues in the United States. No collusion has been found among them for joint profit maximization, and talented players can freely move from one league to the other without any constraint. Each of the leagues involved in the situation cannot engage in wage discrimination by offering the so-called "reservation wages" or the wages that are lower than their market value due to the competition encountered in the market from the other two leagues for the players. One factor that contributes to this perfect elasticity is the number of firms that exist in the market. That is, the more leagues in the same sport, the greater is the elasticity of supply of labor. More detailed discussion will be provided in the following section, "Competitive Labor Markets and Rival Leagues."

Monopsonistic labor markets. A monopsony refers to a market structure in which there is just a single buyer. In a labor market, if there is only one employer for all labor, it is a monopsonistic labor market, and the employer is a monopsonist. For example, the National Football League (NFL) is a monopsonist because it is the only firm that employs professional football players at the major league level. Because it is the only firm that will employ labor in a particular labor market, the monopsonist can capitalize on the situation and make greater profit than can those firms that operate in a competitive labor market. Let us use an illustration (Figure 8-4) to substantiate this point. In Figure 8-4, MCL represents the marginal cost of labor curve, and MRP is the monopsonist's marginal revenue product curve, which coincides with the demand curve for labor. Marginal revenue product is defined as "the amount of added sales revenue derived from employment of an additional unit of input or factor of production." S is the supply curve for labor. From this curve, we know that the monopolist has to pay a higher wage rate in order to bring in more labor. Obviously, this is not a profitable option for the firm. The monopsonist may be better off if it employs fewer workers and pays them at a lower wage rate. The monopsonist can achieve this by setting the marginal revenue product equal to marginal cost of labor. As Figure 8-4 shows, when MCL equals MRP, the monopsonist employs 50 hours of labor, and the hourly rate is $5.00. An economic profit of $5.00 is, therefore, actualized by the firm because the marginal revenue product of labor is $10.00 per hour.

"The ability of a monopsonist to make an economic profit depends on the elasticity of labor supply. The more elastic the supply of labor, the less opportunity a monopsonist has to make an economic profit" (Parkin, 1993, p. 415). However, regardless of the market situation, the supply of labor to a firm does not fall instantaneously to zero if the firm cuts wages. This gives the firm some monopsony power. In the absence of labor unions, a profit-maximizing firm will set a wage below the marginal revenue product of labor so that workers are exploited.

Bilateral monopoly. Bilateral monopoly is "a market in which a single buyer and a single seller bargain to determine the wage rate and market price of a good or service" (Shim &

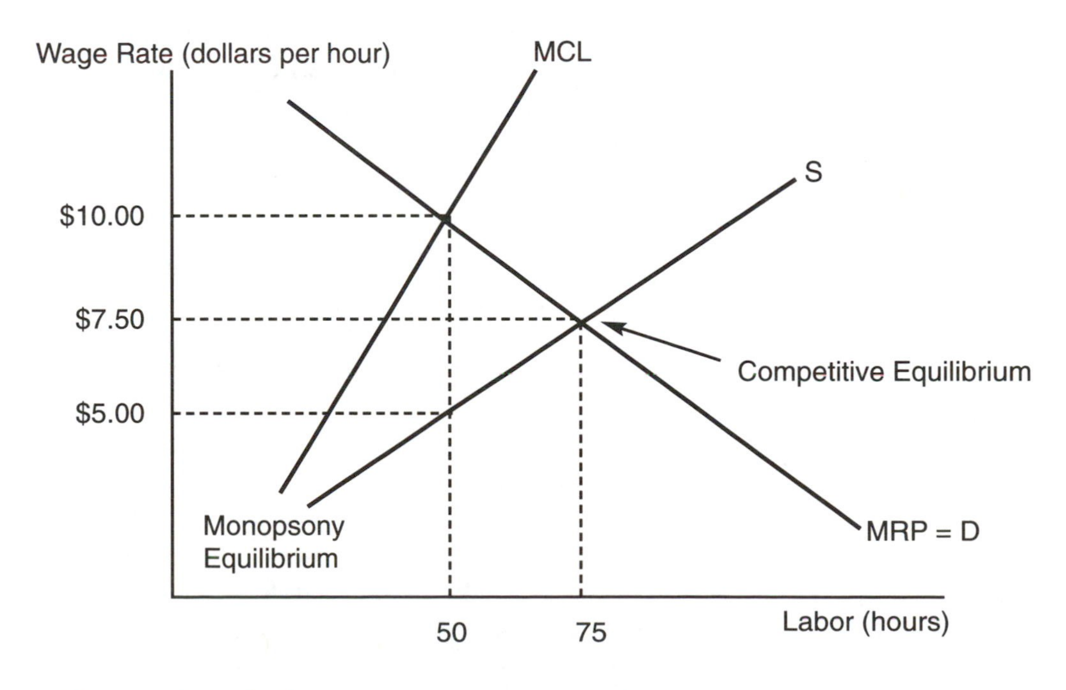

Figure 8-4. A Monopsony Labor Market

Siegel, 1995, p. 34). To better understand this concept, it is necessary to discuss who are the buyer and seller in that particular market. The buyer is a firm that purchases services from the households who supply labor and the seller is a labor union, which is an organized group of workers. The goal of a labor union is to maximize economic gains of its members. Specifically, it attempts to increase workers' compensation (e.g., wages, fringe benefits, retirement pay), to improve working condition (e.g., a health and safe working environment), and to expand job opportunities (e.g., job security). To achieve these objectives, a labor union tends to act like a monopolist in the labor market to restrict competition (Parkin, 1993; Southwick, 1985). The union represents the affiliated workers to negotiate with the management of the firm that buys the labor from those workers in a process called collective bargaining.

The National Labor Relations Act passed by the U.S. Congress in 1935 forms the legal foundation for union representation and collective bargaining. (The impact of the National Labor Relations Act of 1935 on the sport industry will be discussed in greater detail later in this chapter.) The Act grants labor unions the following three basic rights:

1. The right to self-organization, to form, join, or assist labor organizations;
2. The right to bargain collectively through representatives of their own choosing; and
3. The right to engage in "concerted activities" for employees' mutual aid or protection (Staudohar, 1989, p. 11).

With these three rights, the union can collectively bargain with management for its members and can use a strike or other pressure tactics to gain a better position in the collective bargaining process. The main strategy for the firm to use as a weapon in the collective bargaining process is the lockout, in which the firm stops its operation and refuses to continue to hire its workers. The 1998–1999 NBA lockout imposed by the owners illustrates the use of this pressure tactic.

Labor Markets in the Sport Industry

In the sport industry, especially the professional sports segment, players are workers. They are employed by a specific team or a league, or they are self-employed. The labor-market-related issues in the sport industry are reviewed with two situations: (a) the athletes as employees and (b) the athletes as entrepreneurs. The first occurs most commonly in professional team sports where a player signs a contract to play for a team or league for a number of years. The second condition, in which an athlete works as an entrepreneur, usually occurs in professional individual sports, such as tennis, golf, track and field, and figure skating.

Monopsony in Professional Sports

Most professional sports leagues in North America have some monopsonistic power over their players regardless of the business structure under which they operate. This is because many of these leagues are the sole buyers and users of the service rendered by players. For example, if a college football player wants to play professional football at the major league level in the United States, he has to sell his service to the NFL. A female college basketball player has no choice but to make herself available to the WNBA if she wants to play professional basketball in North America. Each professional sports league enjoys being a monopsonist and uses the situation to its best advantage. Specifically, rules for evenly allocating athletic talents are collusively delineated by owners of franchises affiliated with the league for competitive balance.

Reserve clause and control over the player labor market. According to the reserve clause adopted in MLB in1879, once a team drafted a player, the player had to negotiate his contract and salary with that team. The team owned exclusive rights to the services of the player. The player could not sell his services and enter any contractual agreement with other teams unless he was traded or sold to other teams or dropped by the team that initially owned his contract. The reserve clause gave enormous monopsony power to professional sports team owners (Hylan, Lage, & Treglia, 1996). However, such monopsonistic power was substantially weakened in 1975 when arbitrator Peter Seitz granted free agency to two baseball players, Andy Messersmith and Dave McNally, the first free agents in the history of professional sport (McCormick, 1989). Nevertheless, the use of free agency system did not completely ease the monopsonistic control of owners over the player labor market, thanks to the amateur draft system.

Allocations of athletes to potential employers by the draft system. According to the typical draft system, the franchises that had the worst records in the previous season are entitled to a better position in the amateur draft. The process goes on, and the best team gets to pick the latest (a team's draft position sometimes is also subject to trades). The number of rounds in the draft varies by sport. It usually takes several rounds to complete.

As a monopsonist, the league uses the draft rules to set restrictions on employment opportunities of the rookie player. As a result of being drafted, the player does not have to worry about unemployment, and he or she would be more likely to be submissive to a lower salary, a so-called exploitative salary. Once a team drafts a player, other teams in the same league are prohibited from soliciting the player for his or her service under the draft rules and agreement among teams in the league. Such an agreement, according to scholars in antitrust, violates the spirit of the antitrust law (Siegfried, 1995). To avoid antitrust challenges and to continuously exercise their monopsonistic power in the player labor market, professional sport leagues (except Major League Baseball[1]) have worked closely with their respective players unions to gain a labor exemption to the Sherman Act (McCormick, 1989). One of the major outcomes of the collective bargaining process has been the respective unions' allowing the league to keep the draft rules. To a great extent, the rules used in the amateur draft are, therefore, a product of a bilateral monopoly and a result of an agreement between owners and the players who are currently under contracts.

Competitive balance and the draft system. As mentioned above, professional sports leagues have claimed that the main reason an amateur draft system must be in place is the necessity for competitive balance. However, according to Siegfried (1995), such a claim has not been proven true in all sports that use a draft system. There are two counterarguments against the claim. First, the immediate impact created by a drafted player is minimal on the competitiveness of the team in such sports as football and baseball in which each team has a large number of players. In baseball, such impact is modest and indirect as almost all

[1]Major League Baseball is exempted from antitrust regulations with regard to labor because of 1922 ruling of the Supreme Court. It proclaimed that professional baseball games were not 'purely state affairs' and 'not trade or commerce'; therefore, they should not be subject to the scrutiny of the antitrust law (McCormick, 1989). The exemption has been partially revoked by President Clinton in a recent executive order.

drafted players are sent immediately to the minor league affiliates after the draft. As Zimbalist (1994) indicates, there has been more competitive balance among teams since free agency arrived in 1976 in Major League Baseball than in the period before its introduction. In other words, the draft system used before 1976 in MLB was not at all effective in promoting competitive balance. In contrast, the impact of the draft system seems to be more obvious in basketball and hockey. A talented player sometimes can make a difference in a relatively short time. Tim Duncan, the first overall draft pick by the San Antonio Spurs in 1997, instrumentally helped the team win the NBA world championship in 1999.

Second, using an economic theory called the Coase theorem, research has found a sizable increase in social cost due to the implementation of the draft system (Siegfried, 1995). According to the Coase theorem, if property rights are well defined and the costs of buying and selling those rights are not prohibitive, resources will eventually gravitate to their most valuable use, no matter who is given the rights initially (Coase 1960). For example, if the Atlanta Hawks offer a salary to a player that is considered high by other NBA teams that also want the player's service, no transfer earning will occur among the Atlanta Hawks and those NBA teams. In this case, transfer earning is the money required to induce the Atlanta Hawks to offer the player for other NBA teams to use. However, if the Atlanta Hawks sign the player and pay him a low salary, and if other NBA teams also want the right to the player, both the Atlanta Hawks and the teams that want to buy the player's contract can end up better off. This is because the Hawks may receive some economic rent by trading or selling the player, and the other NBA team gets what it wants. During the amateur draft, we often see such a scenario in that an economically and competitively disadvantaged team receives one of the top picks because of its poor performance in the preceding season. No sooner does the team draft the player than it trades him to a wealthy team. Usually, the amount the wealthy team pays for the player is higher than the revenue that the selling team estimates the player will bring in if he stays. The price tag of the wealthy team may include lower round picks and/or players on the current team roster. The result of the trade makes the two involved teams happy because both of them get what they want, even if this may mean that the economically disadvantaged team will continue to have trouble in future competition. The scenario well confirms the Coase theorem. That is, a talented player will be eventually traded to and signed by a team that is willing to make an offer that most closely reflects the true value of the player. This kind of situation has been seen throughout the history of professional sports in the United States.

The discussion above shows that the draft system is fundamentally flawed because it limits the freedom and bargaining power of those players in the draft to sell their service to teams for which they want to play, consequently reducing their value (Siegfried, 1995). Without such restriction imposed by the draft rules, talented rookie players may be able to negotiate and earn what they deserve in an open market. The draft system is fundamentally flawed also because it is a product of an agreement orchestrated by the two parties involved in a bilateral monopoly, the owners and the players' unions. As found in the research of Quirk and Fort (1992), the draft system helps redistribute the wealth between the veterans and rookies. This is logical because the players' union represents mainly the economic interests of the veteran players. The salaries not paid to those newly drafted players may be available for the teams to make bigger and more lucrative offers to those veteran players in the free agent market.

Competitive Labor Markets and Rival Leagues

The players' labor market becomes competitive when a rival league emerges to challenge the existing one. The appearance of the rival league substantially reduces the monopsonistic power that the existing league used to enjoy when it was the only purchaser of players' service in the players' labor market, as well as weakens its bargaining position over players. For the sake of survival, the rival leagues now have to aggressively compete against each other for such resources as players, television revenues, advertising dollars, and fans.

There are many unintended consequences of the competition among rival leagues:

1. Escalating players' salaries. New leagues commonly compete against existing leagues by bidding for talented players. The bidding war among the rivals inevitably escalates the amount of commitment each league has to make to keep or attract good players. The competition for players thus turns the labor market in the players' favor and changes it from a buyer's market into a seller's one. Players can use the threat that they will "jump to another league" as a pressure tactic to boost up their salaries.

2. Reduced the monopsonistic power in the player draft. Bidding for rookies is also another focal point of competition among the rivals. For example, after signing a $36 million contract with CBS in 1964, the American Football League immediately started a bidding war with the NFL by making some large offers for exceptional college players. The United States Football League was another rival to NFL in 1980s. This league adopted the idea of a star system and held its draft before the NFL's. By so doing, it was able to get some talented rookies. Rival leagues have to make reasonable offers that match the ability of the players in the market in order to receive their services.

3. Diluted bargaining power over television networks. When there is only one league in operation, the league is the sole provider of game signals to the television network. To obtain these signals, networks have to compete for a contract with the league. The bidding war among networks raises the television rights fee. The appearance of a rival league gives competing networks an opportunity to choose a potential affiliation. The selection becomes a two-way process. Both rival leagues can negotiate a deal with any of the networks and vice versa.

The Nikki McCray case is good example of the effect of a rival league on the players' labor market. A marquee player in the former ABL, McCray was instrumental in helping the Columbus Quest to win the Championship of the ABL in 1997. Immediately after winning the championship, she requested that the league renegotiate her contract, demanding a considerable increase in her salary and the right of first refusal on all major endorsement deals that the league would sign for its players. The league refused her demand. So, she later signed a 3-year contract with the rival WNBA.

Player Unions and Bilateral Monopoly

As mentioned earlier, if only one professional sports league operates in the market, it is a monopsony buyer. The league may take every possible advantage of the situation in labor negotiations. Nevertheless, the existence of a labor union in that professional sport (e.g., the National Football League Players Association), which acts like a monopoly seller, has changed the dynamic of the players' labor market because it counteracts the monopsony power of the league (Adams & Brock, 1997). The meeting and negotiation between league and the players' union create a bilateral monopoly. Together, the league and union determine the matters regarding player compensation, including minimum pay, pensions, insurance, free agency, and methods for handling grievances.

Let's again use Figure 10-4 to illustrate how the league and the union work in a bilateral monopoly market. The league (mainly the owners) wants to hire 50 hours of labor for a wage of $5.00 an hour. The union, on the other hand, demands an hourly rate of $10.00 with the same number of hours provided by players. This wage rate will equal the marginal revenue product of the involved players. For example, the NBA Players Association, which represents WNBA players, recently sought to increase the league's minimum salary to $45,000 and to get players a share of revenue from the sale of team merchandise, retirement benefits, and the right to challenge disciplinary action. The league has set $15,000 as the minimum salary. To reduce the difference in the wage rate, the league and the players' union had to negotiate through a collective bargaining process. The outcome of such a process usually depends on the negotiation philosophy and strategy the involved trade parties embrace.

Two negotiation models have been widely adopted in professional sport: (a) the adversary model and (b) the cooperative mode (Staudohar, 1989). Using the adversary framework, each side of the negotiations contends for a greater share of the revenues generated from the league's operations. The parties' strategies in negotiation are effectuated through offensive tactics calculated to force the adversary to grant concessions and defensive tactics calculated to prevent the adversary from gaining concessions (Staudohar, 1989).

The offensive strategies include a lockout by the league, and a strike and filling grievance to the National Labor Relations Board by the players' union, respectively. In 1998, the owners of the National Basketball Association used the lockout strategy effectively to force its adversary to agree to some essential matters. The players' strike in Major League Baseball in the 1994–1995 season has proven that a labor strike could be equally effective as well. The players coerced the owners to give up their demand for a salary cap. On the other hand, both the league and the union realize that the best defense is offense. Thus, to prevent its adversary from gaining more at the negotiation table, each party may try to ask for a cutback on benefits that have been agreed upon previously. For example, the 1998 NBA lockout was triggered by an impasse in negotiations between the league and the union because the union rejected the owners' demand for renegotiation of the collective bargaining agreement prior to its expiration. In particular, the owners sought to get rid of the so-called Bird's Rule, which states that the money individual teams use to re-sign their own free agents is not counted against their salary cap limit.

In contrast, the cooperative model is adopted in order to increase the mutual gains of the owners and the players, and the economic wealth of the league as a whole. The adoption of this model requires each party involved to abandon its adversary stance. "Instead of conducting negotiations in atmosphere of crisis confrontation, the parties recognize and accept each other as partners in a cooperative venture" (Staudohar, 1989, p. 177). Mutual gain and survival are the goals of the negotiation. For instance, the escalating salaries in NFL made the owners and players realize that something needed to be done cooperatively between them for the survival and continued prosperity of the league. They then agreed upon the salary cap that was introduced in the league in 1993. Embracing the cooperative model means that the two sides at the negotiation table may be willing to move their demands toward the middle and to find a wage rate that is satisfactory for both. "Hence a bilateral monopoly or cartel naturally militates toward coalescence of power between management and labor, not antagonism or countervailance [*sic*] of power" (Adams & Brock, 1997, p. 721).

Consequently, the owners and the players' union have to cooperate to deal with many labor issues in a way that benefits both the involved parties in the bilateral monopoly. In general, both the owners and players must handle three such issues:

1. How can they find a way that is acceptable to both in allocating the generated revenues from the sport industry? How can they cooperate in order to maximize their respective economic gain?

2. How can they work together to establish an environment conducive to reaching contract agreements in labor negotiation?

3. How can they reconcile the interests of diverse elements within themselves?

Consider the economic gain from the professional sport industry as a pie. Both players and owners have to find a way in which they all feel comfortable sharing the pie. In NBA's case, in 1983, the players' union and the owners together introduced the first salary cap in professional sport history, which guaranteed 53% of league revenues for players. The NFL took a similar measure in 1993. Again, the cooperation between the owners and players in the NBA has led to an unparalleled success and prosperity for the league in the last two decades. Both sides owners and players have benefited tremendously in terms of economic gains. A simple indicator of that is that the highest player in 1977 made $625,000 per year whereas the largest salary in 1996 was $30 million, a 48-fold increase over about a 20-year period.

An environment conducive to reaching contract agreements is extremely crucial in labor negotiation. The lockout in the NBA 1998–1999 season proves to be a good example to illustrate how important a supportive environment is to productive labor negotiation in professional sport. After 3 years of implementing the 1995 collective bargaining agreement, which should have lasted 6 years, the owners demanded a renegotiation of the agreement. The abandonment of Bird's Rule and the subsequent imposition of a hard salary cap were one of the several major issues the owners wanted to renegotiate with the National Basketball Players Association (NBPA). Other issues include free agency, a rookie salary cap, and minimum salaries. Once their demand to renegotiate the agreement was rejected, the owner called a lockout (Staudohar, 1999).

Many different interest groups often exist within each of the two parties involved in a bilateral monopoly. For instance, in 1995, a group of players sought to decertify the NBPA because they believed that if the union were decertified, they then could accuse the team owners of violating the antitrust law. However, players cannot bring a lawsuit against the owners for something that the owners and the union have agreed upon through collective bargaining. Such immunity is called labor exemption (Staudohar, 1999). The decertification effort failed because a majority of players voted against it. The same diverse elements exist with the team ownership. There are always some hard-liners who want to play hard ball at the labor negotiation table. For example, before the 1994–1995 strike, not all the owners in Major League Baseball wanted to impose a salary cap.

Factors Affecting Demand and Supply of Labor in Professional Sports

The demand for players in professional sports is determined in two ways: (a) the total number of players demanded and (b) the demand for specific players or types of players. Such demand in the professional sports labor market is generally inelastic. That means, the percentage change in number of players demanded is smaller than or equal to the percentage change in their compensations, mainly salaries. This is particularly true in the NBA. The price of labor in the NBA has more than doubled in the last 12 years, but demand has remained strong during the same period (Kavanagh, 1999). This could be attributed to the following four reasons:

1. The NBA limit on the number of players allowed to play on a team (12 players per team) determines the magnitude of the league's demand for players. The amount of demand equals the number of teams in the league multiplied by 12. In the 1998–1999 season, this number was 384. The number will remain the same until either the league changes its per-team limit on players or more expansion teams are added to the league.

2. The addition of new franchises to the league increases the demand for players.

3. The use of temporary replacements for injured players creates a demand situation for players. The more players injured, the higher this temporary demand becomes.

4. Even though the league's overall demand for players is relatively stable, the individual team's demand for a specific player changes every season. A player's worth to his team is assessed annually, and the marginal revenue product is re-estimated each year. The change in demand for players at certain positions affects the total availability of revenue used to sign players. A player might affect the revenue of a team in two direct ways. The most direct is the fame of a player. The higher the fan recognition of the player (e.g., Michael Jordan), the higher the impact the player may have on the team's revenues. A player may also affect the marginal revenue product indirectly by improving the win-loss record of a team. This increases the popularity of a team and thus its revenue (Quirk & Fort, 1992).

The marginal revenue product (MRP) is an essential criterion that a team uses in making decisions about whether to sign a player. That is, the team has to evaluate how much in gate receipts, merchandise and concession sales, and parking revenue it may generate as a result of signing a prospective player. But how can we accurately determine the marginal revenue product of a player? This becomes an issue that affects the demand of professional teams for free agents from the labor market. A team may offer a player an amount somewhere close to what the management of the team believes the player's MRP to be. The marginal revenue product of players varies wildly, and their salaries reflect those variations. If a team perceives that a player on another team may help to improve its winning performance, the team may then be willing to trade a player on its roster plus a future draft pick for that player. The marginal revenue products of the to-be-traded player and of the future draft selection are perceived as equal to or less than the MRP of the acquired player.

Two factors affect the supply of labor in a professional sport in the United States: (a) the number of people playing the sport in the country and (b) the popularity and development of that sport around the world (Kavanagh, 1999). The more people playing in high school and college, the greater will be the pool of talented domestic and foreign players available in the draft. This is evidenced by the number of talented high school players drafted by the NBA (Weir, 1999) and the number of non-Americans drafted by Major League Baseball franchises. The form system is also another factor that may affect the supply of talented players.

Determination of a Player's Marginal Revenue Product

The determination or estimation of a player's marginal revenue product has been one of the focuses of research by economists in that last two decades. The study conducted by Scully on Major League Baseball in 1974 led the inquiry in this matter. Scully's work is based on an assumption that "a team's revenues increase when the team wins more games, and the performance of players contributes to team revenue only by changing the team's winning percentage" (Boal & Ransom, 1997, p. 100). So a player's marginal revenue product is defined as "the ability or performance that he contributes to the team and the effect of that performance on gate receipts" (Scully, 1974, p. 916). To estimate a player's marginal revenue product, Scully used a two-step model. First, a regression analysis was performed to identify the factors that might affect a team's revenues. Examples of the factors admitted in the regression equation include team winning percentage, host population, and team's league affiliation. The study concluded that a team's revenues would increase $10,330 for each additional winning percentage point (Scully, 1974). Determining the contribution of individual players on the team to the winning percentage is the second step of the model. Several similar studies have consequently attempted to estimate a player's marginal revenue product in sports that require collaboration and teamwork, such as football and basketball. The approach adopted in Scully's model, which assumes each player's contribution is independent of and distinct from those of his or her teammates, has been criticized and revised accordingly in later studies (Scott, Long, & Somppi, 1991). An overview of all the studies conducted to examine the marginal revenue product of players indicates that four basic steps are crucial in accurately estimating a player's MRP:

1. To quantify the relationship between individual performance and team success

2. To quantify the relationship between team success and team revenue

3. To determine the marginal revenue product of the team in each performance category

4. To determine each player's marginal revenue product in each performance category

Estimating the marginal revenue product of individual players is a rather tedious and complex process. A clear understanding of the sport under study and of the multivariate statistical procedures used in computation is essential for deriving accurate estimations.

Many professional athletes work as entrepreneurs, which means they are owners of their own services and commodity as an athlete in the sport industry. This type of scenario commonly appears in professional or elite individual sports, such as tennis, golf, track and field, and figure skating. As entrepreneurs, these athletes make capital and labor-investment decisions that will help them maximize the profit potential of their services. For example, professional tennis players often have to decide the tournaments in which they want to compete.

Summary

This chapter first gives a detailed overview of concepts and theories in the market for labor. Specifically, the concept of marginal revenue product (MRP) is examined pertaining to what it means and how it can be measured. The relationship between labor and leisure, and between wage rates and labor supply is also analyzed, which may provide explanations about the circumstances under which individual households decide to supply themselves to the labor market. In the overview section, two special, but important, market structures, monopsony and bilateral monopoly, are also addressed.

In addition, this chapter discusses several foundational issues of the player labor market in the sport industry. This first issue is the monopsonistic power of professional sports leagues in North America. Leagues have used the "reserve clause" and the player draft system to enhance their bargaining position in labor negotiations, and ultimately their monopsonistic power. The relationship between competitive balance and the player draft system is another issue discussed. In certain sports such as football and baseball, the player draft system seems to contribute little to efforts to balance the competitive ability of teams within a league. The third issue reviewed is the impact of rival leagues on the player labor market. The role of a players' union on the player labor market is the focus of the four issues. Many economists believe that a bilateral monopoly exists in all major professional sports in North America. The league and the player union collusively determine the wage rates of players and other compensations. Labor issues in a bilateral monopoly and economic rent of that particular market structure are two other issues discussed.

The chapter also examines the labor issues in the sport industry under a special circumstance. That is, how players as entrepreneurs determine how to supply labor to the market.

Chapter Study Questions

1. Using an example, explain the factors affect the supply of labor in the sport industry.
2. Explain how to determine the marginal revenue product of a player.
3. Elaborate on the relationship between labor and leisure, and discuss the condition(s) under which people will reduce their leisure pursuit and increase their supply of labor.
4. Define these two concepts: monopsony and bilateral monopoly.
5. Explain why economists believe professional sports leagues have monopsonistic power over players.
6. Explain why the free agency system reduces the monopsonistic control of leagues over players.
7. Does the player draft system really contribute to enhancing the competitive balance among teams in a league? Why or why not?
8. Discuss the effect of a rival league on the player labor market.
9. Explain the bilateral monopoly situation in professional sport.
10. What are the two models of negotiation used by the leagues and the players' unions in professional sport?

Chapter Nine

INTRODUCTION

Government regulation of commercial activities of private firms has always been a topic of discussion in economics because it is believed that the breadth and depth of government involvement in those activities may have profound impact on the decision-making process of the involved firms (Pappas & Hirschey, 1987). In addition, industry self-regulation is a topic that receives attention from economists. Sport managers need to understand why and how government regulates, what constraints the firms in the sport industry may encounter due to government regulation, and how industry self-regulation works as a supplementary form of regulation. The chapter will examine issues related to both government and industry regulations.

Concept of Regulation

The term *regulation* can be defined in several different ways. Generally, it refers to "the intentional restriction of a subject's choice of activity, by an entity not directly party to or involved in that activity" (Mitnick, 1980, p.5). In the context of the sport industry, the subject is all the firms and organizations in the sport industry, and the party unrelated to the activity conducted by the sport firms and organizations is government. Through regulation, government establishes various requirements of, restrictions for, and constraints on the activities of the sport firms and organizations. Regulations include laws and subordinate rules issued by all levels of government, ranging from federal to local (S. H. Jacobs, 1997). For example, one way that state governments protect wildlife and the environment is to restrict fishing activities. Such restrictions include the requirement on licenses and the limitation on fish type and locations where anglers can fish.

> ***Regulation of Sports***
>
> *The owner of the New Jersey Devils has recently decided to sell the team to a company affiliated with YankeeNets, the parent company of the New York Yankees and New Jersey Nets. The acquisition of the Devils by YankeeNets would make it possible for the three affiliated teams to bundle themselves together in promotion and marketing. This would no doubt give the Yankees a greater advantage over its counterpart, the New York Mets, in terms of market shares and penetration. Is the acquisition anticompetitive? What should government do to ensure that the Yankees do not have any unfair advantage over the Mets?*

The meaning of regulation can also be understood from a different perspective that pertains to the regulatory actions taken by a private industry or nongovernmental, self-regulatory body. This is commonly known as "industry self-regulation." Industry self-regulation is defined as the process of influencing activity of members of an industry through the establishment of rules and procedures, which are administered by a control-agent organization. Thus, in examining the issues related to regulation of sports, the regulatory mechanisms imposed by the government and the regulatory actions voluntarily taken by a specific sector of the sport industry must be discussed. For example, in considering a professional sport franchise as a regulatee, there are two types of regulators: the government and the league-wide regulatory authority. The regulations imposed by the government operate at the level of interorganizational regulation. The purpose of such regulations is to ensure fairness of competition and economic efficiency. Examples of government regulations include the antitrust laws and the National Labor Relations Act. League-wide regulations operate at the intra-organizational level. Regulation at this level is designed to ensure the management efficiency of the league as a business firm and to achieve its goal of profit maximization.

Government Regulations

The involvement of government in a market economy has been a controversial topic for many years. Some argue that if an industry is left alone by the government, open competition will ensure the market will operate efficiently over time. This side favors a laissez-faire approach in which the government intervenes as little as possible and allows mechanisms in the market to move it toward efficiency (Schiller, 1989). Proponents of this view also argue that government regulations are often costly and that, although the intent of the regulations may be good, the result is that the costs exceed the benefits, which will ultimately have a negative impact on the consumer (Hirschey & Pappas, 1995). Moreover, they believe government officials generally lack the industry expertise necessary to understand the impact of the regulations they impose, which results in regulations that often fail to meet their objectives (Hirschey & Pappas, 1995). These government failures may end up being worse than the market failures legislators were trying to correct (Schiller, 1989). The Reagan Administration in the United States is a recent example of a group that held these beliefs and pushed for a reduction in business-related regulations (i.e., deregulation).

However, another side suggests that government regulation is necessary for the market to operate at maximum efficiency. This group argues that although the laissez-faire approach would work fine in a perfectly competitive industry, perfect competition rarely, if ever, exists (Schiller, 1989). In fact, these economists identify a number of imperfections in the market that prevent optimal outcomes from occurring without government regulations (Schiller). These imperfections are called market failure. In other words, market failure refers to the inability of an unregulated market to achieve allocative efficiency in all circumstances. The following are examples of how government regulations prevent market failure:

1. Externalities—As discussed in chapter 5, externalities are indirect benefits or costs of an activity (Schiller, 1989) or the social costs and benefits not included in the price of the product or service (Richardson & McConomy, 1992). In the context of regulation, externalities refer to the indirect benefits or cost as a result of an action taken by the regulatory body (i.e., to regulate or not to regulate). For example, a company that produces a large number of baseball bats may face government regulations because it is killing too many trees, an activity that is damaging the environment and decreasing the supply of wood available for other products. The government may react by limiting the number of bats the company can produce or by taxing the company for each bat that it produces; the company will produce fewer bats, and the environmental damage will abate. However, externalities may also be positive. For example, a youth sport program for disadvantaged youth is expected to provide a number of societal benefits. Because

the financial benefits to a for-profit organization of such a program would be limited, the government may provide these programs or subsidize other organizations so they can afford to provide the programs.

2. Public goods—Public goods are goods or services that cannot be consumed exclusively (Schiller, 1989). The government often provides public goods, such as national defense and roads, to which it forces all taxpayers to contribute. Otherwise, the market would not produce these necessary goods and services because there would be no way to make people pay to eliminate the free riders (i.e., those who use, but do not pay).

3. Market power—Whenever one or more producers have control over industry prices and/or output, it is likely that optimal outcomes will not be reached (Schiller, 1989). These firms will often produce less than the consumer-desired output and charge a higher price for that output (see chapter 4 for discussions of monopolies, cartels, etc.). Numerous government regulations, such as the antitrust laws, seek to control organizations with an excessive amount of market power.

4. Natural monopoly—In some cases, the concentration of market power in one firm may be most efficient (Schiller, 1989). This occurs when one firm can produce all of the output desired by consumers and can do it more cheaply than could a number of firms working separately. The government may allow such monopolies to exist, but regulate the activities of such an organization to make sure they do not abuse their monopoly power.

5. Inequities—In some cases, the market may distribute income in an undesirable way (Schiller, 1989). Without government intervention, some people will have far more than they need, whereas others will lack the necessities (Schiller, 1989). Again, the government can correct some of these inequities through regulation. For example, the minimum wage laws in the United States are designed to prevent employees from being paid a wage so low that they could not afford necessities.

Overall, it appears that in recent years the side supporting government regulation of the market economy appears to be winning. Government regulation "has undergone a period of exponential growth during the past two decades" (Hirschey & Pappas, 1995, p.668). A major goal of some of these regulations is to ensure a healthy level of competition in each industry. To ensure competition, a series of regulations has been enacted since 1989, when the antitrust laws were first introduced. These regulations are designed to prevent firms from having too much market power. As discussed in chapter 4, when a firm has considerable control over the market (e.g., a monopoly, a cartel), it tends to charge consumers higher prices (Shepherd, 1970) and to reduce production below an optimal level (Schiller, 1989). So, although the antitrust laws are often used by firms claiming that competitors are behaving unfairly, they are ultimately designed to protect consumers by ensuring the marketplace remains competitive and firms do not reduce production and charge higher prices. As we will discuss, these regulations have had an impact on the operations of sport organizations.

Learning Activities

1. Return to the beginning of the chapter, and reread the scenario. After reading this chapter, what are your answers to the two questions raised?

2. Compare and contrast government regulation and industry self-regulation in the sport industry with the same sorts of regulation in another industry (e.g., telecommunication, automobile, airline).

3. Organize a class debate on the advantages and disadvantages of government regulation as well as those of industry self-regulation.

Regulatory Systems of Government

The regulatory systems of government in the United States are mainly established at two levels: federal and state. The government, with its three branches, comprises the federal regulatory system. This system, in general, regulates the sport industry by passing various sports laws and laws applicable to the sport industry (by the Congress), monitoring the execution of the laws (by the judicial system), and imposing administrative regulations (by various governmental agencies under the executive branch). It is commonly acknowledged that most government regulation in the sport industry is found in the first two branches of the federal regulatory system, and the regulatory actions taken by these two branches, especially the judicial system, seem to link primarily to the antitrust laws and their applications. In the past, the judicial branch appeared to be unwilling to judge whether violations of the antitrust laws were being committed by a sport organization.

The legislative branch of the federal government plays a critical role in overseeing and regulating the sport industry. It passes various laws that may be applicable to the sport industry (e.g., the antitrust laws and Title IX), enacts sports-related legislation (e.g., The Sports Broadcasting Act), and conducts hearings to gather new information to assist in either developing a new law or amending an existing one. The numerous congressional hearings on whether or not the antitrust exemption granted to Major League Baseball should be revoked illustrate the last regulatory function of the legislative branch in the sport industry. The regulatory influence of the legislative branch of the federal government on the sport industry is also seen through the operations of various federal commissions. For example, the Federal Trade Commission enforces a variety of federal antitrust and consumer protection laws to ensure that the market is functional competitively, is efficient, and is free of undue restrictions. Application and interpretation of the law in the decision of real differences and in decision of cases and controversies are two main powers granted by the U.S. Constitution to the judicial branch. The regulatory power executed by the judicial branch to the sport industry is reflected in the rulings of the U.S. Federal Courts on many cases that involve the interpretation of the antitrust laws and Title IX. The executive branch of the federal government executes its regulatory responsibility in several different ways. For example, the president can issue an executive order to temporarily end a work stoppage as a result of either a player strike or an owners' lockout. The department under each cabinet member, on the other hand, is responsible for the administration and enforcement of some of the federal statutes that may be applicable to the sport industry.

Many restrictions on the sport industry are also set by the state regulatory system, which has developed from the same reasons as those that fostered the federal system. However, the scope of state-imposed regulatory measures is much more limited and state specific than is the scope of federal regulation. Most state-regulated sport-related restrictions occur in areas such as sport agencies, fishing, hunting, and various forms of athletic competitions. For example, a large number of states in the United States have passed statutes to control the sport agency business. Many states have also created athletic commissions to regulate competitions, especially the combative sports competitions such as kickboxing. Rules and regulations are, therefore, adopted for the sake of protecting the athletes as well as the public.

Role of Government

It has been long believed that the government should function as the manager of an economic system under managed capitalism (Elliott, 1985). The managerial functions of government are actualized in the following areas:

1. Through its "framework" activities, a government can establish rules, regulatory legislation, and policies as guidelines for firms. With the guidelines as boundaries of activities or conducts, firms may formulate their operational strategies that are deemed not only economically sound, but also legal and legitimate. An example of this type of government activity is the antitrust laws.

2. Through its preservative intervention and measures, a government can protect and support a particular industry. The Sports Broadcasting Act, passed by the U.S. Congress, to a certain extent, was drafted for the sake of protecting the best interest of professional sports. The legislation exempted the collective negotiation of TV contracts from the reach of the antitrust laws.

3. Through passing various statutes and administrative regulations, a government can control the private businesses. For example, the Labor Relations Act of 1935 controls unfair labor practices by employers and labor unions. An independent Federal agency, the National Labor Relations Board, was created to enforce the law. Players' unions in professional sports have frequently used this law to protect their members and to gain advantages in collective bargaining.

Types/Rationales of Government Regulation

Through regulation, a government usually intends to achieve one or all of the following three basic objectives:

1. To ensure free competition among private firms and ultimately economic efficiency through the application of antitrust policy (Mueller, 1996).

2. To correct the serious flaws in the marketplace that lead to external costs (Warren, 1992), and

3. To protect the public interest.

So, based on its intention, government regulation can be categorized into three basic types: economic, political, and social (S. H. Jacobs, 1997; Pappas & Hirschey, 1987; Weidenbaum, 1992). *Economic regulation* refers to the intervention of the regulatory body for the sake of promoting competition and market entry or exit to enhance the economic efficiency of the market. In short, the government uses economic regulation to prevent market failure and to ensure economic efficiency. An example of economic regulation in all industries, including the one we call sport industry, is the antitrust law, used to limit the growth and size of large competitors (Pappas & Hirschey, 1995). To preserve the power and sovereignty of consumers in the competitive markets is another reason for government regulation. The restrictions exerted by government for this purpose constitute *political regulation*. In competitive markets, consumers' preferences play a very important role in influencing firms' decisions on pricing and quantity. "Firms have substantial incentives to produce products consumers want, and to produce them in desired quantities" (Pappas &

Hirschey, 1995, p.460). Without government regulation and oversight, a firm in a certain product market could keep growing in size, eventually monopolizing that market. In that case, the firm becomes a price maker and has great discretion in its decision pertaining to pricing and output. Under these circumstances, consumers would suffer great losses of power and sovereignty. Social regulation is often used to achieve some noneconomic goals, such as health, safety, environmental protection, and social cohesion. The restrictions set by governments on fishing activities, mentioned earlier, offer a good example of social regulation because these restrictions are intended to protect the environment and wildlife. This chapter mainly discusses the economic and political regulations imposed by the government.

Approaches of Government Regulation

In dealing with matters in the large industries that require its involvement, the government has used three approaches. The use of antitrust laws is one. With the provision of the laws, the government may ensure the fairness in competition among firms. As long as the spirit of the laws is not being violated, the government does not take a stance or act to handle the matter. The other two approaches are *laissez-faire* and *public supervision* (Mueller, 1996).

The adoption of the laissez-faire approach by the government in a free market economy will ultimately lead to the creation of private monopolies. (See chapter 4 for basic economic theories about and characteristics of a monopoly.) This approach has proved to be problematic. Market failure is a major problem associated with private monopolies (see also chapter 4). Monopoly is less efficient than competition because it creates a deadweight loss by restricting output, resulting in reduction in consumer surplus (see Figures 9-1 and 9-2 for details). *Consumer surplus* refers to the difference between the value of a good and its price. It is shown as the shaded area in Figure 9-1. In a competitive market, consumers have to pay only the amount of money signified by the curve Pc for each unit bought (Parkin, 1993). However, in a monopoly, the monopolist usually sets its output at the point where marginal revenue equals marginal cost in order to maximize its profit. Because of the decrease in output, the monopolist turns consumer surplus into its monopoly gain and charges consumers higher prices without fear (monopoly pricing). The monopolist's restriction on output results not only in the loss in the consumer surplus, but also in the producer surplus. *Producer surplus* refers to the difference between a producer's revenue and the opportunity cost of production. It can be calculated by summing differences of the price and the marginal cost of producing each unit of output (Parkin, 1993). A deadweight loss measures the total loss of consumer surplus and producer surplus, and it indicates the allocative inefficiency caused by the monopolist's reduction of output below its efficient level (Parkin, 1995). A comparison of Figure 9-1 and Figure 9-2 reveals two important points:

1. The quantity of a product (i.e., the availability of the product to consumers) is reduced in a monopoly market due to the monopolist's restriction on output.

2. The price for the product will be higher in the monopoly market. The reduction in consumer surplus leads to increase the difference between the value of the product and its sale price.

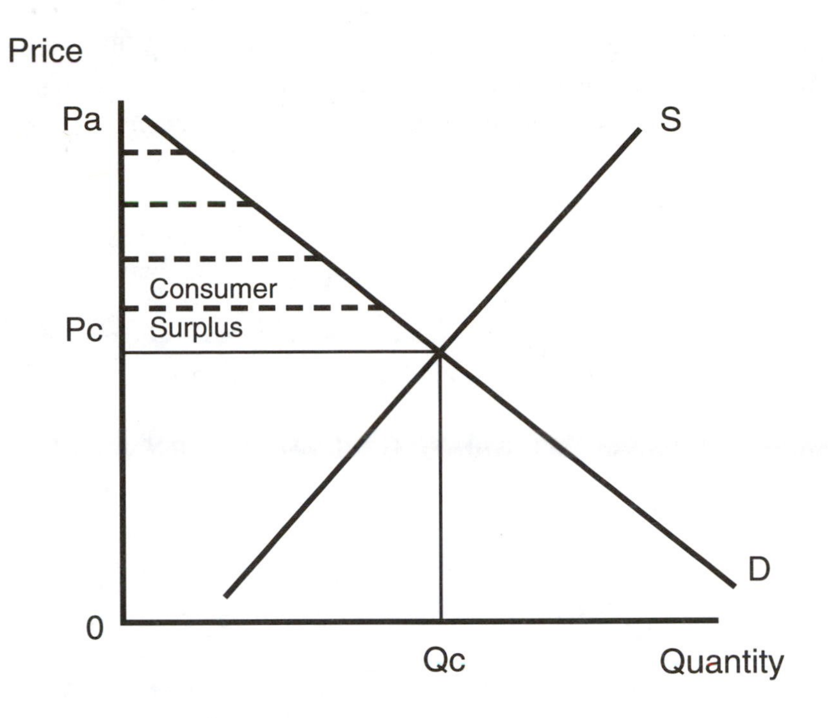

Figure 9-1. A Perfect Competitive Market

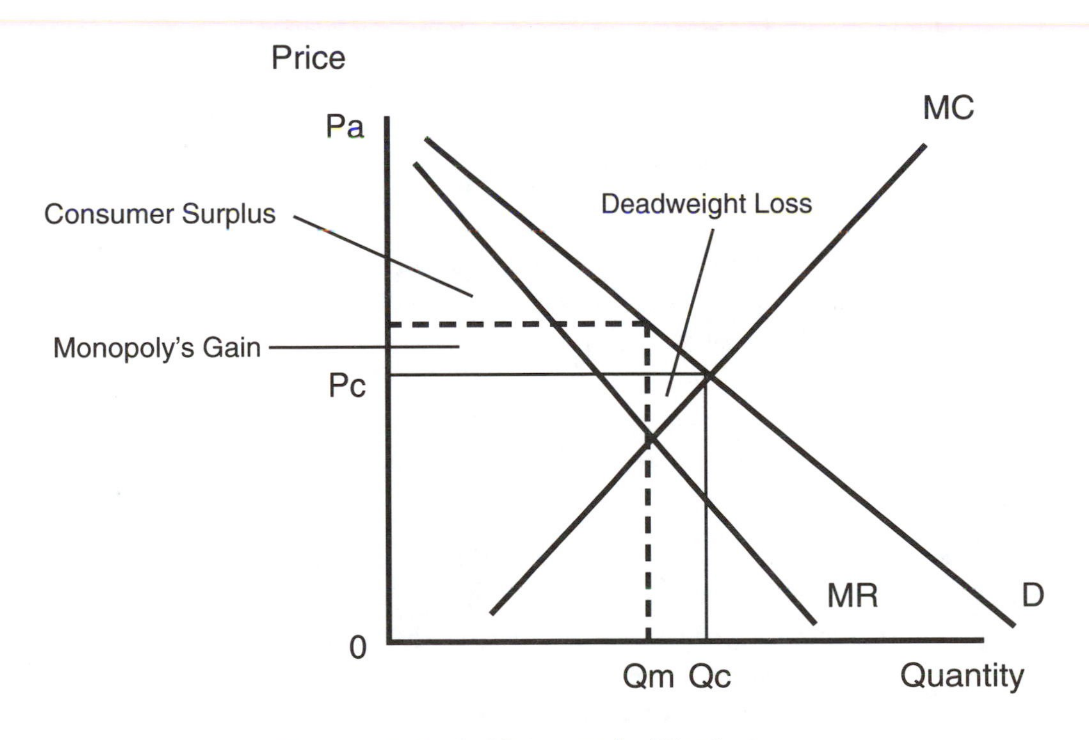

Figure 9-2. A Monopoly Market

The inefficiency existing in a monopoly will, in turn, cause market failure. As Richardson & McConomy (1992) indicate, market failure can happen if the five conditions or criteria for perfect competition (described in chapter 4) are not met. That is, (a) if there are a limited number of sellers in the market, (b) if the firm has power over consumers on pricing of the product, (c) if the product is not standardized and homogenous, (d) if there are barriers to entry into or exit from market, and (e) if information about the product is not widely available to consumers, market failure is an inevitable consequence.

Market failure is commonly observed in the sport industry, especially in professional sports. In almost all cases, there is generally only one seller of each major professional sport in North America (e.g., National Football League in professional football, National Basketball Association in professional basketball, Major League Baseball in professional baseball). This sole seller often takes advantage of the situation to exercise its monopoly power by setting restrictions and barriers to entry. By so doing, it violates the first and second conditions that prevent a market from failure. It is exceptionally hard, if not impossible, for a new league to make inroads into a market that has been exclusively controlled by an existing league. The adjustments that the new league must make are tremendous. For example, it needs to earn (a) respect from a public that has been exposed only to the product of its rivals, so as to establish a solid fan base, and (b) support from sponsors and media that have been very friendly to the present league. The costs involved in forming a new league are considerable, especially when there is a heated competition with the established league for players. Because Americans have long been exposed to the current traditional forms of various professional sports like football, basketball, and baseball, it is extremely difficult for those who want to enter the market and to compete with the well-established, well-known, and well-recognized league in a given sport. For the reasons mentioned above, the new entry will have difficulty competing unless it develops a new product to differentiate it from that of the existing league. If it decides to differentiate its product, the existing league will continue to hold on to its monopoly power and enjoy it fully. Arena Football would be a good example.

Another violation of the conditions for perfect competition occurs in the area of information asymmetries. Again, due to the familiarity of the products (e.g., team names and logos) of the existing league and its affiliated franchises, and the constant marketing bombardment of the league and teams through the media, the general public may not have the knowledge to differentiate the quality and price of the products of the two competing leagues. In other words, people tend to see the existing league and its teams as being of higher quality even if they are not.

Externalities, often high, also exist in professional leagues. The externality costs in professional sports include the use of taxpayers' money by state and municipal governments to subsidize a professional sports franchise in a certain locality, which may include sports facility renovation and construction, tax breaks and concessions, and nominal rental fees. To a certain extent, the more public consumption of the product and service of a professional sports league as a monopolist, the higher the externality costs will be.

Despite the violations of the conditions of perfect competition, the professional sports market is generally unrestricted by the government. In such an unregulated market, a particular league operates in a manner similar to that of a monopolist. It sets restrictions on number of games to be played and the number of franchises to be granted and/or expanded. The fewer franchises a league has, the greater economic rent it can actualize. How large should a professional sports league be to achieve economies of scale and to exhaust all of the efficiencies associated with its size? It seems to the owners and management of a specific professional sports league that the optimal size is "big," big enough to monopolize the market. However, the owners and management never want to expand the league to the optimal size. The principle of the so-called "minimum efficient scale" (MES) calls for the government to determine the optimum size of each professional sports league.

Many monopolists that once dominated their industries have ultimately fallen victim to their own inefficiency, including high salaries for both management and labor (Jones & Ergas, 1993; Mueller, 1996). This is true in the case of professional sports. The size of players' salaries has escalated to a point that many teams have to spend more than 60% of their revenues on salaries. Inefficiency is found in the management of individual franchises as well.

Allocative efficiency will occur when marginal cost equals price, and it will be found only in a regulated industry. It is one of the reasons, or so sports fans argue, that government should attempt to restore and maximize total consumer surplus through the application of other regulatory policies in addition to the antitrust laws.

The economic theories in industrial resource allocation reveal that the development and utilization of modern technology have inevitably led to the creation of oligopoly in many product markets. The competitive firms in the oligopoly market tend to conspire to create a collusive oligopoly market (closely similar to a pure monopoly market) that is necessary not only to the maximization of profit, but also to the maximization of output. The oligopoly situation creates a functional conflict between size of production and efficiency. The history of professional sports in the United States has witnessed the development of several collusive oligopoly markets in professional sports and the problems that have resulted from the creation of such markets. The merging of the National League and American League into Major League Baseball and the association between the NFL and AFL are classic examples that illustrate the collusive oligopoly markets in professional sports. The economic characteristics of a collusive oligopoly market are similar to those of a monopoly market. Inefficiency is, therefore, often associated with this type of market as well.

Public supervision is the third approach that government may adopt to regulate an industry. This approach calls for close government scrutiny of an industry. The basic assumption underlying this approach lies in the public interest theories. The public interest theories of regulation "assume that [government] regulation is established largely in response to public-interest-related objectives" (Mitnick, 1980, p.91). The public interest theory of government regulatory behavior provides another theoretical foundation for government to act to achieve an efficient allocation of resources. For example, professional sports have been perceived as public goods. Public goods are defined as "goods and services which are available to other persons even while being consumed by one person" (Southwick, 1985, p.721). However, some have argued that such "public goods" have taken advantage of the support of the enthusiastic fans and "rip them off" with no mercy (Dell'Apa, 1993). The rip-offs are found in at least the following three areas:

1. Monopoly pricing. Due to the monopoly control of the availability of professional sport games, the owners of sport franchises force the public to pay an extravagant amount of money to use their services and products (Howard, 1999).

2. Control over franchise expansion. Professional sports takes advantage of being operated in a monopoly market and reluctantly adds new franchises. The scarcity of professional sports teams has fueled competition among municipalities to "bribe" teams with considerable subsidies in order to lure a professional sports franchise.

3. Designated area for operations. By dividing the country into exclusive, designated territories for operations, local franchises are ensured that they can "shift television rights from over-the-air stations to cable networks without fear that a local broadcaster would compete by importing another team's games" (Dell'Apa, 1993, p. 6). Individual professional sports teams can, therefore, maximize their local television revenues though such territorial restrictions.

For the reasons mentioned above, public interest advocates argue that professional sports should be regulated much as government has regulated other public-oriented industries (utility, transportation, etc.). This regulation will ultimately eliminate the deadweight loss and inefficiency caused by monopolistic practices.

To ensure lower prices and higher quality that flow from effective competition, and to ensure fairness for business firms, the U.S. government passed the Sherman Act in 1890 and the Clayton and Federal Trade Commission Acts in 1914 to declare both monopolization and the restraint of trade unlawful. The antitrust laws were the legal foundation of government regulation. Chapter 10 will provide detailed discussion of all antitrust-related laws and regulations. Since the passage of these laws, the federal government has appeared to take a laissez-faire stand or a reactive approach to the problems in the sport industry, especially in the professional sports segment, even though congressional inquiries and hearings were conducted into professional sports (Johnson & Frey, 1985). Historical cases in professional sports have demonstrated that it is unrealistic to expect a stable growing economy simply as a result of the existence of such regulatory legislation. With the intention of promoting fairness in competition and preventing monopolistic practices, the U.S. government passed and reinforced the antitrust laws. However, the Sports Broadcasting Act, which was passed in 1961, has allowed professional sports leagues to collectively pool television rights to all games of their member teams and to sell them to the national networks without violating the antitrust legislation. Such a contradiction in public policy creates numerous problems. Professional sports leagues see such legislation as empowerment and encouragement from the government for their monopoly practices. The creation of this act again illustrates the ineffectiveness of government regulation in professional sports. The inability of government to provide regulatory supervision has been affirmed to be problematic.

Industry Self-Regulation

As mentioned previously, industry self-regulation refers to the process of influencing the activity of the associates through the establishment of rules and procedures administered by a control-agent organization (Stern, 1981; Wotruba, 1997). The rules are drafted to serve as norms and/or standards of behavior for the affiliated members of the organization. In other words, they define the limits of acceptable behavior. Industry self-regulation can be implemented at two levels of business activity: company and industry. Most industry self-regulation activities take place at the industry level. Often a control-agent organization develops and administers policies with which all the members agree. These policies are believed to be in the best economic interest of the industry as a whole.

Many regulatory mechanisms (e.g., rules, policies, procedures) found in the sport industry are deliberately developed by individual sports control-agent organizations to regulate the affiliated members (e.g., franchises, institutions) for the sake of economic stability and growth. In professional sports, these regulatory mechanisms include, but are not limited to, revenue sharing, national TV contracts, amateur drafts, and league control over logos and trademarks. In collegiate athletics, various rules set by national governing bodies in player recruitment are also examples of self-regulatory practices. In other segments of the sport industry, industry self-regulation is also widely used. For example, the Automobile Competition Committee for the United States (ACCUS) is recognized by the Federation Internationale de l'Automobile (FIA) as the National Sporting Authority (ASN) for the United States. Championship Auto Racing Teams (CART), Indy Racing League (IRL), National Association for Stock Car Auto Racing (NASCAR), and Professional Sports Car Racing (SPORTS CAR) are some of the member clubs of the ACCUS. Affiliated teams and individuals must comply with all the rules and regulations set by those clubs in such areas as license, equipment, and conduct.

The consumers of sport products and services also play a role in the regulatory process. They can provide feedback to both regulators (the government and the control-agent organization) regarding whether their rights have been violated by an individual firm from which they have purchased products or services. If the complaint is legitimate and a substantial number of consumers are affected, the government may step in to address the issue and put pressure on the firm involved (e.g., an injunction was issued by the court to stop the baseball strike in 1995). The control-agent organization may also react to the consumers' comments by adopting corresponding regulatory policies to deal with the perceived problem. Figure 9-3 shows the regulatory model in the sport industry.

Rationale for Industry Self-Regulation

According to some economists, the problems found in the sport industry, especially in professional sports, could be solved eventually by the market's and the industry's self-regulatory mechanisms. These economists argue that government should leave the sport industry alone and deem any attempted interventions unnecessary. Is industry self-regulation a miraculous cure to all the problems in the sport industry? According to

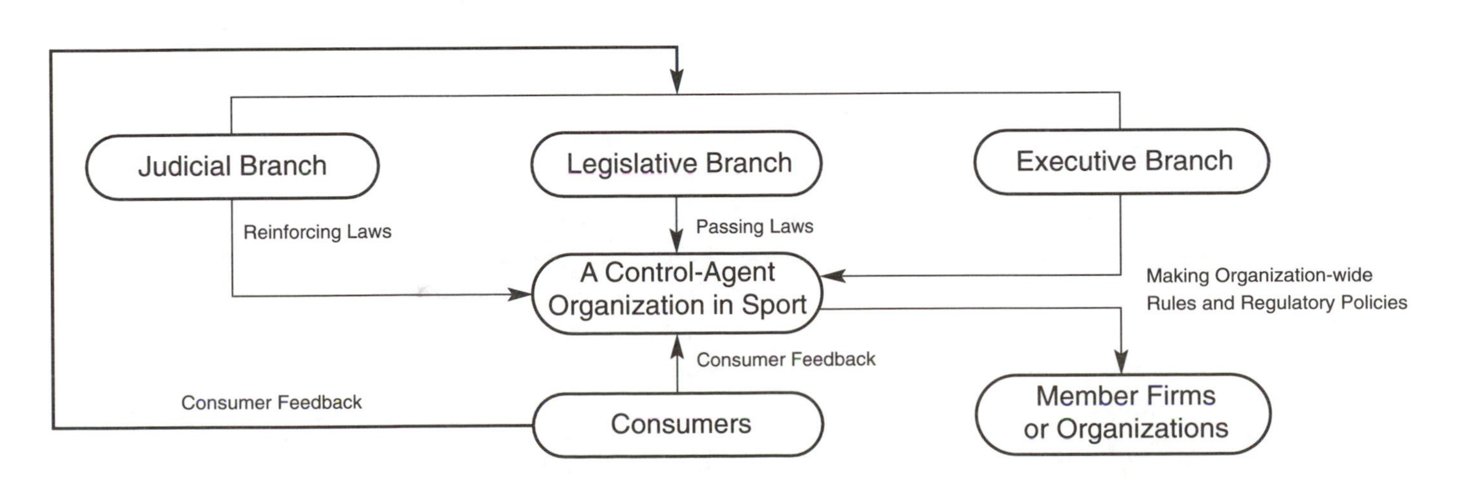

Figure 9-3. A Regulatory Model in the Sport Industry

Wotruba (1997), the basic motive for an industry to embrace and develop self-regulation mechanisms and policies is that self-regulation will benefit members as a whole economically. Industry self-regulation would achieve one or all of the following five basic goals:

1. To promote equity in competition among members. Maintaining a relative balance in financial and athletic ability among affiliated members has been an important task for the control-agent organizations in many segments of the sport industry, especially those involved in athletic performance and competition.

2. To enhance members' competitive positions in the market. The collective negotiation of all professional sports leagues in the United States with the national television networks is an excellent example to illustrate this intention. By controlling the right to negotiate, a professional sports league, like the NFL, has great economic advantage at the negotiating table over any national television network that wants to telecasts its games and takes the market into a seller's one.

3. To promote and maintain outcome uncertainty. Outcome uncertainty is the most essential element of sport competition, regardless of whether it is in professional sport or in amateur athletics. Therefore, all control-agent organizations have rules and regulations to ensure the integrity of competition.

4. To maximize its profit as a business entity. Although recognizing profit maximization as a common goal of all business firms, many control-agent organizations in the sport industry also have specific rules and regulatory policies to ensure that profit maximization for the involved firms as a whole is the ultimate goal.

5. To ensure the safety of participants and spectators. The control-agent organizations for those industry segments (e.g., car racing) that are involved in great physical risks to participants and spectators have to develop rules and regulations specifically to ensure safety. For example, all promoters or organizers of all SPORTS-CAR-sanctioned car-racing events must provide proper liability and participant accident insurance with certain minimum limits.

In some cases, industry self-regulation is also intended to discourage competition among members, ultimately reducing their costs related to competition. Without rules and regulations, individual members may try whatever they can to gain advantage in competition. Often, such competition away from the competition site is very costly. For example, imagine that if the NCAA did not have any restrictions on campus visits by prospective student athletes, what would happen?

Forms and Issues of Self-Regulation in Professional Sports

Self-regulation in professional sports takes two major forms. The first involves establishing regulatory policies within each league. Examples of league-wide regulatory policies include (a) the luxury tax and revenue sharing, (b) the salary cap, (c) the amateur draft, (d) the collective negotiation of national television contracts, and (e) league-wide sponsorship agreements. The use of a syndicated ownership (or single entity ownership) structure is the second form of industry self-regulation observed in professional sports.

League-wide regulatory policies. In general, the league-wide regulatory policies are intended and established for the following five reasons:

1. To more evenly distribute the wealth. The recent establishment of a luxury tax and increased revenue sharing by the owners in Major League Baseball exemplifies such an intention. By so doing, they hope to reduce the disparity among affiliated teams in terms of their economic wealth.

2. To control player salaries through the implementation of a salary cap. A salary cap serves two purposes. It not only helps the owners by slowing and eventually stopping the escalating salaries, but also narrows the gap of spending on players between the wealthier franchises from big markets and the poorer ones from small markets.

3. To more evenly distribute player talent. For example, the worst franchises are given better positions in the amateur draft. By doing this, the league hopes to equalize the opportunities (for success) by individual franchises. In theory, the amateur draft, together with other league-wide regulatory policies, may prevent a highly successful franchise from dominating and a franchise that is currently unsuccessful from staying at the bottom forever.

4. To negotiate more lucrative national television contracts. By negotiating national TV contracts this way, a professional sports league can achieve a major economic goal. It precludes the big market franchises from obtaining all of the television exposure and all of the television revenues. Strictly from a commercial perspective, the national television networks will be much more likely to televise the games played by big market teams to maximize advertising revenues because of the considerable television exposure in those markets. The league's control over the right for negotiating national TV contracts guarantees the small-market teams the opportunity to be exposed to the national television audience and more importantly, to receive an equal share of the television revenues, which is vital to the survival of some franchises.

5. To maximize and evenly distribute licensing revenues through league-wide licensing agreements. The league-wide agreements ensure that the small market teams or the teams with worst records receive equal shares of the revenues obtained from the sales of licensed merchandises. These revenues are desperately needed for these organizations to be financially capable of signing big-name players to stay competitive.

A professional sports league confronts many regulatory issues if its franchises are independently owned and a league functions as a control-agent organization. Franchise relocation is one issue that has become a focal point of discussion lately. From a pure economic standpoint, a professional sports league will use its regulatory power to regulate the relocation of its member franchises only if the action is in the best economic interest of the league (Vrooman, 1997). In other words, a professional sports league may hesitate to prevent its members from relocating if the league will prosper economically with members who do not move obtaining a share from the franchise's stadium extortion and keeping the value of the expansion opportunity untouched. This scenario happens when the franchise moves from a city that has higher expansion value than the proposed new location. It will be in the best economic interest of the league to take a tough stand to oppose any relocation proposal if the direction of the move is reversed, that is, the franchise will relocate to a city that has a greater expansion value.

However, the self-regulatory power of the league has not prevented franchise movement. In 1996 alone, four NFL teams, five MLB franchises, and at least one team in both the

NBA and the NHL moved or threatened to move to another city (McClimon, 1996). By threatening to relocate, these professional sports franchises forced the host cities and communities to commit more resources to the teams. Historically, the federal government, especially its judicial branch, has held the position that franchise relocation was a matter for the professional sports league and the league had the authority to prevent its franchises from relocating. However, the exercise of this authority was often challenged by the franchise intending to move. These franchises claimed that the league's actions were a violation of the antitrust laws, and such an allegation was upheld by the court in the case of the *Los Angeles Memorial Coliseum and Los Angeles Raiders v. National Football League* (1984). As a result, individual professional sports franchises, except in Major League Baseball, were able to take advantage of and counter any restrictive efforts exercised by the league that prohibited them from relocating to other cities. The application of the antitrust laws has inevitably weakened the authority of individual professional sports leagues to use their regulatory power to deal with the franchise relocation issue. Some suggest that the current situation calls for further government intervention and a strong role in handling this matter (Dell'Apa, 1993).

Syndicated ownership (or single entity ownership) structure. Discussion related to this type of industry self-regulation can also be seen in chapter 5. The syndicated ownership structures have been utilized in several professional sports leagues, such as the American Basketball League (folded in 1999) and Major League Soccer. Discussion on the syndicated ownership structure may provide the student with insight into how and why it is considered a new way of self-regulation in the professional sport industry and how it works. In general, all syndicated professional sports leagues have the following common characteristics:

1. The league owns all players contracts, the most valuable assets of a league, and can move players from team to team based on the best economic interest of the league;
2. Players' salaries are determined by the league based on such criteria as performance and seniority;
3. There are two types of ownership of individual affiliated teams: licensees and investors. As a licensee, an owner has to (a) pay a fee to the league for the exclusive right to market and operate a team in a particular area, (b) pay an annual membership fee, and (c) underwrite the costs of marketing the team locally. As an investor of the league, an owner has an exclusive right to operate a franchise in a geographic location.

The adoption of such a syndicated structure in a professional sports league may solve most of the regulatory issues associated with the traditional nonsyndicated structure (e.g., the antitrust challenge brought by players, competitive imbalance). There are several obvious regulatory benefits. A professional sports league that adopts the syndicated ownership structure will virtually operate as a single business entity. The league can legitimately implement a variety of regulatory policies and practices and be free from many antitrust attacks. In other words, players can make no claims on the ground of unreasonable restraints of trade. To operate as a single entity also enables to the league to avoid franchise relocation-related issues and, thus, avoid the associated antitrust scrutiny. Regardless of the form chosen, industry self-regulation is utilized to counter the market forces in a free competitive market. In addition, it is also considered an effective survival strategy for individual leagues in monopolistic competition against their rivals.

Forms and Issues of Self-Regulation in Collegiate Athletics

To a certain extent, all the intercollegiate athletic associations (i.e., NCAA, NAIA, and NJCAA) regulate their members through similar regulatory rules and policies. This chapter mainly discusses the forms and practices of self-regulation in the case of the National Collegiate Athletic Association (NCAA), the biggest national governing body in intercollegiate athletics. As a private, nongovernmental regulatory body, the NCAA is responsible for overseeing athletic programs at more than 1,000 institutions. To obtain its goals, the NCAA has formulated many regulatory policies. It hopes through the implementation of these policies, the affiliated member institutions will benefit economically as a whole. The regulatory practices of the NCAA include, but are not limited to, the following:

1. Setting up restrictions on recruitment of student-athletes, specifically on the number of contacts and campus visits. A national letter of intent is introduced as another regulatory measure to serve the same purpose.

2. Controlling the rights for contract negotiation with television networks for all sports except football.

3. Limiting the size of coaching staff and their salaries.

4. Limiting the number of athletic scholarships that can be awarded to student-athletes in all sports.

5. Regulating the duration and intensity of student-athlete participation (i.e., setting limits on length of season and schedules of practice).

6. Establishing a system to detect and penalize member institutions that violate set policies (DeSchriver & Stotlar, 1996; Koch, 1984; Stern, 1981).

In 1910, when the member institutions formed the NCAA, its primary function was to develop rules of play and set up eligibility codes for its member institutions. As intercollegiate athletics has evolved, it has gradually become a control-agent organization, whose main function is to oversee the implementation of its regulatory rules and policies. Due to its role in the development and enforcement of regulations, the NCAA has become perceived as an economic cartel in many ways (DeSchriver & Stotlar, 1996; Koch, 1984). Chapter 4 has a detailed description of an economic cartel in terms of its characteristics and functions. To be economically effective as a cartel, the NCAA has to implement various rules and policies to regulate and control collectively the behavior of the affiliated member institutions. The main goal for doing this is threefold:

1. To minimize unwanted competition among the members (e.g., the NCAA places restrictions on recruiting and on number of scholarships allowed based on levels of competition).

2. To enhance the competitive position of the organization as a whole in the market, ultimately strengthening the mutual gains of the members. The NCAA collectively negotiates a television package for the championship tournament in all sponsored sports, except in football.

3. To level the playing field and attempt to ensure a competitive balance among its member institutions so as to strive for joint revenue maximization on the part of membership (Stern, 1981). It is believed that the survival of the NCAA depends on its ability

(a) to limit the financial clout of its big-time football and men's basketball members and (b) to redistribute big-time men's basketball income to its general membership.

The implementation of the NCAA's regulatory rules and policies is not problem-free. Many problems are caused by the friction between its organizational structure and cartel policies, and between the intentional opportunism of individual member institutions and the mission of the NCAA as a control-agent organization. The NCAA has faced the following three problems for decades, and they will continue to be irritants in years to come:

1. The NCAA has too many member institutions (more than 1,000 schools) to oversee. It is extremely difficult, if not impossible, to keep track of the activities and transactions of all these institutions. It is believed that the NCAA has not yet developed effective methods to detect and punish the member institutions that violate its cartel rules (DeSchriver, 1997). The strategies the NCAA has used in dealing with problems stemming from the large membership include (a) dividing the membership into divisions and levels of competition (e.g., Division I-A, and I-AA) based on certain criteria and allowing each division to have its own governance structure to make rules that are applicable to institutions in that particular division and (b) setting membership requirements (e.g., Division I-A) as barriers to entry to ensure the homogeneity of institutions affiliated with a certain division. By so doing, the NCAA tries to ensure that member institutions in the same division will have similar interests and financial capabilities.

2. The number of points of initiative is exceedingly large, which could be one reason why there are so many membership violations. One strategy that the NCAA has used is to keep restructuring its membership to produce more homogeneity among the membership of its various divisions. Restructuring is aimed at reducing the number of points of initiative and increasing the cartel effectiveness of the NCAA.

3. The NCAA has had legal challenges from member institutions for violation of their property rights as a result of price-fixing practices. (See the next chapter for more discussion on this matter.)

Forms and Issues of Self Regulation in Other Segments of the Sport Industry

Self-regulation is also common in other segments of the sport industry (e.g., sport and fitness clubs, and sporting goods). Nevertheless, because many of these control-agent organizations are trade-oriented associations, the regulatory issues differ from those of professional sport and collegiate athletics discussed above. The Sporting Goods Manufacturers Association (SGMA), for example, is a trade group founded to promote and stimulate market growth in sporting goods. One of its regulatory responsibilities is to set standards for all sporting goods. It wants to make sure that the sporting goods produced by all affiliated manufacturers meet the standards and that consumers and users accept these goods.

Risk of Self-Regulation

The implementation of various regulatory policies in a specific segment of the sport industry (e.g., professional sport) has helped (to a certain degree) to homogenize the membership to improve its financial and athletic competitive ability. However, it is not problem-free. Economists commonly recognize that an antitrust violation is one of several potential problems or risks of implementing the self-regulation program or policy. The judicial branch of the government often examines all the circumstances to determine whether the activities and policies implemented by an industry for a self-regulatory purpose are anticompetitive (Jacobs & Portman, 1997). Any self-regulation programs, policies, and activities that are anticompetitive and discriminatory or that are implemented without fair procedures are very likely subject to antitrust challenges.

This is certainly true in the case of professional sports. Players have frequently accused the owners and the league management of collusion. Individual owners also sometimes contend that the league-wide regulatory policies violate the antitrust laws (e.g., Dallas Cowboys owner Jerry Jones's antitrust lawsuits against the NFL for the latter's control over all franchise logos, trademarks, and licensing products) ("NFL, Cowboys Drop Suits," December 16, 1996). The contention against the regulatory policies has resulted in ceaseless labor turmoil and work stoppages and has intensified the internal friction among owners, ultimately undermining the economic stability of a professional sports league. Moreover, courts have frequently ruled in favor of players and owners who have accused the league of violating antitrust laws (Bulkeley, 1993). The challenges of the legitimacy of league-wide regulatory policies and the problems that have occurred accordingly raise the issue of the regulatory role that the government should play.

Industry Self-Regulation and Competitive Balance

In a free competitive market, the market force tends to promote a virtuous circle for winning teams (Gratton & Taylor, 1985). The teams with better winning records may generate more and more revenues due to higher attendance. With more money in their hands, the owner can then sign more lucrative contracts with marquee players to retain dominance and success (Gratton & Taylor, 1985). Furthermore, the sizes of markets in which affiliated franchises operate vary in terms of population, average household income, and the size of TV markets. The differences in these areas create disparity among franchises pertaining to the revenues they can possibly generate locally. As part of an entertainment industry that heavily relies on gate receipts, the financial wealth and ability of individual franchises are, to a great extent, affected and determined by the financial backing that they may receive from the local community. One good example that illustrates such disparity in local support (gate receipts, local media contracts, and other revenues from the stadium) exists in Major League Baseball. The annual revenues received by the New York Yankees in 1993 were about $94.6 million, whereas the Milwaukee Brewers' revenues were only $45.3 million in the same year (Ozanian, 1993). Evidently, the former franchise will be much more financially capable of acquiring marquee players than the latter in a free competitive market environment. Hypothetically, if the league does not use any regulatory policies in player signing and players can change teams at will, the economic condition of the league would suffer because the wealthier franchises from bigger markets would be able to obtain all of the talented players and dominate the player market. "Empirical evidence of the historical distribution of the win percent among clubs [in professional baseball] shows a lack of competitive balance" (Scully, 1995, p.83). To maintain the stability of the league, the strategy of revenue sharing is used to take wealth from the rich franchises and give it to the poor franchises for the sake of breaking the so-called virtuous circle for the winning franchise (Gratton & Taylor, 1985). Evidently, if a league operates under a complete free competitive market environment, it would be extremely difficult for franchises with less financial capability and local support to survive. Under this circumstance, league-wide policies must be employed to level the playing field among franchises. Theoretically, the economic efficiency of the operation of a professional sports league will be obtained only if competitive balance between individual franchises and stability of operation is ensured.

Dilemma of Industry Self-Regulation and Roles of Government

It is believed that the best outcome of regulation comes from the use of a regulatory system that incorporates the mechanisms of both government regulation and self-regulation (Wotruba, 1997). Nevertheless, the mixing these two types of regulatory mechanisms in professional sports seems to have unintended and unwanted consequences. As mentioned earlier, the government regulates professional sports mainly through its legislative and judicial branches, whereas the executive branch does not become as involved in regulating the sport industry as in it does in regulating other industries. The antitrust laws were some of the few pieces of legislation that have a great regulatory effect on the sport industry. Compliance with these laws has been monitored and reinforced by the judicial branch of the government. Although the intention of the laws was to promote free competition and economic efficiency, the use of the laws has weakened the power of a professional sports league in its self-regulatory efforts.

Future Models in Sport Regulation

Many chaotic situations in the sport industry, especially in professional sports in the United States, have prompted the public to rethink the role of government and to readjust its theoretical positions about whether government should play a stronger and more specific role in regulating professional sports. It is believed that the weakness of or lack of governmental regulatory mechanisms has indirectly provoked these negative situations.

A long-standing controversy in professional sports management has been whether the government should regulate professional sports as it does other segments of the business world. Advocates of regulation strongly urge that some sort of governmental involvement and regulation occur in professional sports to stabilize the economy in that particular segment of the sport industry and to respond to the "public-interest-related objectives" (Mitnick, 1980, p. 91). Without government intervention, in professional sport, as in other industries, achieving economic efficiency will be difficult; professional sports leagues will continue to monopolize resources and dominate the demand and supply relationship, eventually fixing the price and controlling the public goods. According to Dell'Apa (1993), professional sports have been able to conduct the business side of their operations largely outside of governmental control and public scrutiny. The government's passive stance has continued to cause considerable trouble for professional sports and the public.

However, the opponents of regulation contend that government intervention and "public policies commonly are followed by unintended consequences" (Frey & Johnson, 1985, p. 264). They contend that the problems of professional sports are caused by the imperfection of the free market system. These problems will be solved eventually by the market's as well as the industry's self-regulatory mechanisms. Government interventions are unnecessary.

Should the government be involved and how does it ensure the public interest will not be unfairly hampered? This question still does not have a clear-cut answer.

Summary

This chapter presented economic theories related to both government and industry self-regulation. The government regulates industries for both economic and social reasons. This chapter mainly discusses why and how government regulates the industries from an economic perspective. Allocative inefficiency and market failure are two primary reasons for government regulation of industries. Problems in professional sports are attributed to the lack of government involvement in the sport industry.

Industry self-regulation is another form of regulation addressed in the chapter. This discussion focuses on why an industry regulates itself and how it can do this task effectively. Examples of self-regulation in professional sports and collegiate athletics are provided. Issues related to self-regulation in both professional sports and collegiate athletics are also discussed.

Chapter Study Questions

1. Using an example in the sport industry, explain the concept of government regulation.
2. Elaborate on the three basic types of managerial and economic functions of government.
3. Explain why the government would need to regulate an industry.
4. Using the concepts, "deadweight loss" and "market failure," discuss why monopoly is less efficient than competition.
5. Define the concept "industry self-regulation," and explain why industries want to impose regulations onto their members.
6. Discuss how a professional sports league regulates the affiliated franchises.
7. What are the forms of self-regulation in collegiate sports?
8. Discuss the relationship between industry self-regulation and competitive balance.
9. What are the regulatory policies and practices of the NCAA as a control-agent organization?
10. What problems does the NCAA face as a control-agent organization, and what coping strategies has it used to solve those problems?

Chapter Ten

INTRODUCTION

In chapter 9, we have discussed economic theories related to both government and industry self-regulation. One of the fundamental arguments for government regulation is to ensure fairness in business competition. Antitrust laws are passed specifically for this purpose. This chapter will examine U. S. antitrust laws and their various applications in the sport industry to provide a clear understanding of how the government uses the laws to promote competition in the sport marketplace.

Statutes

The Sherman Act

The antitrust laws are a series of regulations that were enacted beginning in 1890. The overall goals of the laws were to encourage competition and to prevent monopolies and the inefficiencies associated with them (McGuigan & Moyer, 1986). The first antitrust law, passed in 1890, was the Sherman Act. Although many monopolistic and anticompetitive practices were already illegal under common law, during the rapid industrialization of the late 19th century, people began to believe that legislation would be needed to maintain and encourage competition (Mansfield, 1992). Combinations of organizations, called trusts, were engaging in collusion (i.e., forming cartels) in order to restrict output and increase prices, so many felt legislation was needed to prevent the formation of these trusts (Mansfield). The Sherman Act essentially does two things. First, it declares in Section 1 that "every contract, combination in the form of a trust or otherwise, or conspiracy in restraint of commerce among the several States, or with foreign countries" is illegal. This part deals only with agreements in which two or more people are involved.

Second, Section 2 makes it illegal for an individual to "monopolize, or attempt to monopolize, or combine or conspire with any other person or persons, to monopolize any part of the trade or commerce among the several States, or with several nations." This part is broader in that it applies to both individual efforts and activities by more than one person (McGuigan & Moyer,

Competition and Antitrust in the Sport Industry

Rick Sterling is the president of Sterling Sporting Goods, Inc. (SSG). His business has been very successful in large part because it completely dominates the market for lacrosse sticks. All users consider Sterling's sticks superior. However, the company does not sell its product through sporting goods stores; it only sells them directly to high school, university, and professional teams.

Although Rick Sterling is happy with the success of his business, he would like to expand his business in order to realize even greater profits. Recently, SSG has begun producing tennis rackets and hockey sticks. Rick's vice-president for sales, Jill McGowan, says that she has a good idea. She suggests that Rick attempt to tie sales of the Sterling tennis rackets and hockey sticks to the very popular Sterling lacrosse sticks. Under this new arrangement, high schools and universities wishing to buy the Sterling lacrosse sticks would also have to agree to buy their tennis rackets and hockey sticks exclusively from Sterling.

Rick thinks Jill's idea sounds great. The Sterling lacrosse sticks are very popular, and the tennis rackets and hockey sticks are considered at least comparable to the other products on the market. Is this strategy legal and/or ethical? If this strategy is not possible, are there other approaches that would be legal and ethical?

1986). It should also be noted that both sections state that laws apply only to interstate (i.e., between two states) and international commerce, so intrastate (i.e., within one state) commerce is clearly not covered. This means that if all of the actions in question take place within a given state, the Sherman Act does not apply. Although many states have their own antitrust laws to deal with intrastate commerce, this legislation is often weak and is less often applied (Salvatore, 1993).

Violators of either section of the Sherman Act may be subject to both civil actions and criminal prosecution (Hirschey & Pappas, 1995). Although violations were originally considered misdemeanors, a 1974 amendment to the Sherman Act declared violation a felony that can result in up to 3 years in prison and fines for both the individual and the organization. Civil action may result in an even larger financial loss than the fines, in part because damages are automatically tripled. Therefore, a company found liable under the antitrust laws for $1 million in damages must actually pay $3 million. Despite the potential penalties, many expressed dissatisfaction with the Sherman Act in the years following its passage because they found it too general and vague, and enforcement was limited (McGuigan & Moyer, 1986). Moreover, businesses claimed there was considerable confusion over which actions were considered legal and which were illegal (Hirschey & Pappas, 1995). The generality of the act and the confusion related to the legality of certain business practices led to further legislation in the early part of the 20th century.

Clayton Act

In 1914, Congress passed the Clayton Act to deal with the perceived weaknesses of the Sherman Act. Although Congress was attempting to create a "comprehensive list of forbidden monopolistic practices," the Clayton Act was able to identify only four such practices (McGuigan & Moyer, 1986, p. 621). First, Section 2 declared price discrimination among business customers illegal, unless these differences were based on differences in the cost of selling or transporting the goods or services or unless the differences were offered to meet competitive demands.

For example, a New Jersey manufacturer of golf clubs could charge a higher price when selling to California retail stores as opposed to local New Jersey retail stores because of differences in transportation costs, but could not charge different prices among local New Jersey stores. The main focus of this section was to prevent national companies from charging lower prices in some regional markets with the intent of driving local competitors out of business to obtain a monopoly over the regional market (Hirschey & Pappas, 1995). This section was later amended by the Robinson-Patman Act in 1936, which outlaws specific examples of price discrimination (i.e., certain chain-store practices; Hirschey & Pappas, 1995).

Learning Activities

1. Return to the beginning of the chapter, and reread the story about Sterling Sporting Goods, Inc. After reading this chapter, what advice would you give to Rick Sterling? Is Jill's plan legal and/or ethical? If it is illegal, who may try to use the antitrust laws to stop SSG? Are there other ways the company could accomplish its goals but avoid possible litigation?
2. In this chapter, we discussed activities engaged in by the NCAA that have led and could eventually lead to violations of the antitrust laws. If you were in charge, what type of NCAA activities might you change in order to avoid antitrust liability?
3. There has been discussion that perhaps the government should not be a provider of sport. Are there methods to achieve the same goals without the government's being a sport provider? If so, how?

Second, Section 3 declared exclusive and tying agreements illegal when they were designed to reduce competition and create a monopoly. One example of a tying contract would be when a company would tie the purchase of one product to the purchase of another (Hirschey & Pappas, 1995). For example, if the Hillerich & Bradsby Company (Louisville Slugger) were the only producer of aluminum bats and they wanted to use this position of power to help the sales of their PowerBilt golf clubs, they might decide to force high school and university athletic departments to sign a contract that would allow them to buy Louisville Slugger bats only if they also agreed to buy exclusively PowerBilt golf clubs. However, because this type of agreement would reduce competition in the golf club industry, it would be a violation of the Clayton Act.

Third, Section 7, the antimerger section, declared that it was illegal for a firm engaged in commerce to acquire shares or stocks of competing firms if this would result in substantial damage to competition or would tend to create a monopoly. Although this section was designed to prevent competitors from merging if such a merger would result in a significant decrease in competition, it was not intended to prevent all mergers. For example, the merger of the 75th and 76th largest firms in an industry with 100 large firms is unlikely to have the same impact on competition, as would a merger between two firms in an industry with only two major firms.

There were, however, two essential loopholes in Section 7. Section 7 outlawed only horizontal mergers (i.e., mergers between competitors), so vertical (i.e., mergers between companies with a buyer-seller relationship) and conglomerate mergers (i.e., mergers between unrelated companies) were legal even if they lessened competition (McGuigan & Moyer, 1986). In addition, Section 7 failed to outlaw mergers that reduced competition via asset acquisition as opposed to stock acquisition (Hirschey & Pappas, 1995). However, the Celler-Kefauver Act of 1950 later closed both these loopholes.

Finally, Section 8 declared it illegal for individuals to sit on the board of directors of two or more competing firms. Obviously, firms with common directors would be unlikely to compete vigorously against one another (Hirschey & Pappas, 1995). This is the only section of the act in which the practice is automatically illegal, and there is no need to prove damage to competition (McGuigan & Moyer, 1986).

Federal Trade Commission Act

The Federal Trade Commission Act was also passed in 1914 as a supplement to the Clayton Act. Section 5 of the act states "that unfair methods of competition in commerce are hereby declared illegal." Determining what constituted unfair methods of competition became the responsibility of the Federal Trade Commission, an independent government agency created by this act. Section 5 of the FTC Act was later amended by the Wheeler-Lea Act of the 1938. Several court decisions had interpreted Section 5 in such a way that for a firm to be found in violation, there had to be (a) evidence there was damage to the buyer and (b) strong evidence the firm had competitors who would be damaged and who were not also engaging in similar deceptive practices (McGuigan & Moyer, 1986). The Wheeler-Lea Act made deceptive acts or practices illegal, even if no harm to competition is proven, thereby expanding consumer protection and increasing the ease of prosecuting violators (McGuigan & Moyer).

Exemptions

Sports Broadcast Act of 1961. When examining the application of antitrust laws in the sport industry, it is important to note several exemptions to the laws. First, the Sports Broadcast Act of 1961 exempted league-wide television contracts from the antitrust laws (Masteralexis, 1997). The ability to legally negotiate league-wide contracts, as opposed to team-by-team deals, has significantly increased the bargaining power of professional sport leagues in television negotiations and has helped them to negotiate increasingly high television rights fees. However, as will be discussed later, this act did not apply to the NCAA and did not protect its national football contract.

Labor union exemption. Second, organized labor also has an antitrust exemption. Prior to the Clayton Act, labor unions were often the targets of antitrust suits by firms that argued strikes and boycotts were conspiracies to restrain trade (Masteralexis, 1997). The vagueness of the Sherman Act made such a use of the antitrust law a possibility. The Clayton Act corrected the problem by stating that "a human being was not a commodity or article of commerce, and thus, labor's actions were not subject to the Sherman Act" (Masteralexis, 1997, p. 403). Because the courts continued to grant injunctions against boycotts, in 1932, Congress passed the Norris-LaGuardia Act, which further restricted the use of injunctions against union actions during labor disputes (Masteralexis). Moreover, the Wagner Act of 1935, also called the National Labor Relations Act, further expanded the rights of employees and unions and created the National Labor Relations Board to enforce the labor laws (Masteralexis).

However, although the laws exempted actions of labor when workers are acting in their own self-interest, the laws do not exempt union-management agreements that are "conspiracies in restraint of trade" (Masteralexis, 1997). For example, if a union were negotiating with a number of organizations in the sporting goods industry and entered an agreement with one firm that had the effect of driving the other firms out of business, this agreement would not be exempt and the labor union would be liable under the antitrust laws. To use the labor exemption, the following three-part test must be satisfied:

1. The injured party (the plaintiff) must be party to the collective bargaining agreement;
2. The subject being contested on antitrust grounds must be a mandatory subject for bargaining (a mandatory subject is one that deals with hours, wages, and other terms and conditions of employment);
3. The collective bargaining agreement must have been achieved through bona fide arms' length bargaining (Masteralexis, 1997, p. 404).

If any one of these three elements is absent, the labor exemption may not be used, and the actions being contested may be considered violations of the antitrust laws.

The Role of the Courts

As is the case with any law, it is the role of the courts to enforce the antitrust laws (Mansfield, 1992). In general, antitrust proceedings are initiated by the Antitrust Division of the Department of Justice, the Federal Trade Commission, or private parties (individuals or groups; Salvatore, 1993). Although the Department of Justice generally initiates criminal cases and the Federal Trade Commission initiates only civil cases, most of the cases, over 90% of the over 2,000 initiated each year, are actually filed by private parties (Salvatore).

The large percentage of cases attributed to private suits is not surprising when we consider a number of factors.

First, government agencies generally have limited resources and cannot possibly pursue every case. Moreover, they often pursue large firms with substantial resources available to oppose the government, so cases tend to be difficult and lengthy (e.g., the case against Microsoft for antitrust violations). Therefore, the government tends to focus on cases in which the violations appear blatant and the financial impact of these violations is large. By pursuing these cases, government agencies hope to maximize their success and their impact. Cases in which success is less likely or the financial impact of the violator's actions is minimal are then left to the private parties to pursue.

Second, the antitrust laws are broad and general (Salvatore, 1993). The difficulty in determining what is "unfair" and what "substantially lessens competition" has led to divergent opinions on what justifies an antitrust suit (Salvatore). Again, the government tends to ignore cases in which the existence of an antitrust violation is less clear, whereas a private party who has been severely affected may wish to pursue the suit even if there is only some chance for success. Because of the broadness of the laws, "some chance for success" is common. Third, American society in general is becoming more litigious. The number of private parties filling suits has increased rapidly in recent years, so the high percentage of antitrust cases initiated by private parties is consistent with that trend. Again, the lack of clarity about what constitutes an antitrust violation has made this a particularly rich area for litigation.

Dispute Resolution

If the court believes an antitrust violation has occurred, it has a number of potential means for resolving the related dispute. In a criminal proceeding, the court may fine (up to $100,000) or imprison (up to 3 years) individuals found guilty. The court may also fine (up to $1 million) an organization found guilty of violating the antitrust laws. Private parties damaged by the violations are awarded triple damages in civil cases, and there is no limit on the total amount of the damages. The large potential impact on both individuals and organizations is certainly one significant deterrent from violating the antitrust laws.

However, many antitrust disputes are settled instead by (a) dissolution and divestiture, (b) injunction, or (c) consent decree (Salvatore, 1993). In some antimerger cases, the firm has been ordered to dissolve, which causes them to lose their identity, or to divest (i.e., sell its assets acquired in the merger), which essentially voids the merger. An injunction is an order from the court that either forces the company to refrain from anticompetitive actions (e.g., collusion between competing firms to fix prices) or to take actions that increase competition (e.g., license rights to produce a patented product to other companies). A consent decree is an agreement by the firm with the Justice Department, in which the defendant agrees to abide by certain rules specified in the decree. A major advantage of the consent decree is that it allows the Justice Department and the firm to avoid the expense and time-consuming process of a court trial.

Basis for Court Decisions

Although determining which actions violate the antitrust laws is rarely clear-cut, possible violations related to Section 1 of the Sherman Act are particularly difficult to determine.

To deal with the vagueness of this section of the Sherman Act, the Supreme Court has developed three approaches for determining if the actions under examination constitute a violation of the act. The first approach is used when the anticompetitive activity is considered to be illegal per se (Masteralexis, 1997); In these cases "certain types of agreements are so consistently unreasonable that the Court deems them as illegal without any further inquiry in the rational given for their existence" (Drowatzky, 1997, p. 414).

What constitutes a per se violation has been developed by the court over time as a result of dealing with a number of antitrust cases. Although the rather mechanical per se approach is generally quicker and easier to apply, it is more limited and has rarely been applied in the sport setting (Champion, 1993; Drowatzky, 1997). In addition, the second approach, called the consumer welfare approach, has not been applied in sport cases (Masteralexis, 1997). When this approach is used, the plaintiff must demonstrate that the conduct of the organization actually had a negative impact on consumer welfare (Masteralexis).

The third and final approach, referred to as the rule of reason approach, is the approach used most often in and out of the sport industry (Champion, 1997). When using the rule of reason approach, the Court will examine whether the restraint imposed by the action is justifiable based on a legitimate business purpose and whether it is the least restrictive means possible to achieve this purpose (Drowatzky, 1997). Because the action taken, the purpose of the action, and the other possible actions that would have been less restrictive all must be examined, the rule of reason approach is often time-consuming and complex. To examine the action in an orderly fashion, the Court will make its evaluation using three questions (Drowatzky, 1997):

1. Is the rule in keeping with the purposes of the group (or is it intended to protect the association from competition by outsiders)?
2. Is the rule a reasonable means of achieving an otherwise proper goal?
3. Are the procedural aspects of the group's enforcement activities reasonable and appropriate?

The burden of proof in these cases is on the plaintiff. They must prove the defendant's actions were, in fact, improper and the restraint was unreasonable based on the justification given by the defendants. To be successful, the defendant must provide evidence that leads the court to answer "no" to one of the three questions above.

Focus of Antitrust Laws

Mergers

Types of mergers. Mergers have frequently been the focus of antitrust litigation, in part, because of the increasing frequency of large mergers (McGuigan & Moyer, 1986). As previously noted, there are three types of mergers. *Horizontal mergers* occur between two or more competing organizations. An example of a horizontal merger would be if two athletic footwear companies, such as Nike and Reebok, were to merge. *Vertical mergers* involve firms with a buyer-seller relationship. If, for example, Adidas were to merge with Foot Locker retail stores, this would be an example of a vertical merger.

Finally, *conglomerate mergers* occur when the companies involved are not competitors and have no significant buyer-seller relationship. These could include mergers between companies producing the same product in different geographic markets (i.e., geographic market-extension mergers), mergers between companies producing related products (i.e., product-extension mergers), and mergers between firms that are basically unrelated in any meaningful way (i.e., pure conglomerate mergers). As examples, a merger between a chain of fitness clubs in Kentucky and a chain in Indiana would be a geographic market-extension merger, the merger between Disney and the Anaheim Angels is a products-extension merger (both are in the entertainment industry), and a merger between Rawlings Sporting Goods and Julio Gallo wines would be a pure conglomerate merger (the companies are completely unrelated).

Legality of mergers. As previously discussed, mergers are not automatically illegal. They often have a legitimate purpose and are not anticompetitive. For example, horizontal mergers are often designed to improve the efficiency of production, vertical mergers are generally used to improve the efficiency of distribution, and many conglomerate mergers are focused on diversifying the firm's operations and thereby spreading the risk (i.e., failure in one area of the firm can be offset by success in another area; McGuigan & Moyer, 1986). If a merger has little or no impact on the level of competition in the marketplace, the merger will not be a violation of the antitrust laws and will be allowed. The problem lies with trying to determine which mergers will cause the level of competition in the marketplace to experience a significant decline.

Horizontal mergers. Many antitrust cases have focused on horizontal mergers, and these cases have certainly slowed the rate of horizontal mergers (McGuigan & Moyer, 1986). In fact, the Clayton Act (1914) covered only horizontal mergers; all vertical and conglomerate mergers were legal for the first half of the 20th century. Moreover, although determining the impact of mergers on competition is never easy, the impact of horizontal mergers is often the most clear. To determine the impact of a horizontal merger on competition, a number of factors are generally examined, including the size of the organization after the proposed merger, the number of competing firms in the industry, and the market share of the firm (McGuigan & Moyer, 1986).

Also, the current market concentration ratio (see chapter 4) is often critical in the examination of the merger's impact. Research suggests that as the four-firm concentration ratio increases above 70%, the market price for a product or service tends to increase by at least 10% (Bain, 1951; Schwartzman, 1959, 1961). Other research indicates that for each 10% increase in the four-firm concentration ratio, prices tend to increase by 1.1 to 1.4% (Collins & Preston, 1968). Obviously, it is in the consumers' best interest to prevent mergers that lead to high levels of market concentration because such mergers tend to result in excessively higher prices.

Vertical mergers. In 1950, the Celler-Kefauver Act extended the jurisdiction of the antitrust laws over mergers to include both vertical and conglomerate mergers. However, the impacts of such mergers are generally much harder to determine. When examining vertical mergers, we must try to determine how increasing control over the distribution system may allow a company to increase market power. In theory, the example of the Adidas merger with FootLocker should have little or no immediate impact on the four-firm market concentration or Nike's market share. However, if Adidas only allowed Adidas products to be sold at FootLocker stores and thereby significantly increased their sales, while decreasing the sales of their competitors (e.g., Reebok, Nike), the merger would clearly have an impact on competition in the market and would decrease the choices given to the consumer.

Conglomerate mergers. Examining the impact of conglomerate mergers is particularly hard, because rather than examining only one industry, the federal agency or court must determine the impact on aggregate economic concentration (McGuigan & Moyer, 1986). In other words, they must determine the impact of the merger on the economy as a whole. For example, a merger between Microsoft and Ford might be scrutinized because of the large size of both organizations even though they are not in the same industry. However, few pure sport organizations (i.e., those whose business is entirely sport related) are so large that their merger with a company in another industry would have much impact on total business in the United States. Sport organizations involved in large conglomerate mergers (e.g., ESPN, Atlanta Braves) have generally been only a small part of these mergers.

Monopolization

The focus on mergers is closely related to a concern about the potential for monopolization. Again, firms in unrestricted monopolies generally have the power to charge prices well above their costs and to restrict output. Therefore, it is in the public's best interest to prevent actions that would push an industry closer to a monopoly and to encourage actions that would tend to move the industry in the opposite direction of the continuum, toward perfect competition. Although a merger is one way an organization can monopolize, it is not the only option. Firms have frequently been accused of trying to run competitors out of business so that they can become a monopoly in a certain geographic location.

For example, some have suggested that national sporting good chains sometimes come into communities and charge very low prices in an effort to destroy the local "mom and pop" operations. Although these national chains can afford to charge lower prices because of the discounts they obtain from buying in large quantities from suppliers and because they can use profits from one store to offset a temporary loss at another (i.e., predatory pricing), the small business simply cannot afford to compete with the lower prices. Once all of the small businesses are gone, the national sporting goods chains will have a local monopoly and will be able to charge higher prices because of the lack of competition. Because consumers will then be left with higher prices and no options, preventing such efforts to monopolize is in the best interests of the local residents.

Anticompetitive Practices

Cartels and collusion. The antitrust laws are also designed to prevent a number of anticompetitive practices that include mergers in an attempt to control the market, actions designed to destroy the business of competitors, and other attempts to monopolize an industry. There are, however, other anticompetitive practices. For example, much of the collusion done by cartels is considered anticompetitive because it allows a group of organizations to act in a manner similar to a monopoly with regard to high prices and artificially restricted output. Although explicit collusion agreements are clearly anticompetitive and a violation of the antitrust laws, even informal understandings between competitors in a cartel may be considered illegal if these understandings substantially reduce competition (Salvatore, 1993).

High barriers to entry. In addition, another anticompetitive practice is for a firm to create high barriers to entry so new firms can not enter the market. Some means for creating high barriers to entry include

1. Patenting an invention and then refusing to license the product or process.

2. Obtaining control over all or most of the supply of a necessary input.

3. Entering exclusive agreements with all or most of the buyers of the product or service.

4. Inflating start-up costs for any new firms wishing to enter the market.

Actions of monopsonies. Finally, anticompetitive practices used to maintain unreasonably low prices for a given supply are also illegal. As discussed in chapter 4, monopsonies are firms that are the sole purchasers of a given supply. This position allows the monopsony to have considerable power over the market, and like a monopoly, the firm can use this power to affect prices. However, in contrast to a monopoly that is trying to increase the prices paid for their good or service, the goal of the monopsony is to keep prices they pay for a good or service low. Actions by a firm that are designed to maintain their position as a monopsony may also be considered anticompetitive, and therefore, a violation of the antitrust laws.

For example, if only one firm owned all of the athletic footwear stores in the United States, they could keep the price they paid for the athletic footwear very low. To maintain this power, they could try to prevent any competitors from entering the market, or they could enter into a collusive agreement with new competitors, in which they agree to continue to offer only the current low price for the athletic footwear supply. Such actions would prevent true competition from occurring in that industry.

It should be noted, however, that some argue the actions designed to monopsonize and keep prices low should generally be allowed and should not be considered violations of the antitrust laws (Hirschey & Pappas, 1995). This argument suggests if a firm, or group of firms, can keep the prices of their supply low, they will be able to pass those savings on to the consumers. Because one of the major goals of the antitrust laws is to protect consumers from inflated prices, the actions of monopsonies would not be considered a violation of the antitrust laws because they would ultimately benefit the consumers. Actions by the government or private party to end a monopsony would eventually lead to an increase in prices and damage to the consumers. For example, one could argue the decrease in monopsony-like control of professional sport leagues over the labor market resulted in increased prices for consumers (Howard, 1999).

However, others have argued the practices of monopsonies also lead to a reduction in production (Weiler & Roberts, 1993). Because of the low prices paid to suppliers, these suppliers will produce less, resulting in decreased production by the monopsony, which ultimately is detrimental for the consumer. In addition to protecting the consumers, the antitrust laws are designed to prevent other firms and labor from anticompetitive practices, and the actions of monopsony could damage these groups. In fact, many of the cases brought against firms acting as monopsonies have been brought forward by other firms or by labor groups, not by the government. Moreover, it is not uncommon that certain actions (e.g., running a competitor out of business) may be designed to both monopolize and monopsonize and, therefore, should clearly be violations of the antitrust laws. In general, any anticompetitive activities by an organization could be considered violations of the antitrust laws and subject to litigation.

Antitrust Enforcement and Professional Sports

Although some antitrust litigation has addressed individual sports such as boxing (*United States v. International Boxing Club,* 1955), most of the antitrust cases in professional sports have involved professional team sports. In fact, all of the four major professional team sport leagues have been involved in antitrust-related litigation during their existence (Masteralexis, 1997). This is not surprising because professional sport leagues could be described as monopolists or cartels (see chapter 4), and the antitrust laws are designed to restrict the actions of monopolies and cartels. However, the antitrust laws are not applied equally to the professional sport leagues.

Although court decisions indicate the antitrust laws apply to professional football, basketball, and hockey, professional baseball has been exempt from the antitrust laws since the Supreme Court decision in *Federal Baseball Club of Baltimore, Inc. v. National League of Professional Baseball Clubs, et al.* (1922; Berry & Wong, 1986). The Court concluded in the *Federal Baseball* case that the antitrust laws did not apply to professional baseball because two key elements were missing (Masteralexis, 1997). First, the Court said that baseball was intrastate, not interstate. The majority opinion of the Court argued that games were merely local exhibitions and, therefore, only intrastate activities. Second, the Court argued that professional baseball was not commerce. The inability to see sport as "real" business was very common in the early part of the 20th century. People believed the major significance of the games was the competition among the players, not the money made by the owners.

Although later Supreme Court rulings have clearly stated that professional sport is both interstate and commerce and should, therefore, be subject to the antitrust laws (e.g., *Radovich v. National Football League,* 1957), baseball has retained its exemption based on the precedent of the *Federal Baseball* decision. The Court stated in later decisions (*Flood v. Kuhn,* 1972; *Toolson v. New York Yankees,* 1953) that after the Court's initial ruling, it became the responsibility of Congress to pass legislation to revoke baseball's antitrust exemption and the fact that Congress had not passed legislation was an indication that Congress does not believe the *Federal Baseball* decision should be overturned.

Recently, Congress did pass the Curt Flood Act, which revoked baseball's antitrust exemption only as it applies to player employment issues (Curtis, 1998; King, 1998a). Although baseball executives were supportive of the Curt Flood Act, they have continually lobbied Congress to allow them to retain the remainder of their antitrust exemption (King, 1998a). This exemption allows professional baseball to engage in monopolistic or cartel-like activities without fear of being sued based on the antitrust laws. This is certainly a position that is the envy of many businesses. In fact, when a more recent Federal District Court decision stated the antitrust exemption should not be applied to the business of baseball (*Piazza v. Major League Baseball,* 1993), the league settled the case out of court so the decision would have no precedential value and would, therefore, not endanger the league's exemption (Masteralexis, 1997). The economic impact of antitrust enforcement and the different antitrust status of the leagues will be discussed throughout the next section.

Specific Areas of Antitrust Enforcement in Professional Sports

Mergers

Mergers in professional sports are not unusual. Because established leagues have plenty of incentive to maintain their power over their respective professional sport, whenever rival leagues emerge to challenge more established leagues, the result is that the established league either runs the new league out of business or the two leagues merge (Champion, 1993). Despite the fact that most professional sport leagues completely control their respective markets (e.g., professional football in the United States), mergers in professional sports have not generally been unopposed by the government. At first glance, this behavior by the government may seem unusual.

As previously discussed, among the major criteria the government uses to determine whether a merger should be allowed are the relative market share of the merging firms and the four-firm concentration ratio (McGuigan & Moyer, 1986). In the case of many of the recent sport league mergers (e.g., the American Basketball Association (ABA) with the National Basketball Association (NBA); the American Football League (AFL) with the National Football League (NFL), there were only two major leagues in the given sport before the merger and only one after the merger. Based on the complete control of the respective sport market of the merged league, such mergers would clearly appear to violate the antitrust laws and should be stopped by the government. In fact, antitrust lawyers working for the NFL advised against the AFL-NFL merger because they believed that such a merger would certainly lead to antitrust litigation, which they felt certain the league would lose (Chester, 1999).

Reactions by the government to league mergers. However, mergers have generally been unopposed by the government, and there are a number of possible reasons for this inactivity:

1. The 1966 Act of Congress, 15 U.S.C. Sec. 291 specifically permitted the merger of two or more professional football leagues thus exempting football mergers from the antitrust laws.

2. The leagues are generally not legally viewed as single entities (Champion, 1993), so a merger between two leagues differs slightly from a merger between two firms in another industry. For example, the merger between the NFL and AFL did not reduce the number of separately owned and operated franchises. Therefore, the market share of each team would be relatively unaffected and the four-firm (or team) concentration ratio would also remain unchanged.

3. In some cases (e.g., the ABA-NBA merger), the secondary league and its teams may not have survived without the merger. The government is generally reluctant to prevent a merger if one of the companies will cease to exist without the merger. In fact, professional sport league mergers in these cases will actually maintain a greater number of franchises than would exist without the merger, so the merger is arguably increasing competition in the market.

4. The market share of the league and the market concentration ratio depend on how one defines the market. A narrow definition of the market would suggest that the Major League Baseball is a monopoly or cartel in the professional baseball market. However, the market could be defined more broadly as (a) the professional sport market, which would include all professional sport associations (e.g., NBA, NFL, NHL, MLS, WNBA);

(b) the baseball market, which would include baseball at all levels (e.g., intercollegiate, high school); or (c) the sport entertainment market, which would include any sport association that provides sport entertainment (e.g., Ladies' Professional Golf Association, National Collegiate Athletic Association, National Hockey League). In each case, the market share and market concentration ratio for Major League Baseball would be much lower and, particularly in the third case, the merger would appear to have little impact on the overall competition in the industry.

5. The economic and financial impact of mergers between professional sport leagues is very small when compared to mergers in other industries. For example, a merger between long-distance companies AT&T, MCI, and Sprint would have a far greater impact and would, therefore, concern consumers more than would any sport-related merger. Because the government has a limited amount of time, it tends to pursue only cases with the greatest impact, thereby ignoring mergers with a more limited impact.

Reactions by private parties to league mergers. Although the government may be reluctant to oppose sport league mergers, three parties have some incentive to stop such mergers. First, franchises in the new league that are not included in the proposed merger have an incentive to try to stop the merger or to seek compensation for their losses during the merger. Such an attempt has been seen in professional baseball (*Federal Baseball Club of Baltimore, Inc. v. National League of Professional Baseball Clubs, et al.*, 1922). The Federal Baseball Club of Baltimore failed because the Court determined that antitrust laws did not apply to professional baseball, but former ABA teams were at least successful in gaining some compensation in an out of court settlement in the 1970's.

Second, fans have an incentive to oppose such mergers. When there are two competing leagues, fans are likely to have more television viewing options and more teams in the local area, and they are also more likely to be able to buy tickets at a lower price. However, no fan or group of fans has yet attempted to use legal means to stop a merger, and the chances for success of such litigation are, therefore, still uncertain.

Third, players have an incentive to try to stop a proposed merger. When only one league exists, competition for the services of the players is more limited. There is only one amateur draft and, with the exception of free agents, only one team with which players can negotiate a contract (i.e., a monopsony). Prior to the existence of free agency, rapid salary increases in sport occurred only when there was more than one league. For example, competition between the NFL and the World Football League (WFL) in the 1970s and the United States Football League (USFL) in the 1980s helped to improve the bargaining power of professional football players and led to salary increases for the players.

In *Robertson et al. v. National Basketball Association* (1975), players actually succeeded in blocking a proposed merger between the ABA and NBA by claiming that such "a merger would be anticompetitive, creating a monopoly and imperiling jobs" (quoted in Berry & Wong, 1986, p. 393) and was, therefore, a violation of the antitrust laws. Although the players and the NBA later reached a settlement allowing the merger to occur (Berry & Wong), the success of the NBA players in this case indicates the Court believes sport league mergers are subject to the antitrust laws, and such mergers can be stopped in certain cases.

Monopolization

Whether professional sport leagues are monopolists or cartels, clearly, their status has provided them with considerable market power. For example, the television rights sold by the NFL have increased in value dramatically in recent years (Coakley, 1998). If there were other professional football leagues competing with the NFL, or if the NFL sold the television rights on a team-by-team basis, it is unlikely they would be able to charge such high fees for their broadcasts. However, the Sports Broadcast Act of 1961 specifically exempts this activity from the antitrust laws, providing the leagues with a major economic advantage.

In addition, the leagues try to provide most of their teams with local monopoly status. By limiting the number of teams and establishing regulations that attempt to control and limit franchise relocation, the leagues give most teams significant market power within a given geographic region. As would be suggested by economic theory, the monopoly status of many of these teams in regional markets has allowed them to charge increasingly higher prices. For example, the cost of attending an NHL game increased 77% in just 6 years, from 1991 to 1997 (Howard, 1999). It is unlikely such increases would have occurred if there had been multiple teams in each city, especially in the midsized cities.

Moreover, the market power possessed by the teams because of the limited number of teams has allowed teams to force cities to subsidize the construction of their facilities (Howard & Crompton, 1995). Despite research that suggests building sport facilities does not have a positive economic impact on the community (Baade & Dye, 1990; Noll & Zimbalist, 1997), many cities remain willing to use substantial amounts of tax revenue to help build these facilities because they fear losing their teams. If there were an unlimited number of teams, it is unlikely that teams would have the power to "blackmail" cities into building the facilities that teams want.

Local monopolization litigation. Thus far, two types of cases related to local monopolization have emerged. First, some potential owners have sued the league for limiting the number of franchises and, thereby, preventing the individual or group from starting its own team. For example, the Mid-South Grizzlies, formerly of the WFL, sued the NFL for refusing to admit the team into the league (*The Mid-South Grizzlies v. The National Football League,* 1983). Although the Mid-South Grizzlies were unsuccessful, this situation did not involve a threat to a local monopoly because the closest team was 280 miles away (Berry & Wong, 1986). It would be interesting to see if the case would have been more successful if the owners had wanted a franchise in Chicago, where it would have been a direct competitor for the Chicago Bears. Overall, professional sport leagues have often chosen to expand and place a team in a community if they believed their threat of a suit was serious, so the number of suits has been limited.

Second, owners and facilities have filed suits claiming the leagues' franchise-relocation restrictions violate the antitrust laws. Although the team owners in *San Francisco Seals, Ltd. v. NHL* (1974) were not successful in challenging the league rules, a different finding emerged from *Los Angeles Memorial Coliseum Commission v. NFL* (1984; Champion, 1993). In that case, Oakland Raiders owner Al Davis sought to relocate his team to Los Angeles to play in the Coliseum. The NFL denied his request to move, in part, because it would have ended the Los Angeles Rams' monopoly in the Los Angeles area. The Raiders and the Coliseum successfully challenged the rules based on the antitrust laws, and the

Raiders moved to Los Angeles without the NFL's approval. The result in this case makes the legality of the franchise relocation rules questionable (except in MLB, which is exempt). However, as long as the leagues can limit the number of teams, they still possess considerable market power.

Government reluctance to oppose sport monopolization. Although future cases may challenge the legality of these local monopolies, the ability of professional sport leagues to operate like cartels has largely been unopposed by the government. Leagues have been allowed to work together in a variety of ways including the negotiation of league-wide television rights agreements, sponsorship agreements, collective bargaining agreements, and licensing agreements. The reluctance to address the issue of professional sport league cartels can be explained by a couple of factors.

First, a certain amount of cartel behavior is necessary for the operation of professional sports. Although the countries involved in OPEC did not need to work together (see chapter 4), professional sport leagues must collaborate on issues such as the scheduling of games and game rules. Therefore, it is nearly impossible for the team sports to operate without some means of working together and agreeing on certain issues. Once the establishment of the cartel as "necessary" is achieved, it has then been easier for the league to expand its cartel activities into other areas (e.g., licensing agreements, television rights agreements) and maintain that this expansion is also "necessary" for league survival.

Second, sport has considerable public support, and legislators are reluctant to interfere with their operations for fear they will be blamed if the changes result in damage to the league or individual teams. The reluctance of Congress to completely remove baseball's antitrust exemption, for which there is no rational justification, can be explained by this fear. In fact, the partial removal of the antitrust exemption in 1998 was supported by Congress only after all the affected parties (i.e., players and owners) indicated their support (King, 1998a). Congress has also passed legislation that has helped the leagues by allowing them to negotiate television rights as a group (Masteralexis, 1997) and by allowing football leagues to merge (Berry & Wong, 1986).

The only times that politicians seem to act is when the region they represent has been negatively affected by losing a team or by the league's refusing to let a team move to their area or when the league is in turmoil (e.g., the 1994 baseball strike led to Congressional hearings). However, local politicians are unlikely to get the support of unaffected politicians from other communities, so if their goal is to pass national legislation, they are likely to fail. Moreover, the turmoil is generally temporary, a shorter period of time than it would take to pass legislation, and once the temporary turmoil is over, Congress will again become reluctant to act. Regardless of the reasons for allowing the cartel-like behavior of the leagues, it is clear this behavior has had numerous economic benefits for the leagues and its teams by allowing them to maintain high levels of market power, resulting in higher prices and lower output.

Anticompetitive Practices

Although the number of anticompetitive activities engaged in by professional sport leagues and teams is numerous, we will identify only a few and discuss the positive economic impact of these activities on the organizations and the legal implications of these actions. In general, anticompetitive practices relate to either (a) the acquisition of goods and services by a league and its teams or (b) the sale of goods and services by a league and its teams.

Anticompetitive practices related to players. Most of the controversy regarding the acquisition of goods and services has related to the acquisition of players. In the past, the leagues clearly engaged in many anticompetitive activities designed to depress player salaries (Berry & Wong, 1986). Such activities included

1. Restrictions to the amateur drafts—By only allowing incoming players to negotiate with only one team, the leagues were able to significantly reduce players' power in contract negotiations and thereby reduce their salaries.

2. The reserve clause—The reserve clause gave the team the power to unilaterally renew each player's contract for one year. As long as the team continued to renew the player's contract, the player could not negotiate with any other team, thereby binding the player to one team until the team decided to trade the player. Once traded, the player would then become indefinitely bound to the new team.

3. Blacklisting and refusals to deal—Players said the owners would frequently blacklist or refuse to deal with players who either refused to sign the Standard Player Contract, which included the reserve clause, or signed with a rival league. These actions prevented players from playing out the remainder of their contract and then becoming free agents and from trying to negotiate with teams in two different leagues to improve their bargaining power (Berry & Wong, 1986).

Factors leading to a decrease in litigation related to players. Although litigation related to these anticompetitive activities was common in the past (see Berry & Wong, 1986), lawsuits are less likely in the future because some of these anticompetitive activities (e.g., the reserve clause) no longer exist; others (e.g., the amateur draft), however, are still included in the collective bargaining agreements between the owners and the players. Even the maximum salary limitations (per team and per player) in the recent NBA collective bargaining agreement would not be considered anticompetitive because it was the result of an arm's length (i.e., fairly negotiated) agreement between the owners and the players.

The only way a player or the union could use the antitrust laws to stop such a practice would be to show the league had an excessive amount of power in the negotiations and forced the players to accept the limitations, while giving nothing in return. The increasing power of the player unions makes this highly unlikely. Moreover, an unspoken refusal to deal and collusive actions that try to circumvent the collective bargaining agreement are also unlikely. The Major League Baseball owners tried to do this in the mid-1980s in an attempt to hold down player salaries, and their actions ended up costing them millions of dollars (Durland & Sommers, 1991).

Litigation by competing leagues. The controversy over anticompetitive activities regarding the sale of goods and services by the leagues and their teams has often involved league actions related to competing leagues. As previously discussed, when there have been two leagues in the major professional sports, either they have merged, or the weaker league has folded. A recent example of this occurred in women's basketball: The Women's National Basketball League (WNBA) and the American Basketball League (ABL) coexisted for over 2 years before the ABL declared bankruptcy in 1998 (Cavanaugh, 1999).

Although some suggest mergers and league bankruptcies have occurred because the established leagues operate, in essence, in natural monopolies (i.e., demand is not sufficient to support two leagues) that are not illegal (Champion, 1993), others have argued that the anticompetitive actions of the more powerful league have led to these results (Cavanaugh, 1999). For example, the WNBA and its parent organization, the NBA, are currently facing legal action from the state attorney general of Connecticut, who claims the actions of these organizations led to the bankruptcy of the ABL and the local team in Connecticut, the New England Blizzard (Cavanaugh).

Reasons for litigation by competitors. The litigation in this area has generally been related to a variety of issues. First, the more established leagues have been accused of attempting to control geographic markets (Berry & Wong, 1986). For example, in *American Football League v. National Football League* (1963), the American Football League (AFL) accused the NFL of trying to monopolize the best markets. Shortly before the creation of the AFL, the NFL added franchises in Minnesota and Dallas, two prime sites that the AFL was targeting. However, the court ruled that the NFL had as much right as the new league to those geographic markets and was under no obligation to simply cede those areas to the AFL (Champion, 1993). In fact, both leagues could still put teams in those locations and equally compete for fans.

Second, established leagues have been accused of trying to control the player market (Berry & Wong, 1986). For example, the World Hockey League (WHL) successfully argued in *Philadelphia World Hockey, Inc. v. Philadelphia Hockey Club, Inc.* (1972) that the NHL's reserve clause made it impossible for players to leave their NHL team for a WHL team (Masteralexis, 1997). The NHL was, therefore, monopolizing the player market and preventing the WHL from signing the marquee players the league needed to be successful.

Third, the more powerful leagues have been sued for their attempts to control stadium usage (Berry & Wong, 1986). Because a given area may have only one suitable facility, if a team from the established league owns the stadium or signs an exclusive use agreement with the facility, a new league may not be able to place a franchise in that area. The cost of a new facility would be a significant barrier to entry that may be impossible to overcome. The decision in *Hecht v. Pro-Football, Inc.* (1977) clearly indicates the courts believe that actions by teams to maintain exclusive control over a facility are limited by the antitrust laws (Berry & Wong, 1986).

Fourth, the leagues have been accused of trying to control television markets in order to eliminate competition (Berry & Wong, 1986). Because television revenues are a significant percentage of total team revenue, over 50% in some leagues (Howard & Crompton, 1995), if the established league can keep the new league from obtaining a lucrative national television rights agreement, they can keep the new league from being able to successfully compete. The most famous case involving control over the television market was the *United States Football League v. National Football League* (1986). Although the jury agreed that the NFL had monopolized the television market, it did not believe the harm done to the USFL by the NFL actions was significant and awarded the USFL only $1, automatically tripled to $3 (Maurice & Smithson, 1988). The jury felt that the USFL's trouble with obtaining a good television contract was more related to the weakness of the league than to any NFL actions. In other words, a stronger new league may have been more successful in a similar lawsuit.

Finally, the more powerful leagues have been accused in recent years of trying to control access to corporate sponsors (Cavanaugh, 1999). As sponsorships have become a more significant source of income for leagues, the importance of access to sponsorship money has become more critical for league survival.

Litigation by team owners. Ironically, the second major group responsible for lawsuits and controversy over anticompetitive activities has been the owners in the respective leagues. As previously discussed, Raiders' owner Al Davis, along with officials from the Los Angeles Memorial Coliseum, successfully sued the NFL over its efforts to keep the Raiders from relocating from Oakland to Los Angeles. In another case, *Chicago Bulls and WGN v. National Basketball Association* (1992), an NBA team and a local television station sued the league over its restriction on the number of games a team could broadcast nationally on a superstation (Masteralexis, 1997).

In a more recent controversy, Dallas Cowboys owner Jerry Jones challenged the NFL's right to negotiate league-wide marketing and licensing deals and then to split the revenue equally among the teams (Masteralexis, 1997). Jones believed teams would be better off if they abandoned their league-wide philosophy and handled their own marketing and licensing. Although such an arrangement would probably benefit teams like the Cowboys, which is in a major market and has a large national following, a complete abandonment of the league-wide philosophy would not be better for many of the smaller market teams and the league as a whole would probably not benefit financially. Major League Baseball's current status with a few rich and competitive teams and an increasing number of struggling teams is a clear demonstration of what can happen in the absence of a league-wide philosophy.

Moreover, the ability to operate as a cartel is a huge economic advantage (see chapter 4), and although some members of the cartel may believe they would be better off on their own, that is generally true only for a very small group of dominant firms. In fact, in some cases even the dominant firms suffer when the cartel is dissolved. As will be discussed later in this chapter, the NCAA's loss of its ability to act as a cartel with regard to football broadcasts was a significant financial loss for the association and its member schools.

The Application of Antitrust Laws to Other Professional Sports

As discussed earlier, although the antitrust laws have been more frequently applied to the four major professional team sport leagues, they have also been applied to a number of other professional sports, such as boxing, tennis, golf, automobile racing, horse racing, and wrestling (Wise & Meyer, 1997a). Some of the applications were very similar to the ones related to the NFL, NBA, NHL, and Major League Baseball. For example, tennis player Cliff Drysdale claimed the World Team Tennis player draft was designed to restrain trade by allowing him to negotiate with only one team (*Drysdale v. Florida Team Tennis, Inc.*, 1976).

However, others differed from the cases previously discussed. For example, lawsuits have occurred relative to rules limiting the type of equipment that could be used at sanctioned events (*Gunter Harz Sports, Inc. v. United States Tennis Association*, 1981; *STS Corporation v. United States Auto Club, Inc.*, 1968) and eligibility rules for association events (*Dessen v. Professional Golfers Ass'n of America*, 1966; *Hartley v. American Quarter Horse Association*, 1977). In general, the sport organizations often succeeded in arguing that they had a right to make eligibility rules and to specify the type of equipment that could be used, especially when the rules were related to safety concerns (Wise & Meyer, 1997a). Still, a review of litigation clearly indicates that the antitrust laws have a far greater application to professional sports than to just a few team sports.

Antitrust Enforcement in Intercollegiate Athletics

When one recognizes that the NCAA operates like a monopoly or cartel, depending on whether it is seen as single entity or a group of organizations working together, it is not surprising the NCAA has been subject to antitrust litigation. In one critical case, the NCAA was successful in defending its actions when it assumed control of women's sports in the mid-1980s, an action that led to the end of the Association for Intercollegiate Athletics for Women (*Association for Intercollegiate Athletics for Women v. National Collegiate Athletic Association,* 1983). However, the NCAA has lost two major antitrust cases that clearly indicate that not only is the association subject to antitrust regulations, but that anticompetitive activity by the association will not be tolerated and also could be quite costly.

Football Television Broadcasts

Prior to the mid-1980s, the NCAA negotiated a national television contract for college football on behalf of its member institutions (*National Collegiate Athletic Association v. Board of Regents of the University of Oklahoma and University of Georgia Athletic Assn.,* 1984). This arrangement, a classic example of cartel behavior, resembled the current practice of the NFL. The association-wide negotiations allowed the NCAA to limit the output (i.e., number of games televised), while increasing the price charged (i.e., the television rights fees paid by the stations to broadcast games). The agreement even limited the output per organization (i.e., number of games on television for each school) and attempted to spread the revenue more evenly among the members, also common practices in a cartel.

However, as commonly happens in cartels, some of the more powerful members believed they could do better without the agreement. In other words, they could sell more output (i.e., televise more games) and increase the total revenue they would receive (i.e., individual share of the television rights fees). In fact, many of the major football powers formed the College Football Association (CFA) to negotiate a contract that would increase revenue and the number of games televised (Drowatzky, 1997). This second contract resulted in litigation between the NCAA and the CFA member schools led by the Universities of Oklahoma and Georgia (*National Collegiate Athletic Association v. Board of Regents of the University of Oklahoma and University of Georgia Athletic Assn.,* 1984).

The Supreme Court agreed with the schools that the NCAA's association-wide television agreement was anticompetitive and led to an increase in prices and a decrease in output (Drowatzky, 1997). This restraint of trade was a clear violation of the antitrust laws under the rule of reason because the Court did not believe there was a strong purpose being served by this process (Drowatzky). The Court also believed that in addition to the agreement's not being in the best interest of the NCAA member institutions, it was damaging to the television stations, which had to pay higher rights fees on a per game basis, and to the public, which did not have the opportunity to see as many games as they would in a free market system. The antitrust laws were designed to protect the interests of all of these groups, so the association-wide television agreement was declared illegal.

The impact of the case is also typical of what happens when cartel agreements are voided. As predicted by the Court, the rights fees on a per game basis decreased, and the number of games on television increased significantly. However, the institutions, with the notable exception of Notre Dame, that were sure they would be better off without the NCAA's cartel-like television agreement, were generally disappointed with the results of the court decision (Fizel & Bennett, 1989). As basic economic theory would suggest (see chapter 4), organizations are in a more powerful position and will, therefore, generally benefit more when they can work together as a cartel than when they act separately as competitors.

Restricted Earnings Coaches

The second, and more recent, case involved the NCAA's efforts to control the earnings of some basketball coaches at member institutions. In 1991, the NCAA, based on a recommendation from its Cost Reduction Committee, passed a bylaw that established a restricted-earnings basketball coach position at Division I institutions (Drowatzky, 1997). A coach in this position could be paid only $12,000 during the school year and $4,000 during the summer ("Restricted-earnings," 1999). Claiming the rule was anticompetitive and therefore a violation of the antitrust laws, the affected coaches then began a class-action suit against the NCAA (Drowatzky, 1997). In *Law v. National Collegiate Athletic Association* (1995), the court agreed with the coaches. The court stated the rule had depressed prices for coaches' salaries and it was not justified by a legitimate organizational purpose, as required under the rule of reason (Drowatzky). The reduction in salary for only one coach had done little to reduce costs within college athletics (Drowatzky).

Although the NCAA was certainly concerned by the ruling that the bylaw violated the antitrust laws, it was the amount of the judgment that received the most attention. Damages were found by the court to be over $22 million, which under the antitrust laws was automatically tripled to approximately $67 million ("Restricted-earnings," 1999). After this was later increased to almost $75 million to adjust for inflation, the NCAA finally settled the case for $54.5 million ("Restricted-earnings").

Other Potential Antitrust Problems

Because of the huge financial loss suffered by the NCAA as a result of *Law v. National Collegiate Athletic Association* (1995), the organization may be forced to reevaluate much of its current cartel-like behavior to make sure it does not leave itself vulnerable in future cases. In fact, the NCAA recently faced antitrust litigation from Adidas, which believe the NCAA's control over licensing agreements is also a violation of the antitrust laws (Mullen, 1998).

Moreover, the NCAA could someday face the most damaging antitrust litigation from student-athletes, particularly those in the revenue-producing sports. NCAA rules restrict the compensation of student-athletes to figures that are sometimes well below the value of these players in a free market (Bowers, 1999; Brown, 1993, 1994). In addition, the rules limit the money the athletes can earn from other sources. Moreover, some of these limitations have clear benefits for the school. For example, athletes cannot endorse athletic footwear; instead the school endorses this product and receives revenue that would have gone to the athlete had the rule not existed.

When surveyed in the early 1990s, economists said they believed that controlling athlete compensation in intercollegiate athletics is the most blatant monopoly-like activity in the United States (Barro, 1991) and that the rules of the NCAA and its members are clear violations of the antitrust laws. The NCAA has long argued that its athlete compensation rules are not anticompetitive but are, instead, designed to protect the athlete and to maintain the integrity of amateur athletics. Also, the NCAA suggests that player "compensation" cannot be classified as a salary because the athletes are not employees. In addition, the organization argues that college athletics generally is not a money-making operation (Fulks, 1996), so the money to pay athletes would not be available even if the rules changed.

However, if the players who have suffered financially due to the NCAA restrictions decided to file a class action suit, which could include decades worth of players, and the NCAA was to lose this case, the amount that the players would be compensated could be astronomical and essentially bankrupt the NCAA. In fact, most economists, as well as many antitrust experts, believe the current NCAA rules are "morally repugnant" and would see such a ruling against the NCAA as fair and in accordance with the antitrust laws (Barro, 1991, p. A12). Overall, although the cartel-like activities of the NCAA have economically benefited the association and its member institutions for many years, these activities leave the organization very vulnerable to antitrust legislation, and the NCAA needs to be cautious in the future.

Antitrust Enforcement in Other Areas of the Sport Industry

Although the application of the antitrust laws to professional and college sports has been unusual due to their unique structures and situations, the application of the laws and the evaluation of anticompetitive activities in other areas of sport are more typical. For example, a merger in the athletic footwear industry between Nike, Reebok, and Adidas would be treated in a manner similar to that of a merger in the computer industry. The government and/or the courts would try to determine the impact of such a merger on competition in the athletic footwear market based on the size and market share of the proposed organization and the four-firm market concentration ratio. Because of the dominance of these three firms and the fact that such a merger could ultimately lead to the near monopolization of the athletic footwear industry, it is possible that such a merger would not be allowed.

In another example, if all of the fitness clubs in a community formed a cartel and then fixed prices at a higher than normal rate, this activity would also be seen as a violation of the antitrust laws and would likely lead to litigation. Overall, a review of the section on the general focus of the antitrust laws toward the beginning of this chapter provides a good understanding of how the antitrust laws affect most organizations in the sport industry.

Although actual antitrust cases in other areas of the sport industry are not overly common, there have been enough to indicate there is the potential for application (Wise & Meyer, 1997c). Two notable cases have occurred in the sporting goods industry, but the plaintiff was not able to prove that the defendants were engaging in illegal activities under the antitrust laws (*Sports Center, Inc. v. Riddell, Inc.*, 1982; *Trans Sport, Inc. v. Starter Sportswear, Inc.*, 1992). However, in *Aspen Skiing Co. v. Aspen Highlands Skiing Corp.* (1985), the plaintiff was able to prove the acts of its competitor "in light of its market power, were predatory, aimed at squeezing (the plaintiff's) profits and making it difficult for (the plaintiff) to survive in the marketplace" (Wise & Meyer, 1997c, p. 1911). This case shows that attempts at local monopolies by sport organizations are potential violations of the antitrust laws.

Antitrust Enforcement Outside of the United States

Although antitrust laws do not exist in every part of the world, they are fairly common. For example, Canada has the Competition Act, which has been applied to sport on several occasions (Wise & Meyer, 1997b). European countries are affected by Articles 85 and 86 of the European Community Treaty, as well as various antitrust laws in individual countries (Wise & Meyer, 1997b). Articles 85 and 86 have been applied to a number of situations in sport including whether a player's former team can force his new team to pay a transfer fee, whether leagues can place limits on the number of nonnationals who can play on teams in their national leagues, whether sport federations can make the use of "official" equipment mandatory, and whether sporting event organizers can grant exclusive rights for the distribution of sales (Wise & Meyer, 1997b). Although the plaintiffs have not always been successful in changing the actions of the sport organization, there are potential applications of Articles 85 and 86 to a variety of sport organizations in Europe. Other countries, such as Japan, have strong antitrust laws, but they are rarely, if ever, applied to sport (Wise & Meyer, 1997b).

Government Influences on the Marketplace

As previously noted, a perfectly competitive market does not guarantee "perfect" results. For example, positive and negative externalities may emerge from a given activity that will increase the benefits or the costs of the activity. Because the firms are not always concerned with these social externalities, they may produce more of the good or service than is best for society when the externalities lead to an increase in societal costs and less of the good or service than is optimal when the externalities lead to societal benefits. Because sport is believed to have a number of positive externalities, or benefits (e.g., improved physical health, character building), many argue more sport activities should be provided than would be available in a perfectly competitive market.

In addition, because firms are primarily concerned with profit maximization (see chapter 2), there will be inequalities in the availability of sport activities. In particular, individuals from lower socioeconomic groups or those with disabilities will generally not be given the same opportunities in a free market. Finally, some sport-related items might be viewed as public goods. For example, there are perceived benefits (i.e., improved morale, enjoyment from following the team in the papers and on television, economic development) to having a professional sport team in town (Howard & Crompton, 1995) that accrue to all of the residents, even those who never attend a game and, therefore, never pay for a ticket. Those who receive benefits without having to pay for them are referred to by economists as "free riders" (Schiller, 1989). Although most economists have argued that these perceived benefits, particularly those related to economic development, are highly inflated (Baade & Dye, 1990; Noll & Zimbalist, 1997), city officials and team owners have suggested the team and the facility needed to keep or obtain the team could be classified as public goods. Therefore, it would make sense that the public should have to financially support the availability of these public goods.

Because government officials understand that inefficiencies exist even in a free market system, they will do a cost-benefit analysis of certain activities to determine if the societal benefits of providing more of an activity would exceed the societal costs. To deal with the imperfections that would result in a free market system from the failure to maximize societal benefits, the government has a few options to correct the system including (a) granting nonprofit status to certain sport organizations (e.g., Special Olympics, YMCAs), (b) subsidizing the operations of certain sport organizations (e.g., sport facility construction), or (c) offering sport activities through government agencies.

Nonprofit Status

One means the government has to encourage sport organizations to provide goods or services to society is to grant the organization nonprofit status. Nonprofit sport organizations include intercollegiate athletic departments, the Special Olympics, and a variety of amateur sport organizations (e.g., the United States Olympic Committee or USOC, Amateur Athletic Union, USA Volleyball).

Advantages. This status provides the organization with two tax-related advantages. First, donations to the organization are tax deductible. This can be a major benefit to the nonprofit organization's fund-raising efforts. Firms will be more willing to donate money, and the amount they will be willing to donate will be greater, if their donation provides them with a tax deduction. For example, most agree donations to intercollegiate athletic departments would decrease significantly without this tax-related benefit to donors. In addition, encouraging these donations also decreases government costs. In most countries throughout the world, amateur sports are heavily supported by financial contributions from the government (Hugh-Jones, 1992). In the United States, the government relies on private support in the form of donations to support the activities of many of the amateur sport organizations (e.g., USOC, intercollegiate athletics), thereby reducing the need for financial support from the government.

The second tax advantage for nonprofit sport organizations is that they do not have to pay taxes (e.g., income taxes, property taxes). The fact that the organization has no taxes to pay has definite economic implications. Essentially, the removal of tax liability causes operating costs to decrease, which results in a decrease in price and an increase in output. For example, a nonprofit ski resort could afford to charge less for lift passes and offer more participation opportunities due to the removal of tax liability. As shown in Figure 10-1, the downward shift of the marginal cost curve results in and increase of output (i.e., participation opportunities) from 4,000 to 6,000 and a reduction in the lift ticket price from $20 to $15. In this case, the lower price will theoretically allow more people from lower socioeconomic classes to participate.

Nonprofit controversies in sport. However, many have questioned the nonprofit status of some sport organizations. Miller and Fielding (1995) argue the nonprofit status of YMCAs is not appropriate. They detail how most YMCAs operate in a similar manner as the for-profit health clubs and openly compete with these clubs. Although the YMCAs argue they are different from commercial clubs because they use membership fees from their more affluent members to subsidize the membership fees of the underprivileged, discounted and free memberships have continually declined during the 20th century, and

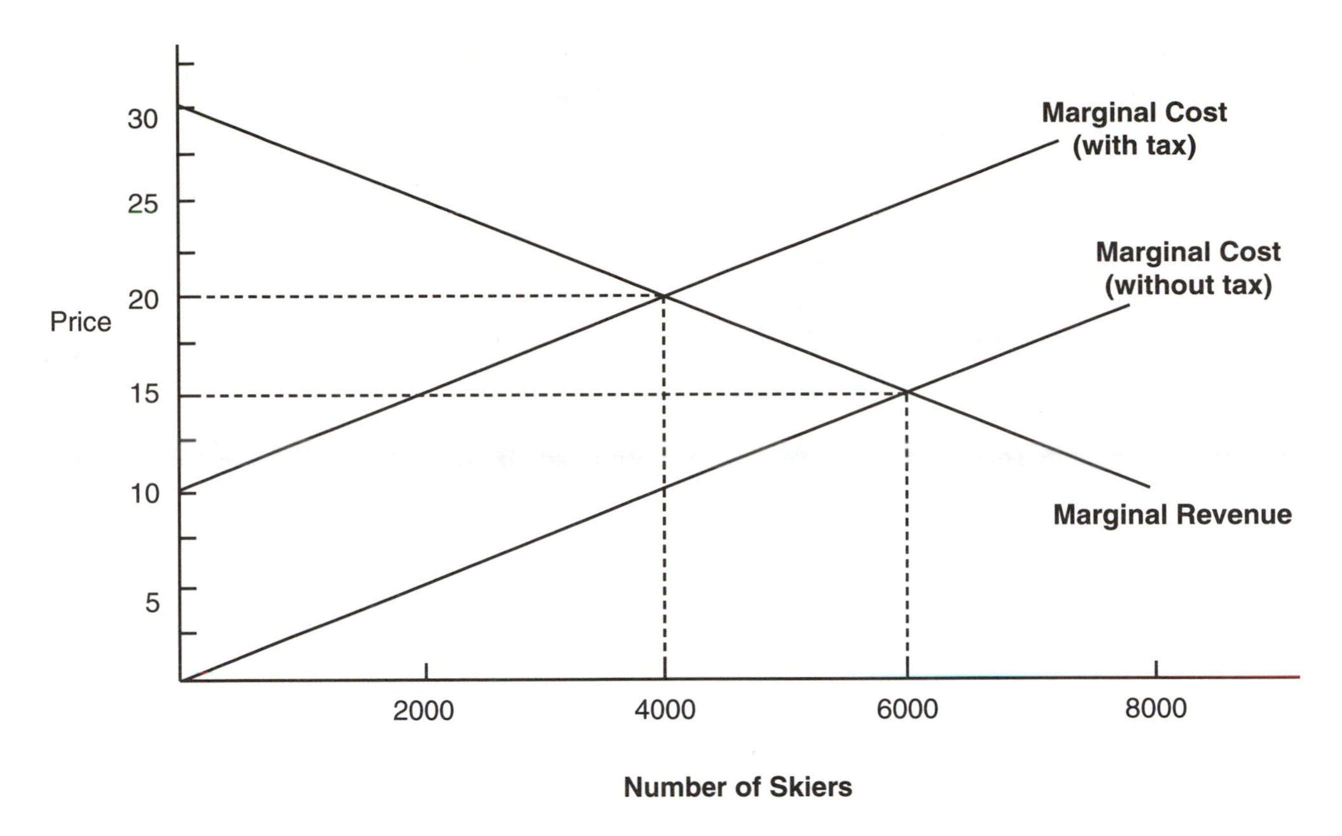

Figure 10-1.

the YMCAs have "almost completely eliminated programs for the underprivileged" (Miller & Fielding, 1995, p. 103).

In addition, others have argued the nonprofit status of intercollegiate athletics, particularly at the NCAA Division I level, is also questionable. Although Division I athletic departments claim their nonprofit status based on the educational purpose of the university, athletic department operations closely resemble the operations of professional sports, and many decisions of athletic department managers seem to focus more on profit maximization than on educational enhancement (e.g., scheduling television games during final exams). For example, University of Florida football coach Steve Spurrier's contract has incentives for both graduating athletes and on-field success. However, the incentives related to on-field success, which are closely tied to profitability, are far more lucrative (Jones, 1997).

Moreover, donations to the athletic departments are often tied to the purchase of tickets, so they generally have less to do with an altruistic desire to support education and are really just a means for charging more for tickets. In fact, the IRS currently allows only an 80% deduction for athletic department donations tied to tickets, and some believe the percentage should be decreased further or simply eliminated. Further, some have suggested the nonprofit status of these sport organizations be revoked, or at least that the income they receive that is not related to their nonprofit purpose be subject to Unrelated Business Income (UBI) tax (Craig & Weisman, 1994; Miller & Fielding, 1995). However, we can expect both the YMCAs and intercollegiate athletic departments to oppose any efforts to revoke their nonprofit status or to subject even some of their income to UBI tax because of the significant tax advantages of being a nonprofit organization.

Government Subsidies

In addition to or instead of granting an organization nonprofit status, the government can provide a variety of subsidies to sport organizations providing positive externalities, reducing inequalities, and/or providing public goods. These subsidies come in two forms. First, the subsidy may reduce the costs for the sport organization. For example, nonprofit organizations receive postal rate discounts (Miller & Fielding, 1995). In addition, some for-profit organizations are granted a limited tax waiver (Howard & Crompton, 1995). For example, some professional sport teams do not have to pay property taxes on their facility. As previously discussed, these reductions in cost cause a downward shift in the marginal cost curve. Therefore, more output will be generated at a lower price.

Second, the subsidy may provide additional sources of revenue or other resources for the sport organization. For example, the government will often provide land, land improvements, or tax revenue to support the construction of a sport facility (Howard & Crompton, 1995). These subsidies can lead to the construction of a sport facility that would not have occurred otherwise. If the community does not provide some subsidies, an organization (e.g., a professional sport team, recreation facility) may decide to operate in another community. Although the benefits of sport organizations, particularly professional sport teams, to a community are questionable (Baade & Dye, 1990; Noll & Zimbalist, 1997), the use of government subsidies to support the construction of a facility is not unique. For example, local governments frequently subsidize local airports because of the anticipated external benefits to the community of the airport (McGuigan & Moyer, 1986).

In addition, the government has occasionally given resources directly to a sport organization to be used for its general operations. In 1980, the United States government gave millions of dollars to the USOC to support the organization's operations (Clumpner, 1986). Moreover, Florida law offers "big-league" sport franchises that operate in the state a $2 million subsidy for 30 years (Hugh-Jones, 1992). Overall, the subsidies from the government decrease the percentage of the costs provided by the sport organization, which again will allow the organization to produce more output for a lower cost.

However, two points need to be made regarding government subsidies. First, the U.S. government generally tries to avoid subsidizing sport organizations and instead tends to prefer to leave support to private sources (e.g., corporations, private citizens). The large amount of private money available in the United States provides the government with an opportunity to shift financial responsibility in a way that is not available in most other countries. Much subsidization takes place when two or more local governments are competing for a sport organization (e.g., professional sport team, recreation facility).

Second, most governments in the world, including the United States, have been accused of providing more subsidies for elite sport over participant sport. Governments appear far more willing to provide a significant amount of money for a stadium or to support a national sport organization capable of winning Olympic medals than to provide the minimal amount of money needed for activities like Midnight Basketball (i.e., a basketball program for underprivileged youth). Although many would argue the benefits relative to the costs of Midnight Basketball are greater, the local and national governments receive far more attention for their support of elite sport and more opportunity to demonstrate the success of their subsidies to the larger communities. The argument over the relative support for elite vs. participant sport will continue to be a topic of debate for years to come.

Government Enterprises as Providers of Sport

The final option for the government when it is seeking to maximize societal benefits is to provide the goods or services through governmental agencies. Because of failures in the marketplace to provide the output necessary to maximize societal benefits, the government has consistently increased its role within the marketplace (Schiller, 1989). For example, the federal government has gone from employing 14,000 people in the early 1900s to over 5 million today (Schiller). In the sport industry, the government has been largely responsible for providing participation opportunities for the community, particularly for the underprivileged. Even organizations that have been granted nonprofit status or given various subsidies (e.g., YMCAs, youth sport programs) still tend to charge participation fees that prevent some people from being able to participate. The government can use tax revenue to support the work of various agencies, which ensures that everyone will have access to certain sport opportunities (e.g., youth sport leagues, parks, swimming pools, and other recreation facilities).

The government may also operate other sport or recreational facilities that compete with private sport organizations. For example, many communities now have municipal golf courses that compete with privately owned courses. The difference generally is that the government-run courses charge lower greens fees, a strategy that allows some residents to participate who could not afford the greens fees and membership fees charged by the private courses. Government agencies also operate large sport facilities that may bring sport or other entertainment events to the community. If these facilities can attract more events that would have gone to other communities, they can increase economic activity in the community and have a positive economic impact.

It should be noted, however, that some in the United States argue that we should move away from having a large number of government agencies toward privatization of many of the government activities (Hirschey & Pappas, 1995). The people behind this movement believe government operations have become inefficient over time, due in part to the lack of clear measurable goals (see chapter 2). They suggest that private organizations could run the operations more efficiently (e.g., decrease costs) and society would receive more benefits relative to costs.

However, there are concerns that privatization will change the goal of the organization to profit maximization and that, in turn, will lead to higher prices and, in the case of monopolies, to lower than optimum output. For example, Miller and Fielding (1995) argued that an increasing focus by the nonprofit YMCAs on revenue generation has brought them to a point where they do little for the underprivileged groups they were supposed to be helping according to their nonprofit purpose. If a nonprofit organization can lose sight of the potential societal benefits that their organization was designed to achieve, a profit-oriented organization is even more likely to ignore potential societal benefits or costs of their activities. Essentially, the government loses its ability to control the activities of an organization after it is privatized, and its original goals may be ignored.

Overall, the government has a number of options related to maximizing societal benefits and minimizing societal costs. Although providing goods or services through governmental organizations is likely to provide the government with the most control, some of the other options may be better for minimizing government costs and the need to collect additional taxes. Regardless, each option is designed to reduce prices and increase output for sport-related goods and services that provide benefits to society.

Increasing Competition in the Sport Industry

Estimates suggest the sport industry increased from being the 23rd largest industry in the United States at $63.1 billion industry in 1988 (Compte & Stogel, 1990) to being the 11th largest industry at $152 billion in 1995 (Meek, 1997) and $213 billion by the end of the 20th Century (Broughton, et al., 1999). Although such an increase in economic activity seems to suggest that this is a great period for companies in the sport industry, this is not necessarily true. It appears that much of this growth is related to an increasing number of organizations operating in the sport industry rather than simply to growth by already existing sport organizations. This increase in the number of organizations has led to increased competition in the sport environment. For example, the number of professional sport leagues has risen dramatically in recent years (Howard, 1999). In the last 20 years, we have seen the emergence of new professional leagues in a variety of sports including women's basketball, men's and women's volleyball, arena football, women's softball, and men's soccer. Competition among sporting goods companies has become more intense, and many of those organizations are struggling financially (Kaplan, 1998).

Because increased competition in an industry has a tendency to decrease prices, we can expect that sport organizations may react in a variety of ways to avoid this increasing level of competition. For example, mergers and acquisitions within the sport industry have become increasingly common. We have seen both horizontal mergers, such as those occurring between sport agent firms (Gotthelf, 1998), and vertical mergers, such as those occurring between media outlets and professional sport teams (Schoenfeld, 1998). In addition, the NFL recently acquired an interest in the Arena Football League (Lombardo, 1999), and the NBA started its own women's basketball league, the WNBA, in an effort to control their respective professional sport marketplace.

The competitive environment also will probably lead to an increase in anticompetitive activity, such as collusion between firms and efforts designed to run other firms out of business. For example, at least some people believe that the failure of the ABL was related to anticompetitive practices by the WNBA. Because of the current competitive environment, we can expect the government to monitor the sport industry more closely as the dollars involved and the incentive to "cheat" increase. Antitrust laws may have an even greater impact on the way sport organizations operate in the future.

In addition, this focus on revenue maximization suggests many sport organizations will focus their activities on attracting those with more money to spend, thereby ignoring those without the necessary financial resources. Therefore, the government will continue to play an important role in ensuring access to sport activities either through subsidization or government agencies. Overall, it is likely that the involvement of government in the sport industry will increase rather than decrease in the years to come.

Summary

Because perfect competition is better for societies than monopolies, there is incentive for the government to move industries away from monopoly-like status and to encourage competition. The purpose of this chapter was to discuss attempts by the government to encourage competition and how these attempts have affected the sport industry. We focused primarily on the antitrust laws and how they have been applied to various segments of the sport industry. In particular, the imapct of the laws on the operations of professional team sports and college athletics was discussed in detail. The chapter also discussed the presence of antitrust laws in other parts of the world and their impact on sports in those locations. Finally, the chapter discussed other ways that government can influence the marketplace in a way that benefits the general public.

Chapter Study Questions

1. Briefly explain the purpose of the antitrust laws and how they are designed to benefit society.
2. Identify and briefly explain the exemptions available to sport organizations relative to the antitrust laws.
3. Discuss the three types of mergers, and cite actual and possible examples of these merger types in the sport industry.
4. Professional sport leagues have been accused of anticompetitive activity on a number of occasions. Give a few examples of this activity, and discuss which groups may be negatively affected by this behavior.
5. Discuss some ways in which the government has provided benefits for sport organizations. Do you believe all of these benefits are/were appropriate? Why or why not?

Chapter Eleven

INTRODUCTION

Sport management professionals today face many issues that have never been dealt with before. Some of those issues have an intentional connotation, such as globalization. Globalization has made the world economy more interdependent, more open and transparent, and more competitive. The globalization of sport has paralleled and been influenced by this trend. Today, sport is widely viewed as a cultural universal or global phenomenon. The increased internationalization of sport business activities and the demand from the sport industry for managers who are educated and trained to be capable of handling various international business matters have grown considerably. The globalization of sport calls for sport management professionals to devote more of their attention to international issues. This chapter is intended to provide the students in sport management with information that may help them understand those issues. Specifically, the chapter will address the following:

International Issues

Susie Ford, a student who graduated from one of the NASPE-NASSM-approved graduate sport management programs, was recently hired as an assistant to the chief operating officer by NGS International, a sporting company. Due to the heavy competition in the domestic sporting goods market as well as the relative saturation in the kind of sporting goods that the company produces, company management wants to open up a new market in South America. So Susie's first assignment is to develop a plan for the company to expand into the market in South America. What kind of information should Susie collect to complete this project? What will the expansion plan look like?

1. Why does an economic system affect the sport governance in a certain nation?
2. What is the theoretical foundation in economics for globalization of sport?
3. How can sport organizations expand internationally?
4. What are the organizational patterns of sports clubs in the world?

Types of Economic Systems and Sport Governance

Introduction to Economic Systems

An economic system is

> A set of relations among decision-makers and between decision-makers and economic variables. It consists of the sum of ideas, goals, methods, and institutions used in society to resolve these economic issues in some more or less organized or "systematic way" (Elliott, 1985, p. 3).

The economic systems embraced and adopted by various countries are distinguishable in three major areas (Elliott, 1985; Parkin, 1993):

1. The structure of an economic system. The "structure [of economics systems] refers to

salient features that characterize an economic system and distinguish it from others" (Elliott, 1985, p. 5), which may include, but are not limited to, ownership, control of the means of production, locus and organization of economic power, and social processes for economic coordination. For example, in the People's Republic of China, whose economic system most approximates centralized socialism, the government used to own and control all enterprises. Economic power is unilaterally possessed by the government because it decides what to produce, how to produce it, and how much to produce. As a result of economic reform, some decentralization has occurred in the Chinese system, and private ownerships have been permitted to join the state enterprises in production in the last two decades.

2. Various aspects of economizing behaviors of an economic system. Using various incentive arrangements, a specific economic system has its own methods of allocating resources, distributing income, and maintaining economic stability. These methods are referred to as the economic behaviors of the system. Scarcity of resources forces an economic system to choose a method, which can satisfy to the greatest extent the needs of society, to allocate and use the scarce resources and to distribute income among different economic classes so as to maintain ultimately the economic stability of the system. Generally, the economic behavior of the economy in the United States can be best interpreted by the term *managed capitalism*. The federal government often uses various monetary and fiscal policies (adjustments made to the interest) to promote economic stability.

3. The performance of an economic system. How efficiently and equally the resources are distributed is one main criterion used to evaluate the performance of an economic system. The other areas related to the performance of an economic system are employment, price stability, and growth.

Learning Activities

1. Return to the beginning of the chapter, and reread the story. Assume you are Susie. Explain the information you would collect and describe your expansion plan.

2. Identify one sport club in Germany or in Italy or in a European nation that sponsors professional teams and gather as much information as possible about the club in terms of its organizational structure and policies.

3. Compare and contrast this club with a professional franchise in the United States.

In general, socialism, welfare state capitalism, and capitalism are the three most represented and endorsed economic systems (Parkin, 1993).

Socialism represents the type of economic system that is based on state ownership of capital, means of production, and land; and resources are allocated based on a central economic plan (Parkin, 1993). Two main versions of socialism are derived from the classic socialist theories: (a) centrally planned socialism and (b) decentralized socialism. Prior to the economic reforms of the 1980s, the economy of the People's Republic of China was in principle typical, centrally planned socialism. Considerable changes have taken place in this system in recent years. More and more privately owned enterprises are joining the public counterparts in production. To a certain extent, the current form of the economic system in the People's Republic of China would probably be better labeled as decentralized socialism, another version of socialism. In the decentralized system, private elements are included in the ownership and control of the means of production. The public sector, however, still maintains its control over the economy. Decentralized socialism shares some traits with both centrally planned socialism and capitalism.

Capitalism, on the other hand, is "an economic system in which the means of production and distribution are privately owned by individuals or corporations who receive the income earned thereon" (Shim & Siegel, 1995, p. 53). The evolution and alterations of the classic theories on capitalism have created several versions of capitalism. *Managed capitalism* is one version of capitalism that warrants some further discussion. Managed capitalism is a particular condition that can be used to denote the type of economic system found in the United States, Japan, and Australia. The government controls the economic activities of the private sector by regulation, subsidy, support, and mediation.

Welfare state capitalism, also referred to as "the social democracy system," is an economic system that stands inbetween the capitalist and socialist systems. This system has been adopted in the United Kingdom and in several Scandinavian countries, such as Norway, Denmark, and Sweden. The social democracy system is still a capitalistic-based system. A certain level of social ownership (or state government) in the industry and its control over the private sector are maintained for the sake of reducing social inequality in society and promoting societal cooperation and stability. Representations of social ownership are typically found in such industries as public utilities, basic industries, and financial enterprises. Industries in these areas are usually nationalized to prevent exploitation of consumers. Economic decisions are based on four basic social processes—price system, democracy, bureaucracy, and bargaining—and the government has consciously regulated the market to ensure competition and economic efficiency (Elliott, 1985). Table 11-1 compares the characteristics of managed capitalism and centralized socialism.

Table 11-1. Comparison of the Characteristics of Managed Capitalism and Centralized Socialism

Dimensions	Economic Systems and Characteristics	
	Managed Capitalism	Centralized Socialism
Level of economics development	Highly developed	Underdeveloped, but developing
Resource base	Highly capitalistic	In the process of transformation into capitalistic
Ownership-control of instrument	Predominantly private-capitalist and corporate; separation of ownership and control	Dominantly government ownership-control of production
Locus of economic power	Dispersed, yet concentrated in large-scale private and public organizations	Government, central planning board (CPB)
Organization of economic power	Mixture of centralization and decentralization	Dominantly centralized
Social processes for making and coordinating economic decisions	Mixture of competitive/monopolistic price system, democracy, bureaucracy, and bargaining	Dominantly government hierarchy
Motivational system	Individual economic gain	Government promotion of social goal

Note: The table is modified from Elliott (1985), *Comparative Economic Systems*, Table 9-1, page 165.

Sport Governance Under Various Economic Systems

The sport governance system in a nation is a function of the structure and behavior of its own economic system. Based on this assumption, three major types of sport governance systems have been identified accordingly as corresponding to the economic systems discussed above: (a) the centralized sport governance system, (b) the decentralized sport governance system, and (c) a combination of the other two types of governance systems.

The centralized sport governance system, commonly adopted by the economies that embrace socialism, refers to the sport managing system in a nation in which a specific government unit at every level of government is responsible for overseeing sport-related affairs and operations. The sport governance system in the People's Republic of China is an example of the centralized sport governance system. The Sport Bureau (formerly the State Sports Commission) is empowered by the Chinese government to handle all matters in the sport industry in the nation. Its responsibilities include, but are not limited to, (a) establishing sport policies and overseeing their implementation, (b) developing strategic plans for sports development, (c) preparing and coordinating competitions for all high-performance sports, and (d) setting up specific policies for the sport industry and promoting the development of a sport market.

The decentralized sport governance system refers to the sport managing system in a nation in which government has no or very limited involvement in managing sport, and no government units at both the federal/national and state/provincial levels are specifically established for sport. The government utilizes the same legislation passed for the business community to regulate the sport industry. Various nongovernment entities, such as individual national sports-governing bodies and administrative associations, split the power and assume the responsibility of regulating a specific segment of the sport industry. The sport governance system in the United States illustrates precisely the decentralized sport governance system. For example, collegiate sports are regulated and controlled respectively by three different national associations (i.e., NCAA, NAIA, and NJCAA). There is no specific entity in either federal or state government functionally set up for managing sport at all. There are no or limited policies developed by the government to handle sport-related matters. There are no or limited financial subsidies provided by the government to sport development in the country.

The sport governing systems in many nations can be characterized as a combination of the two previously mentioned types of sport governance systems. The sport governance systems in both Canada and Australia exemplify this type of combination system. Governments in these countries have a great deal of involvement in developing sport policies for the public sector, but they exercise very limited supervision over the sport operations controlled by the private sector. In other words, their governments do not regulate and police the private sport sector as much as they do the public sport sector. For example, as a government entity at the federal level, the Australian Sports Commission is responsible for (a) providing leadership for sport development in the country, (b) developing policies to regulate the public sport sector, and (c) overseeing and financing national sport organizations (Australian Sports Commission, 2000). Similar circumstances can be found in Canada. Sport Canada is an agency within the government's fitness and amateur sport directorate. Its major responsibilities include (a) funding various sports undertakings (e.g., creating a partnership with the Canadian Olympic Association to create a network of training facilities across Canada to enhance the training environment for high-performance stream athletes, (b) subsidizing athletes financially (e.g., providing funding to qualified international-caliber athletes through a taxfree monthly living and training allowance), and (c) brokering the acquisition of sponsorships for all National Sport Organizations (Sport Canada, 2000). Table 11-2 summarizes the characteristics of the three main sport governance systems in the world.

Table 11-2. Characteristics of the Three Basic Types of Sport Governance Systems in the World

	Centralized System	Decentralized System	Combination
National Policies	There are policies outlined by government for sport development in all sectors of the sport industry	No specific policies are made by government for sport development	National policies are drawn specifically for mass sport development and for national pride
Funding	Government provides funding to sports organizations at all levels	No government subsidies are provided to sport organizations	Funding is provided by government to national sports organizations
Organization/Structure	There are government units at all levels of government responsible for overseeing sport development	No government units are set up specifically for sport development; sport development is the main responsibility of various national sport organizations	Similar to the centralized system, but the government units are set up mainly for promoting sport and fitness among its citizenry
Control/Regulation	Government regulates sport organizations in both the public and private sectors	Government regulates the sport industry as it does other industries	Government regulates the public sector of the sport industry

Globalization of Sport

Because of the continuing development of new technology, the last decade of the 20th century saw tremendous global interactions and international competitions in many areas. No exception was found in the sport industry, especially in the elite sports segment. The intensified races and competitions among nations in such events as the Olympic Games and the world championships sponsored by various international sport federations and among teams within a professional sports league that crosses national borders have been noticed everywhere (Thoma & Chalip, 1996; Wilcox, 1994). To accomplish the objective of winning international competitions, many nations and sport enterprises in those nations have taken advantage of the globalization of sport.

Theoretical Foundation of the Globalization of Sport

Globalization is a process of political, economic, and cultural penetrations among nations. In the context of sport, globalization refers to the increased interactions and integration among sport organizations and enterprises around the world. The law of comparative advantages, also known as the law of comparative costs, is an economic doctrine that provides a theoretical explanation of the process of globalization in sport (Yeh & Li, 1998).

The theoretical crux of this law is summarized in the following two points:

1. Whether or not one of two regions is absolutely more efficient in the production of every commodity that is in order, if each specializes in the products in which it has a comparative advantage (greater relative efficiency), trade will be mutually profitable.
2. An illdesigned prohibitive tariff, far from helping the protected factor of production, will reduce the real wage by making imports expensive and by making the whole world less productive through eliminating the sufficiency inherent in the best pattern of specialization and division of labor.

Therefore, these two regions can share benefits because the total number of products manufactured by these two regions increases and the total costs of producing the products decrease (Samuelson, 1970).

This law can be further explained with an example. A and B are two different regions. Both regions need products X and Y. Table 11-3 illustrates their initial production and demand before trading with each other.

Table 11-3. Production and Demand for Region A and B (Before Trade)

Region	Cost	Demand	Total Cost
A	@X = $1	X = 40	$40
	@Y = $3	Y = 20	$60
			$100
B	@X = $3	X = 20	$60
	@Y = $1	Y = 40	$40
			$100
A + B			$200

As Table 11-3 shows, both A and B have their strengths (X for A and Y for B); however, A and B also have their weaknesses (Y for region A and X for region B). If there are no trade barriers between these regions, and their production factors (e.g., wages or transportation fees) are the same, each region can identify its own advantages and disadvantages and produce only one product, which will cost it less (X for region A, and Y for region B), then trade its surplus products to the other region. Table11-4 indicates their situation after trade.

Region A produces X, and region B produces Y. Both regions produce more units than their domestic demands require; then their total costs reduce to $60. They can exchange the extra 20 units and satisfy their mutual demands.

Having been refined by various economists, the law of comparative advantages has become one of the important principles observed closely in international trade for almost 200 years. Its application in globalizing the world economy is fourfold. First, in order to save costs on materials and on transportation, many business conglomerates tend to establish overseas divisions to produce parts for their products or directly sell them locally.

Table 11-4. Production and Demand for Region A and B (After Trade)

Region	Cost	Produce	Total Cost
A	@X = $1	X = 60	$60
	@Y = $3	Y = 0	$0
			$60
B	@X = $3	X = 0	$0
	@Y = $1	Y = 60	$60
			$60
A + B			$120

Second, cooperation agreements or exchange contracts are also made by various nations, regions, and organizations for mutual benefits. Third, to protect the draining of their resources, either natural materials or human resources, many nations set up tariff barriers to prevent their domestic resources from being exported massively or to prevent "dumping" from other countries that may damage their domestic industries. As a result, competition and cooperation coexist among international business interactions and in the process of globalization. To reduce their trade costs, many nations eventually end up entering into an alliance, such as the European Community (EC) and the General Agreement on Tariff and Trade (GATT). Within these communities, as a result of cooperation, such as setting up similar tariffs or production prices among various nations, their members have many equal economic opportunities. People in the membership countries also can mobilize from one nation to another easily for business reasons that may assist in improving the economic situation of the whole economy (Nicolaides, 1989).

Globalization of Sport in Elite Sports

From the perspective of sport economics, sport events and games are viewed as intangible products. The production of those events and games involves several unique elements, such as human resources (e.g., athletes, umpires, coaches, and officials), facilities and equipment, and money. Professional sports and other highly competitive "nonprofessional" sports included in the sport programming of such events as the Olympic Games, the Pan America Games, the Asian Games, the Commonwealth Games, and in the tournaments sponsored by various international sport federations are two major forms of elite sports.

There are three ways that the law of comparative advantages can be used to interpret and explain matters associated with the globalization of sport. First, the law can help a nation select its ideal sports for implementation. Strategically, in order to win medals in international competitions, it is important for the sport leadership of a country to compare its resources with those of its counterparts in such areas as number of talented athletes, levels of talent, budgets, and facilities. The comparison could lead to the proper selection of specific sports that are compatible biologically with its athletes and economically with the country's financial capability, ultimately enhancing the possibility for its athletes to win in international competitions. This strategy is extremely critical for those nations that have limited financial resources and athletic population. Clumpner (1994) indicated that some more populous nations, such as China, Germany, and the United States, may have advantages in drawing more talented athletes from their own population than might other less populated countries. However, the size of population may not automatically guarantee success in those sports that require specific physical attributes. Due to special environmental and traditional living styles and body compositions, people from certain areas of the world have the advantage in certain sports events such as long-distance running for African athletes, table tennis, gymnastics, and diving for Asian athletes, and winter sporting events for the athletes from the countries in the frigid zone (Miller & Redhead, 1994). The geographical and anthropological advantages may increase the possibility for athletes from these regions to win international competitions.

The law can also be used to explain the global movement of labor in the sport industry, such as talented athletes, experienced coaches, and other sports-related personnel. Importing human resources can help a nation or a sports organization save costs and enhance its competitive advantage. As mentioned previously, from the perspective of international economics, human resources are an important production element that can be mobilized internationally in the modern era. This also holds true in the world of elite sports. To reduce the costs of player development, franchises in Major League Baseball and Major League Soccer (MLS) often recruit a relatively large number of players from Central and South America. Similarly, the National Hockey League (NHL) has recruited players from Russia and Canada. Canadian ice-hockey players are also exported to Europe, Australia, and Asia (Genest, 1994). The importation of foreign players can help a league not only reduce its costs on personnel development, but also alter its line-up of foreign players and assist its effort in expansion internationally to a prospective foreign region. Similar applications can be seen in amateur elite sports. Through international exchange agreements, talented athletes can train in the nation with advanced training facilities and technology. For example, colleges and universities in the United States each year recruit many elite athletes from other countries. This practice has been considered a win-win strategy for both the host institution and the student-athlete. The institution can use the athlete's athletic talent to serve its interest. The athlete can enjoy the high-quality training facilities provided by the institution and the opportunity to compete and improve his or her athletic competitiveness.

The final application of the law is found in the area of international expansion. Professional sports leagues and/or sports franchises are always looking for opportunities and alternatives to increase sources of revenue. One commonly adopted approach is to extend their markets into other countries and regions. According to the law of comparative advantages, it is more efficient and profitable to extend a market overseas than to keep it domestically. Great examples are the increased extension of NFL, MLB, NHL, and NBA influence in Japan and the NFL's marketing efforts in Europe. Eitzen and Sage (1997) anticipated that the international market for the professional sport industry would be considerably expanded due to the improvements in economy and technology in many regions. Johnson (1991) predicted that by 2001, the NBA will be "the global game with 128 teams in 30 countries and more popular than soccer before" (p. 46). Although this prediction seems somewhat inaccurate, it does catch the spirit of global expansion in professional sport. The international market for the professional sport industry in the future is optimistic.

Issues in Globalization of Sport

Some issues must be dealt with in the future to facilitate the process of globalization of sport. Monopoly and dumping are two of those issues that warrant a further discussion. The existence of monopolies in the world of elite sports has created controversy. For example, a Japanese baseball pitcher named Hideki Irabu was traded to the San Diego Padres as the result of an agreement between the Lottes, a professional baseball team in Japan, and the Padres. Irabu has long desired to play for the New York Yankees. So he demanded to be traded to Yankees. Nevertheless, according to MLB's policies, the only team that he can play for is the Padres unless the Padres agree to release or trade him, or he retires from the Lottes. In other words, Irabu did not have the opportunities to pitch for any other MLB team at will due to the monopolistic agreement between the Japanese professional baseball team and the San Diego Padres. A similar situation occurred in Europe. Since the 1970s, free movement of players from team to team within the European Professional Football (soccer) League has been broadly discussed among the representatives of players, owners, the European Community, and the European Free Trade Association. The use of a quota system to determine the number of foreign players that a team could recruit, and the method of compensation (transfer fees) made to the team that loses a player from the team that receives that player are two main issues of the discussion (Miller & Redhead, 1994). Although the rules on player transferring have been challenged for the purpose of creating a free labor market in the sport industry within the European Community since 1974, yet during these 20 years, this situation was not improved until the recent ruling of the European Court of Justice, which declared the transfer rules illegal.

It is commonly acknowledged that athletes from certain regions or nations are usually more athletically skillful in some sports than those from other parts of the world. Some advantage is also found in coaches from those regions or nations. In other words, they seem to have a better understanding of those sports, such as table tennis in China, tae kun do in South Korea, and basketball in the United States. Since the early 1980s, many Chinese table tennis players have immigrated to other nations and represented those nations in various international competitions. Accordingly, a large majority of players competing in some international championships and tournaments in table tennis are Chinese. Although in many cases, the athletes did not violate the rules set by the international sport governing body, their achievements in the competition had little or no impact on the development of table tennis in those countries. The immigration of athletes from a country to other nations in the world due to their athletic superiority in that sport is called *dumping*. The dumping phenomenon is also found in basketball. Many American basketball players are recruited by professional basketball teams in many other countries and regions, such as Taiwan, Japan, and the Philippines. The dumping and importation of foreign players have raised some concerns in those nations because of the effect on the welfare of native players. Young native players may get fewer opportunities to play at the professional level. To protect their native players, governing bodies in basketball in some nations (e.g., the Chinese Basketball League in Taiwan) have developed policies to limit the number of foreign players allowed to play on each team. From the perspective of international economics, the implementation of such protectionist policies, however, is not problem free. First, these policies are deemed to restrict an enterprise, such as a professional sport franchise, from looking for better resources (i.e., outstanding overseas players). Second, these policies erect barriers to prohibit international free trade (Yeh & Li, 1998).

International Expansions

Rationale for International Expansion

International expansion refers to the expansion of a firm or organization into targeted foreign nations for economic growth. Fighting for market shares and growth has been considered one of the major reasons for firms and organizations in sport wanting to get involved in international expansion. According to Allen (1993), there are more opportunities to grow and gain market shares in a new and low-competition market that is still growing than in a saturated and fully mature market, as the latter is usually much more competitive. In addition, the increasing prosperity and demand for new sports in many regions overseas are another two reasons for international expansion (Maynard, 1995). The increased interest in sport and the subsequent growth in sport population have added fuel to the bandwagon of globalization in sport. The growth in the population of sport participation, in turn, will create tremendous opportunities in international expansion for firms in the sport industry. International expansion is no longer simply an option for many businesses, but a vital means for survival. It is believed that the benefits of international expansion are enormous. These benefits include, but are not limited to

1. additional growth opportunities;
2. added revenues or profits and financial gain;
3. increased market penetration and shares; and
4. greater international identity and more name recognition (Go & Christensen, 1989).

Additional growth opportunities. The development of a subsidiary league in a foreign region or the expansion of a franchise to a new foreign market are two commonly observed applications for firms in the sport industry to expand internationally. For example, the development and operation of the NFL Europe (former the World League in Europe) serves two basic strategic purposes for the National Football League in the United States: (a) exportation and promotion of American football in Europe and (b) international expansion and growth. The World League or the later NFL Europe is an introductory version of the NFL. Through this subsidiary's presence and presentation in Europe, NFL management intends to educate Europeans about American football and hopes to cultivate fans, ultimately forming a favorable fan base in that market. Further expansion efforts (e.g., adding new franchises in various European cities) will be made once the situation warrants.

Added revenues or profits. The increase in growth opportunities will inevitably boost the sales of television rights and licensed merchandise of the firms (e.g., professional sports leagues) that expand internationally. Sports apparel giants, such as Nike or Reebok, have also become strategically involved in global expansion to capture more profits from their overseas operations. For example, Nike has recently invested about $10 million in Melbourne, Australia, to develop the first superstore outside of North America ("Nike to Open," 1997).

More market penetration and more market shares. To obtain more market penetration and more global market shares is another perceived and acclaimed benefit of international expansion. The NBA and its properties group have set up offices in Hong Kong, Melbourne, Tokyo, Barcelona, and Geneva to penetrate unsaturated markets in Asia and Europe for the sake of increasing sales in NBA merchandise. The acquisition of the

Washington-based Advantage International and the London-based API Group by the global advertising giant Interpublic (IPG) in 1997 also exemplifies the trend of international expansion in this particular regard (Jensen, 1997). The growth and development of cable and satellite television systems have given professional sports all over the world an increased international presence. Many firms in the sport industry have taken advantage of technological development to promote their names and products in the hope of becoming global brands, eventually hiking their global market shares. The management of Manchester United, one of the top English soccer clubs, has realized the massive popularity of the club in Asia and accordingly taken a proactive approach to promote itself in that region. Some of the strategies include participating in exhibition games and staging a sales office in Hong Kong (Bawden, 1999).

Monopolistic market control. To gain monopolistic market control in a particular segment of the sport industry is another reason that some firms develop plans to expand internationally. The World Golf Championship by the PGA Tour starting in 1999 is a good example of this rationale. Greg Norman and a private promoter wanted to start a world tour of eight annual events. Fearful of losing its control over the market and its players, the PGA Tour immediately launched the event called World Golf Championship ("PGA Sets Scene," 1997).

Forms of International Expansion

Experts in international law have pointed out that when thinking of expansion internationally, a company should consider three strategic factors: rationale for expansion, urgency, and format for expansion (Graham, Ruggieri, Clements, & Cody, 1994). The format of expansion refers to the various forms of international expansion that sport enterprises may adopt in their efforts to develop globally. The following are some of the common forms utilized by the sport enterprise in international expansion.

Overseas subsidiary operations. Establishing an overseas operations (e.g., subsidiary leagues or divisions) has been proven to be an effective, self-generated growth for sport enterprises. After its establishment, the subsidiary can then expand in the region by further granting franchises and providing direct services to its affiliates. As mentioned previously, the NFL Europe sponsored by the National Football League in Europe has helped promote American football outside of North America. The league currently has franchises in London, Amsterdam, Scotland, Barcelona, Dusseldorf, and Frankfurt. Using overseas divisions to increase market penetration and share is a popular practice among sport enterprises.

Acquisitions or mergers. The takeover of or merging with a company in a foreign territory is another common form of international expansion in the sport industry. Through acquiring a foreign company, the sport enterprise will either increase its market share or gain competitive edge in the world monopolistic competition for control of a certain product. The merger with a sport business firm in the targeted region or nation to form an alliance represents another aspect of this expansion approach.

Franchising or licensing. Franchising is the third form employed by the sport enterprises, especially by the sporting goods firms, to expand into the global market. For example, Chicago-based Sportmart has 12 franchised stores in Japan. The sport enterprise using this type of expansion acts as a franchisor, granting a license to a company or individual as a "licensee" who pays fees or royalties to the licensor (i.e., the franchisor) to operate an outlet that uses the franchisor's name and logo and sells the franchisor's designated products.

To expand into other countries and regions, many sport enterprises use one or more of the following three franchising approaches: joint venture, master licensing, and direct licensing. The strategy in joint venture calls for joining forces with local investors, local governments, or even local competitors in the targeted nation or region to gain market entry. The sport enterprise establishes a joint venture agreement or partnership with a company or individual in a foreign market, and the partner will be in charge of the on-site operation. The Golf Channel and International Management Group worked together to expand the network in Southeast Asia in 1996. Specifically, Japan, Taiwan, and Australia are three nations or regions affected by the expansion effort. A joint venture was set up in Japan to distribute the signal. In using master licensing as a strategy, a license is granted to a company or individual in the intended market for expansion by the franchisor. The licensee can then operate the franchise under its ownership. In addition to granting a license for operation to a company and individual in the intended market, the franchisor will also provide the franchisee with financial backup and support of personnel. This type of strategy is called direct licensing (Go & Christensen, 1989).

Direct expert. This approach calls for the sport enterprise to create dedicated export sales representative positions or to employ traveling export sales representatives in a foreign city to coordinate direct foreign sales in a designated region. An alternative to this is to hire a local distributor or agents in that region to represent the company.

Issues of International Expansions

The sport enterprise that intends to expand internationally may find that its expansion efforts could be blocked by the differences existing in many areas between its home country and the intended market or nation for expansion. An understanding of these differences and the issues that arise as a result of the differences would help the sport enterprise become better prepared and develop a strategic plan to deal with those issues prior to their expansion entry into the market or nation. Of many issues that could be faced by the expanding sport enterprises, the ones in finance and legality are of greatest importance and are worth further discussion. In addition, the logistic aspect of international expansion is also an issue that must be dealt with.

Financial issues. Exchange risks and different taxation systems and banking laws are some of the issues that sport enterprises need to consider when developing their expansion plans. Exchange risks are the first issue that needs careful attention. An exchange risk refers to the risk that adheres to fluctuations in exchange rates, eventually affecting the performance of a company involved in international expansion. In other words, "an asset denominated in or valued in terms of foreign currency cash flows will change in value if that foreign currency changes in value over time" (Folks & Aggarwal, 1988, p. 89). Companies are exposed to three types of risk: translation exposure, transaction exposure, and economic exposure (Folks & Aggarwal, 1988).

1. Translation exposure refers to the effect on the balance sheet of the company as a result of the adverse, substantial changes occurring in the exchange rate between the company's home currency and the one of the targeted foreign market.

2. Transaction exposure is experienced by the company because of the fluctuation in the translated amount of the foreign currency between the invoice date and the payment

date. This type of exposure usually happens to a firm involved in an importing or exporting business.

3. Economic exposure reflects the degree of decline in the overall economic value of a company that is involved in the international business due to the changes in exchange rates. Speaking in the terms of international expansion in sporting goods, the extent of the risk exposed by a sporting goods company in exchange rate changes depends on how competitive the markets of its major inputs (e.g., where it purchases its raw materials) are with those of its major outputs (where it sells its products).

The second issue that an expanding sport enterprise must face is tax levy and collection. As previously noted, one of the two essential goals for international expansion is to make a profit from the overseas operations and repatriate it back to the home country. The actualization of this goal, nevertheless, requires the involved sport enterprise to have a clear understanding of the tax system and structures and of the government regulations and policies of the targeted nation on repatriation. In particular, attention needs to be paid to the exchange control and taxation policies.

1. The government of the nation that the sport enterprise has expanded to may have certain regulations and policies to prevent funds from entering or leaving its country. The rationale for the policy set to restrict fund inflows is to prevent devaluation of the host nation's currency. On the other hand, the prevention of fund outflows is used when the host government is short of foreign exchange or has heavily borrowed from external sources. By prohibiting fund outflows, the government can ensure that a certain amount of foreign hard currency will be available when needed.

2. The tax regulations and policies play an important role in the process of fund transfers (e.g., repatriation). The dividends, interest payments, or royalties that a sport enterprise earns from its operations in a foreign nation may be subject to a so-called "withholding tax" by the host government.

3. Business structures may affect the amount of tax liability that a company owes to the government of the targeted nation. (The four major forms of business structures that may be used by the sport enterprise in international expansion have been discussed previously.) First, in addition to various levels of government income taxes, the subsidiary of a sport enterprise is also subject to a withholding tax if aftertax cash will be repatriated. The withholding tax rate for a foreign subsidiary in the United States is 30%, which may be reduced from 5 to 10% by treaties. According to the Canadian tax laws, a so-called "branch tax" has been imposed on the Canadian branch operation or a Canadian subsidiary of a foreign company although the latter repatriates its profits to the parent company. In other words, should the subsidiary decide not to reinvest the aftertax earnings in its Canadian operation, it will be required to pay a branch tax, which was 25% in 1997. Tax treaties between the Canadian government and other nations may reduce this tax from 25% to anywhere between 10% and 15%. Second, the sport enterprise that enters the targeted foreign market as a corporation or partnership will be subject to the same tax conditions as those of a foreign subsidiary. Third, in general, the income earned by a sport enterprise that uses the direct expert approach (i.e., using an independent distributor to conduct business for it as its representative or agent in the targeted market) will not be subject to the host country's taxation.

Legal issues. One legal issue that sport managers may face involves the different ways of applying and interpreting the antitrust policies. Sport firms that are considering international expansion must be aware that the target region or nation may have its own version of laws that are mainly adopted to promote free and fair competition. The application, implementation, interpretation, and reinforcement of these laws may vary from country to country. Although the primary goal of antitrust legislation is the same in many countries, that is, to prohibit anticompetitive agreements that set restraints to deliberately hamper competition, the definition of restraints differ (Hawk, 1988). It is imperative that people involving in international expansion understand the differences between the antitrust laws of their countries and those of the host nation.

The competition policy adopted by the European Union (EU) deserves special mention. All member states of the EU form a single market, and a competition policy was enacted in 1993 to ensure that the competition among companies from all EU nations would be free from restraints. The antitrust laws adopted by member states themselves are deemed supplemental to the unified antitrust policies. A comparison of the competition law of the European Union and the antitrust laws of the United States is given below. Through the comparison, concerned professionals in the sport industry can gain an understanding of the antitrust legislation in these two regions.

1. Both the European Union's and the United States' antitrust laws recognize the promotion of competition as a principle. Nevertheless, the antitrust law of the former has been developed primarily for the promotion of integration of separate economics of Member States in the European Union whereas the antitrust law of the latter was drafted mainly to promote true competition.

2. Although the EU's antitrust law emphasizes the political and social values of competition (e.g., fairness), U.S. antitrust law highlights the economics value of competition (e.g., allocative efficiency).

3. The European Commission is the sole enforcer of the antitrust law implementation in the European Union. In the United States, multiple enforcers of the antitrust law coexist, including the Justice Department (hard-core cartel behavior and large horizontal mergers), the Federal Trade Commission (large horizontal mergers and anticompetitive practices), the enforcement arms of individual States, and private enforcement and actions (outside the merger area).

The differences in existing government policies and regulations may create barriers for a sport enterprise to expand internationally. For example, according to the North American Free Trade Agreement (NAFTA), each nation involved in the agreement should not discriminate against companies from other NAFTA nations to keep them from gaining access to and using telecommunications transport networks and services in their territory. In fact, Canada and Mexico expressed reservations about implementing the agreement. The Mexican government today still controls satellite communications and mandates that radio broadcasting and radio and television services be reserved for Mexican nationals (Rogers & Arriola, 1997). The same kind of protectionism is also noticed in Canada. The Canadian government specifically sets Content Rules to limit the distribution of U.S. media products like ESPN in Canada. According to the Content Rules, 50% of any distributed broadcast signals in Canada must be Canadian related (McCarthy & Wilcox, 1997).

Steps and Strategies for International Expansion

According to experts in international economics and trade, a plan for publicity must be developed prior to the commencement of any expansion action (Hayes, 1993). Having exhibition games played abroad is a common practice of American professional sports leagues intending to expand internationally. An example of this would be the game played by two NFL franchises each year in Mexico.

Selection of an expansion market has been perceived as a critical concern for sports firms that are considering international expansion. When sports enterprises consider a market or nation for expansion, its potential must be examined in the following areas (Love, 1995):

1. The size of the population and the population's financial situation.
2. The population's knowledge and appreciation of the industry to be expanded.
3. The favorable disposition of the host country's culture toward the industry to be expanded.
4. The favorable nature of government regulations toward and restriction on the industry to be expanded.
5. The competition from the domestic segment of the same industry.
6. The growth potential of the market.
7. The political and economic stability of the host country.
8. The availability and cost of human resources.

A Perspective of Sport Club Systems in the World

Sport clubs are major players in sport development in many countries in the world. Based on their mission and goals, sport clubs can be classified into three common types: amateur sport clubs, professional sport clubs, and commercial sport clubs.

Amateur Sport Clubs

Amateur sports clubs refer to those membership-owned sport clubs formed primarily for providing their members with opportunities to play sports in their leisure time. This type of club is very popular in Germany and other European nations. Amateur sport clubs share several features. First, a club is owned by its membership and the membership elects the management team for the club. Second, in most cases, the club is involved only in a single sport, such as soccer or table tennis. Third, the club operations are supported by the membership dues, the revenues from its operations (sponsorships, ticket sales, advertisements, rental, etc.), and the voluntary services of its members. Fourth, the club is a non-profit entity. Fifth, based upon their athletic ability and ages, members are grouped into teams at various competitive levels that form a hierarchical structure. Sixth, all the clubs are affiliated with local or regional associations in their respective sports, and competitions among clubs at each level are therefore coordinated by those associations.

Professional Sport Clubs

There are several systems or models in professional sport club operations. Each is created to operate specifically in a certain economic and societal environment, and it has, therefore, some distinctive characteristics that make it different from others. Nevertheless, some commonalities exist among these models. Only those clubs in certain sports that are widely viewed and beloved by consumers can survive in the market economy.

Model I: Most teams are owned independently by affluent individuals or corporations. This type of professional sport club operations is most commonly seen in the world. Three versions of this model exist.

1. A control-agent organization, usually known as a league or an association, is formed, and individual teams are registered to the league as its franchises. The league is a product of a joint venture or "conspiracy" of individual owners. The league is generally operated under a basic economic principle, that is, to maximize its economic profit for the league as a whole. Thus, the league is vested with power not only to handle such matters as scheduling and properties but also to make rules and policies to regulate and sanction individual team owners or franchisees deemed to be rule violators. The four major sports leagues in the United States (i.e., the NBA, NFL, MLB, and NHL) exemplify this type of operations.

2. A league or association, usually a semigovernmental entity, is created to handle all matters from making draft rules to launching disciplinary action against affiliated teams and players for rule infringements. This type of model is often seen in nations that embrace centralized systems of government system. For example, the Chinese Professional Soccer Association, even though it is claimed to be independent from government, has tremendous power over its associated teams and players.

3. All the teams involved are affiliated with two independently run leagues. To forge competition between them, the two involved leagues enter into an agreement, and an association is created to enforce the agreement. Nevertheless, the association is not a legal entity and has no any power over the two leagues that create it. Professional baseball operations in Japan follow this deviation.

Model II: Professional sport teams are owned by amateur sport clubs. The evaluation of some amateur sport clubs has led to the creation of a mixture of both amateur and professional operations in their clubs. The clubs are still owned by their memberships, and their operations are still amateur oriented. However, the teams that compete in their respective professional leagues follow a separate model in their operations.

Model III: All teams are owned by a single league that is incorporated. The structure and operations of the Major League Soccer (MLS) in the United States reflects precisely the spirit of this model. Individual team owners are also the investors of the league. They not only have exclusive control over their teams' operations, but also share the financial wealth of the corporation. The league signs all players and negotiates and owns ultimately all players' contracts. All the teams have opportunities to select players from a pool in the annual draft. A salary cap is imposed on each team. As a result of these special configurations, the management of the league may enjoy the following six economic benefits (Major League Soccer, 2000):

1. Limit the financial disparities between large and small markets,

2. Offer commercial affiliates an integrated sponsorship and licensing program,

3. Decrease the opportunity for sponsorship ambush,

4. Gain economies of scales in purchasing power and cost control,

5. Make decisions in the best interest of the entire league rather than just one team,

6. Avoid the teams fighting for star players, which eventually escalates player salaries.

Commercial Sport Clubs

Commercial sport clubs are those sport clubs owned by entrepreneurs who intend to use the establishments for their own financial gains. In general, there are two types of commercial sport clubs. One requires a membership, and the other does not. For having the opportunity to use the club facility and receiving the services rendered by the club that requires a membership fee, users usually have to pay a relatively large initiation fee up front and a membership due each month thereafter. Examples of this type of commercial clubs include sport and fitness clubs. On the other hand, many sport clubs such as bowling alleys, ice-skating rinks, and public golf courts are open to everyone as long as he or she pays a fee for the use of the facility.

Summary

In this chapter, international issues in sport economics were discussed. Specifically, several types of economic systems (e.g., capitalism, welfare state capitalism, market socialism, and socialism) and their respective sport governance systems were examined so as to provide information about how individual economic systems dictate the selection and use of various sport governance systems. Globalization of sport, as an important economic issue, has also been discussed in this chapter. Specifically, the law of comparative advantage, the theoretical foundation for sport businesses to expand globally, was reviewed. Two basic applications of this law involved international monopoly and dumping. International expansion was another major issue in sport economics addressed in this chapter. Fighting for market share, growth, and profit supplies several reasons for a sport enterprise's wishing to expand internationally. The benefits of international expansion are enormous. Additional growth opportunities, added revenues or profits and financial gain, more market penetration and share, international identity and more name recognition, just to name a few, are commonly recognized benefits of international expansion. Sport enterprises commonly use four types of international expansion in their efforts to develop globally:

1. overseas subsidiary operations,

2. acquisition and merger,

3. franchising and licensing, and

4. direct export.

Several important issues related to international expansion were also reviewed. Exchange rate risks and differences in taxation systems and regulations, labor laws, and antitrust applications were examined. To expand into the international market successfully, a model for expansion was recommended. A summative description of the sport clubs systems in the world was given in the last part of this chapter.

Chapter Study Questions

1. Explain and distinguish various economic systems.
2. What are the three common types of sport governance systems and their basic economic characteristics?
3. Explain the reasons for international expansion. List its four main benefits.
4. Using an example, discuss each of the four major forms of expansion that the sport enterprise may adopt in its endeavor to grow internationally.
5. What are the common financial issues confronted by the sport enterprises that want to extend their market globally?
6. What are the common legal issues facing sport enterprises that want to extend their market globally?
7. Elaborate on the strategies that could be incorporated by a sport enterprise into its expansion plan to penetrate a foreign market.
8. Compare and contrast the three common types of sport club systems.
9. Compare and contrast the three models of professional sport club operations.
10. Compare and contrast the three versions of professional sport club operations under Model 1.

Chapter Twelve

INTRODUCTION

If someone from 30 years ago were to look into a crystal ball and observe the sport industry of the late 1990s, it would be difficult for that person to fathom the changes that have occurred. If someone from today were to look into another crystal ball to observe the sport industry of 30 years in the future, just how much change, and of what kind, will have occurred? People of 30 years ago would have been unlikely to predict what was to happen, just as today we are unlikely to be able to predict exactly what the future holds. The previous chapters have demonstrated how an economic perspective can be used to analyze the sport industry as it currently exists. It is also important to look beyond the current environment to the future, to explore what it holds for the sport industry.

Future Direction of the Sport Industry: An Economic Perspective

Sport management professionals should be concerned about the future. Some business firms develop plans for 20 to 30 years into the future. The sport industry has generally not looked that far out. For many sport organizations, 5 years forward represents long-term planning. However, those who want to start firms or those who want to ensure that their current firms will survive need to understand the nature of current trends, their meaning for the future, and the ways in which they will impact sport organizations. Managers of firms, both general and sport, are becoming more concerned about the time dimension of economic decisions. Firms must think not just about short-term revenue maximization but about how today's decisions will contribute to long-term survival. For example, if professional baseball or the tennis industry is to survive, it must continue to attract fans. Where are those fans going to come from, and how can baseball and tennis develop the next generation of fans?

> ***Projecting Future Demands***
>
> *It's 2002 and Lee John, CEO of johnssports.com, is considering the future. His two-year-old company develops sports-themed software for computer games and has grown each year. Software is a rapidly-changing industry, and John wants to ensure that his business survives. The company focuses on mainstream sports with a customer base largely composed of males in their teens to mid-twenties. John wants to stay in the sports area but is thinking about whether he needs to expand into other sports or audiences. In his attempt to determine where future demand will be, what might he consider?*

Economic concepts will not change. In 30 years, economists analyzing the sport industry will still talk about market structures, supply and demand, and labor market inputs. However, the specific issues under analysis may very well change.

The sport industry is part of the larger world, and the changes of the world thus impact sport. Many industries are trying to look into the crystal ball. Manufacturing, health care, and education are all industries struggling with decisions about what the future holds. Mark R. Daniels, president of a Canadian insurance association, suggests several trends in the financial services sector (Daniels, 1999):

1. global structural change, marked by decreased government expenditures and tight fiscal management;
2. intense competition, from domestic and international firms and from nontraditional sources;
3. rapidly changing technology; and
4. changing demographics and changing markets.

These trends for financial services are similar to those the sport industry will encounter. In this chapter, we will first look at population changes as a foundation for discussing other changes. Then we will consider suppliers of sport, technology, and competition as three areas of importance for sport organizations and the industry.

A caveat is that change is unpredictable. Trying to describe what our society and the sport industry will be like in 10 . . . 20 . . . 30 years is difficult. There is no crystal ball and no way to be certain what will happen. We will make one assumption for the following discussion, that the basic institutional structures in our society will remain the same. We do not anticipate radical change in our political, economic, or family structures. Given that assumption, we will make some predictions for the sport industry (see Table 12-1).

Learning Activities

1. Create a time capsule for the year 2020. Make predictions about what you think the sport industry will look like. What will the most popular sports be, both from a spectator and participant perspective? Who will be the most powerful people (titles rather than names)? How much will tickets to the NCAA Final Four cost? What will the role of the Internet be?
2. Choose a sport organization. Write a memo to the CEO of the organization outlining how changing demographic trends are going to impact that organization.

Table 12-1. The Future of the Sport Industry

Changing demographics

- Slower population growth
- Aging population, with different demand pattern
- More diverse population, with different demand pattern
- Changed family structure, with different needs and time resources

Less government-supplied sport; more community-based and private enterprise supplied

- Self-regulation of sport as opposed to government regulation

Increased competition

- Niche marketing
- Consolidation of producers, through mergers and acquisitions
- Continued escalation of professional salaries and franchise valuations, although at a slower rate

Slowing down of the explosive growth of the sport industry

Increasing technology, including extensive use of the Internet

Changing Demographics and Changing Markets

Population Distribution Changes and Impacts

A number of trends for the future are already clear and will impact virtually every industry in the economy. These trends provide a foundation for any predictions about the future of the sport industry. First, there will be slower population growth. The U.S. population grew 102% over the previous 50 years; the projected increase for the next 50 years is 57% (U.S. Census Bureau, 1999). There will be fewer consumers in general, including sports fans and participants, in our society. The impact will be on total consumption of goods and services. Will the sport industry experience reduced demand for its goods and services?

The ways in which this population is distributed are changing. Two of the main areas in which the population will differ are age and ethnic diversity, but other patterns are also changing.

Age Distribution

In the United States, it is estimated that 16% of the population will be over 65 years of age by the year 2020, compared to 13% today (Table 12-2). Part of the growth is attributable to increases in life expectancy and part to the large mass of baby boomers growing older.

Table 12-2. U.S. Population Projections, By Age (%)

Age	2000	2020
18+	74.1	76.3
10–49	58.7	51.1
55+	21.1	29.5
65+	12.7	16.5

U.S. Department of the Census, 2000

What do these changes mean for the general economy? Dowd, Monaco, and Janoska (1998) suggest three main effects on an economy of an aging population:

1. The labor force growth slows as older citizens keep their jobs and younger workers have difficulty entering the work force. This reduces the economy's potential both to produce and consume.

2. Government spending is impacted as much of government budgets are dedicated to entitlement programs, many of which are directed at older citizens.

3. Spending shifts with changing demand. Especially noticeable is a shift from consumption of goods to consumption of services (especially health care).

The sport industry has experienced explosive growth over the past two decades. To a large extent, its growth has matched demand created by the baby boom generation as it moves through its consumer life cycle. What will happen to segments of the sport industry as the increase in numbers of consumers slows and the distribution patterns change? These patterns will affect the industry. For example, consumption patterns differ when examining different age-groups. As people become older, they change their consumption patterns (Kelly & Godbey, 1992). Instead of playing hockey, they turn to golf; instead of watching football on television, they watch news programs; instead of taking ski vacations, they go on cruises. The traditional sport audience is moving into an age where it will not consume in the way sport organizations have been accustomed to them consuming (Hofacre & Burman, 1992). Although the sport industry as a whole may not suffer, specific segments may be greatly impacted.

How is demand going to change? How will sport organizations adjust supply to meet changing demand? For example, different age-groups have different values and look for different experiences from their consumption. Younger people are developing interests in new sports, finding many of the ones the older generations enjoyed "boring." According to National Sporting Goods Association studies (Agoglia, 1999), the fastest growing sports in the United States in the 1990s were nontraditional ones such as roller hockey (+110%) and inline skating (+644%). Sporting goods manufacturers are producing new products for these audiences, ski resorts have targeted snowboarders, the International Olympic Committee added wind surfing and aerials as sports, and television programming now includes the X-Games.

Table 12-3. U.S. Population Estimates and Projections, By Race/Ethnicity (%)

	1900	1950	1980	2000	2020
White	87.9	89.5	80.9	71.4	63.8
Black	11.6	10.0	11.8	12.2	12.8
Hispanic	NA	NA	6.4	11.8	17.0

NA = not recorded separately

U.S. Department of the Census, 2000

Ethnic/Racial Distribution

Demand also changes as with changes in ethnic racial group population patterns. A second trend is increasing diversity (U.S. Census Bureau, 1999). Table 12-3 demonstrates that Hispanics are the fastest growing ethnic/racial group in the United States, projected to increase from today's 12% of the population to 17% in 2020. The African American population will increase from 12% to 13%. Other ethnic groups will also experience growth. Overall, the traditional majority white population is projected to decline from 70% to 64% of the U.S. population in the next 20 years. Will this change influence demand for sporting goods and service and, if so, how? Producers of sport, whether sporting goods or activities, will have to recognize the potential impact of the change. Some organizations have already begun. The USTA and USGA have created programs to appeal to minority groups (Taylor, 1999), and Major League Soccer and Major League Baseball are developing promotions and advertising to create demand.

Other Patterns

Perhaps one of the largest changes in sport demand and supply patterns has occurred with sports for girls and women. In the past decade, opportunities for females have greatly expanded. Women now participate in college athletics in record numbers, young girls play soccer and t-ball in record numbers, over 90,000 fans fill a stadium to watch the U.S. Women's Soccer team win the World Cup, female athletes are in demand as product endorsers, and sporting goods manufacturers create products designed specifically for women. A major contributor to these opportunities has been Title IX as well as the increased role of women in a number of areas of the economy.

Family patterns have changed from the two-parent, stay-at-home-mother family with children (61% in 1950, 53% in 1999, U.S. Census Bureau, 1999). A growing number of single-parent families and families where both parents work outside the home affects demand for sport goods and services. On the one hand, parents are looking for places to send children for supervision. A University of Michigan study showed children 12 and under have 75% of their weekdays programmed for them (Agoglia, 1999). Such programming might include sport camps, club teams, and after-school recreation programs, provided by government, community organizations and/or private enterprise. On the other hand, the opportunity costs to support voluntary sport organizations, as coaches, organizers, and fund-raisers, may be high.

In any society, income is not distributed equally (Kelly, 1985). There is concern in the United States that not everyone shared in the economic boom of the 1990s. What will the future hold? What groups will have resources (e.g., financial, time) to be able participate in various segments of the sport industry? Within the spectator segment of the industry, there is concern that many individual fans are being priced out of the ability to go to games and events whereas corporations, with their ability to afford (and get tax deductions for) tickets, corporate boxes, advertising, sponsorships, and fund-raising will dominate the audience.

Suppliers of Sport

One of the issues an economy needs to consider is the balance between "human investment" and production (Kelly, 1985). The question is how many resources (wealth) should go directly to "taking care of people," as in government-supplied education, social, and sport/recreation services, and how much should be directed to production so that goods and services can be supplied to citizens? When economic times are good (as was true for much of the 1990s), these decisions may be easier in that there are more resources available. However, when economic times are tough (as was true in the 1980s), these decisions are more difficult. Thus, economists attempt to forecast economic cycles to assist in making decisions about the future. However, as discussed in chapter 3, forecasting is difficult. How a society supplies its citizens with goods and services is an issue.

In previous chapters, we have talked about the reasons that government, nonprofit community-based organizations, and private firms all provide recreation programs and sports facilities. In spite of the attention paid to recent government support for sport facilities, the future appears to hold less government involvement in sport.

Changing population patterns will effect political decision-making. It is likely that government officials and legislatures will become both older and more ethnically diverse (Jones, 1999), corresponding to the general population shift. This sets the stage for more disagreement: older versus younger, traditional white majority versus minority. Historically, government has provided much support for recreation and sport, either directly or indirectly. That traditional support may change. Older citizens are more likely to vote than are younger citizens. For the elected official who wants to continue in office and has to weigh interests of competing groups, self-interest dictates listening to those who vote. At the minimum, we will see more political coalitions formed, with the resulting negotiation and compromise.

Increased governmental regulation of sport seems unlikely. Politicians appear reluctant to make any serious change in the way the sport industry operates. Even when the federal government has been active, as with Title IX and the Civil Rights Restoration Act, it took a great deal of time to enforce the law. For all the discussion about Congress's reexamining baseball's antitrust exemption, the only modification to the exemption, in 1998, occurred because it was supported by Major League Baseball. The role of government in the future may be to provide a threat under which leagues, conferences, and associations enact self-regulation.

If government does not supply sport, it will fall to community organizations and private enterprise to do so. Evidence for this already exists for community organizations such as Little League and Pop Warner Football, which have seen a consistent 8 to 10% growth rate in the 1990s (Agoglia, 1999). The future will see more sport provided through these mechanisms.

Competition

Competition is an element of sport participation. It is also an element in the provision of sport. Professional sport teams and leagues compete, YMCAs and private athletic clubs compete, sporting goods manufacturers compete, and television sports channels compete. As discussed in chapters 9 and 10, one role of government is to ensure that competition exists through its antitrust laws.

With a slowing population growth rate, competition will become more intense within the industry. With fewer, and a changing mix of, consumers, many sport organizations will not survive the competition. Those that do will have to find a strategy that enables them to continue to operate. Some may do this by finding a niche market. For example, Major League Soccer will have difficulty rising to the level of the other four major professional sports in North America. However, it may do very well with a more limited role in the professional sport scene. Another means of survival will come through mergers and acquisitions. As discussed, the rationale for such activity is that mergers and acquisitions provide more efficiencies for the firms involved. Although government will continue to oversee such behavior for monopoly considerations, the future will see a consolidation of firms involved in supplying sport.

Undoubtedly the most public attention in the United States is given to the issue of competition within professional sports leagues. Although only a small part of the general issue of competition within the sport industry, it receives disproportionate media coverage. Small-market versus large-market teams, revenue sharing, and salary caps have become well-used words in the vocabulary of those involved in professional sports, either as fans or administrators. Professional sports leagues continue to talk about future expansion, thus diluting an already limited supply of very good players. Competition will continue to increase for that limited supply, resulting in higher salaries and larger gaps between those teams that can afford the salaries and those that cannot. Government will not regulate professional sport, so it is up to owners to self-regulate, via revenue sharing and/or salary caps. The mixed history of owners' being willing to engage in self-regulation does not promise much for the future.

Technology Trends

Technological innovation is a given in North American society, and the pace continuously accelerates. At the minimum, it changes some of our decisions; that is, taking an airplane to a destination ski resort for a weekend instead of going by car for 2 weeks or going to a local resort; or it may make old skills, traditional organizations, and stable markets obsolete.

Technology changes rapidly. For our person from 30 years ago, technology was instant-replay cameras, aluminum tennis racquets, Astroturf, and waffle soles on running shoes. Today it is minute-to-minute Internet updates of sporting events, satellite distribution of worldwide sporting events, and golf clubs that add 40 yards length off the tee. What will it be in 30 years?

Technology creates new products (e.g., titanium bats), new services (e.g., virtual reality golf courses), new channels of distribution (e.g., the Internet), and new alliances (e.g., CBS and SportsLine). Arguably, the greatest technology issue facing the sport industry is the Internet.

In 1999, the National Sporting Goods Association annual management conference held a 1-hour panel discussion on the Internet and the sporting goods industry. In 1998, an estimated $78 million worth of sporting goods was sold over the Internet; industry estimates are that $3 billion dollars will be sold within 5 years (McEvoy, 1999a). Companies such as Nike, Dick's Sporting Goods, and regional retail chains are setting up Web sites themselves or outsourcing site construction. The benefit to the firm is the ease of reaching consumers. A concern is that manufacturers may elect to sell directly to consumers, bypassing conventional retailers and shortening the chain of production.

Sport firms are using the Internet to provide information about their organizations, to sell directly to consumers, to create promotions, and to create sponsorships. The CEO of the Salt Lake Organizing Committee for the Olympic Games says that "the Olympics needs to become the e-Olympics" (Horovitz, 1999, p. B3). For the Salt Lake City Games, the Internet could be used for on-line ticket sales, ticket auctions, merchandise purchases, donations, obtaining volunteers, and sponsorship tie-ins. Internet firms are supporting the sport industry with advertising and sponsorship dollars. PSINet signed a naming right deal with the NFL Baltimore Ravens worth $105.5 million over 20 years whereas Yahoo! sponsors the America's Cup team and the U.S. Postal Service Cycling Team ("Special Report: Sponsorship," 2000).

The prevalence of new technologies reflects changes in demand. For example, at the 1999 Extreme Games, of the 168 credentialed media, 70 were Internet sites (Ruibal, 1999). For the younger generation, the Internet is as relevant as sports magazines or television is to an earlier generation.

Many sport organizations have learned that they must keep up with technology to be competitive. At a metropolitan YMCA, members have their handprints scanned before they can enter the building. They begin their weight-cycle workout by checking a computer kiosk that tells them what their past workouts have been and what they need to do for the current workout. As they move to the stair climber, where they watch television programs off satellites, their heart rate is automatically monitored by sensors. At each stop in the facility, information is entered into a database that records what activities they participated in and for how long.

Although technological advancement presents many opportunities for firms, both to use and to produce new technologies, it also presents problems for sport organizations. Disputes arise over the proper role of technology. The NCAA, for example, banned the newest titanium baseball bats as being too dangerous for fielders. For the NCAA, the costs of using the bats (injuries) are higher than the benefits (more offense) (McEvoy, 1999b). Bat manufacturers sued, alleging restraint of trade. In other cases, the issue is that technology is not regulated by any outside agency. The number of offshore Internet sports betting sites has exploded, worrying sport officials who see increased potential for contest-related problems due to the amounts bet. In the future, government must address the issue of whether it is appropriate to have government regulation or whether the technology industry and its various elements will self-regulate.

Globalization

Finally, as discussed in chapter 11, internationalization of sport is escalating. This trend will be a major factor in the sport economy of this new century. Sport enterprises in the world will continue their efforts in internalization through mergers, acquisitions, and other means. The slogan "globalize or perish" is applicable to many segments of the sport industry. Nevertheless, globalization in sport will continue to encounter many political, cultural, and sociological obstacles.

Views of Leaders in the Sport Industry

In 1999, in an interview in *SportsBusiness Journal*, several sport industry leaders gave their view of the future of the sport industry (Schoenfeld, 1999). The panelists included Todd Leiweke (Staples Center), Bob Whitsitt (Seahawks and TrailBlazers CEO), and Kay Yow (University of Maryland Athletic Director). Although these leaders came from the spectator sport segment of the industry, some of their perspective relates to the entire industry. Their predictions follow.

First, dollars will continue to increase throughout the industry, including valuations of professional franchises; gross gate receipts; and remuneration for players, coaches, and executives. Each time it seems as though the numbers cannot go any higher, a franchise sells for a record amount or a player sets a new high for yearly salary. As discussed with demand and supply, excess demand for limited supply, whether of franchises or very good players, drives up prices.

Second, corporations will become increasingly involved at every level of sport. Corporate involvement will increase in several areas. One is ownership, which is already occurring, from media companies' purchasing sports teams to corporations' accumulating health clubs and golf courses. In major sports, ownership as ego gratification will fall by the wayside, in large part because of the dollars required. Individuals looking for that involvement may gravitate to minor leagues, which could see expansion. Sport firms will be diversified. As Whitsitt says, "Sports teams are in the arena business, the t-shirt business, the shopping mall business, the hotel business" (Whitsitt in Schoenfeld, 1999, p. 38). Another involvement is in sponsorship, not only at the professional, commercial level, but down to high schools and recreational activities. Firms see their participation as a good economic decision, where benefits exceed costs.

Third, the panel sees the massive growth spurt of the 1980s and 1990s slowing. That period of time saw tremendous expansion in leagues and teams, in television coverage, and in dollars spent. However, a maximum point is being reached. For example, the amount of time Americans spend watching television is near saturation. Television can provide more options but not more viewing time in a day. Although the panel did not talk about population changes, the slowing population growth and shift from the traditional 18- to 49-year-old white male sport fan will impact sport. The panel did see markets in which sport can grow; however, they view the growth as more restrained. Although other countries provide growth opportunities, international expansion for U.S. sports will come "indirectly, through targeted marketing, promotions, targeted marketing, new media, and special events" (Schoenfeld, 1999, p. 34). Growth in technology will continue.

Fourth, the television system will continue to fragment, but major sport properties will maintain their values. Cable television has allowed many sport activities (e.g., aerobics, extreme sports, beach volleyball) to receive exposure to a wider audience than would have been possible relying on in-person viewers. However, these are niche sports, and they are all competing for limited time and dollars. Over-the-air television will remain a stronghold for major sports events.

Fifth, revenue discrepancies between small and large markets in professional sports will be addressed with more income-sharing. The panel is perhaps more optimistic than are the authors of this text.

Sixth, technology advances will allow the sport industry to "operate more efficiently, but also will augment the total sports experience, both live and through a variety of media" (Schoenfeld, 1999, p. 34). Technology is changing the way in which people view and buy sports. Although the panel correctly sees technology impacting demand and supply, the costs and benefits will need to be addressed.

Summary

The sport industry in the United States and North America faces many challenges as it enters the 21st century. The explosive industry growth experienced in the last two decades of the 20th century is unlikely to continue. Population changes and resulting changes in demand will create a different environment for firms and organizations. Economic issues will include the nature of sport suppliers, the impact of competition, and changing technology. A requirement for managers of sport organizations is that they must anticipate and plan if they are to make effective decisions for the future.

Chapter Study Questions

1. How are sport organizations already beginning to adjust to the changing environment?
2. How have changes in sport industry technology impacted your sport experience?

Credits

Figure 1-2 adapted with permission from Fitness Information Technology, Inc., from B. G. Pitts, L. W. Fielding, and L. K. Miller, 1994, "Industry Segmentation Theory and the Sport Industry: Developing a Sport Industry Segment Model." Sport Marketing Quarterly, *3*(1).

Tables 3-1 and 3-2 adapted with permission of R. G. Walsh, 1986, *Recreation Economic Decisions: Comparing Benefits and Costs* (State College, PA: Venture Publishing).

Table 5-3 adapted with permission from Street & Smith's *SportsBusiness Journal* (May 10–16, 1999).

Table 5-4 adapted with permission of K. J. Myers, 1998, *Sports Market Place* (Mesa, Arizona: Custom Publishing, Inc.).

Table 6-1 adapted with permission of Fitness Information Technology, Inc., from A. Meek, 1997, "An Estimate of the Size and Supported Economic Activity of the Sport Industry in the United States. *Sport Marketing Quarterly, 6*(4).

Table 7-3 adapted with permission by D. W. Turco, 1995, from a paper, "Measuring the Economic Impact of a Sporting Event," presented at the 1995 North American Society for Sport Management Annual Conference, Athens, GA.

Figure 8-3 adapted by permission of L. Southwick, Jr., 1985, *Managerial Economics* (Plano, TX: Business Publications, Inc.).

Table 11-1 adapted with permission from J. E. Elliott, 1985, *Comparative Economic Systems* (Belmont, CA: Wadsworth Publishing Company).

References

Adams, W., & Brock, J. W. (1997). Monopoly, monopsony, and vertical collusion: Antitrust policy and professional sports. *Antitrust Bulletin, 42*(3), 721–747.

Agoglia, J. (1999, June 21). The lost generation? *Sports Goods Business,* 34–35.

Allen, R. L. (1993). The why and how of global retailing. *Business Quarterly, 57*(4), 117–122.

Amateur Athletic Union (AAU). (2000). *About AAU* [Online]. Available: www.aausports.org/ysnim/home/aau_index.jsp

American Football League v. National Football League, 323 F.2d 124 (4th Cir. 1963).

American Recreation Coalition. (July, 1998). Insights into trends, developments and other curiosities in the world of recreation. Washington, DC: Author.

Anonymous. (1998, May 16). Leaders: Soccer and stockmarkets. *The Economist, 347*(8068), 18.

Aspen Skiing Co. v. Aspen Highlands Skiing Corp., 472 U.S. 585 (1985).

Association for Intercollegiate Athletics for Women v. National Collegiate Athletic Association, 558 F. Supp. 487 (D.C. D.C. 1983), aff'd 735 F.2d. 577 (D.D.C. 1984).

Aubrey, J. (1999, August 2). Bad sign for Canadian clubs. *Ottawa Citizen Online* [Online], p. 2. Available: www.ottowacitizen.com/sports.html

Auerbach, A., & Kotlikoff, L. (1995). *Macroeconomics: An integrated approach.* Cincinnati: South-Western College Publishing.

Auger, D. A. (1999). Privatization, contracting, and the states: Lessons from state government. *Public Productivity & Management Review, 22*(4), 435–454.

Australian Sports Commission. (2000). *Overview* [Online]. Available: www.ausport.gov.au/ascmain.html

Baade, R., & Dye, R. F. (1990, Spring). The impact of stadiums and professional sports on metropolitan area development. *Growth and Change, 21*(2), 1–14.

Back, R., Elliot, D., Meisel, J., & Wagner, M. (1995). Economic impact studies of regional public colleges and universities. *Growth & Change, 26*(2), 245–260.

Bain, J. S. (1951). The relation of profit rates to industry concentration: American manufacturing. *Quarterly Journal of Economics, 65*, 293–324.

Barro, R. J. (1991, August 27). Let's play monopoly. *The Wall Street Journal,* p. A12.

Baumol, W. J. (1959) *Business behavior, value and growth.* New York: MacMillan.

Bawden, T. (1999, May 6). Man Utd aims brand at Asian goal. *Marketing Week, 22*(14), 6.

Behavior Research Center, Inc. (1993). *Cactus League attender survey: Executive summary.* Phoenix, AZ: Author.

Berle, A. A., & Means, G. C. (1932). *The modern corporation and private property.* New York: Commerce Clearing House.

Bernstein, A. (1998, November 23–29). Reebok's future not in the stars. *Street & Smith's SportsBusiness Journal,* p. 7.

Bernstein, M. F. (1998). Sports stadium boondoggle. *Public Interest,* (132), 45–57.

Berry, R. C., & Wong, G. M. (1986). *Law and business of the sport industries: Volume I.* Dover, MA: Auburn House Publishing Company.

Boal, W. M., & Ransom, M. R. (1997). Monopsony in the labor market. *Journal of Economic Literature, 35*, 86–112.

Bowers, T. (1999, March 15–21). Scholarship limits offer a handy excuse to exploit athletes. *Street & Smith's SportsBusiness Journal,* pp. 34–35.

Boyne, G. A. (1998). Bureaucratic theory meets reality: Public choice and service contracting in U.S. local government. *Public Administration Review, 58*(6), 474–484.

Brandman, J. (1999, September). Sport securitization: Start your engines. *Global Finance, 13*(9), 69–70.

Brickley, J. A., Smith, C. W., Jr., & Zimmerman, J. L. (1997). *Managerial economics and organizational architecture.* Chicago, IL: Irwin.

Bridges, F. J., & Roquemore, L. (1996). *Management for athletic/sport administration* (2nd ed.). Decatur, GA: ESM Books.

Broughton, D., Lee, J., & Nethery, R. (1999, December 20–26). The question: How big is the U.S. sports industry? *Street & Smith's SportsBusiness Journal,* 2(35), 23–29.

Brown, R. W. (1993). An estimate of the rent generated by a premium college football player. *Economic Inquiry, 31,* 671–684.

Brown, R. W. (1994). Measuring cartel rents in college basketball player recruitment market. *Applied Economics, 26,* 27–34.

Bulkeley, W. M. (1993, October 25). NFL restrictions on ownership violate antitrust law, jury finds. *Wall Street Journal,* B8.

Bureau of Economic Analysis. (1997). *Regional multipliers: A user handbook for the regional inputoutput modeling system (RIMS II*; 3rd ed.) [Online]. Available: www.bea.doc.gov/bea/regional/articles.htm

Burgi, M. (1997, March 10). A garden of cable delight. *Mediaweek, 7*(10), 5.

Burton, R., Quester, P. G., & Farrelly, F. J. (1998). Organizational power games. *Marketing Management. 7*(1), 27–36. [Online]. Available: callisto.gsu.edu:400/QUERY:fcl=1: . . . entity NewArticle=1:next=html/Article.html

Cady, E. H. (1978). *The big game college sports and American life.* Knoxville, TN: The University of Tennessee Press.

Cairns, J., Jennett, N., & Sloane, P. J. (1986). The economics of professional team sports: A survey of theory and evidence. *Journal of Economic Studies, 13*(1), 3–80.

Carr, R. (2000, May). Nike gets hit from all sides. *Sporting Goods Business, 33*(8), 9.

Cavanaugh, J. (1999, January 25–31). ABL action more likely in court than on. *Street & Smith's SportsBusiness Journal,* p. 43.

CBS SportsLine. (1999). *CBS SportsLine.com* [Online]. Available: www.sportsline.com

Chamberlin, E. H. (1933). *The theory of monopolistic competition.* Cambridge, MA: Harvard University Press.

Champion, W. T., Jr. (1993). *Sports law: In a nutshell.* St. Paul, MN: West Publishing.

Chester, G. J. (1999, February 1–7). Break up the NBA! And MLB, the NFL, NHL too. *Street & Smith's SportsBusiness Journal,* p. 39.

Chicago Bulls and WGN v. National Basketball Association, 961 F.2d 667 (7th Cir. 1992).

Clifford, F. (1993, October 2). Curry Co. turns over Yosemite concessions. *Los Angeles Times,* p. A18.

Clumpner, R. A. (1986). Pragmatic coercion: The role of government in sport in the United States. In G. Redmond (Ed.), *Sport and politics* (pp. 5–12). Champaign, IL: Human Kinetics, Inc.

Clumpner, R. A. (1994). 21st century success in international competition. In R. Wilcox (Ed.), *Sport in the global village* (pp. 353–363). Morgantown, WV: Fitness Information Technology, Inc.

Coakley, J. J. (1994). *Sport in society: Issues and controversies* (5th ed.). St. Louis, MO: Mosby.

Coakley, J. J. (1998). *Sport in society: Issues & controversies* (6th ed.). Boston: McGraw-Hill.

Coase, R.H. (1960). The problem of social cost. *Journal of Law and Economics, 3,* 144.

Colander, D. (1998). *Economics* (3rd ed.). Boston, MA: McGraw-Hill.

College football. (1997). *USA Today* [Online]. Available: www.usatoday.com/sports/football

Collins, N. R., & Preston, L. E. (1968). *Concentration and price-cost margins in manufacturing industries.* Berkeley, CA: University of California Press.

Compte, E., & Stogel, C. (1990, January 1). Sports: A $63.1 billion industry. *The Sporting News,* pp. 60–61.

Coughlin, C. C., & Erekson, O. H. (1985). Contributions to intercollegiate athletic programs: Further evidence. *Social Science Quarterly, 66,* 194–202.

Coughlin, C. C., & Mandelbaum, T. B. (1991). A consumer's guide to regional economic multipliers. *Federal Bank of St. Louis Review, 73*(1), 19–32.

Craig, C. K., & Weisman, K. (1994). Collegiate athletics and the unrelated business income tax. *Journal of Sport Management, 8,* 36–48.

Crompton, J. L. (1995). Economic impact analysis of sports facilities and events: Eleven sources of misapplication. *Journal of Sport Management, 9*(1), 14–35.

Crowe, S. (1999, March 13). Heavy intrigue: Holyfield–Lewis bout a big draw. *Los Angeles Daily News,* p. S1.

Curtis, T. (1998, November/December). Partial repeal of Major League Baseball's antitrust exemption is enacted. *The Sports Lawyer,* pp. 1, 6–8.

Datapol, Inc. (1988). *Economic impact of Major League Baseball spring training on the greater Mesa, Arizona, area.* Mesa, AZ: Author.

Deckard, L. (1990, September). Many roles and reasons for sports authorities. *Amusement Business,* 16–17.

Dell'Apa, F. (1993, May/June). Do pro sports take advantage of their fans? *Public Citizen,* 10+.

Delpy, L., & Li, M. (1998). The art and science of conducting economic impact studies. *Journal of Vacation Marketing, 4*(3), 230–254.

Demmert, H. G. (1973). *The economics of professional team sports.* Lexington, MA: Lexington Books.

DeSchriver, T. D. (1997). *Cartel behavior within the NCAA.* Paper presented at the 12th Annual Conference of the North American Society for Sport Management, St. Antonio, Texas.

DeSchriver, T. D., & Stotlar, D. K. (1996). An economic analysis of cartel behavior within the NCAA. *Journal of Sport Management, 10,* 388–400.

Dessen v. Professional Golfers Ass'n of America, 358 F.2d 165 (9th Cir. 1966).

Division of Research. (1990). *The economic impact of the MCI Heritage Classic on the economy of Hilton Head Island, South Carolina.* Columbia, SC: College of Business Administration, the University of South Carolina.

Dowd, T. A., Monaco, R. M., & Janoska, J. J. (1998, September). Effects of future demographic changes on the U.S. economy: Evidence from a long-term simulation model. *Economic Systems Research,* 239–262.

Drowatzky, J. N. (1997). Antitrust law and amateur sports. In D. C. Cotten & T. J. Wilde (Eds.), *Sport law for sport managers* (pp. 408–422). Dubuque, IA: Kendall/Hunt Publishing Company.

Drysdale v. Florida Team Tennis, Inc., 410 F. Supp. 843 (W.D. Pa. 1976).

Durland, D., & Sommers, P. M. (1991). Collusion in Major League Baseball: An empirical test. *Journal of Sport Behavior, 14,* 19–29.

Eitzen, D. S., & Sage, G. H. (1997). *Sociology of North American sport* (6th ed.). Madison, WI: Brown & Benchmark Publishers.

El Nasser, H. (1999, June 16). Commotion kicking up over space for soccer. *USA Today,* p. 17A.

Elliott, J. E. (1985). *Comparative economic systems* (2nd ed.). Belmont, CA: Wadsworth Publishing Company.

Federal Baseball Club of Baltimore, Inc. v. National League of Professional Baseball Clubs, et al., 259 U.S. 200 (1922).

Finalfourseats.com. (2000). E-mail ticket request form [Online]. Available: www.finalfourseats.com/index.html

Fizel, J. L., & Bennett, R. W. (1989). The impact of college football telecasts on college football attendance. *Social Science Quarterly, 70,* 980–988.

Fleisher, A. A., Goff, B. L., & Tollison, R. D. (1992). *The National Collegiate Athletic Association.* Chicago: The University of Chicago Press.

Fleming, W. R., & Toepper, L. (1990). Economic impact studies: Relating the positive and negative impacts to tourism development. *Journal of Travel Research, 29*(1), 35–42.

Flood v. Kuhn, 407 U.S. 258 (1972).

Florida Sports Foundation. (1998). *About Florida sports* [Online]. Available: www.flasports.com/afs.htm

Folks, W. R., Jr., & Aggarwal, R. (1988). *International dimensions of financial management.* Boston, MA: PWS-Kent Publishing Company.

Frechtling, D. C. (1994). Assessing the economic impact of travel and tourism—measuring economic benefits. In J. R. B. Ritchie & C. R. Goeldner (Eds.), *Travel, tourism, and hospitality research: A handbook for managers and researchers* (2nd ed., pp. 368–391). New York: John Wiley and Sons.

Frey, J. H., & Johnson, A. T. (1985). Conclusion: Sports, regulation, and the public interest. In A. T. Johnson & J. H. Frey (Eds.), *Government and sport* (pp. 261–264). Totowa, NJ: Rowman & Allanheld Publishers.

Fulks, D. L. (1996). *Revenues and expenses of Divisions I and II intercollegiate athletics programs: Financial trends and relationships—1995.* Overland Park, KS: The National Collegiate Athletic Association.

Galbraith, J. K. (1952). *American capitalism: The concept of countervailing power.* Boston, MA: Houghton Mifflin.

Galbraith, J. K. (1958). *The affluent society.* Boston, MA: Houghton Mifflin.

Galbraith, J. K. (1967). *The new industrial state.* Boston, MA: Houghton Mifflin.

Genest, S. (1994). Skating on thin ice? The international migration of Canadian ice hockey players. In J. Bale & J. Maguire (Eds.), *The global sports arena: Athletic talent migration in an interdependent world* (pp. 125–131). London: Frank Cass & Co. Ltd.

Gilley, B. (1998, December). Sweating it out. *Far Eastern Economic Review, 161*(50), 66–67.

Gilpin, K. (1996, Nov. 29). Seven ski resorts merge. *New York Times,* p. D13.

Go, F., & Christensen, J. (1989). Going global. *Cornell Hotel & Restaurant Administration Quarterly, 30*(3), 72–79.

Golf Research Group. (1997, August). *The US golf development report* [Online]. Available: www.golf-research.com/usgolf.htm

Gorman, J., & Calhoun, K. (1994). *The name of the game.* New York: John Wiley & Sons.

Gotthelf, J. (1998, June 1–7). NBA agents in acquisition talks. *Street & Smith's SportsBusiness Journal,* pp. 1, 48.

Graham, E., Ruggieri, C. A., Clements, P. J., & Cody, A. (1994). Introduction. International Corporate Law/Mergers & Acquisitions Yearbook, 2–5.

Gratton, C., & Taylor, P. (1985). *Sport and recreation: An economic analysis.* New York: E. and F.N. Spon.

Gratton, C., & Taylor, P. (1992). *Government and the economics of sport.* Essex, England: Longmon Group.

Gray, S. J., McDermott, M. C., & Walsh, E. J. (1990). *Handbook of international business and management.* Oxford, UK: Basil Blackwell Ltd.

Gruen, A. (1976). An inquiry into the economics of racetrack gambling. In D. Watson & M.Getz (Eds.), *Price theory in action* (4th ed., pp. 65–73). Boston, MA: Houghton Mifflin.

Gunter Harz Sports, Inc. v. United States Tennis Association, 665 F.2d 222 (8th Cir. 1981).

Hall, J. S., & Mahony, D. F. (1997). Factors affecting methods used by annual giving programs: A qualitative study of NCAA Division I athletic departments. *Sport Marketing Quarterly, 6*(3), 21–30.

Hall, M. (1967). Sales revenue maximization: An empirical investigation. *Journal of Industrial Economics, 15,* 143–156.

Hartley v. American Quarter Horse Association, 552 F.2d 646 (5th Cir. 1977).

Hawk, B. (1988). European economic community and United States antitrust law: Contrasts and convergences. *Australian Business Law Review, 16*(4), 282–325.

Hayes, J. P. (1993). International expansion: A four-point PR program. *Franchising World, 25*(5), 9–11.

Hecht v. Pro-Football, Inc., 570 F.2d 982 (D.C. Cir. 1977).

Hirschey, M., & Pappas, J. L. (1995). *Fundamentals of managerial economics* (5th ed.). Fort Worth, TX: The Dryden Press.

Hofacre, S., & Burman, T. (1992). Demographic changes in the U.S. into the 21st century: Their impact on sport marketing. *Sport Marketing Quarterly, 1*(1),

Holl, P. (1977). Control type and the market for corporate control in large U.S. corporations. *Journal of Industrial Economics, 25,* 259–273.

Horovitz, B. (1999, August 5). Olympics chief looks to Web for solutions. *USA Today,* p. 3.

Howard, D. R. (1999). The changing fanscape for big-league sports: Implications for sport managers. *Journal of Sport Management, 13,* 78–91.

Howard, D. R., & Crompton, J. L. (1995). *Financing sport.* Morgantown, WV: Fitness Information Technology, Inc.

Hugh-Jones, S. (1992, July 25). A survey of sports businesses. *The Economist,* pp. S3–S17.

Humphreys, J. M., & Plummer, M. K. (1995). *The economic impact on the State of Georgia of hosting the 1996 Summer Olympic Games* [Executive summary prepared for the Atlanta Committee for the Olympic Games]. Athens: University of Georgia, Selig Center for Economic Growth.

Hylan, T. R., Lage, M. J., & Treglia, M. (1996). The Coase theorem, free agency, and Major League Baseball: A panel study of pitcher mobility from 1961 to 1992. *Southern Economic Journal, 62*(4), 1029–1042.

Intille, S. S. (1996). *Sport online* [Online]. Available: www.white.media.mit.edu/~intille/st/sp.html

International Event Group (IEG). (1997). *IEG sponsorship report.* Chicago, IL: Author.

Jacobs, J. A., & Portman, R. M. (1997). Risk of self-regulation. *Association Management, 49*(3), 89–90.

Jacobs, S. H. (1997). Regulatory reform: Times for action. *OECD Observer, 206,* 5–9.

Jensen, J. (1997). Sports, event marketing shops seeking mainstream alliances. *Advertising Age, 68*(31), 14–15.

Johnson, A. T., & Frey, J. H. (1985). *Government and sport.* Totowa, NJ: Rowman & Allanheld Publishers.

Johnson, W. O. (1991, July 22). Sport in the year 2001. *Sports Illustrated, 75,* p. 46.

Jones, D. (1997, September 9). Spurrier surpasses coaching elite with $12M deal. *USA Today, 15,* p. 1C.

Jones, K. (1999, July/August). The next generation of legislatures. *State Legislatures,* 38–41.

Jones, L. P., & Ergas, H. (1993). Appropriate regulatory technology: The interplay of economic and institutional conditions. *World Bank Research Observer,* 181–213.

Kanters, M. A. (1999). *The economic impact of the WRAL Southeastern Wake County athletic complex* [Technical report]. Raleigh, NC: Department of Parks, Recreation, and Tourism Management, North Carolina State University.

Kaplan, D. (1998, August 24–30). Tough times for shoe companies, retailers. *Street & Smith's SportsBusiness Journal,* p. 6.

Kaplan, D. (1999). Going public makes company an open book. *Street & Smith's SportsBusiness Journal, 2*(7), 21–23.

Kaplan, D., & Mullen, L. (1999). Angry Ascent shareholders seek suitors. *Street & Smith's SportsBusiness Journal, 2*(8), pp. 1, 47.

Kavanagh, L. (1999). *The NBA labor market* [Online]. Available: tudents.uiuc.edu/-lkavanag/NBA.html.

Keat, P., & Young, P. K. Y. (1992). *Managerial economics.* New York: Macmillan.

Kelly, J. R. (1982). *Recreation business.* New York: John Wiley & Sons.

Kely, J. R., & Godbey, G (1992). *The sociology of leisure.* State College, PA: Venture Publishing.

King, B. (1998a, August 3–9). An antitrust bill in name only. *Street & Smith's SportsBusiness Journal,* p. 3.

King, B. (1998b, December 21–27). Patience richly rewarded: Timing boosts contracts for Brown, Williams. *Street & Smith's SportsBusiness Journal,* pp. 1, 43.

Knowles, G., Sherony, K., & Haupert, M. (1992). The demand for Major League Baseball: A test of the uncertainty of outcome hypothesis. *The American Economist, 36*(2), 72–80.

Koch, J. V. (1984). Intercollegiate athletics: An economic explanation. *Social Science Quarterly,* 360–373.

Koepp, S. (1986, February 17). The price war is here: Saudi Arabia's oil production binge may cost its competitors dearly. *Time,* p. 54.

Kraus, R. G. (1984). *Recreation and leisure in modern society.* Glenview, IL: Scott, Foresman.

Laing, J. R. (1996, August). Foul play? *Barron's, 76*(34), 23.

Law v. National Collegiate Athletic Association, 902 F. Supp. 1394 (D. Kan. 1995).

Leonard, W. M. (1998). *A sociological perspective of sport* (5th ed.). Boston, MA: Allyn and Bacon.

Leontief, W. W. (1966). *Input-output economics.* New York: Oxford University Press.

Leontief, W. W. (1985, March-April). Why economics needs input-output model? *Challenge,* 27–35.

Lieberman, P. (1994, April 11). For some golfers it's worse than a bogey. *Los Angeles Times,* p. A1.

Lipsey, R. G., Courant, P. N., & Ragan, C. T. S. (1999). *Economics* (12th ed.). Reading, MA: Addison-Wesley.

Lombardo, J. (1999, February 8–14). NFL taking stake in arena ball. *Street & Smith's SportsBusiness Journal,* pp. 1, 46.

Los Angeles Memorial Coliseum and the Los Angeles Raiders v. National Football League, 726 F.2d 1381 (9th Cir. 1984).

Love, W. D. (1995). Been there, done that. *LIMRA's MarketFacts, 14*(6), 38–40.

Mahony, D. F., Fink, J., & Pastore, D. (in press). Rules violations in college athletics: A comparison of men's and women's sports. *Professional Ethics Journal.*

Mahtesian, C. (1997, October). Revenue in the rough. *Governing, 11*(1), 42–44.

Major League Soccer. (2000). *About MLS* [Online]. Available: www.mlsnet.com/about/index.html

Mankiw, N. G. (1998). *Principles of microeconomics.* Fort Worth, TX: The Dryden Press.

Mansfield, E. (1992). *Principles of microeconomics* (7th ed.). New York: W. W. Norton and Company.

Mason, R. T. (1971). Executive motivations, earnings, and consequent equity performance. *Journal of Political Economy, 79,* 1278–1292.

Masteralexis, L. P. (1997). Antitrust law and labor law: Professional sport. In D. C. Cotten & T. J. Wilde (Eds.), *Sport law for sport managers* (pp. 394–407). Dubuque, IA: Kendall/Hunt Publishing Company.

Maurice, S. C., & Smithson, C. W. (1988). *Managerial economics: Applied microeconomics for decision making* (3rd ed.). Homewood, IL: Richard D. Irwin, Inc.

Maynard, R. (1995). Why franchisers look abroad. *Nation's Business, 83*(10), 65–67+.

McCarthy, L., & Wilcox, R. (1997). *NAFTA and the North American sport industry.* Paper presented at the 12th Annual Conference of the North American Society for Sport Management, San Antonio, TX.

McCarty, M. H. (1986). *Managerial economics with applications.* Glenview, IL: Scott, Foresman and Company.

McClimon, T. (1996). Sports franchises. *Washington update* [Online]. Available: www.btg.com/wash_update/documents/Sports_Franchises_060596.html

McCormick, R. A. (1989). Labor relations in professional sports—Lessons in collective bargaining. *Employee Relations, 14*(4), 501–512.

McEvoy, C. (1999a, July 16). The SGB interview: Tim Harrington. *Sporting Goods Business, 32*(11), 48–51.

McEvoy, C. (1999b, November 5). Batting around NCAA standards. *Sporting Goods Business, 32*(16), 39.

McGuigan, J. R., & Moyer, R. C. (1986). *Managerial economics* (4th ed.). St. Paul, MN: West Publishing Company.

McGuire, J. W., Chiu, J. S., & Elbing, A. O. (1962). Executive incomes, sales and profits. *American Economic Review, 52,* 753–761.

Mcnow, G. (1989, May). From calamity to conglomerate. *Nation's Business, 77*(5), 48–51.

Meek, A. (1997). An estimate of the size and supported economic activity of the sports industry in the United States. *Sport Marketing Quarterly, 6*(4), 15–21.

Mid-South Grizzlies v. National Football League, 720 F.2d 772 (3d Cir. 1983).

Miller, F., & Redhead, S. (1994). In J. Bale & J. Maguire (Eds.), *The global sports arena: Athletic talent migration in an interdependent world* (p. 142). London: Frank Cass. & Co. Ltd.

Miller, L. K., & Fielding, L. W. (1995). The battle between the for-profit health club and the "commercial" YMCA. *Journal of Sport and Social Issues, 19,* 76–107.

Miller, M. (2000, March 13–19). Why owners would demand a union. *Street & Smith's SportsBusiness Journal,* p. 58.

Minnesota IMPLAN Group, Inc. (2000). *What is IMPLAN?* [Online]. Available: www.msu.edu/course/prr/840/econimpact/

Mitchell & King. (1999, May 10–16). Leagues spurn congressional reins on stadium financing. *Street & Smith's SportsBusiness Journal, 2*(3), 5.

Mitnick, B. M. (1980). *The political economy of regulation: Creating, designing, and removing regulatory forms.* New York: Columbia University Press.

Monsen, R. J., Chiu, J. S., & Cooley, D. E. (1968). The effect of separation of ownership and control on the performance of the large firm. *Quarterly Journal of Economics, 82,* 435–451.

Mueller, C. E. (1996). Laissez-faire, monopoly, and global income inequality: Law, economic, history, and politics of antitrust. *Antitrust Law and Economic Review* [Online]. Available: www.metrolink.net/~cmueller/i-overvw.htm

Mullen, L. (1998, November 23–29). Antitrust action has NCAA edgy. *Street & Smith's SportsBusiness Journal,* p. 6.

Mullin, L. (1999, May 31–June 6). Churchill to bankroll spree with new stock offering. *Street and Smith's SportsBusiness Journal,* 9.

Mullin, B., Hardy, S., & Sutton, W. A. (1993). *Sport marketing.* Champaign, IL: Human Kinetics.

Murphy, P. E., & Carmicheal, B. A. (1991). Assessing the tourism benefits of an open access sports tournament: The 1989 B.C. Winter Games. *Journal of Travel Research, 30,* 32–35.

Myers, K. J. (Ed.). (1998). *Sports market place.* Mesa, AZ: Custom Publishing, Inc.

National Collegiate Athletic Association v. Board of Regents of the University of Oklahoma and University of Georgia Athletic Association., 468 U.S. 85, 82 L.ED.2d 70, 104 S. Ct. 2948 (1984).

NCAA. (1996). *NCAA online* [Online]. Available: www.ncaa.org/index.cgi

National Federation of State High School Association (NFSH). (2000). *NFSH official Web site* [Online]. Available: www.nfhs.org

NFL, Cowboys drop suits in sponsorship dispute. (1996, December 16). *Wall Street Journal,* pp. B2, B6.

Nicolaides, P. (1989). Globalisation of services and developing countries. In R. O'Brien & T. Datta (Eds.), *International economics and financial markets* (pp. 172–194). New York: Oxford University Press.

Nike to open 10m store in Melburne. (1997, October 31). *Sport Business* [Online]. Available: www.sportbusiness.com/dailynews/news007.htm

Noll, R. G. (1974). Attendance and price setting. In R. G. Noll (Ed.), *Government and the sports business* (pp. 115–158). Washington, DC: Brookings Institution.

Noll, R. G., & Zimbalist, A. (Eds.). (1997). *Sports, jobs, & taxes: The economic impact of sports teams and stadiums.* Washington, DC: Brookings Institution Press.

Office of Business and Economic Research. (1995). The impact of the Redskins football stadium on the economy of Maryland. Office of Business and Economic Research, Department of Business and Economic Development, Maryland.

Office of Management and Budget. (1997). *North American industry classification system (NAICS)—1997.* Washington, DC: U.S. Department of Commerce.

Ozanian, M. K. (1992). W's valuation scoreboard. *Financial World, 161*(14), 44.

Ozanian, M. K. (1993). Foul ball. *Financial Management, 162*(11), 18–31.

Ozanian, M. K. (1997). Valuation scoreboard. *Financial World* [Online]. Available: www.financialworld.com/archives/1997/June/sportsvalues.html

Pappas, J. L., & Hirschey, M. (1987). *Managerial economics* (5th ed.). Chicago, IL: The Dryden Press.

Parkin, M. (1993). *Economics* (2nd ed.). Reading, MA: Addison-Wesley Publishing Company, Inc.

Patino, M. J. (1999). *The sport summit/sport business directory* (5th ed.). Bethesda, MD: E. J. Krause & Associates, Inc.

Penrose, E. (1959). *The theory of the growth of the firm.* Oxford: Basil Blackwell & Mott.

PGA sets scene for world tour. (1997, October 31). *Sport Business* [Online]. Available: www.sportbusiness.com/dailynews/news007.htm

Philadelphia World Hockey, Inc. v. Philadelphia Hockey Club, Inc., 351 F. Supp. 462 (E.D. Pa. 1972).

Piazza v. Major League Baseball, 831 F. Supp. 420 (E.D. Pa. 1993).

Pitts, B. G., Fielding, L. W., & Miller, L. K. (1994). Industry segmentation theory and the sport industry: Developing a sport industry segment model. *Sport Marketing Quarterly, 3*(1), 15–24.

Pitts, B. G., & Stotlar, D. K. (1996). *Fundamentals of sport marketing.* Morgantown, WV: Fitness Information Technology, Inc.

Pomeroy, R. S., Uysal, M., & Lamberte, A. (1988). An input-output analysis of South Carolina's economy: With special reference to coastal tourism and recreation. *Leisure Science, 10,* 281–288.

Quirk, J., & Fort, R. D. (1992). *Pay dirt: The business of professional team sports.* Princeton, NJ: Princeton University Press.

Radovich v. National Football League, 352 U.S. 445 (1957).

Regan, T. H. (1996). Financing sport. In Bonnie L. Parkhouse (Ed.), *The management of sport* (pp. 363–373). St. Louis, MO: Mosby-Year Book.

Reid, S. R. (1968). *Mergers, managers and the economy.* New York: McGraw-Hill, Inc.

Restricted-earnings case settled for $54 million. (1999, March 15). *The NCAA News,* pp. 1, 18.

Richardson, A. J., & McConomy, B. J. (1992). Three styles of rule. *CA Magazine, 125*(5), 40–44.

Rickman, D. S., & Schwer, R. K. (1993). A systematic comparison of the REMI and IMPLAN models: The case of southern Nevada. *The Review of Regional Studies, 23*(2), 142–161.

Robertson et al. v. National Basketball Association, 389 F. Supp. 867, 872–874 (S.D. N.Y. 1975).

Rogers, J. E., & Arriola, A. Z. (1997). Telecommunications: An international legal guide supplement (Mexico). *International Financial Law Review,* 48–50.

Ruibal, S. (1999, June 28). Extreme sports make mark on line. *USA Today,* p. 8C.

Sack, A. L. (1988). College sport and the student-athlete. *Journal of Sport and Social Issues, 11,* 31–48.

Sailes, G. (1999, April). Basketball at midnight. *The Unesco Courier,* pp. 25–26.

Salvatore, D. (1993). *Managerial economics in a global economy* (2nd ed.). New York: McGraw-Hill, Inc.

Samuelson, P. A. (1970). Economics (8th ed.). New York: McGraw-Hill, Inc.

Samuelson, P. A., & Nordhaus, W. D. (1995). *Economics* (15th ed.). New York: McGraw-Hill, Inc.

San Francisco Seals, Ltd. v. National Hockey League, 379 F. Supp. 966 (C.D. Cal. 1974).

Sandomir, R. (1988, November 14). The $50-billion sports industry. *Sports Inc.*, 14–23.

Schiller, B. R. (1989). *The microeconomy today* (4th ed.). New York: McGraw-Hill, Inc.

Schoenfeld, B. (1998, May 25–31). Ownership is a corporate thing. *Street & Smith's Sports-Business Journal,* pp. 1, 48.

Schoenfeld, B. (1999, January 4–10). Smartest in sports see new golden age. *Street & Smith's SportsBusiness Jounal, 1*(37), pp. 1, 34–39.

Schwartzman, D. (1959). The effect of monopoly on price. *Journal of Political Economy, 67,* 352–362.

Schwartzman, D. (1961). A correction. *Journal of Political Economy, 69,* 494.

Scott, F. A., Long, J. E., & Somppi, K. (1991). Salary vs. marginal revenue product under monopsony and competition: The case of professional basketball. *Atlantic Economic Journal, 13*(3), 50–59.

Scully, G. W. (1974). Pay and performance in Major League Baseball. *American Economic Review, 64,* 915–930.

Scully, G. W. (1995). *The market structure of sports.* Chicago: The University of Chicago Press.

Seeley, A. M. (1997). Bringing fitness to the masses. *Parks & Recreation, 32*(10), 72–76.

Seo, K. K. (1984). *Managerial economics: Text, problems, and short cases* (6th ed.). Homewood, IL: Richard D. Irwin, Inc.

SFX Entertainment, Inc. (1999). *SFX sports group* [Online]. Available: sfx.com/fp.asp?layout=sfxsports1

Shepherd, W. G. (1970). *Market power and economic performance.* New York: Random House.

Shim, J. K., & Siegel, J. G. (1995). *Dictionary of economics.* New York: John Wiley & Sons, Inc.

Siegfried, J. J. (1995). Sports player drafts and reserve systems. *Cato Journal* [Online], *14*(3). Available: www.cato.org/pubs/journal/cj14n34.html

Siegried, J. J., & Eisenberg, J. D. (1980). The demand for minor league baseball. *Atlantic Economic Journal, 82*(2), 59–69.

Sigelman, L., & Brookheimer, S. (1983). Is it whether you win or lose? Monetary contributions to big-time college athletic programs. *Social Science Quarterly, 64,* 347–359.

Simon, H. A. (1959). Theories of decision-making in economics. *American Economic Review, 49,* 253.

Slesinger, J. B. (1972). About input-output analysis. *New Mexico Business,* 18.

Smith, K. (July 28, 1995). *Denver Business Journal. 46,* p. A4.

Southwick, L., Jr. (1985). *Managerial economics.* Plano, TX: Business Publications, Inc.

Spalding Sports Worldwide, Inc. (1999). *History* [Online]. Available: www.spalding.com/history2.html

Spanberg, E. (1999, April 5–11). Retail sales leave stocks in the rough. *Sports Business Journal,* p. 20[illegible]

Special report: Sponsorship. (2000). *Street & Smith's SportsBusiness Journal, 2*(46), 25–38.

Sperber, M. (1990). *College sports, inc.: The athletic department vs. the university.* New York: Henry Holt and Company.

Sport Canada. (2000). *What is Sport Canada?* [Online]. Available: www.pch.gc.ca/sport canada/SC_E/EscA.htm

Sporting Goods Manufacturers Association. (1997). *Recreation executive report number 9.* Author.

Sporting Goods Manufacturers Association. (1997, January). *Press release* [Online]. Available: www.sportlink.com/research/1998_research/industry/export9801.html

Sporting Goods Manufacturers Association (1997, March). *Press release* [Online]. Available: www.sportlink.com/press_room/1997_releases/m973.html

Sporting Goods Manufacturers Association. (1998). *1998 state of the industry report* [Online]. Available: www.sportlink.com/research/1998_research/industry/98soti.html

Sports Center, Inc. v. Riddell, Inc., 673 F.2d 786 (5th Cir. 1982).

Statistics Canada. (2000). *Government revenues, expenditure and debt* [Online]. Available: www.statcan.ca/english/Pgdb/State/govern.htm#rev

Staudohar, P. D. (1989). *The sports industry and collective bargaining* (2nd ed.). Ithaca, NY: ILR Press.

Staudohar, P. D. (1999). Labor relations in basketball: The lockout of 1998–99. *Monthly Labor Review, 122*(4), 3–9.

Stern, R. N. (1981). Competitive influences on the inter-organizational regulation of college athletics. *Administrative Science Quarterly, 26*, 15–31.

STS Corporation v. United States Auto Club, Inc., 286 F.Supp. 146 (S.D. Ind. 1968).

Stynes, D. J. (1999). *Economic impact concepts* [Online]. Available: www.msu.edu/course/prr/840/econimpact/

Stynes, D. J. (1999). Economic impacts of tourism. *Bulletins on Concepts and Methods.* Department of Parks, Recreation, and Tourism Resources, Michigan State University.

Sweezy, P. (1939). Demand under conditions of oligopoly. *Journal of Political Economy, 47,* 568–573.

Taylor, A. (1999, August 25). Tennis no match for net of full life. *Black World Today* [Online]. Available: www.tbwt.com/views/andre

Thoma, J. E., & Chalip, L. (1996). *Sport governance in the global community.* Morgantown, WV: Fitness Information Technology, Inc.

A tighter rein on privatization. (1998, January 4). *Los Angeles Times,* p. 4.

Toolson v. New York Yankees, 346 U.S. 356 (1953).

Trans Sport, Inc. v. Starter Sportswear, Inc., 964 F.2d 186 (2d Cir. 1992).

Turco, D. M. (1993). Assessing the economic impact and financial return on investment of a national sporting event. *Sport Marketing Quarterly, 2(3)*, 17–22.

Turco, D. M. (1995, June). *Measuring the economic impact of a sporting event.* Paper presented at the 1995 North American Society for Sport Management Annual Conference, New Brunswick, Canada.

United Soccer League. (1999). *About USL* [Online]. Available: www.usisl.com/about/index.html

U.S. Census Bureau. (1994). *Finance data for the largest city and county governments* [Online]. Available: www.census.gov/govs/county/94cnty01.txt

U.S. Census Bureau. (1997). *1997 economic census.* Washington, DC: Bureau of Economic Analysis.

U.S. Census Bureau. (1997). *Statistical abstract of the United States (1997).* Washington, DC: Bureau of Economic Analysis

U.S. Census Bureau. (1997). *Statistical abstract of the United States 1997* [Online]. Available: www.census.gov/stat_abstract.

U.S. Census Bureau. (1998). *Statistical abstract of the United States 1998* [Online]. Available: www.census.gov/stat_abstract.

U.S. Census Bureau. (1998). *Statistical abstracts of the United States* (118th ed.). Washington, DC:

U.S. Census Bureau. (1999). *Frequently requested population tables* [Online]. Available: www.census.gov/statab/www/pop.html

U.S. Census Bureau. (2000). *Index of population/projections/nation/summary* [Online]. Available: www.census.gov/population/projections/nation/summary/np-t4-a.txt

United States Football League v. National Football League, 634 F. Supp. 1155 (S.D. N.Y. 1986).

United States Olympic Committee. (2000). *About USOC* [Online]. Available: www.olympic-usa.org/about.html

United States v. International Boxing Club, 348 U.S. 236 (1955).

Vitullo-Martin, J. (1998, May 20). The private sector shows how to run a city. *The Wall Street Journal*, p. A14.

Vrooman, J. (1997). Franchise free agency in professional sports leagues. *Southern Economic Journal, 64*(1), 191–219.

Walker, S. (1999, July 30). Country clubs get snubbed. *The Wall Street Journal*, pp. W1, W9.

Walsh, R. G. (1986). *Recreation economic decisions: Comparing benefits and costs.* State College, PA: Venture Publishing.

Wang, P., & Irwin, R. L. (1993) An assessment of economic impact techniques for small sporting events. *Sport Marketing Quarterly, 2*(3), 33–37.

Warren, M. (1992). *Government regulation and American business.* St. Louis, MO: Center for the Study of American Business, Washington University.

Weiler, P. C., & Roberts, G. R. (1993). *Cases, materials, and problems on sports and the law.* St. Paul, MN: West Publishing Co.

Weir, T. (1999, June 30). Too young to play: Analysis finds players who join NBA early reap big benefits. *USA Today*, p. 1C.

Weisbrod, B. A. (1977). *The voluntary nonprofit sector: An economic analysis.* Lexington, MA: Lexington Books.

Wilcox, R. C. (1994). Preface. In R. C. Wilcox (Ed.), *Sport in the Global Village.* Morgantown, WV: Fitness Information Technology, Inc.

Williamson, O. E. (1963). A model of rational managerial behavior. In R. M. Cyert and J. G. March (Eds.), *A behavioral theory of the firm* (pp. 237–252). Englewood Cliffs, NJ: Prentice-Hall.

Wise, A. N., & Meyer, B. S. (1997a). *International sports law and business: Volume 1.* The Hague, The Netherlands: Kluwer Law International.

Wise, A. N., & Meyer, B. S. (1997b). *International sports law and business: Volume 2.* The Hague, The Netherlands: Kluwer Law International.

Wise, A. N., & Meyer, B. S. (1997c). *International sports law and business: Volume 3.* The Hague, The Netherlands: Kluwer Law International.

Women's Sports Foundation. (2000). *Grants* [Online]. Available: www.womenssportsfoundation.org/templete/grants/index.html

Wotruba, T. R. (1997). Industry self-regulation: a review and extension to a global setting. *Journal of Public Policy and Marketing, 16*(1), 38–54.

Yeh, K. T. (1997). *The assessment of economic impact studies on sport-related events in North America: a content analysis.* Unpublished doctoral dissertation, University of Northern Colorado, Greeley, CO.

Yeh, K. T., & Li, M. (1998). Globalization of sport: What sport management professionals should know. *Journal of the International Council for Health, Physical Education, Recreation, Sport and Dance, 34*(2), 29–33.

Zikmund, W. G. (1994). *Business research methods.* Fort Worth, TX: The Dryden Press.

Zimbalist, A. S. (1994). *Baseball and billions: A probing look inside the big business of our national pastime.* (Ed.). New York: Basic Books.

Zuckerman, G. (October 28, 1999). Baseball cards see sales slump in Pokemon era. *Wall Street Journal*, p. 1.

About the Authors

Dr. Ming Li is an associate professor of recreation and sport management at Georgia Southern University. He coordinates the sport management program and teaches courses on sport management the economics of sport, financial management of sport, facility and event management, international sport management, management of sport organizations, research methods and statistical applications in recreation and sport management. His major interests are in financial and economic aspects of sport and comparative sport management. He received his bachelor's degree in education from Guangzhou Institute of Physical Culture (PRC), his master's degree in education from Hangzhou University (PRC), and his Doctor of Education in sport administration from the University of Kansas. He used to be a member-at-large on the Executive Board of the North American Society for Sport Management (NASSM), chair the Sport Management Council of the National Association for Sport and Physical Education (NASPE), and act as director of the Sport Management and Administration Commission of the International Council for Health, Physical Education, Recreation, Sport and Dance (ICHPER•SD). Dr. Li is currently serving on the Sport Management Program Review Council (SMPRC). He also has memberships on the editorial boards of three professional journals: *Journal of Sport Management, International Sports Journal,* and *International Journal of Sport Management. In 1996, he worked for the Atlanta Committee for the Olympic Games (ACOG) as an Olympic Envoy. Dr. Li has published more than 20 articles in refereed journals in various professional journals, such as Sport Marketing Quarterly, International Sports Journal, and Journal of Sport Management, and made a number of presentations at state, national,* and international conferences.

Susan Hofacre, PhD, is the director of the sport management program and a professor of sport management at Robert Morris College in Pittsburgh, PA. Her research focuses on marketing and economics of sport. She has taught courses on the economics of sport in the U.S. and in Greece. She has served as a featured speaker at sport industry conferences and works as a consultant for sport and recreation organizations in conducting economic impact and marketing studies. Dr. Hofacre received her doctorate from the University of California, Riverside, and a master's in sports administration from Ohio University.

Dr. Dan Mahony is an assistant professor in sport administration and director of the sport administration program at the University of Louisville. Dr. Mahony has a BS in accounting from Virginia Tech, an MS in sport management from West Virginia University, and a PhD in sport management from Ohio State University. He has previously worked for the accounting firm of Peat Marwick Main & Co., the North Hunterdon High School Athletic Department, the West Virginia University Athletic Department, the University of Cincinnati Athletic Department, and the Cincinnati Reds. Dr. Mahony currently teaches classes in sport finance, sport sociology, management in sport, and athletics and higher education. Dr. Mahony is an active researcher and has had recent articles published in *Sport Marketing Quarterly, International Sports Journal, Sport Management Review, International Journal of Sport Marketing and Sponsorship, Journal of Sport Management, and Journal of Sport and Social Issues. He has also made a number of presentations at the North American Society for Sport Management's annual conference and at the European Congress on Sport Management.*

Index

D

E

F

G